'*Power and Crime* advances the n(
between the licit and illicit – the leg
criminal – provides a haven of sere
sibilities linking crime with power. ıt argues boldly that criminology's
monopoly as a discipline to explain this phenomenon is less well
deserved than most in it think. Insights from social theory, economics,
politics, ethics and law furnish criminology with the analytical prospects
for unpacking that grey area, rendering it visible. The prose is as per-
suasive as it is beautifully crafted, drawing upon disparate sources and
disciplines rarely read together. The narrative power of this method
illustrates why Vincenzo Ruggiero is one of the world's leading scholars,
sporting an impressive intellectual command over a wide terrain of the
social sciences. This book is essential reading for a wide range of scholars
and students across the social sciences.'

Professor Kerry Carrington, *Head of School of Justice,*
Faculty of Law, Queensland University of Technology,
Australia

'Ruggiero's book provides an extremely important, comprehensive interpretation of a much-neglected subject. He moves beyond traditional
criminological explanations regarding power and crime, and crimes of
the powerful, in order to provide a unique and much-needed analysis
of the causes and effects of these processes. Ruggiero's approach will
interest students and scholars of criminology/criminal justice, sociology,
and political science.'

Jeffrey Ian Ross, *Ph.D., Professor,*
University of Baltimore, USA

'A penetrating, passionate and profound critical analysis of the intimate
inter-relations of crime and power. Whilst the everyday criminal "justice"
process and the sadistic scapegoating of the popular media continue to
demonise the deviance of the powerless, in the wake of the financial
crisis and proliferating elite scandals this smokescreen is ever harder to
maintain. Ruggiero marshals his considerable learning in many fields –
philosophy, social and political theory, economics, literature, as well as
conventional criminology – to demonstrate that contrary to the obfus-
cations of official statistics and the mass media, crime in the broadest

sense is the twin of power. The book is an impressive illumination of vital issues, from one of the most sophisticated and erudite contemporary criminological theorists.'

Robert Reiner, *Emeritus Professor of Criminology,*
Law Department, London School of Economics, UK

POWER AND CRIME

This book provides an analysis of the two concepts of power and crime and posits that criminologists can learn more about these concepts by incorporating ideas from disciplines outside of criminology. Although arguably a 'rendezvous' discipline, Vincenzo Ruggiero argues that criminology can gain much insight from other fields such as the political sciences, ethics, social theory, critical legal studies, economic theory and classical literature.

In this book Ruggiero offers an authoritative synthesis of a range of intellectual conceptions of crime and power, drawing on the works and theories of classical as well as contemporary thinkers in the above fields of knowledge, arguing that criminology can 'humbly' renounce claims to intellectual independence, and adopt notions and perspectives from other disciplines.

The theories presented locate the crimes of the powerful in different disciplinary contexts, and make the book essential reading for academics and students involved in the study of criminology, sociology, law, politics and philosophy.

Vincenzo Ruggiero is Professor of Sociology at Middlesex University in London. He has conducted research on behalf of many national and international agencies, including the Economic and Social Research Council, the European Commission and the United Nations. He has published extensively on illicit economies, corporate crime and corruption, penal systems, social movements, fiction and crime. His latest book is *The Crimes of the Economy* (2013).

NEW DIRECTIONS IN CRITICAL CRIMINOLOGY
Edited by Walter S. DeKeseredy, *West Virginia University, USA*

This series presents new cutting-edge critical criminological empirical, theoretical, and policy work on a broad range of social problems, including drug policy, rural crime and social control, policing and the media, ecocide, intersectionality, and the gendered nature of crime. It aims to highlight the most up-to-date authoritative essays written by new and established scholars in the field. Rather than offering a survey of the literature, each book takes a strong position on topics of major concern to those interested in seeking new ways of thinking critically about crime.

POWER AND CRIME

Vincenzo Ruggiero

Routledge
Taylor & Francis Group

LONDON AND NEW YORK

First published 2015
by Routledge
2 Park Square, Milton Park, Abingdon, Oxon, OX14 4RN

and by Routledge
711 Third Avenue, New York, NY 10017

Routledge is an imprint of the Taylor & Francis Group, an informa business

British Library Cataloguing in Publication Data
A catalogue record for this book is available from the British Library

Library of Congress Cataloging-in-Publication Data
Ruggiero, Vincenzo.
Power and crime / Vincenzo Ruggiero.
pages cm. -- (New directions in critical criminology.)
Includes bibliographical references.
ISBN 978-1-138-79237-1 (hardback) -- ISBN
978-1-138-79238-8 (pbk.) -- ISBN 978-1-315-76215-9 (ebook)
1. Crime--Sociological aspects. 2. Power (Social sciences)
3. Critical criminology. I. Title.
HV6025.R84 2015
364.01--dc23
2014038524

ISBN: 978-1-138-79237-1 (hbk)
ISBN: 978-1-138-79238-8 (pbk)
ISBN: 978-1-315-76215-9 (ebk)

Typeset in Bembo
by Integra Software Services Pvt. Ltd.

Printed and bound in Great Britain by
TJ International Ltd, Padstow, Cornwall

CONTENTS

1

INTRODUCTION

I am not sure whether this book fits into the series the publishers designate as 'New Directions in Critical Criminology', for the simple reason that the directions it follows are far from 'new'. The book examines the relationship between power and crime (and/or the crimes of the powerful) from a number of perspectives. A canonical initial chapter, of course, is devoted to the contribution which criminology, critical or not, has made to the analysis of the subject matter. We cannot exempt ourselves from the obligation we make imperative to our students: an acceptable review of the literature is likely to result in a better grade. But, after paying respect to the discipline, one may feel authorized to undertake an excursion into other fields of inquiry, where perhaps the notions and ideas elaborated in the criminological arena find a different theoretical context which invalidates, corrects, corroborates or strengthens them. Such an exercise may convince purists that criminology does not need the support or the refutation of other areas of knowledge, as its logic, method and understandings are independently cast in its own specialist vantage point. Purists, for example, may rejoice when faced with what they see as the success experienced by criminology over the past decades: students apply for degrees in droves, new journals are founded and a hail of books hits the field every year. This apparent success, however, decisions to violate laws (Vaughan, 2007). Cultural rules, it is argued, define legitimate goals, and determine action and meaning. In the economic sphere actors experience a relative autonomy whereby agency determines whether obligations to obey the law or to follow business norms justifying violations prevail (Aubert, 1956). This is consistent with Sutherland's (1983) theory of differential association, whereby individuals learn within their own professional enclave the techniques and the rationalizations necessary to deviate. Organizations and their members, however, may not simply follow a rational choice model, but find motivation for offending within the uncertain position in which they feel they are situated. More than sheer greed or striving for success, offenders experience anxiety and 'fear of falling' or 'status panic', as organizations and their members try to either rise, remain the same, or fall in the rank of the organizational system (Vaughan, 1983). It is within this culture of anxiety and panic that offenders are made to feel conformist rather than deviant in relation to their own professional setting. Offending, in this sense, is not the result of calculated choice, but the routine outcome of an organizational culture which tends to normalize deviance.

It should be noted that this consideration is far removed from the analytical field of 'techniques of neutralization', the latter indicating that offenders are aware that their acts are wrong and try to justify them. On the contrary, when deviance is normalized, the conduct is not seen as wrong, nor is it concealed from other members of the organization: 'it is, in fact, culturally approved and therefore rewarded' (Vaughan, 2007: 12).

According to this analysis, therefore, violations are encouraged less by the 'objective' dynamics of the free enterprise system than by the contingent economic and political conditions. Economic actors may, in fact, be led to offend by their own assessment of their immediate financial circumstance, by their forecast of future economic development, and by their perception that their acts will be met with impunity (Yeager, 2007). In a related analysis both the social power and risk-taking attitude of materially privileged classes are pinpointed as crucial variables contributing to crime and delinquency. Such classes, moreover, inhabit specific *generative worlds* guided by key cultural elements facilitating criminality: unbridled competition, a pervasive sense of arrogance and an ethic of entitlement. According to Shover (2007: 88), these are among the reasons why 'not only taverns and jails but also worlds of privilege and

1

INTRODUCTION

I am not sure whether this book fits into the series the publishers designate as 'New Directions in Critical Criminology', for the simple reason that the directions it follows are far from 'new'. The book examines the relationship between power and crime (and/or the crimes of the powerful) from a number of perspectives. A canonical initial chapter, of course, is devoted to the contribution which criminology, critical or not, has made to the analysis of the subject matter. We cannot exempt ourselves from the obligation we make imperative to our students: an acceptable review of the literature is likely to result in a better grade. But, after paying respect to the discipline, one may feel authorized to undertake an excursion into other fields of inquiry, where perhaps the notions and ideas elaborated in the criminological arena find a different theoretical context which invalidates, corrects, corroborates or strengthens them. Such an exercise may convince purists that criminology does not need the support or the refutation of other areas of knowledge, as its logic, method and understandings are independently cast in its own specialist vantage point. Purists, for example, may rejoice when faced with what they see as the success experienced by criminology over the past decades: students apply for degrees in droves, new journals are founded and a hail of books hits the field every year. This apparent success, however, may also be a consequence of the growing belief that technical, administrative, environmental, architectural or policing strategies are the only ones capable of responding to crimes. The success of criminology, in this sense, may be bad rather than good news, a supplementary reason to move away from it.

This is what this book attempts to do, namely to migrate to other areas of expertise with a view to learning about principles and views, absorbing analyses and theories which may at times make our discipline a little less vapid than what it appears to be to many. This migration could be particularly fruitful when addressing the crimes of the powerful, which do not lend themselves to the conventional understandings by now too well consolidated in the discipline. Can we explain the crimes of the powerful with strain theory, namely with coping mechanisms adopted by individuals who fail to achieve valued goals? Do powerful offenders have a background of child abuse or other forms of victimization or discrimination? Do they offend due to lack of bonds with conventional society?

> Individuals break the rules when the bonds that attach them to others, commit them to conventional lines of action, involve them in conventional activities, and sustain their belief in the rules themselves weaken or break. As individuals' social bonds drop away, in essence they are free to do as they want.
>
> *(Rosenfeld and Messner, 2013: 29)*

This explanation belies the reality that powerful offenders *are* committed to conventional lines of action, *are* involved in conventional activities, and *are* attached to others who sustain their beliefs.

Offending, on the other hand, is commonly associated with low socioeconomic status and lack of social welfare provisions. Powerful offenders, however, enjoy high socioeconomic status and generous state provisions in the form of tax exemptions and tolerated tax avoidance and evasion. Conventional analysis of their criminality may resort to biological arguments or other individual characteristics such as low self-control, manifested through impulsivity and insensitivity to the feelings of others (Gottfredson and Hirschi, 1990). Similarly, assuming that unemployment and murder are connected, how can we explain murder committed by employers? Rational choice theory would contend that situational contingencies make crime a viable option, particularly when targets are vulnerable and control measures are found wanting (Felson, 2002).

After the canonic homage to criminology in Chapter 2 ('A criminological classification'), as we shall see in Chapter 3 ('Fearing the future'), social theory offers a variety of alternative interpretations: powerful violators of law implicitly declare their loyalty to their own system of norms, triggering 'herd behaviour'; that is, imitative conduct encouraged by their ostentatious success. From classical social theory we also learn that power itself contains a nucleus which is antithetic to peaceful, non-violent coexistence, and possesses an element of substantial irrationality that is antagonistic to the well-being of communities. Ultimately, the crimes of the powerful, in this perspective, aim to perpetuate and augment the privileges enjoyed by offenders, who fear they will be deprived of them in the future.

Powerful actors do not constitute an underclass: they do not experience long-term inactivity, social instability or alienation from formal authority. And yet, the codes of conduct they adopt echo the street codes of their powerless counterparts. Conventional analysis would posit that when powerful actors offend, social institutions are to blame, as they fail to enact agreed rules governing behaviour. Regulatory deficits are commonly referred to as causes of the crimes of the powerful, which purportedly occur thanks to the 'anomic ethic' spreading among privileged groups. The rules of the game are said to lack moral authority and legitimacy, hence the need to establish consensual regulations benefiting the collectivity. In Chapter 4 ('The law of power'), this discussion is undertaken from a legal perspective, starting off with a schematic distinction between law as a set of universal values applying to all and law as a set of techniques for the perpetuation of power. These contrasting views of law, originally expressed by Plato and Thrasymachus respectively, return in contemporary debates around the conduct of the powerful and its regulation. The crimes of the powerful, as will be argued, may find justification in both of these contrasting views of law.

Economic deprivation and social instability may be singled out as possible causes of crime. When applied to conventional offenders these variables are connected to a general incapacity on the part of communities to express collective efficacy (Sampson, 2006). This argument includes a political element, as it seems to suggest that criminal conduct results from the inability of communities to take collective action, engage in meaningful interactions and improve the general conditions of their everyday life. In brief, political apathy may be said to degenerate into dysfunctional social relationships, with absenteeism from public life hatching individualism and crime. 'Bowling alone' is now a common expression to describe this decline of public spirit, loss of the sense of community and growing selfishness (Putnam, 2000). Political thought, as I will argue in Chapter 5 ('Domination, hegemony and violence'), offers alternative insights that help explicate the conduct of powerful offenders. Many classics suggest that political power itself, rather than lack of it, can be the source of crime. Learning from political thought, we may well equate the crimes of the powerful to 'states of mind' or to forms of 'radical evil'; we can endorse the notion that they are caused by the implicit criminality of political power, and even assimilate them to ordinary acts of government.

There is a large body of literature dealing with the relationship between crime and the economy, focusing on productive performance, cycles of growth, or labour market dynamics (for an extended bibliography, see Albertson and Fox, 2012; Rosenfeld and Messner, 2013). The economy has also provided the backdrop to celebrated analyses of incarceration rates (Rusche and Kirchheimer, 1968; Melossi and Pavarini, 1977). Chapter 6 ('Inglorious human activities') approaches the issue from a different perspective: it attempts a criminological critique of economic thought itself, probing how some categories elaborated by the 'dismal science' may be used for the analysis of the crimes of the powerful. These types of crimes, as will become clear in the chapter, may be tolerated due to their 'utility', a miraculous economic category absolving all wrongdoing in the name of performance, accumulation and growth.

As suggested above, powerful offenders are often attached to others who sustain their beliefs. And, while mainstream criminological thought may be unable to explicate what these beliefs are, philosophy has many suggestions in this respect. Chapter 7 ('The ethics of power') assesses how ethics can provide crucial tools for the analysis of the subject matter. Powerful offenders, in the argument presented, seek justification for their conduct through a selective interpretation of classical Western philosophy. This interpretive process is led by the purpose of expanding their social opportunities, including opportunities for further offences, while making the latter acceptable to their peers and others. The process entails the implicit claim that offences are, in fact, respectful of the very norms being violated.

For Aristotle (1996), the difference between a historian and a poet is not that one writes prose and the other verse. The real difference, in his view, is that the former tells what happened, while the latter foretells what might happen. For this reason poetry, and for that matter fiction, are more scientific and serious than history, as they tend to give general truths, whereas history only gives particular facts. By general truth, Aristotle meant the sort of thing that certain types of people will do or say, either probably or necessarily (Bull, 2013). Giambattista Vico (1999) echoes this view when he equates fiction to the *verisimile*, namely an ideal truth that conforms to the common sense of all citizens. Chapter 8 ('Balzac: power as crime') looks at some of the vast work produced by Honoré de Balzac, seeking in his wonderful 'human comedy' new insights for a better understanding of the crimes of the powerful.

Two preliminary, short, points of clarification. First, in Chapter 2, which provides an overview of criminological arguments around the crimes of the powerful, we come across a key section devoted to the *legal–illegal continuum*, namely the grey area where these types of crime often occur. It is the very existence of this grey area that demands the aid of interpretations transcending those commonly offered by established criminological knowledge. Hence the choice, in this book, to seek such aid in the realms of social theory, legal theory, politics, economics, ethics and fiction. Second, definitions of power are never straightforward and uncontroversial, as shown in the chapters that follow. Surely, domestic violence requires a power imbalance between the perpetrator and the victim, as does hate crime. Armed robbers, at least while performing their task, wield more power than those they rob, even if the latter may be more socially, economically and politically powerful than the former. However, this should not lead to the conclusion that all crimes are to be regarded as crimes of the powerful. Perpetrators of domestic violence, hate crime or armed robbery, after committing their offences, are likely to return to the status of powerless individuals characterizing them in other social spheres. The conducts considered in the following pages, on the contrary, are those adopted by actors for whom power is a resource available in all areas of life and for all types of action, those actors who, after using power to commit crime, can easily return to other spheres of existence and action where they will continue to exercise that power.

2

A CRIMINOLOGICAL CLASSIFICATION

The field of criminology may or may not remain disproportionately preoccupied with socially vulnerable offenders involved in conventional crime. True: examinations of the major US and British journals of criminology and criminal justice reveal that a mere 3 per cent of research articles focus on criminal activities of corporations and governments (Michalowski and Kramer, 2007; Ruggiero and Welch, 2009). However, when focusing on the specific literature addressing the relationship between power and crime, one may have the opposite impression. Given the avalanche and increasing variety of crimes perpetrated by states and other powerful actors, scholars are faced with a fuzzy analytical framework, with the result that some may be tempted to describe as crime everything they, understandably, find disturbing. The complexity, evasiveness and deceptive profile of the crimes of the powerful contribute to this process, so that the expansion of criminology into the terrain of powerful offenders risks turning our object of study into 'everything we might not like at the time' (Cohen, 1993: 98).

The evasiveness and deceptive nature of these types of conduct were clearly pointed out by Edwin Sutherland (1945), who asked whether white-collar crimes had indeed to be deemed crimes. We are still wondering, in this respect, whether he only intended to pose a mere rhetorical question and enjoy the interminable debate and controversies such a question was bound to generate. And it is from Sutherland's work on white-collar crime that we must start if we want to draw an outline of criminological contributions to the analysis of the crimes of the powerful. This chapter, after proposing such an outline, attempts to classify the diverse offences committed by powerful actors, with a view to drawing a tentative template within which each offence may be identified as a distinct type of illegitimate or harmful conduct. Prior to attempting such classification, however, a preliminary proviso is necessary as to which specific conducts the proposed typology will include.

Power crimes

The formulation 'white-collar crimes are crimes committed by persons of respectability and high social status in the course of their occupation' (Sutherland, 1983: 8) continues to be regarded as too broad, because white-collar offences entail diverse combinations of respectability, social status and occupation. Critics argue that the original definition encompasses too many diverse and often unrelated behaviours and should therefore be broken down into more precise categories. As alternatives to white-collar crime, definitions such as elite deviance, official deviance and corporate deviance have been used (Simon and Eitzen, 1982; Ermann and Lundman, 1978, 1982; Douglas and Johnson, 1977). Other definitions aimed at narrowing the original conceptualization and identifying more specific behaviours are corporate crime, business crime, political crime and government crime (Clinard and Yeager, 1980; Roebuck and Weeber, 1978; Conklin, 1977; Yeager, 1995).

The debate also centres on the social status of offenders. As Croall (1992) explains, this controversial aspect may hamper research and analysis as offenders of diverse social status and respectability may commit white-collar offences. On the other hand, it is felt that the definition 'occupational crime', whose original formulation is due among others to Quinney (1964), may resolve the issue by including both white-collar and blue-collar crime.

Green (1990: 13) defines as occupational crime 'any act punishable by law which is committed through opportunity created in the course of an occupation that is legal'. He argues that the criterion of legal occupation is necessary because without it the term 'occupational crime' could conceivably include all crimes. The author identifies four categories of occupational crime: crimes for the benefit of an employing organization (organizational occupational crime), crimes by officials through the exercise of their state-based authority (state authority occupational crime), crimes by professionals in their capacity as professionals (professional occupational crime), and crimes by individuals as individuals (individual occupational crime).

It should be noted that Green's definition is in complete accordance with Sutherland's original formulation. Sutherland, in effect, stresses that white- collar crime excludes many crimes of the upper classes such as most cases of murder, intoxication or adultery, since these are not a part of the occupational procedures. 'Also, it excludes the confidence games of wealthy members of the underworld, since they are not persons of respectability and high social status' (Sutherland, 1983: 7).

A further elaboration of Sutherland's seminal work pertains to the nature and definition of corporate crime. According to a relatively accepted formulation, this consists of illegal acts performed within a legitimate organization, and in accordance with the organization goals, which victimize employees, customers or the general public (Schrager and Short, 1977). Related to this formulation is the distinction between crimes for corporations and crimes against corporations, the latter representing what is commonly associated with 'corporate crime' (Box, 1983). But, although useful, this distinction is said to implicitly overstate the homogeneity of 'crimes against business'. If such crimes include fraud, for example, 'Even if one excludes from consideration many forms of business "malpractice" that are either not criminal at all or whose criminality is ambiguous, to write about commercial fraud is to write about a number of very different sorts of activities' (Levi, 1987: xix).

If white-collar crime embraces illegal behaviour adopted within a legal occupation, the nature of this occupation and the degree of power that this carries vary significantly. Some types of white-collar crime may be committed by secretaries or truck drivers, as well as by high-ranking officials or presidents within the same organization (Geis and Jesilow, 1993). Levi (1987: xix) also argues that the social composition of white-collar criminals is not homogeneous, as it includes members endowed with varying degrees of power and respectability. 'Even upmarket-sounding

crimes like insider dealing – where shares are bought or sold unlawfully
on the basis of confidential inside information – may be committed by
the company chauffeur or the company typist'.

As I stressed in the Introduction, the premise of this book is that the
crimes of the powerful are not 'equal opportunity crimes'; hence the
necessity, for any study of the subject matter, to clearly delimit the terrain
to which the inquiry is referred. The argument developed below does not
consider crimes committed by company chauffeurs or company typists,
but is confined to offences committed by actors such as states, corporations, financial institutions and other similarly powerful organizations,
namely offenders who possess an exorbitantly exceeding amount of
material and symbolic resources when compared with those possessed by
their victims. These offenders exercise power not only when committing
crime, but also in all other spheres of their social, economic and political
life. Their offences may be termed 'power crimes', a phrase which in
turn requires further qualification and precise connotation (Ruggiero and
Welch, 2009). The phrase should be located against the background of
differentiated opportunities which are offered to social groups. Social
inequalities determine varied degrees of freedom, whereby individuals are
granted a specific number of choices and a specific range of potential
actions which they may carry out. Each degree of freedom offers an
ability to act, to choose the objectives of one's action, and the means to
make choices realistic. The greater the degree of freedom enjoyed, the
wider the range of choices available, along with the potential decisions to
be made and the possibility of realistically predicting their outcomes.
This asymmetric distribution of freedom makes some turn the acts
performed by others into means for their own goals (Bauman, 1990).
This may be realized through coercion or legitimacy, which award
those endowed with more resources the prerogative to establish which
means and which ends are to be considered acceptable. We may argue,
with respect to the crimes of the elite, that criminal designations are
controversial and highly problematic due to the higher degree of freedom
enjoyed by the elite. The capacity to control the effects of their actions
allows those who have more freedom to conceal (or negotiate) their
criminal nature. If we translate the notion of freedom into that of
resources, we can argue that those possessing a larger quantity and variety
of these resources also have greater possibilities of attributing criminal

definitions to others and repelling those that others attribute to them. They also have greater ability to control the effects of their criminal activity, and usually do not allow this to appear and be designated as such. The notion of 'power crime' therefore applies to actors endowed with high degrees of freedom and resources, a notion that echoes Sutherland's variables 'high status and respectability'.

A different conceptualization of the crimes of the powerful is found in criminological contributions from control balance theory. Tittle's (1995) theory takes as its organizing theoretical variable the degree of control actors exercise in relation to the amount of control they experience. According to his formulation, control surpluses (an excess of control exercised relative to control experienced) give rise to autonomous forms of deviance, namely deviance aimed at extending the existing control surplus. This includes offences that do not entail direct interaction with victims, ranging from acts of exploitation (corporate price fixing, influence peddling by political figures) to acts of plunder (pollution, destruction of forests and animals), and a variety of forms of indirect predation (Piquero and Piquero, 2006). Exploitative deviance, for example, may consist of corporate executives authorizing the dumping of toxic waste into rivers while predicting that those most immediately affected (farmers and fishers) will be unable to react: 'Businesspeople do these things when they become aware that they, through the corporate vehicle, enjoy a surplus of control, which can be extended by any means' (Tittle, 1995: 164).

Although perhaps still incomplete, the identification of the crimes of the powerful with those committed by actors who enjoy an excess of freedom, resources and control may suffice for the purpose of distinguishing the types of illegalities dealt with below within the wide range of criminal conducts that the literature on white-collar crime takes into account. Moving our focus onto precise powerful actors, we find in the criminological literature more material upon which to reflect.

State agents and economic actors

We can isolate a set of conceptualizations of the crimes of the powerful as those arising from the analysis of the state. Particularly focused on violence, these conceptualizations see the crimes of the powerful as original foundational events, as secular forms of Promethean acts leading to state formation. These acts, it is argued, constitute authorized force and amount to lawmaking violence. They may be foundational, when they establish new systems and designate a new authority. But they may also amount to law-conserving violence, when they protect the stability of systems and reinforce authority (Derrida, 1992; Benjamin, 1996). Tilly's (1985) work is, in this respect, well known for its emphasis on the centrality of direct organized force to the process of state-making (Whyte, 2009). The crimes of the powerful, from this perspective, give us a picture of how power is formed and distributed within society and how such distribution can be altered (Geis and Meier, 1977). Pursuing this strand of analysis, some scholars have looked at extra-legal activities of the modern state and how these may be located within legal-political theory (Sabuktay, 2009), while other experts of state crime in general have remarked that the core capitalist states remain the greatest source of state-supported harm, violence and injury (Rothe and Ross, 2009; Chambliss *et al.*, 2010).

It is in contributions pertaining to the economic sphere, and indeed to capitalism, that we find the second set of concepts. Rereading Frank Pearce's (1976) seminal book, one notes that it took the author more than seventy pages before 'audaciously' introducing the phrase 'crimes of the powerful'. At stake was the delineation of a theoretical paradigm which, while incorporating some elements of the sociology of deviance of the time, intended to decisively supersede it. Hence Pearce's appreciation of labelling theory but also his sustained criticism of Lemert's analysis of radicalism, which according to the latter was represented by 'structurally marginal people [who] cannot influence others through any rational methods but only through propaganda, manipulation, infiltration and distortion' (ibid.: 31). Pearce's radicalism, on the other hand, was based on variables and concepts belonging to classical Marxism such as mode of production, surplus value and class struggle. Conflict as an explanatory variable, therefore, inevitably became paramount for the analysis of the crimes of the powerful, in that definitions of crime themselves were deemed the result of battles engaged in the legal arena, with powerful individuals and groups distancing themselves from imputations of criminal conduct while attributing them to the powerless. Finally, Pearce specified that, after starting his analysis of corporate crime within a very legalistic framework, he was forced to progressively move away 'from the confines of positive criminology', and in analysing crimes of corporation he was 'ultimately led to ask fundamental questions about the nature of American and the world's free enterprise system' (ibid.: 105).

To be sure, the work produced on the subject matter throughout the 1970s into the 1990s built on the solid foundations laid down by Sutherland (1983), who described corporations as recidivist offenders and concluded that disadvantage as well as privilege may instigate learning processes leading to crime. In the last analysis, looking at the social damage caused by corporate actors, it is legitimate to wonder why the focus on conventional crime historically adopted by criminology is still prevailing.

Anomie, control and techniques of neutralization

Supplementing approaches centred on state formation or focused on economic variables are perspectives inspired by criminological theory itself. Anomie and control theory, for example, have both been mobilized to explain the crimes of the powerful. The former may posit that the settings in which the elite operates are already largely normless, thus encouraging experimental conducts and allowing for the arbitrary expansion of practices. Passas (2009: 153), for instance, argues that pressure to attain goals is constantly experienced by people in the upper social reaches, and that, therefore, 'they are far from immune to pressures towards deviance'. Control theory, in its turn, has suggested that a number of characteristics belonging to offenders may explain all types of crimes, be they committed by powerful or powerless individuals. Such characteristics include physical as well as psychological traits ranging from impulsivity and recklessness to the incapacity to delay gratification and a propensity to blame others first and oneself last (Gottfredson and Hirschi, 1990). Sykes' and Matza's techniques of neutralization appear to lend themselves ideally to explanatory efforts addressed to the crimes of the powerful. For instance, such techniques may be used to deny that powerful offenders cause harm or victimize specifically identifiable subjects, to claim that other conducts are far more harmful than those which one adopts, or that in any case whatever conduct one adopts this expresses a form of loyalty to one's social group and, therefore, cannot be deemed criminal. Techniques of neutralization comprise other aspects that will be addressed later.

Organizations and their members

An important strand of analysis focuses mainly on micro-sociological aspects, for example, observing the dynamics guiding the behaviour of organizations and their members. As organizations become more complex, responsibilities are decentralized, while their human components find themselves inhabiting an increasingly opaque environment in which the goals to pursue and the modalities through which one is expected to pursue them become vague and negotiable. Organizations may be 'mechanistic' or 'organic', the former operating in conditions of relative stability, the latter adapting themselves to changing conditions (Burns, 1963). Illegal practices may be the outcome of such changing conditions, as organizations are required to incessantly devise new ways of reaching their ends and, consequently, to innovate by reinventing or violating rules. Organizations, on the other hand, are composed of individuals and groups pursuing their own interests although internal conflicts are rarely officially displayed and are hidden behind public images of harmony (Dalton, 1959; Mouzelis, 1967). Alliances taking shape and dissolving, contingent interests and a permanent antagonistic climate characterize the daily existence of organizations, whose goals are as indefinite as is the outcome of the power struggles taking place within them.

By 'decoupling themselves' from their constituent parts, organizations attempt to meet their goals while operating in a highly unpredictable environment. In this way they assume 'a structure consisting of loosely coupled entities' (Keane, 1995: 169). The different entities keep a relative independence, and a loosely coupled structure allows organizations to deal with the vagaries of business. Decoupling, particularly encouraged by geographical expansion, mergers and acquisitions, also entails that the parent companies dissociate themselves from the practices adopted by their subsidiaries or partners. Where such practices are illegal, organizations may therefore claim their innocence and invoke ignorance of the types of operations being conducted by subsidiaries or partners.

In further developments, attempts have been made to merge macro- and micro-levels of analysis, leading to the growing inclusion in the study of the crimes of the powerful of formal and complex organizations. These types of crimes are equated to manifestations of 'situated action', and explanatory efforts have addressed how contextual cultures affect decisions to violate laws (Vaughan, 2007). Cultural rules, it is argued, define legitimate goals, and determine action and meaning. In the economic sphere actors experience a relative autonomy whereby agency determines whether obligations to obey the law or to follow business norms justifying violations prevail (Aubert, 1956). This is consistent with Sutherland's (1983) theory of differential association, whereby individuals learn within their own professional enclave the techniques and the rationalizations necessary to deviate. Organizations and their members, however, may not simply follow a rational choice model, but find motivation for offending within the uncertain position in which they feel they are situated. More than sheer greed or striving for success, offenders experience anxiety and 'fear of falling' or 'status panic', as organizations and their members try to either rise, remain the same, or fall in the rank of the organizational system (Vaughan, 1983). It is within this culture of anxiety and panic that offenders are made to feel conformist rather than deviant in relation to their own professional setting. Offending, in this sense, is not the result of calculated choice, but the routine outcome of an organizational culture which tends to normalize deviance.

It should be noted that this consideration is far removed from the analytical field of 'techniques of neutralization', the latter indicating that offenders are aware that their acts are wrong and try to justify them. On the contrary, when deviance is normalized, the conduct is not seen as wrong, nor is it concealed from other members of the organization: 'it is, in fact, culturally approved and therefore rewarded' (Vaughan, 2007: 12).

According to this analysis, therefore, violations are encouraged less by the 'objective' dynamics of the free enterprise system than by the contingent economic and political conditions. Economic actors may, in fact, be led to offend by their own assessment of their immediate financial circumstance, by their forecast of future economic development, and by their perception that their acts will be met with impunity (Yeager, 2007). In a related analysis both the social power and risk-taking attitude of materially privileged classes are pinpointed as crucial variables contributing to crime and delinquency. Such classes, moreover, inhabit specific *generative worlds* guided by key cultural elements facilitating criminality: unbridled competition, a pervasive sense of arrogance and an ethic of entitlement. According to Shover (2007: 88), these are among the reasons why 'not only taverns and jails but also worlds of privilege and corporate offices can be breeding grounds for transgression'. With the variable 'competition' we find an echo of previous analyses focused on free market economies as criminogenic environments. The variable 'arrogance', in turn, alludes to the confidence accumulated through 'the habit to give orders' and the insolence gained through the lack of defiant responses. Finally, 'entitlement' implies offenders believing that external forces interfere with their just desert, namely their right to pursue wealth without external restraint. 'What is instructive about this is confirmation that an *ethos* of entitlement can become so pervasive among occupational practitioners or organizational managers that it becomes taken for granted and erodes willingness to comply with law' (ibid.: 92, emphasis added).

The legal–illegal continuum

It is widely argued that the crimes of the powerful cannot be solely identified on the basis of a coded prohibition, because the law may fail to prohibit them clearly and strictly. Are these crimes narrowly definable in relation to a precise breach of rules and laws? In answering this question some authors resort to different conceptualizations based on deviance rather than criminality. Quinney (1970), for instance, considers the correspondence between deviant and criminal behaviour as crucial in the study of the crimes of the powerful. The question he poses is whether or not the behaviour defined as criminal is also a deviation from the normative structure of the role one occupies: 'If it can be established that the behaviours are regarded as deviant, as well as criminal, by the occupational members, the criminal violations can truly be studied as deviations from occupational norms' (ibid.: 33). In brief, according to Quinney, the behaviour studied by criminologists as criminal must be so regarded by the groups being studied.

This formulation raises old dilemmas and echoes the controversies engaging Sutherland and his critics. Sutherland holds little doubt about the criminality of powerful offenders, and stresses that the difference between these and their conventional counterparts has to be found in the responses they respectively elicit from institutional authority. Power crimes are socially injurious and may be legally so described, although the administrative procedure to which they are subject symbolically fades their seriousness. In a well-known diatribe around this specific view, Tappan (1947) retorts that crime entails an intentional will to violate norms of conduct prescribed by codes, jurisprudence and custom, and as such prosecuted and punished by the state. Intentionality, a criminal mind, legally definable harm, along with successful prosecution and implementation of penalty: these are the legitimate requisites and by-products of criminal behaviour.

> In Tappan's view, it is illegitimate of Sutherland to describe people as criminal when they have not been successfully prosecuted for a crime and, moreover, he illegitimately extends the concept of crime to cover acts that do not violate the criminal law.
>
> *(Slapper and Tombs, 1999: 6)*

This long-running dispute illustrates the divergence between legal, social and political definitions of criminality, simultaneously reminding us of the artificiality of all definitions of crime (Nelken, 1994). The concept of harm appears to rescue the debate, in that it allows us to identify a continuum linking administrative and criminal violations, *mala in se* and *mala prohibita*, ultimately: legality and illegality.

> Once one extends the label crime beyond those who have been formally and successfully processed as criminals, one enters the sphere of normative reasoning, or moralising … the shift from a focus upon unequivocally defined criminal laws is a shift along a *continuum* which extends to social harms at the other extreme.
>
> *(Slapper and Tombs, 1999: 6, emphasis added)*

It is this continuum that deserves careful examination, in that subjectivity, social and intellectual identity and political strategy are engrained in the very process which extends the criminal label from clearly defined illegitimate acts to harmful acts. This process may cloud the very object of study it aims to clarify, for example, producing the simplification often needed in political campaigns but which is counterproductive in sociological enquiry. It should be noted, however, that this may result from the very nature and characteristics of the crimes of the powerful, which are often, and rightly, described as hazy, evasive, invisible, thus inducing similarly hazy conceptualizations and suggesting nebulous categories or fields of study.

One of the crucial characteristics of white-collar and corporate crime is part of what Nelken (1994) identifies as the fundamental ambiguity of these offences. The fact, for example, that the perpetrator has justification for being present at the scene where the crime takes place distinguishes this type of offending from conventional predatory crime (Clarke, 1990). On the surface, the ambiguity of the crimes of the powerful makes them very similar to ordinary legal behaviour: 'For example, for fraud to succeed, it must obviously succeed in mimicking the appearance of legitimate transactions, and it is not unusual for those guilty of this crime to remain undetected for years, even a lifetime' (Nelken, 1994: 373). In sum, difficulties in classifying powerful offenders are compounded by difficulties in discovering that an offence has been committed in the first place.

Invisibility, in turn, contributes to making the field of study indistinct, classification formless and typologies fuzzy. It has long been noted that invisibility describes the condition of both powerful criminals and their victims. The perpetrator is made invisible by the circumstance whereby the setting of the offence does not coincide with the setting where its effects will be felt. This is also the case because the time when the crime is performed and the time when the damage caused becomes apparent do not correspond. On the other hand, victims themselves may be described as invisible in that they are both absent from the scene of the crime and are frequently unaware of their own victimization.

In the analysis of the moral and managerial component of human behaviour within organizations, Punch (1996: 2) highlights the culture of competition providing opportunities, motivations and rationalizations for rule-breakers. He also emphasizes the ambiguous and manipulative nature of management, matched by the incoherent character of organizations themselves, which may present a clear image of their objectives and practices to the outside world, but in fact operate in a contingent manner whereby the legitimacy of ends and conducts is constantly redefined. Summing up his argument, 'the corporation, and the business environment, are potentially criminogenic'. This statement is perhaps the clearest formulation we can find in the specialist literature of the legal–illegal continuum characterizing the practices of organizations and powerful actors.

I believe it is necessary to identify and isolate at least some elements which constitute such a continuum.

A provisional classification

There is an important precedent to the effort made in this book, one that remains symptomatic of two different ways of approaching the study of powerful people's conduct and, more specifically, of their crimes. In the heydays of radical, new criminology, Quinney (1970) remarked that powerful organizations should be observed in their everyday functioning, their culture and the precise ways in which they operate. In sum, he intended to stress the importance of the occupational aspects and the ideology of those belonging to such organizations. A detailed analysis, in his view, would show how agents formulate their own definitions of whether and when behaviour, including their own, is deemed criminal. The new criminologists were unhappy with this formulation, because once the notion is established that powerful organizations (for example, the police) are 'the agents of the bourgeoisie', studies concerned with their specific social composition and occupational culture constitute unnecessary diversions from that notion (Taylor *et al.*, 1973). Similarly, one could argue that detailed analyses and classifications of the crimes of the powerful are redundant, because they may lead radicals astray. I hope this does not apply to the classification below.

Operative crimes of the powerful

The first type of crime of the powerful I would like to focus on manifests itself when powerful groups and individuals violate their own rules and philosophies. These types of violations bring to mind the concept of 'mock organization' proposed by Gouldner (1954), according to whom rules governing organizations may be a dead letter, in that under normal circumstances they may be ignored by most of their members. Mock bureaucracies or organizations may include the paradoxical feature whereby deviation from rules is status-enhancing and conformity is status-impairing. Organizations that violate their own rules and philosophies include corporations officially standing up for market freedom while in practice showing little credence in such freedom.

According to an important distinction proposed by Parsons, every system or organization relies on a normative order and simultaneously on a factual order. The former refers to a given set of ends, rules or other norms. 'Order in this sense means that the process takes place in conformity with the paths laid down in the normative system' (Parsons, 1982: 98). A normative order may be breeched, giving rise to a different order in the factual sense, a situation where organizations reproduce themselves despite the apparent 'chaos from a normative point of view' (ibid.: 98).

Perrow's more specific analysis of organizations introduces the concept of 'operative goals' in contrast to 'official goals'. The latter constitute the general purpose of the organization as presented in official statements and documents. The former 'designate the ends sought through the actual operating policies of the organization; they tell us what the organization is actually trying to do' (Perrow, 1961: 856). The contrast between these two types of goals mirrors the multiplicity and conflicting nature of organizational goals in a general sense. As Perrow indicates, organizations are never stable, and the apparent tension among goals is a sign of health. 'Despite inevitable costs, such tension helps ensure ready channels for changes in goals, when appropriate' (Perrow, 1970: 174).

Organizations deviating from the rules and philosophies they officially profess commit operative crime; their conduct mirrors an intimate tension among goals: as Perrow would put it, their crime is a sign of health, because it points to possible channels of change when official rules of conduct prove unsatisfactory.

Gangster crimes of the powerful

I would group under this heading all those episodes in which powerful actors commit conventional crime. I am thinking of official entrepreneurs stealing, investing finances in illicit drugs, or funding kidnappings because they are in urgent need of cash (Ruggiero, 1992, 1996). These conducts should be understood in contexts where illegal supplementary incomes are made available which offer the possibility of rapid profits. In this respect, the existence of 'illegal islands' may be hypothesized which allow licit entrepreneurs occasional or intermittent incursions into the criminal arena.

The term 'gangster power crime' conveys a notion of conventional criminality committed by powerful actors in pursuit of supplementary financial gain. Non-patrimonial organizations, however, may also engage in this type of criminality, particularly when their goals include the conservation or enhancement of power.

The crimes of the powerful of a gangster type are, in a sense, copycat offences, because the perpetrators implement the techniques and the rationalizations they learn from conventional criminals in a mutual educational process. In this respect, Sutherland's view that criminal behaviour is learned within specific, circumscribed, occupational circles requires some revising. This type of crime of the powerful shows that criminal conducts possess a degree of modularity, as they migrate from one social enclave to the other, crossing occupational and cultural barriers.

Organizational theories can help locate this criminal variety analytically. While Etzioni's (1964) organization man, who tests reality and defers gratification, may not be the eponymous gangster, March's (1990: 335) morally uncertain man may well describe this type of powerful criminal. Uncertainty alludes to the incomplete rationality of organizations in a perpetually mobile landscape. March suggests that organizations should supplement the technology of reason with a *technology of foolishness*: 'Individuals and organizations need ways of doing things for which they have no good reason. Not always. Not usually. They need to act before they think'. The notion of foolishness should convey that of playfulness, which in turn entails a temporary relaxation or suspension of rules. This temporary absence of rules may favour the exploration of new possibilities, so that new, alternative rules may eventually be identified. Consistency is also suspended while a sort of transitional hypocrisy is adopted. In entering a moral limbo, powerful groups and individuals may therefore delete their memory: forgetting past rules and goals is a guarantee for the discovery of new ones.

Crimes of the powerful by proxy

This type of crime has a long tradition, bringing us back to some excellent pieces of work produced by Chicago School sociologists. The classic study conducted by Landesco (1973 [1929]), for example, shows how official political groups become promoters of criminal activity. Landesco describes the manipulation of elections by 'machine politicians' with underworld assistance, and the violent operations against rival candidates and parties 'contracted out' to organized criminal groups for the benefit of institutional actors (Ruggiero, 2006). In cases such as this, the crimes of the powerful by proxy entail the use by official powerful actors of an illegitimate or clandestine strong arm.

These types of crime, however, do not necessarily possess a violent nature, as in cases in which conventional criminal groups are used by entrepreneurs for the illegal transfer of goods or finances. In such cases, crime is to be understood as a specific illegal service provided to entrepreneurs or other powerful actors. This type of crime suggests that the encounter between powerful and criminal groups is not an unnatural interaction between a lawful, harmonious entity and a dysfunctional one, but rather a consortium of difficult detection due to the mediatory role of a number of actors. It is nevertheless a consortium that benefits all participants, although the subordinate position of conventional criminals remains one of its traits. The category that follows displays a more direct relationship between powerful and criminal groups, who engage in joint ventures where the dominant and subordinate roles are difficult to attribute.

Criminal power partnerships

Under this rubric I would include the crimes of the powerful that are committed jointly by licit and illicit groups and individuals. We are still in the domain of service provision, in the sense that the illegality is performed on behalf of legitimate entities, but in this case the agreement between the two parties is explicit. Cases falling within this category include the disposal of industrial waste in illegal sites, the illicit transfer of arms by organized criminal groups, or national and international fraudulent operations jointly performed by powerful groups and criminals. In some cases the items handled (e.g. arms, waste) are legally produced, but the routes through which they are moved are strictly regulated, hence the establishment of partnerships between producers and criminal groups aimed at bypassing regulations and ensuring movement. In other cases the 'items' are human beings, and the partnership may be explicit or unspoken, with the similar result that the parties involved promote each other's business and determine their respective profits. This specific type of criminal partnership between human smugglers and employers contains some traits characterizing the category that follows, a category describing criminals as benefactors.

Philanthropic crimes of the powerful

'Modern states kill and plunder on a scale that no robber band could hope to emulate' (Green and Ward, 2004: 1). Governments do not limit themselves to violent offending; they also make a major contribution to predatory crime, for example, in the form of corruption. However, powerful actors pursuing their interests do not always resort to coercion, nor do they need to justify their violations, whose perception as criminal acts depends on the strength of the legitimacy they enjoy. Successful power crime, therefore, needs to present itself as a philanthropic deed, in the sense that its effects must appear as benefiting others more than the perpetrator. Philanthropic criminals, in brief, manage to repel the criminal label from their activity and to persuade others that their goals correspond to those of the collectivity.

Foundational crimes of the powerful

The previous category is connected in a continuum with a number of other legitimate but harmful activities. There is a grey area in which conducts await the outcome of the criminalization–decriminalization conflict, in the sense that they may be subject to regulation or may become accepted routine. Some crimes possess a decriminalization impetus; for example, environmental crime for which prosecution is so rare that it appears as crime without criminals. Other criminal conducts implicitly invoke legal pragmatism, in that they challenge legal reasoning and require departure from precedents (Waldron, 2006). An influential version of pragmatism in academic law 'holds that anyone with political power should use that power to try to make things better in whatever way is possible given his institutional position and the degree of his power' (Dworkin, 2006: 23). Judges should, therefore, ignore the legality of certain acts and the jurisprudence determining it, but pursue single-mindedly the goal of strengthening their political community. 'All paraphernalia of traditional jurisprudence are swept away in the fresh wind of forward-looking, instrumental, means–end calculation' (ibid.: 24).

I describe crimes invoking legal pragmatism as foundational crimes, namely conducts inspired by an 'experimental' logic and driven by a consequentialist philosophy. Powerful actors so driven adopt illicit practices with the awareness that they are indeed illicit, but with an eye to the social and institutional reactions that may ensue. It is the intensity of such responses which will determine whether violations are to become part of a 'viable' routine or are to be carefully avoided. Some violations, in sum, possess a 'founding force', namely they are capable of transforming the previous jurisprudence and establishing new laws and new types of legitimacy (Derrida, 1992). Foundational power crime restructures the legal and the political spheres while playing a legislative role.

A variety of foundational crimes of the powerful fall into the economic domain and pertain, for example, to labour legislations, which suffer the experimental logic of employers. Others occur in corporate practice, whereby forcing the rules often results in new rules being devised, in a race which sees the law chasing the economy rather than vice versa. However, the most significant terrain in which foundational power crime is found is the one denoted by the use of a crucial resource: violence.

It is violence itself that may become lawmaking machinery: torture, military invasion, secret flights, kidnappings by secret services and the use of prohibited weapons appear to confirm that the crimes committed by powerful actors rewrite the international law and refound the principles of justice. Foundational crimes of the powerful also include responses to real or imagined threats which give the authorities an opportunity to modify the balance between security and freedom. Potential terrorist attacks, for example, engender a re-examination of that balance. 'Profound fear of further attack weighs heavily in favour of security and against the protection of civil liberties' (Zedner, 2005: 511). In the name of emergency, however, the liberties sacrificed may never be regained: the idea of trading off freedom for safety on a sliding scale is not only a scientific chimera, it is also a foundational practice redrawing human and civil rights and decriminalizing their violations.

It's the economy, stupid!

In an unforgettable TV appearance, Bill Clinton was challenged by a rival candidate to the presidency who quibbled on the programme of the Democratic Party and its capacity to govern the country. After a lively exchange on issues relating to the morality of public and private life, the would-be president concisely identified the arena in which the well-being of citizens should be measured: 'It's the economy, stupid!'

Through this metaphor I would designate all crimes of the powerful that are located in the most extreme ring of the legal–illegal chain, namely in the area where criminal and economic behaviour display intimate similarities. I am thinking of legitimate but harmful practices, and referring to conducts inspired by the cardinal values of market economies. These may be associated with labour exploitation, the perpetuation and accentuation of social inequality, and with all those innovative devices introduced in the economy that prompt Schumpeter to describe the latter as a process of creative destruction. Here, scholars may want to focus on the implicit criminal nature of the distance between costs and prices (as in Weber), on the criminal origin of capitalist accumulation (as in Marx), or on the specific psychological qualities of entrepreneurs impelling them to plunder their neighbours (as in Sombart). The investigation may also focus on more remote epochs, for example, the years when merchants and traders had to convince themselves and others that their activity was different from fraud, or the years when the first bankers in Florence and Genoa had to persuade the Church that their financial initiative could not be confused with sinful usury. This type of archaeological investigation will have to study the Gregorian reformation, which came into being during the course of the twelfth century, when the Church tried to cleanse itself of its compromises with money and various other impurities (Braudel, 1982; Le Goff, 2003). Here, one may study how the damage caused by the economy itself came to be accepted in the collective sensibility (Ruggiero, 2013). In this respect, the concept of 'externality' deserves painstaking examination, a concept that gave a powerful impetus to the perception of economic damage as collateral damage. Externality designates the effect of a transaction on a third party who has not consented to, or played any role in, carrying out that transaction. Working in this specific domain, analysts may want to ascertain whether the concept of externality deserves the scientific status it claims. Finally, and similarly, scholars who are interested in excavating the origin of the concept of 'just war' may want to peruse the writings of Saint Augustine who, while the Church was officially horrified by blood, justified the old and, inadvertently, the new Crusades (Tyerman, 2006).

Conclusion

The word *nasty* is not synonymous with criminal, and the concept of crime may be useless if it is indiscriminately applied to anything objectionable by whoever uses the term (Turk, 2000). In a nutshell, this is the theoretical predicament experienced by students of the crimes of the powerful and campaigners mobilizing against them. Such a predicament is expressed by analysts who search for the origin of corporate misconduct in the implicit 'boldness' of enterprise or in the risk-taking gamble of business that makes a manager resemble an Icarus in the boardroom (Skeel, 2005). It is manifested by scholars who highlight the difficulty of obtaining evidence of corporate wrongdoing, the legal privileges of powerful actors, and the ambivalence of the law in ascribing blame to organizations (Laufer, 2006). As Sutherland realized, research on the crimes of the powerful is difficult without a willingness to expand one's sample well beyond the legal definitions of crime. The crimes of the powerful are deemed examples of how conducts that are bad in themselves and conducts that are bad because they are prohibited by law may cohabit under the same rubric and within the same research agenda. 'State crime then incorporates acts both *mala in se* and *mala prohibita*, as well as those behaviours that have not reached the point where a formal law prohibits them' (Ross, 2000: 5).

This chapter has presented some of the main criminological contributions to the analysis of the crimes of the powerful and discussed the legal–illegal continuum characterizing the practices of organizations and powerful actors. An attempt has been made to isolate some of the distinct stages of such a continuum, thus identifying a number of criminal conducts displaying their own specific characteristics. The very existence of a grey area in which licit and illicit conducts intertwine indicates that contributions outside the field of criminology are necessary for a more complete explanation of the crimes of the powerful. This is the purpose of the following chapters.

3

FEARING THE FUTURE

Hubristic claims of independence by criminology cannot hide the evidence that its main cognitive tools, ideas and elaborations derive from its mother discipline: social theory. This chapter is a journey traversing this discipline in search of ideas which may deepen our understanding of the crimes of the powerful.

'Social' and 'society' maintain the nucleus of the Latin word *socius*, as we know, a term used to designate an individual involved in a trading partnership or, in a more general sense, in an economic transaction. This is ironic, as we shall see in the following pages, in that the values we encounter in the economic sphere are often profoundly antithetic to those we normally associate with the words 'social' and 'society'.

Ethical communion and unethical aggregations

Classical social theory, from its optimistic, evolutionist perspective, envisages a future of ethical communion, characterized by growing solidarity and cooperation. For Comte (1953) the civilization of labour, trade and industry is destined to bring harmony, as in Spencer (1969) liberal democracy is bound to abolish conflicts. Even war, let alone the crimes of the powerful, will wither away as a mode of pursuing national, economic or political interests. Evolution, in Comte, after crossing the theological and the metaphysical 'stage', will reach the final kingdom of science, where a secular civil religion will bind people in permanent peaceful cohabitation.

In the work of Vilfredo Pareto (1935, 1966), by contrast, societies are unethical aggregations governed by minority elites. The governing classes, he argues, are not tight, well-knit and clearly circumscribed organizations, but rather very unsystematic systems, much like feudal systems. 'The essence of all democracies is the patron–client relationship, a relationship based for the most part (and increasingly) on economic interests' (Pareto, 1996: 67). In such systems, democratic participation is achieved by courtesy of 'a vast number of mutually dependent hubs of influence and patronage, which keeps together by the fact that each hub is dependent to some extent on the good graces of another such hub' (ibid.). The task of these systems, in order to maintain their stability, is to aggregate the various centres of patronage, the various clienteles, in such a way that they are all satisfied (Ruggiero, 2000). Powerful offenders may be located within both the categories Pareto identifies: the *foxes*, who are short-term opportunists, skilled at combining diverse interests and pursing them through cunning strategies, and the *lions*, who are bound in persistent aggregations and pursue long-term goals (Harrington, 2005).

Except for the work of Gaetano Mosca (1939), who studies the ruling classes and how they reproduce themselves in self-perpetuating cliques, the elite disappears for a while from the scene, while the concerns of social theorists are mainly directed to order and anomie. The problem of modern society, for Durkheim (1960, 1996), is the slow erosion of moral authority generated by sudden change. Its transitional character makes the two opposite natures of human beings visible: *homo duplex* is the expression used by Durkheim to describe humans as simultaneously violent and sociable. When solidarity declines due to the withering away of a shared system of beliefs and morals, human beings are exposed to their unregulated desires and ambitions. As a consequence, egoism, ambition and unlimited aspirations are encouraged, spreading social malaise. The crimes of the powerful may be situated within this analytical framework, which Durkheim mainly associates with the economic sphere. The economy, he argues, experiences a constant pathological state, because development and incessant change, in this specific area of collective life, appear to evade the moderating action of moral regulation. A chronic climate of competition prevails whereby individuals find themselves freed from any restraints guiding and selecting their aspirations.

In this analysis, the sphere of the state remains untouched, as Durkheim attributes to the state a role of moral guarantor: it is only the state apparatus, he argues, which possesses sufficient authority and collective power to create and protect individual rights. As an organ of moral discipline, by definition, the state cannot list powerful offenders among its representatives. It is only when dealing with war, and after the killing of his son in the First World War, that Durkheim tangentially addresses this aspect: states engaged in war, he says, reduce societies, even the most cultivated, to a moral condition that recalls that of the lower societies (Durkheim, 1985). Individuals are obscured, they cease to count: 'it is the mass which becomes the supreme social factor; a rigid authoritarian discipline is imposed on all volitions'. War, which epitomizes an excessive attachment to one's nation, to one's group or culture, casts 'into the background all feelings of sympathy for the individual' (Durkheim, 1996: 117).

That his concerns exclude the crimes of the powerful is vividly shown by the solutions Durkheim proposes in response to the decline of solidarity. His remedies for anomie include the creation of social institutions such as professional groups and other intermediary agencies capable of engaging in a dialogue aimed at the collective well-being. These groups may differ from the medieval guilds, but they still represent social spaces 'where people with common interests and concerns can gather together, establish direct lines of communication, and form collective identities' (Harrington, 2005: 55). How such professional groups and intermediary associations will reduce inequality, that for Durkheim 'is the source of the evil', is hard to explain. What he proposes, it would appear, is the formation of those very groups, enclaves or cliques that are already in operation, and that Pareto and Mosca regard as the social aggregates underpinning the crimes of the elite.

This chapter started off by noting an antithesis between the 'social' and the 'economic': it is time to examine the contribution of social theory in this regard.

Markets vs. communities

Max Weber argues that markets are antithetic to all other communities, because the latter, not the former, presuppose 'brotherhood' among people.

In trade, the guarantee of legality on the part of two individuals involved is based on the presupposition, often shared by both, that each of them will have an interest in continuing the exchange in the future, and that therefore each will respect the pacts and the promise given. However, because trade is a form of socialization with strangers, therefore with enemies, at the origin, Weber notes, the supervision of legality was entrusted to the religious authority, under the tutelage of the temple, which with time became the state. Supervising legality, however, does not guarantee the rationality of economic initiative, which by pursuing maximum profitability is constantly urged to cross the boundaries of legality itself. There is, therefore, an element of substantive irrationality in the economic order, determined by attempts to make short-term speculative profit, described by Weber as 'pure gambling interest', which 'is one of the sources of the phenomena known as the "crises" of the modern market economy' (Weber, 1978: 40).

Chapter 6 of this book will deal specifically with the crimes of the powerful from an economic perspective. Here, focusing on the work of Weber, it should be noted that in his argument humans are creatures of habit, but are also strongly motivated by their material and ideal interests to circumvent conventional and legal rules, and 'in all societies the economically powerful tend to have a strong influence on the enactment and interpretation of the law' (Roth, 1978: lxix). For this reason, Weber's work on the sociology of law is in a sense a sociology of domination, in which the gradual usurpation of collective power results in legitimate institutional force.

Following a Weberian classification, power implies the use or threat of coercive force on those who are given orders, whereas domination is to be understood as legitimized, internalized propensity to obey orders.

> Power is the probability that one actor within a social relationship will be in a position to carry out his own will despite resistance. Domination is the probability that a command with a given specific content will be obeyed by a given group of persons.

> Discipline is the probability that by virtue of habituation a command will receive prompt and automatic obedience in stereotyped forms, on the part of a given group of persons.
>
> *(Weber, 1978: 53)*

Legitimacy, however, though internalized, needs constant justification on the part of those who have authority, wealth and honour to give reasons for their good fortune. Weber does not propose a joint analysis of legitimacy and the crimes of the powerful, but the scene he sets appears to be ideally conducive to law violations. He is, however, more explicit in this respect when linking the economy to social norms.

There are legal and sociological points of view. Through the former, we ask: What is intrinsically valid as law? That is to say: What significance or what *normative* meaning ought to be attributed to a verbal pattern having the form of a legal proposition? In a sociological perspective, the question becomes:

> What *actually* happens in a group owing to the *probability* that persons engaged in social action, especially those exerting a socially relevant amount of power, subjectively consider certain norms as valid and practically act according to them, in other words, orient their own conduct towards these norms?
>
> *(Ibid.: 311)*

This distinction also determines the relationship between law and economy. Jurists, Weber explains, take for granted the empirical validity of legal propositions; therefore they examine each of them and try to determine the logic and the meaning those propositions have within a coherent system. Jurists, in brief, are concerned with the 'legal order'. Sociological economics, on the other hand, considers actual human activities as they are conditioned by the necessity to take into account the facts of economic life. 'The legal order of legal theory has nothing directly to do with the world of real economic conduct, since both exist on different levels. One exists in the realm of the *ought*, while the other deals with the world of the *is*' (ibid.). The crimes of the powerful, we are authorized to infer, belong to the world of the *is*, and constitute strategies prompted by the difficulties and uncertainties actors face in the economic arena. Such strategies spread, multiply, mushroom, becoming what Weber describes as 'habituation' and 'custom', and although illicit, they determine 'unreflective conducts' morally approved within the surrounding environment.

Mere custom can be of far-reaching economic significance: 'Adherence to what has become customary is such a strong component of all conduct and, consequently, of all social action, that legal coercion, where it opposes custom, frequently fails in the attempt to influence actual conduct' (ibid.: 320). Convention is equally effective, if not more so. Weber argues that individuals are affected by responses to their action emanating from their peers rather than an earthly or transcendental authority. The existence of a 'convention' may thus be far more determinative of conducts than the existence of a legal enforcement machinery. Of course, it is hard to clearly establish the point at which certain actions become custom and certain modes of conduct take on a binding nature. Nevertheless, Weber sees 'abnormality' (or, in our lexicon, deviance) as 'the most important source of innovation ... capable of exercising a special influence on others' (ibid.: 320–321).

Innovation, in economic initiative as well as in deviance, is constituted by a number of elements. First, there is 'inspiration', namely a sudden awareness that a certain action ought to be effected, irrespective of the drastic, or illegitimate, means it requires. Second, empathy or identification, that is, influencing others into acting and at the same time being influenced by their action. When conducts begin to observe a degree of regularity, the third element, *oughtness*, emerges, 'producing consensus and ultimately law' (ibid.: 323).

> Obviously, legal guarantees are directly at the service of economic interests to a very large degree. Even where this does not seem to be, or actually is not, the case, economic interests are among the strongest factors influencing the creation of law. ... The power of law over economic conduct has in many respects grown weaker rather than stronger.
>
> *(Ibid.: 334–335)*

Weber is suggesting that the patterns of relationships among economic actors are determined by experimentation that then turns into habit and are impervious to normative adjustments (Roth, 1978; Ruggiero, 2013). The inclination to forgo economic opportunity simply in order to act legally is obviously slight, he remarks, unless circumvention of the formal law is strongly disapproved of by powerful actors and collectivities. 'Besides, it is often not difficult to disguise the circumvention of a law in the economic sphere' (Weber, 1978: 335).

Applying a Weberian classification to the crimes of the powerful, we propose that some of these crimes implement forms of traditional action deriving from long-established patterns of interaction and habit. Others are guided by emotion, feeling and affect, therefore reflecting status and internal cohesion within specific elites. Others, on the other hand, may be linked to value-rational action, in the sense that their motivations are found in the belief in a particular, unquestionable set of values. Finally, other such crimes may be solely motivated by material interest, being the outcome of instrumentally rational enterprise.

Durable formations and domination

Adjectives describing the sociology of Georg Simmel (1950) vary from residualist to formalist, interactionist to analogic, ambivalent to tragic (Dal Lago, 1994). Residualism refers to Simmel's interest in what are usually regarded as lesser manifestations of social life, while formalism alludes to his study not so much of social events as of the form in which they present themselves to observers. His addressing relationships rather than structures and how relationships are reproduced from one ambit to another accounts for the description of his research as simultaneously interactionist and analogic. Finally, a tragic ambivalence is detected in his refusal to commit himself to general explanatory paradigms, his unorthodox views about scientific thinking, and his relying on 'unfounded certainties' as a response to the crisis of modernity (Cassano, 1983). For our purposes his analysis is important for the way in which it unveils how informal conventions regulate the life and conduct of social groups. Simmel shows that 'molecular' relationships determine social phenomena as we witness them, and that larger formations 'preserve their visibility and perform their function only insofar as they are sustained on a day-to-day basis by a multitude of minute, inconspicuous episodes of interaction' (Harrington, 2005: 79). Powerful groups, from this perspective, reproduce themselves and the ways in which they operate thanks to the inconspicuous modalities by which they elect their goals and choose the means to achieve them. These groups are both close to and distant from society as a whole and its institutions, they are drawn towards and away from them, they may temporarily comply with general norms, conditionally violate them or totally reinvent them.

Contemporary application of this framework of analysis is found in the work on 'networks of trust', constituted by people connected by similar ties, carrying on major long-term initiatives, and competing with society at large for power and resources. The operations of such networks are possible when the boundaries between 'them' and 'us' are maintained or strengthened, and when informal mechanisms lead to agreements about proper and improper behaviour. 'Over the long historical run trust networks' most persistent and effective predators have been duly constituted governmental agents who were just doing their jobs' (Tilly, 2005: 86). Trust networks may capture relevant governmental activities: for example, purchase favours from bureaucrats and politicians, secure public office for private interests, and create 'governmental agencies devoted entirely to the advantage of specific groups' (ibid.: 159).

Simmel's 'molecular relationships', from which networks of trust analysis seems to derive, explain therefore the durable social formations which are the source of the crimes of the powerful, suggesting that criminal conducts are specific features of domination. We need now to address Simmel's views on domination to collect more analytical tools that will help us in our task.

Even the abstract will to dominate, for Simmel, is a case of interaction. The 'superordinates' will draw satisfaction from the fact that the acting or the suffering of 'subordinates' are effects of their will. The significance of the act of domination for the superordinates consists, therefore, of the consciousness of their own efficacy in dominating. Still, the desire for domination incorporates some concern for the person being dominated, and the notion of society only disappears when the independent significance of one of the two interacting parties is eliminated. Simmel provides the example of the lowest paid workers in large enterprises, where:

> the difference in the strategic positions of workers and employers is so overwhelming that the work contract ceases to be a contract

in the ordinary sense of the word, because the former are
unconditionally at the mercy of the latter.

(Simmel, 1971a: 97)

Even in such situations of oppressive and cruel subordination, however,
there is a considerable measure of freedom for the subordinate. In brief,
authority presupposes to a higher extent than is usually recognized 'a freedom on the part of the person subjected to authority' (ibid.: 98). We shall
see shortly how these observations are developed in the thought of Michel
Foucault. We should note here that this analysis of domination and 'relationships of authority', if applied to the crimes of the powerful, would
suggest that such crimes are not based exclusively on coercion but also on
some degree of consensus. Extending this suggestion, we may hypothesize
that their perception rather than their actual incidence plays a crucial role,
as the crimes of the powerful, in some contexts, may be widespread and,
at the same time, very visible. In such contexts these crimes are granted a
form of silent, complicit legitimacy, while the way in which they are
perceived does not lead to deterrence but to tolerance or even imitation.

We have seen, both in Weber and in Simmel, that social interactions
may escape normative control and even when coercion appears to be pre-
eminent a degree of cooperation among parties persists. The relationship
between power and crime could be observed against this relational backdrop. There are, of course, social theorists who would refute this analytical
perspective. Talcott Parsons (1960), for instance, sees no connection
between power and crime: in his harmonic view of social systems, there
seems to be no space for anomalies or illicit deviations of the organisms
forming them. The very phrase 'illegitimate power' is an oxymoron, in
that without legitimation or justification, according to Parsons, power is
no longer what it claims to be (Lukes, 1986). Reviewing other insights,
however, we encounter definitions of the crimes of the powerful that
derive from a critical reading of the definitions of power itself. It is to
such definitions that I now turn.

Romantic pluralism

Wright Mills (1956) argues that some groups make decisions that greatly
affect the everyday existence of ordinary women and men. On the other

hand, the failure of these groups to act and make decisions may produce greater consequences than their action or the decisions they do make. This view constitutes an implicit refutation of the 'theory of balance', which describes governments as 'automatic machines' regulated by an equilibrium among competing interests. 'This image of politics is simply a carry-over from the official image of the economy; in both, an equilibrium is achieved by the pulling and hauling of many interests' (ibid.: 242). Wright Mills terms this an expression of romantic pluralism, whereby it is implied that someone's interests coincide with those of the community as a whole. In reality, he stresses, interests are strictly intertwined with social roles and when these are challenged the elites may just 'smash one structure and set up another in which they then enact quite different roles' (ibid.: 25). In fact, such destruction and creative reinvention of social roles are typical manifestations, or prime marks, of what is commonly termed great leadership.

   On the relationship between power and modern democratic forms of government, Wright Mills echoes the analysis of Pareto presented above. In Wright Mills' version of Pareto's argument, we are told of the 'truly vested interests pushed and protected' by political representatives, who merely heed the parochial demands of local communities. 'Parochial interests are compromised and balanced by other parochial interests', and the prime task of the Congressman, therefore, is to seek what 'favour he can do for one interest that will not hurt any of the other interests he must balance' (ibid.: 256). Wright Mills extends Pareto's criticism, however, to cover both the economic and the political spheres. In the former, he sees changes of power relations and abuses in the disappearance of small entrepreneurs and the creation of a handful of large corporations. In addressing the latter, he argues that his notion of 'higher immorality' is not to be understood as primarily a matter of corrupt individuals in fundamentally sound institutions. 'Political corruption is one aspect of a more general immorality' (ibid.: 343). He does not specify what a higher immorality consists of, nor does he sociologically define it. What he suggests is that the level of moral sensibility 'that now prevails is not merely a matter of corrupt men'. Corruption, he adds, is a systematic feature of the American elite and 'its general acceptance is an essential feature of the mass society' (ibid.). In brief, in both spheres, namely the economic and the political, his definition of power overlaps with that of the crimes of the powerful. Let us examine this aspect in more detail.

Wright Mills concurs that there may be sound institutions hiring corrupt individuals, but is more inclined to detect the capacity of institutions themselves to corrupt those who occupy a position in them. In the corporate era, he remarks, relationships are impersonal and leaders as well as executives are partly relieved from individual, direct responsibilities. As a consequence, 'the private conscience is attenuated – and the higher immorality is institutionalized' (ibid.). Political careers, in this climate, require the hasty adoption of a somewhat blunted moral sensibility. And in an explicit evocation of the crimes of the powerful, he concludes: 'Many of the problems of white-collar crime and relaxed public morality, of high-priced vice and of fading personal integrity, are problems of structural immorality' (ibid.).

Techniques of neutralization, in this context, do not take the form of ad hoc justifications for illicit conducts, but demand the appeal to some threatening force, some ineluctable menace to which conducts are called to provide responses. One such threatening force is 'crisis', a 'bankrupt' concept and term, in Wright Mills' opinion, constantly evoked by the elites 'in order to cover up their extraordinary policies and deed'. In fact, it is precisely the absence of crises, understood as challenges to the status quo and the distribution of power, that characterizes the higher immorality. In the absence of crises so understood, another, more insidious process is likely to take place, one leading to generalized distrust and cynicism, defined by Wright Mills as 'Machiavellianism-for-the-little-man'. The allusion here is to a form of popular consensus expressed through a vicarious enjoyment of the privileges of the rich and a morbid interest in the lifestyle of celebrities. When it comes to honour and repute, therefore, 'money-makers' have no rivals, while all values and choices end up being exclusively weighed in relation to the individual gains they bring. Hence the increasingly limited number of people who are entrusted with taking decisions which affect all and the growing effort to imitate the privileged few. This is the trajectory of democracy.

> A society that is in its higher circles and on its middle level widely believed to be a network of smart rackets does not produce men with an inner moral sense; a society that is merely expedient does not produce men of conscience. A society that narrows the

meaning of success to the big money and in its terms condemns failure as the chief vice, raising money to the plane of absolute value, will produce the sharp operator and the shady deal.

(Ibid.: 347)

This form of consensus, ultimately, hints at the widespread acceptance of success as a result of immorality. Echoes of Simmel's work on dominance and authority are clearly perceptible. Wright Mills' emphasis on how the meaning of success is narrowed to coincide with big money, moreover, finds a precedent in Simmel's comparison of money with prostitution: the indifference with which money lends itself to any use, the infidelity with which it switches partners, its incapacity to create ties, 'its complete objectification that excludes any attachment and makes it suitable as a pure means – all this suggests a portentous analogy between money and prostitution' (Simmel, 1971c: 122).

But with these formulations we are now entering a different theoretical area, where power tends to become diffuse and the crimes of the powerful take on a set of different features. One wonders whether Wright Mills was aware of how social theorists succeeding him on the scene would extend his embryonic argument. We shall discuss this extension later, after examining the contribution of other classics in the history of social theory.

Latent functions and choice

Robert Merton warns that his analysis runs counter to prevailing moral evaluations, as these tend to be based on the manifest consequences of conducts. The latent functions he identifies in the political machine or the 'political racket', therefore, may be judged as unequivocally bad and undesirable. The grounds for such judgement vary: political rackets violate moral codes, bribery hampers smooth interactions and 'protection for crime clearly violates the law and the mores' (Merton, 1968: 125). From his viewpoint, however, such conducts may perform positive functions which are not adequately fulfilled by behaviour complying with the law. Focused on corruption, his analysis proceeds with the remark that the structural function of a corrupt politician or 'boss' is to organize, centralize and maintain in good working conditions the 'scattered fragments of power which are at present dispersed through our political organization' (ibid.: 126). Among the subgroups identified by Merton as the beneficiaries of political bosses are businesspeople who are offered privileges entailing economic gain. In such cases, the political machine rationalizes the relationships between public and private business. In brief, even corrupt political machines and rackets, like gangster Al Capone, represent the triumph of amoral intelligence over morally prescribed failure.

Merton's functionalism inspired several authors according to whom corruption is mainly found in transitional societies, where it contributes to the humanization and personalization of new social bonds. From this perspective, political machines are said to flourish during periods of rapid growth, when the sense of community is weakened and fragmentation makes particularistic ties virtually the only feasible means of cooperation. A tolerant attitude towards corruption, therefore, may be the only way in which institutions geared towards economic and social progress can be established. These institutions, though corrupt, will still provide conduits of integration for individuals who would otherwise systematically resort to violence in order to express their political and social demands. In a nutshell: who would blame people who bribe their way out of a concentration camp?

Corrupt powerful individuals, from this standpoint, may play a crucial social function, although we may object that their being corrupt does not restrain them from systematically resorting to violence. Merton, however, also examines the structural context in which powerful individuals and groups operate and it is perhaps in this specific examination that we can find some pointers for the analysis of the crimes of the powerful. His celebrated classification of 'deviant adaptations' needs only a brief summary here: crime is a response to 'a heavy emphasis on wealth as a basic symbol of success, without a corresponding emphasis upon the legitimate means on which to march toward this goal' (ibid.: 193). Applied to privileged groups, this formula should be read against the specific political culture predominating in the US, where the legal possibility of highly centralized power is, according to Merton, precluded. Centralized authority is distrusted as an obstacle to liberty: as a consequence, power is spread thinly and barriers are erected against its concentration. Authorities, therefore, are unable to take positive action, and as a consequence deviant actors may replace them. Business corporations, for example, seek 'special political dispensations which will enable them to stabilize their situation and to near their objective of maximizing profits' (ibid.: 129). In this respect, Merton notes the basic similarity between legitimate and illegitimate business, as both are concerned with providing goods and services for which there is a demand. Ultimately, his analysis of the crimes of the powerful relies on the importance of technical expediency, and of the available procedures, whether legitimate or not, which are 'most efficient in netting the culturally approved values' (ibid.: 189). The crimes of the powerful are the outcomes of a culture that eulogizes 'winning' rather than winning under the rules of the game.

Merton's theoretical apparatus is not universally embraced. Social theory hinging on rational choice, for example, rejects explanations of human behaviour based on the influence of external forces (Inglis with Thorpe, 2012). Emphasizing human agency, Coleman (1990: 13) stresses that 'persons act purposively toward a goal, with the goal (and thus the actions) shaped by values and preferences'. Purposive agents, it is argued, manipulate and accumulate resources and, in so doing, they interact in systemic competition. In debt to Weber's methodological individualism for its focus on social relationships as they occur, rational choice theory as elaborated by James Coleman implies that individuals adhere to norms when they benefit from their regulative power, and that some groups gain the power to decide which norms should prevail. This is achieved through the unilateral transfer of power, so that some actors become dependent on others; for example, ordinary individuals become subordinated to large corporations and governments. 'Primordial institutions' such as the family, class, ethnic group and communities are replaced by purposive structures such as economic and political organizations. This rearrangement and constant polarization of power, we may conclude, is the source of the crimes of the powerful.

We have returned to the line of argument established by Simmel, Wright Mills and others, and it is to power itself that we will now turn.

Locating power and its crimes

Social power relations entail the ability of some actors to lay routine, enforceable boundaries upon the activities of others. This ability may rest on the resources possessed by the former allowing them to deprive others of freedom, bodily integrity, 'reliable access to nourishment, shelter or other primary material goods; the enjoyment of a degree of assurance of one's worth and significance' (Poggi, 2001: 14). Such deprivations, at times, may be disguised behind a 'service conception' of power, adopted by actors who claim that they are not pursuing their own goals but those of others or of the community as a whole. 'Needless to say, this service conception is usually and especially favoured by the powerful and those employed in defending and promoting their power' (Lukes, 1986: 7).

The service conception of power, therefore, may be deemed to be a pure ideological artifice. This notwithstanding, powerful groups and individuals are unlikely to be credible on exclusively ideological grounds unless they are prepared to grant concessions, be they material or symbolical, to the powerless. Such concessions describe an apparent process of decentring and diffusion, whereby resources and status seem to percolate throughout a system and among its members. Diffusion, on the other hand, renders the location of power difficult, making it problematic to call, as Wright Mills suggests, men of power to account. The controversy engaging Wright Mills and Raymond Aron is, in this respect, illuminating. Mills argues that power lies with those who occupy key positions allowing them to make choices that affect large sections of society. If such choices fail to benefit the collectivity, it is 'sociologically realistic, morally fair and politically imperative to make demands upon men of power and to hold them responsible for specific courses of events' (Wright Mills, 1959: 100). For Raymond Aron (1964), on the other hand, it makes no sense to single out individual power holders in societies where, through pluralism and democracy, namely through the very dispersion of power, maintenance of privilege and inequality are achieved.

Michel Foucault (1977, 1986) brings the analysis of dispersion to its most radical consequences. In his approach, the production of dis-courses of truth connotes the limits of power. Truth must be produced like wealth, 'indeed we must produce truth in order to produce wealth in the first place' (Foucault, 1986: 230). It is the monopoly in the production of truth that creates domination, not that of the king upon his subjects, but that among subjects in their ordinary interactions. Power, in this way, is expressed through a chain of disciplinary tools leading to constant and growing subjugation, ultimately governing bodies, behaviours and thoughts:

> Subjects are gradually, progressively, really and materially con-stituted through a multiplicity of organisms, forces, energies, materials, desires, thoughts, etc. We should try to grasp subjection in its material instance as a constitution of subjects.
>
> *(Ibid.: 233)*

These micro-mechanisms of power delimit our field of action and knowledge, making us participants in our own subjugation (Drayfus and Rabinow, 1983).

Foucault's argument, therefore, is that power 'circulates', it is never localized here, there or in someone's hands, never appropriated as a commodity or piece of wealth. Individuals 'circulate' too, as they simultaneously endure and exercise power: 'They are not only its inert or consenting target; they are always also the elements of its articulation. In other words, individuals are the vehicles of power, not its points of application' (Foucault, 1986: 234).

While this analysis depicts power as domination and subjugation, it fails to indicate where and in what circumstances conducts of powerful groups and individuals may be described as criminal. Some tentative suggestions in this respect derive from an extension of Foucault's arguments.

Akin to the notion of individuals participating in the process of their own subjugation is the phenomenon of status imitation, whereby the powerless adopt the values of the powerful. The 'trickling down' of status symbols, for instance, manifests itself through a form of 'layering', so that an exchange of sort takes place and complicity is established between parties that, nevertheless, remain engaged in drastically asym-metrical relationships. 'The very widespread phenomenon of clientele can be interpreted in this sense' (Poggi, 2001: 36). This type of exchange reproduces the large power differences between those involved, yet brings both in a common field of action and, ultimately, in a shared universe of meaning. The subordinate person offering complicity, in many cases, may be granted material advantages, privileged access to public resources, or a degree of immunity from public exactions.

'Generally speaking, the chief effect of the combination is to strengthen the relationship's core feature, which remains the substantial power inequality between the parties' (ibid.: 36). Examples are found in societies where opportunities are granted to ordinary citizens to benefit from minor episodes of corruption. In such societies ordinary citizens may be led to condone large-scale corruption enacted by the elite: rather than 'condemning the condemners' (yet another technique of neutralization) we are faced here with a process of 'condoning the condoners' (Ruggiero, 2000).

Power, in such cases, is not confined to exacting obedience or pursuing egoistic interests, but spreads into the arena in which priorities are established and where others are mobilized to assist the powerful in their own practices. This consists in the capacity of one party to determine the action and reaction of others according to its gain. If we embrace this perspective we are forced to modify Weber's definitions, which characterize the 'others' as simple opponents of power holders, and subscribe to the view that the 'others' may well be victimized by being induced to implement the will of the power holders.

In brief, if we extend Foucault's analysis, we reach the point where individuals are vehicles not only of power but also of the crimes of the powerful. Let us see in the final part of this chapter whether we can find some insights within social theory warranting such a conclusion.

Economic power, social norms and herd behaviour

Our understanding of the world and the possibility of acting in it depend on concepts and categories of meaning. A group that manages to elaborate a more or less coherent set of concepts and categories, and to make it acceptable to others, will gain empowerment over the rest of society (Mann, 1986). Such a group may also identify norms, namely 'shared understandings of how people should act morally in relation to one another' and gain power as these norms are sanctioned by society (Poggi, 2001: 60).

Drawing on Foucault's suggestions, power may be distinguished as authoritative or diffused. The former pertains to institutions issuing commands and requiring conscious obedience. The latter is unconscious, decentred, and spreads spontaneously throughout a population, resulting in practices that are not explicitly commanded. Diffused power, typically, is not formed of the couplet command–obedience, but rests on the assumption that the practices adopted are normal, natural, the result of self-evident common interest (Mann, 1986). Practices, in brief, reflect norms as shared understandings of how people are expected to act. Some final considerations pertaining to the normative realm may further clarify the analysis conducted so far.

It is a common understanding that people are prevented from preying on each other due to the force of state laws. A person will lie, steal, drive carelessly or kill unless the state erects a deterrent in the form of laws against fraud, theft, negligence and murder. This description of the world, in Posner's (2000) analysis, is partly true, but mostly wrong. Most people, in fact, often refrain from harmful conducts even when laws do not prohibit them. To understand how conformity to social norms occurs it is necessary to observe the relationship between law and non-legal mechanisms of cooperation.

People engage in signalling games in order to show that they are desirable partners in cooperative endeavours. Such games establish behavioural regularities and guarantee the predictability of the effects of interactions. Good or bad reputations, depending on the signaller, are built as people attempt to publicize their skills and potential to benefit others in joint ventures. When criminals send signals they find a way of displaying their credentials, identifying each other, advertising the goods they trade and their reputation, while at the same time 'maintaining secrecy vis-à-vis rivals and law enforcers' (Gambetta, 2009: vii). Law-abiding people, similarly, identify possible partners by signalling their own reputation as cooperative individuals in the face of incentives to free-ride on group endeavours. Legal rules, it may be suggested, attempt to harness these informal norms of interaction by providing a more or less precise behavioural template. Ideally, in order to safeguard the interests of all parties interacting, these rules should incorporate or direct the independent regulatory force of social norms. Social norms, however, are unlikely 'to change as a result of simple, discrete, low-cost interventions by the government' (Posner, 2000: 8). This is because actors may have invested large amounts of time and resources in perfecting their social norms of interaction and, therefore, would expect to reap enough future payoffs before being prepared to abide by the laws.

Those who violate social norms may value the immediate benefit of their behaviour more than its reputational consequences, thus discounting the future heavily. Violators, at times, may also be motivated by the fact that others cannot afford to ostracize them, and that even their bad reputation will not reduce the desire of others to interact with them: at times cutting off relationships with violators can result in loss. This perception is caused by the idea that those who violate social norms are wealthy and powerful enough to be able to afford violations, and that they deserve cooperation or imitation.

> A common modern form of hubris is for increasingly successful people to violate norms until they go too far and are finally shunned by anyone whose cooperation they would find desirable. They violate norms as a challenge: it is their way of saying: you need me more than I need you.
>
> *(Ibid.: 28)*

Ostentatious violators of social norms include conventional as well as powerful criminals, both implicitly declaring their loyalty to their own system of values as alternative systems to the dominant ones. What is important to note, moreover, is that such violators may trigger 'herd behaviour', namely imitative conduct based on the observation that the behaviour of violators is undeniably successful. In such circumstances, shaming violators by communicating their undesirable character proves ineffective, as it is unlikely to provoke genuine ostracism. Even the peers of violators will hesitate to act as whistleblowers, fearing the loss of future opportunities that interactions with them will certainly bring. In brief, the act of shaming is often too costly. In extreme cases, even formal punishment may fail to build a bad reputation for those punished, who may instead use it as a 'badge of status', a sign of distinction which augments rather than dents their popularity.

Conclusion

We have reached the end of our swift journey. Criminological analysis of the crimes of the powerful has relied on economic variables or focused on state formation. It has been inspired by anomie and conflict theory and, at times, has addressed the dynamics guiding the behaviour of organizations and their members. Going through some key contributions emanating from social theory, we have gathered additional insights. We have learned that powerful offenders can be *foxes* or *lions*, that the elite has a propensity to offend due to the mode in which it reproduces itself in closed cliques and to the competitive climate in which it operates. While Durkheim sees in *homo duplex* the co-presence of violence and sociability, Max Weber detects in markets something substantially antithetic to the very notion of community, namely an element of substantive irrationality encouraging speculation and 'pure gambling interest'. We have apprehended that molecular relationships and networks of trust underlie criminal conducts, and that these conducts require specific relationships of domination and authority. It is also in the very trajectory of democracy, as we have seen, that the higher immorality of powerful offenders may be inscribed. The notion of 'winning' rather than 'winning according to the rules' has provided yet another supplementary viewpoint, while the increasing polarization of power has been listed among the causative conditions. The review proposed in this chapter has been enriched with definitions and analyses of the crime of the powerful derived from definitions of power itself, providing an arena of investigation and thinking that will need further future efforts. Here we have learned that the diffusion and relational constitution of power, along with imitative behaviour, can help locate theoretically, with more precision, the crimes of the powerful.

Ultimately, it is worth drawing attention to 'uncertainty' as a crucial aspect of the life of powerful offenders, who are not only led to violations by the 'objective' dynamics of the free enterprise, but also by the contingent economic and political conditions, by the assessment of their immediate financial circumstances, and by their forecast of future economic development. The crimes of the powerful, therefore, may be partly deemed to be the outcome of fear for the future. Fear, however, is also an element of power itself. As Poggi (2001: 11) has perceptively argued:

> Power has to do with the future, with expectations, with hopes and fears. In this sense, it has anthropological significance. ... Hobbes was right in saying that humans alone, among animals,

can feel tomorrow's hunger today. We can think of power as a way of confronting and controlling the inexorable sense of contingency and insecurity generated by our awareness of the future.

Social theory as applied in this chapter allows us to view the crimes of the powerful in the same fashion. The crimes of the powerful are the result of an obsessive relationship of powerful individuals and groups with their future, they are forms of accumulation and accretion of the power they already possess inspired by fear that in the future events may lead to them losing that power.

4

THE LAW OF POWER

Fearing the future, as we have seen in the previous chapter, could be listed among the motivations for offending. Powerful offenders, moreover, could be led to act illegally because others fail to ostracize them, or simply feel that they can afford to violate laws. The powerful, therefore, are capable of sparking cooperation, if not imitation. This process entails a view of the law that recalls an ancient, yet contemporary, diatribe.

Plato and Thrasymachus express two contrasting views of the law whose echo constantly returns, to the point that contemporary views of the crimes of the powerful could be situated within the analytical framework drawn by the former or the latter respectively. Plato fears social disunity and, as a consequence, looks for norms to which everyone is willing to submit. Compliance, in his view, is brought about by persuasion, which locates the law in a sphere of equality and promotes the image of people as free individuals among free peers. Plato is concerned with *isonomia*, namely equality of rights, legal universalism. Thrasymachus, by contrast, argues that 'the just is nothing else than the advantage of the stronger: each form of government enacts the laws with a view to its own advantage' (Plato, 1937: 39). The thinkers and law scholars discussed in this chapter may be grouped under the philosophical tradition of the former or the latter, which does not imply disrespecting their contribution for having added little to the contrasting paradigms drawn thousands of years ago. In fact, having one's thought associated with such giant father founders, if anything, should be flattering. This chapter contrasts law as guarantee against power with law as perpetuation of power and encouragement for its relentless accumulation.

Justice and consensus

Plato's concerns are relived in the numerous attempts to establish an autonomous science of jurisprudence, a pure theory of law independent of empirical social disciplines as well as moral theory. Kelsen (1945) makes one such attempt in his celebrated work separating morality from the theory of justice. Laws are valid, in his argument, if and only if they are enacted in accordance with the procedures authorized by a basic norm (Vinx, 2007). As a logical system of norms, law is closed in on itself, although it constantly refers to *Grundnorm*, a foundational set of legal principles. This logical system is autopoietic, in the sense that, as we see in biology and cybernetics, it maintains itself by reproducing its own components.

Jurisprudence, therefore, is a normative science because it is devoid of ideology and because it reflects constitutional arrangements and pre-established legal principles. In Kelsen, lack of ideology equates to independence from myth, and his 'pure' theory of law is congruent with the formation of stable and humane communities (Williams, 2007). His theory, ultimately, is meant to support liberal democracy and individual freedom.

Kelsen may advocate non-ideological laws and constitutional principles, but his aspiration to create stable and humane communities may be regarded as an effect of his own political ideology. In other words, his 'pure' theory contains an evaluative choice which situates him among the defenders of parliamentary democracy and of liberal constitutionalism. Moreover, his advocacy of an international legal order that would provide for binding mechanisms of peaceful conflict resolution among states makes his theory consistent with the idea of the rule of law, at national as well as at international level.

In Kelsen's perspective, it would appear, the crimes of the powerful are jurisprudentially inconceivable, as they are above the law and, when taking the form of state illegal action, they violate the content of the positive, basic norms constitutionally established. This formulation is an endorsement of the principle that state power should be limited by stringent legal restraints. However, Kelsen also concedes that basic norms themselves are open to change, although he fails to examine how such change might take place and what consequences it might generate. Ultimately, Kelsen's legal utopia envisages the strengthening of constitutional systems in which legality turns into duty for all, because all are 'subject, as far as this is possible, only to the objective rule of laws, and not to the rule of men' (Vinx, 2007: 25). Contemporary commentators would object that, in most modern democracies, there is a physiological illegitimacy in many new laws being created when these are examined against the constitutional principles which should inspire them. The disjuncture is described as a crisis determined by the development of extra-state or supra-state entities such as economic and financial powers which regularly evade legal control (Ferrajoli, 2013).

In opposition to Kelsen's 'utopia of legality', dualist theories hold that the political authority of the state is prior to the law 'and that a capacity to act without legal authorization or even in disregard of the law is an essential element of statehood' (Vinx, 2007: 16). Whether this formulation justifies or encourages state crime is open to debate, although it certainly constitutes an obstacle in the path of the full realization of the rule of law. Corporate actors and other powerful offenders, in their turn, may find inspiration in this argument, as their power too may be deemed prior to the law, if not altogether independent from the process of its constitution. We would suggest, however, that so far in this chapter Kelsen's Platonism has not encountered its Thrasymachus, namely its radical opponent, but only a mild objection in the form of theoretical uncertainty and political dilemma.

Dilemmas return in the shape of conflict, when the inner nature of law is looked at and when the realization is reached that its linguistic repertoire is limited. Semantically indeterminate, the law may be seen as possessing an open texture that renders its clear and consistent application uncertain. Hart (1961) terms Kelsen's basic norms 'the norms of recognition', which provide the general inescapable framework within which legislative production has to find legitimacy and validity. Norms of recognition, however, possess in their turn a degree of indeterminacy, and our relative incapacity to 'frame general rules in advance makes it necessary and desirable to exercise choice in subsequent application of the rules' (ibid.: 121–123). The only outcome of this conflict inherent in the law, therefore, is discretion in its application. The crimes of the powerful, against this background, may find favourable conditions to develop if they are met with 'favourable discretion' on the part of the authorities. They can neutralize their illegal character thanks to the 'penumbra of uncertainty' surrounding all legal rules (Hart, 1977). This is the same uncertainty described by Merton (1976: 6) as the 'sociological ambivalence of the normative expectations assigned to a status or incorporated in a single role'.

The fight against the crimes of the powerful, from this perspective, amounts to a struggle for legality as a way of responding to the 'penumbra of uncertainty' or the 'ambivalence' of roles. This solution posits that the law may be changed by obeying it, which implies that the rule of law is an unqualified human good, something that even the privileged have to respect in order to legitimate their power (Thompson, 1977). By adopting agreed standards of justice, the elite is said to inhibit its dominant role or run the risk of being exposed. Alexis de Tocqueville (2003), for example, highlights the positive social benefits of the law as a form of constraint placed upon the power of dominant groups. Conflict, in this case, arises from the contradiction between formal rules and their application by the rulers, while the ruled, in pursuing the unqualified good of the law, may perform radical political action.

I would call this a paradigm of consensus, which regards law as an institution produced through a series of interactions and processes, but at the same time as 'a system with its own operations, forms of communication and above all a claim to autonomy from the social forces which produced it in the first place' (Banakar and Travers, 2013: 4). In this view, law incorporates a shared set of values and amounts to a mere neutral artifice holding society together. Lawyers are not simply another occupational group – they are custodians of a cultural tradition to which we loyally adhere.

Once law is explored from a consensus-oriented standpoint, it balances rights and obligations, protects us from crime and social harm, brings a degree of certitude to our collaborative and contractual relations, and facilitates the exchange of goods and services in a capitalist economy.

(Ibid.: 4)

In brief, what the paradigm of consensus implies is that the crimes of the powerful can be prevented and fought through the very laws created by powerful individuals and groups.

Law as fraud

Critics of consensus-oriented views of the law would see in this formulation an ideological device allowing for the perpetuation of privilege and the germination of crime by the privileged. The neutral utopia of legality posited by Kelsen becomes, in this way, a fraudulent conceptualization maintaining and strengthening the status quo. The law, be it positive, uncertain, covered by a robe of penumbra or indeterminacy, still constitutes a vehicle through which hegemonic ideologies and social inequalities are reproduced.

Here comes Thrasymachus, well interpreted by the Marxist tradition, whose understanding of law revolves around the unequal social relations obscured by legal categories: injustice is reproduced and exacerbated by statutes and constitutions. Ironically, if we stretch this argument, we may suggest that capitalism is a 'just' society, in the sense that its laws perfectly reflect its dynamics aimed at perpetuating inequality, and that the dream available to antagonists to such a system is an 'unjust' society, namely one that abandons the dominant discourse of law altogether. In the Marxist tradition, the law is rooted in commodity exchange, and incorporates the advantages enjoyed by one of the parties in the exchange, conferring legal form on the unequal relationship between capital and labour (Marx, 1976a, 1992; Engels, 1943; Cain and Hunt, 1979). The rights legally guaranteed to the disadvantaged are, therefore, a deceptive semblance, alien to the content of the transaction, 'an empty illusion, a mirror of economic relations' (Fine, 2013: 99). In brief, while legality appears to regulate relationships between independent and equal persons, it actually hides the dominion of one class over another.

How social injustice is mediated through the rule of law constitutes one of the traditional concerns of Marxist analysis (Arthur, 1978). The 'legal relation between subjects is simply the reverse side of the relation between products of labour which have become commodities', argues Pashukanis (1978: 85), thus reiterating that law is an aggregate of artificial norms, a lifeless abstraction justifying exploitation. Norms would have no meaning without the existence of commodities and of the money economy, and the legal subject, consequently, 'has its material base in the person operating egoistically' (ibid.: 93).

Let us pause for a moment. Marxist analysis as presented thus far does not contemplate the crimes of the powerful, the powerful being criminal by definition, even when totally compliant with the rules their power allows them to establish. Studying the crimes of the powerful, from this perspective, may become a misleading, even dangerous, deviation from the core duty of those fighting against capitalism and its laws. Sure, as the product of labour becomes a commodity and a bearer of value, labourers acquire the capacity to be legal subjects and the bearers of rights. Relations are reified, while people assume no greater significance than objects, thus gaining the right to enter legal relationships.

> At a particular stage of development, the social relations of pro-
> duction assume a doubly mysterious form. On the one hand they
> appear as relations between things (commodities), and on the
> other, as relations between the wills of autonomous entities equal
> to each other – of legal subjects.
>
> *(Ibid.: 117)*

What follows from this argument is that criminal law, like law in general, is a form of intercourse between isolated egoistic subjects, the bearers of autonomous but unequal private interests.

Karl Korsch (1978) terms this approach a didactic, scholarly-dogmatic, 'revolutionary' theory lagging behind the very theoretical ideas expressed by Marx and Engels in an earlier historical period. Looking at those ideas, however, the relationship between power and crime appears to be as nebulous as it remains today. Let us look at some examples.

Marx unravels the criminality of primitive accumulation but also eulogizes the achievements of 'progress'. He does underline the social harm produced by enclosures and privatization of land; the victimization of the rural population is vividly highlighted in his work, when 'great masses of men are suddenly and forcibly torn from their means of subsistence, and hurled onto the labour market as free, unprotected and rightless proletarians'. But this is also described as an 'epoch-making revolution', a 'lever for the capitalist class in the course of its formation' (Marx, 1992: 876). The crimes of the powerful, in this conceptual framework, constitute a form of 'development', as they end up contributing to the formation of a modern industrial working class, which is also a 'revolutionary' process. The birth of large property, the destruction of customary rights and the privatization of land, in other words, contain a criminal core which is nevertheless evolutionary in its nature and modernizing in its direction. A similar argument accompanies Marxist analysis of the destruction of the Indian economy, when traditional social arrangements are dissolved as a result of military force and trade initiative. Marx describes those social arrangements as the core elements of the subsistence economy upon which 'semi-barbaric and semi-civilised' small communities have survived for centuries, concluding that the English invasion causes the most gigantic, and to be sure the only social revolution that Asia has ever known. He explains that those 'idyllic villages' have been the solid base of oriental despotism, narrowing human spirit and making it docile, prone to superstition, 'enslaving it to customary norms, stripping it of any historic energy, of any greatness' (Marx, 1960: 61). The question is: can humanity accomplish its fate without a profound revolution in social relationships in Asia? 'If the answer is no, then whatever the crimes committed by England might be, she was, by provoking such revolution, the unconscious instrument of history' (ibid.: 62).

Again, the crimes of the powerful are deemed to be, first, a natural component of labour relationships based on the extraction of surplus value; and second, the basis for the development of a class destined to overthrow the 'criminals' who appropriate surplus value. In brief, those victimized by powerful offenders are unconscious martyrs of a future social revolution, the human toll of the inevitable progress towards a new world (Ruggiero, 2013).

The crimes connected to primitive accumulation are, in a sense, legalized and incorporated in the very logic of exploitation and accumulation: what this reading neglects, however, is how the very legality established by the powerful is constantly superseded by those who establish it. Legality, in other words, contains a deviant nucleus providing exceptions, openings and artifices for its own supersession. Legality, therefore, may be insufficient for the reproduction and intensification of inequality, and in a relentless dynamic may require adjustments, self-negations, reinventions and profound ethical revisions.

Insatiability and the rules of exception

In the Aristotelian tradition, an awareness of the effects of inequality is constantly present. True, it is up to individuals whether their life is successful or not. However, proper *eudaimonia*, that is, personal and human flourishing making a life worthwhile, requires 'external goods, for it is impossible, or at least not easy, to play a noble part unless furnished with the necessary equipment' (Appiah, 2008: 172). Among such 'external goods' are social connections, resources, political power, 'good birth' (Aristotle, 1995). Inequality, in sum, allows us to 'differentiate criminal offences from normal behaviour'. To a great extent, the legal system can constantly create crimes and criminals through its arbitrary categorization of certain human conducts as illegal. There is total awareness, in the Marxist tradition, of these mechanisms, according to which the criteria used to distinguish criminality from other forms of behaviour reflect the interests of powerful social strata rather than social consensus on what distinguishes right from wrong actions. Legal categories are politically charged, and 'societal elites, then, have rarely, if ever, been concerned with law and order in the abstract, but with historically specific laws and social orders which promote their economic, political, or status interests' (Chambliss and Mankoff, 1976: viii). Thrasymachus is here completely vindicated, while his views are expanded in the following manner.

The liberal idea of the law reflects, as we have seen, a form of atomistic individualism which prevails in its correspondent type of society. Individuals stand before the law as abstract holders of rights, as legal persons, irrespective of status and social background. There is a presumed equivalence between parties because everyone who comes before the law is granted the quality of a juridical subject (Bankowski,

1983). It should be reiterated that Marxist analysis regards this formulation as a gigantic confidence trick, because in fact the law offers an image of universal equality while keeping economic and social inequality intact. But something is missing from this picture.

The laws, according to the dualist approach mentioned above, are general commands emitted by representatives of the state. Such representatives, for the most part, will govern on the basis of the general, legitimate commands they emit, but may also choose to disregard them and exercise political authority in other ways than through mechanisms of legality. Law as an omnipotent tool reflects the omnipotence of God, and if jurisprudence is a sacred text, it must feature exceptions similar to how religious texts feature miracles (Schmitt, 2006, 2014). It is otiose to identify the state with the impersonal application of codified law and to regard laws as self-referring norms, the validity of which is supposedly only found in procedural consistency. For Schmitt, laws have to be situationally understood and cannot take the place of a sovereign authority, which is often required to ignore procedural standards, express leadership and, therefore, make decisions in the shifting circumstances of politics (Gottfried, 1990). In brief, Schmitt suggests that rationality is the last characteristic we can expect from law.

This suggestion is critiqued by Franz Neumann (1957) in his analysis of authoritarianism focused on the Nazi period. He notes that laws grow irrational during the transition from competitive to monopolistic markets. Rational laws, in his view, mirror the freedom of transactions and their predictability in competitive regimes, and are unnecessary when planning and monopoly control predominate. With this shift, it is labour that should express an interest in rational law, as it retains a set of guarantees to be used for the improvement of conditions.

> While totalitarian movements opposed positive law in their exercise of terror, Neumann argued that Marxism could not be blind to the fact that rational law was not merely a lesser evil but a genuine repository of democratic values.
>
> *(Fine, 2013: 101–102)*

Law as a repository of democratic values is also an aspect of Arendt's (1973) argument that we find in her theoretical excursus through totalitarianism. In her view, power completely disregards laws – economic as well as ethical – when it engages in the sole task of appropriating wealth, pursuing the 'ugly dream' and the 'empty desire' to have money beget money. With wealth it is power itself which is accumulated, in a never-ending process foreshadowing the rise of imperialism. Arendt does not refer to the naive delusion of a limitless growth of property, but to the idea that power accumulation is the only guarantee for the stability of so-called economic laws. The imperialist-minded businessman is annoyed because he cannot appropriate stars, but he soon realizes that 'power organized for its own sake will beget more power' (ibid.: 143–144). Among the 'heroes' of British imperialism, for instance, Arendt singles out Cecil Rhodes, whose 'monstrous innate vanity' leads him to the discovery that imperial expansion is not only driven by 'the specific appetite for a specific country' but is also guided by an endless process in which every country serves as a stepping stone for further expansion. The desire for acquisitions and glory, therefore, is never satisfied, but turns into the maelstrom of an unending process of expansion and accumulation. In our own terms, we suggest that the crimes of the powerful create and expand new forms of power. Those involved in the process will only obey their own rules and identify themselves with the anonymous forces that feed the maelstrom. They will think of themselves as mere functions, anonymous agents of progress who need not feel any obligation to fulfil established norms. Their lawfulness, in their own mind, is proven by their success.

Positive law, for Arendt, may therefore create obstacles to the endless expansion of power, although the dynamics she describes would also suggest that such law is easily swept away by anonymous agents engaged in permanent expansion and accumulation. How realistic her defence of lawfulness is, for this reason, remains an enigma. Some clarification, perhaps, is provided by her analysis of human rights as rights which characterize the human condition that no tyrant can take away.

> Its loss entails the loss of the relevance of speech (and man, since Aristotle, has been defined as a being commanding the power of speech and thought) and loss of all human relationship (and man, again since Aristotle, has been thought of as the 'political

animal') … the loss, in other words, of some of the most essential
characteristics of human life.

(Ibid.: 297)

The crimes of the powerful, from this perspective, deny a political
community the enjoyment of any right whatsoever, and by destroying
a polity they expel humans from humanity itself. We are here in the
domain of crimes against human rights of course, but it is worth trying
to draw from this point a tentative generalization covering the crimes of
the powerful tout court.

As we have seen in a previous chapter, one of the rationalizations of this
type of crime is the offenders' claim that their conduct benefits others as
well as themselves. I have termed these illicit conducts 'philanthropic
power crimes'. In addition, totalitarian regimes, as Arendt reminds us,
present their acts as beneficial to all, thus echoing Hitler's motto that
'right is what is good for the German people'. In this sense it is quite
conceivable, and even within the realm of practical political possibilities,
that some authority, highly organized, mechanized and democratically
elected, might propose that 'for humanity as a whole it would be better
to liquidate certain parts thereof' (ibid.: 299). Such authority, while
defying legality, will pretend to establish the direct reign of justice on
earth by executing the law of history or of nature.

According to Arendt, underlying the Nazis' race laws as the expression
of the law of nature is Darwin's idea of human beings as the product of a
natural development which does not necessarily stop with the present
species of human beings. Similarly, in her view, behind the Bolsheviks'
belief in class struggle as the expression of the law of history lies a
notion of society as the product of a gigantic historical movement of
evolution and emancipation. Human beings and their social arrangements are seen as evolving in a unilinear fashion, following an infinitely
progressing direction, so that 'nature is, as it were, swept into history',
and natural life is considered to be historical. 'The natural law of the
survival of the fittest is just as much a historical law and could be used
as such by racism' as well as by theorists of the survival of the most
progressive class (ibid.: 463).

Powerful offenders can appoint themselves as agents of this unstoppable
evolutionary process, and identify their victims as the objective enemies

of history or nature. Those who are victimized are those who stand in the way of progress and are prone to succumb. But offenders and victims are all subjectively innocent: the former because they follow a superior historical mission, the latter because they do not challenge the legitimacy of that mission. Powerful offenders do not claim to be just or wise, but only to execute historical or natural laws.

The crimes committed in the name of the law of history and nature, however, lend themselves to a dual interpretation: they may be seen as violations of the *consensus iuris* which, according to Cicero, constitutes a people, but also as the result of a new *consensus iuris* among powerful offenders and others, including their victims. Arendt wavers between these interpretations, describing law as restraint of power, on the one hand, and power as permanent defiance of law, on the other. In her conclusion, however, she shifts towards a more optimistic, if idealistic, view: law constitutes the civilized world insofar as it remains the foundation-stone of conducts, and insofar as it presupposes a basic consent. Totalitarianism, and for our purposes the crimes of the powerful, do not replace one set of laws with another, they do not establish their own *consensus iuris*; they do not therefore create a new form of legality. They defy all types of human legality, promising to derive law directly from action and will, bringing 'justice on earth because [they] claim to make mankind itself the embodiment of the law' (ibid.: 462). A defence of positive law, from this perspective, is congruent with the aim of bringing a degree of stability to the volatile movements of individuals and groups.

Positive law in constitutional government is said to erect boundaries and establish channels of communication within communities which are continually endangered by the new people being born into them. 'With each new birth, a new beginning is born into the world, a new world has potentially come into being' (ibid.: 465). The stability of the laws is necessary vis-à-vis the constant motion of all human affairs, a motion which can never end as long as human beings are born and die. The laws protect us from new and unpredictable conducts and events; they constitute for our political existence what memory is for our identity:

> they guarantee the pre-existence of a common world, the reality of some continuity which transcends the individual life

span of each generation, absorbs all new origins and is nourished by them.

(Ibid.: 466)

Crimes committed by authorities demolish the boundaries and channels of communication constituted by laws; they abolish the fences of laws between human beings, taking away their freedom and destroying their political possibilities. Form this perspective, the crimes of the powerful may be regarded as the result of a deficit of control or vigilance over positive law. The limited guarantees powerless groups are granted are not sufficiently safeguarded and defended by their bearers. Overlooking such guarantees is a mistake, and may be the result of a political attitude determined, among other things, by the view that laws are inevitably helping the powerful, therefore they are not worth defending at all. Fighting the crimes of the powerful, in sum, does not mean changing the laws so that they favour the powerless, but defending those limiting and restraining the powerful. The fight, in a nutshell, is for the conservation of humanity, as the powerful tend to create a system in which humans are superfluous (Adler, 2005).

Homo juridicus and *homo oeconomicus*

Positive and rational law, according to the analysis discussed above, constitutes a crucial patrimony to be protected. The law, it may be argued, connects our mental universe with our physical existence, thus fulfilling the anthropological function of instituting us as rational beings. It is by transforming each of us into a *homo juridicus* that 'the biological and symbolic dimensions that make up our being have been linked together' (Supiot, 2007: ix). We have also seen, however, that it is often through the law that juridical persons are annihilated, as Arendt reminds us. This is why establishing certainty in law may help identify and thwart abuses and crimes of power. However, legal theorists who see law as nothing but the product of political or economic forces, treating it as nothing but a technique of power serving the interests of the powerful, do not deem this effort to be worthwhile. They may argue, for instance, that only after radically transforming the economic and political spheres can laws treating all citizens with equity be constituted: only then will law coincide with justice. In response, Supiot (ibid.) remarks that law is neither a divine revelation nor a scientific discovery, and that every society must develop a vision of justice that is shared by all its members, 'in order to avoid civil war, and this is what the legal framework provides' (ibid.: xx). True, he continues, conceptions of justice differ from epoch to epoch and from context to context, but the need for a shared representation of justice is constant and immutable. The legal system is where this representation takes shape, a system which confers meaning and orientation to our actions. The crimes of the powerful, therefore, thrive when shared meaning and orientation are discarded as unrealistic, when law is deemed to be a mere technique of domination and when, as a consequence, every 'value choice' is associated with individual morality and excluded from the legal sphere. In these cases 'law's essential quality is neglected, namely that it can temper the most varied forms of political power or technological prowess with a measure of reason' (ibid.: xxv). With this we have now temporarily returned to Plato.

Theorists who separate law from justice, seeing the former as a simple tool for the perpetuation of inequality, unwittingly endorse a 'law and economics' doctrine, which relates every rule to a calculation of utility: human society is thus turned into a sum of individual utilities. Economists who view all spheres of human life through the prism of the market, be that politics, marriage or sex, can easily include the law among their objects of analysis. Their intention is to turn *lex mercatoria* into natural law, and transcend the state and the rule of law while making economics itself a natural science. Let us examine some aspects of *legal economism* by focusing on two variables: efficiency and value.

Economic resources are fully or efficiently exploited when value is maximized, namely when they are turned into aggregate consumer willingness to pay for goods and services. Economists claim that they can predict the effect of legal rules on the basis of the distribution of income and wealth, and that a legal system should be called upon to promote the efficient allocation of resources (Posner, 1972). Thus, for instance, attempts to limit theft may be inefficient: society could obtain more prevention, at lower cost, by using different methods. Victims of theft may be forced to spend large amounts of money to protect their property, while thieves may have to invest amounts of money just as large in order to neutralize their victims' preventive efforts. Both adopt an inefficient way of dealing with property crime. On the contrary, theft should be 'efficient', in the sense that thieves should be required to prove that the value to them of the item they have taken is higher than the value to the previous owner. Powerful thieves such as corrupt politicians, entrepreneurs and corporate actors can easily prove that what they steal acquires greater value once they have stolen it, because it will be invested and will generate yet more value. By the same token, environmental damage and even death caused by powerful offenders may be efficient if the value of the items and human beings destroyed is smaller than the value of the resources necessary to prevent that destruction.

Raising the costs of unlawful conduct is itself very costly, as is the cost of ascertaining criminal responsibility and determining the deterrent force of legal measures. Some conducts are hard to deter and criminal sanctions to prevent or punish them may prove wasteful. True, ordinary criminals may partially desist from property offences if their legitimate income increases. But applying the same logic to powerful criminals would lead to the belief that the only way to dissuade them from offending is allowing them to increase their profits. And that, on the contrary, by punishing them we decrease their profits and simultaneously force them to commit further crimes.

The costs of apprehending and convicting criminals rise with the probability of apprehension: 'higher probabilities imply greater numbers of police, as well as more court officials, attorneys, etc.' (ibid.: 167). As powerful offenders are difficult to apprehend and convict, economic efficiency would suggest that those costs could be reduced arbitrarily close to zero. Hence the choice to entrust to powerful offenders themselves the task of preventing and detecting their own offences through self-regulation. Imprisonment, in its turn, imposes pecuniary costs upon violators by reducing their income during the period of confinement and, in many cases, by reducing their earning capacity after release. This so-called 'criminal record effect' is particularly significant for people with high incomes, who are prevented by incarceration from producing large amounts of value: this makes their punishment anti-economic or inefficient. Incarceration as a response to murder, however, may be totally inadequate, because 'the cost to the victim is very high, and may indeed approach infinity, since many people would be unwilling to surrender their lives for any finite sum of money' (ibid.: 169). This suggests a possible economic justification for capital punishment, a form of punishment that imposes upon the defendants a cost roughly commensurate with the harm caused by their conduct. This is why, perhaps, murder committed by powerful offenders, in illegitimate wars, through violations of health and safety legislations, or through environmental devastation, is not regarded as murder, but as unintended outcome, collateral damage or diseconomy. *Legal economism*, as we have seen thus far, is the ideal theoretical ally of powerful offenders. But let us carry on.

In economic terms, altruism means to derive utility from somebody else's utility. In this sense, powerful offenders are altruistic, although they will have to comply with existing rules and legislations. On the other hand, rules and regulations evolve and at times can be radically altered. Moreover, let us bear in mind that the basic function of law, in an economic perspective, is to alter incentives. This implies that law does not command the impossible, since a command that is impossible to fulfil will not alter behaviour: ultimately, not all commands backed by the state are entitled to claim obedience as law. Rules are the outcome of decisions, which with time become 'precedents' and a 'body of precedents in an area of law constitutes a capital stock, that is, a stock of capital goods' (ibid.: 419). Such 'goods', like all other commodities, depreciate, as they become unable to regulate or guide conduct. Therefore, criminal conduct by powerful people may simply prove that the existing stock of precedents is obsolete and that new decisions and rules have to be made and established. With this argument we are entering the domain of philosophical pragmatism, which encourages us to give up the 'idea that legal or moral or even scientific inquiry is an attempt to discover what is really so' (Dworkin, 2006). Our 'vocabulary of concepts', pragmatists suggest, may become obsolete and useless, and we should be prepared to change it (Rorty, 1991). In previous chapters we have discussed how this is achieved through forms of judicial innovation justifying the commission of foundational crimes, which violate laws while creating precedents for further future violations.

One further point highlighted by legal economists may help in the analysis of the crimes of the powerful. This pertains to the vagueness of rules, whereby 'violators will discount the punishment cost of the violation not only by the probability that they will be caught but by the additional probability that the rule will be held applicable to the specific conduct in which they engage' (Posner, 1972: 424). The more rapid the pace of social, political and economic change in society, the more rules are likely to appear as vague. Enforcement agencies, under such circumstances, are required to decide where to concentrate their resources, thus acting as rational maximizers. The powerful, in this view, help enforcement agencies in their decisions to concentrate resources on conventional offences, as social, political and economic change will make the rules guiding their own conduct increasingly vague. Vagueness of law encourages powerful offenders to invest large amounts of funds in their judicial defence, which in turn makes costs for law enforcement mushroom. Thus, other things being equal, the rational maximizing agency will prefer to invest resources in cases where laws are clear and defendants do not invest in self-defence.

> Since it may be cheaper to convict a defendant who is not represented by counsel than one who is, even if the former is innocent and the latter guilty, prosecutors might have an incentive to prosecute innocent people who are indigent.
>
> *(Ibid.: 477)*

We have reached a tentative explanation of the crimes of the powerful linking structure and action as constituents of the legal realm. We need now to look at some important related aspects.

Law and action

When examining the relationship between action and structure, we can focus on systems (Parsons, 1964; Luhman, 1985), on practices, communicative action or fields (Althusser, 1971; Habermas, 1984; Bourdieu, 2013). We can draw a grand model of society which establishes limits, constraints and chances for individuals and groups. We can endorse the view that institutions are shaped by social action, but that action is constrained by the structural resources available (Giddens, 1986). On the other hand, we may find that these grand models of society offer an impoverished view of human action and neglect agency. People, in fact, make judgements about others and account for their own actions by justifying them.

Powerful offenders are often able to justify their acts by presenting them as beneficial to others as well as to themselves. Their defiance of the law seeks complicity among peers as well as in society as a whole. Their acts, in brief, pursue public recognition of their utility for the general well-being. Among peers, powerful offenders rely on proximity, personal ties, attachment to organizations and cultures. These physical, social and ideological bonds shape and reproduce identities and ethical standards, providing rationalizations for action and justification of its outcome (Boltanski and Thévenot, 2006). In relation to society in general, powerful offenders mobilize philosophies centred on the common good, appeal to a sense of common humanity, and point to the benefits their action brings to those who are unequal to them. This is not mere deceit, in the sense that violators do not contrive false pretexts or hide some secret motive: theirs is not an ex-post search for an alibi. Rather, 'they seek to carry out their actions in a such a way that these can withstand the test of justification' (ibid.: 37). This requires the identification of a 'higher common principle' making criminal behaviour legitimate and the law an absurd obstacle for action.

Powerful offenders are helped in their endeavour by the plasticity of legal truth itself, which consists in shifting constantly its pro *veritate abetur*, namely in providing a range of truths connected to a variety of human actions. This plasticity implies that the law cannot be defined as a separate world or delimited by its own principles: its agility makes it sensitive to acts performed in other spheres external to it, be these politics, economics or everyday life.

> As a result, just when we think we have discovered it as a particular sphere, with its own regulatory modes, we notice that the legal institution is so porous that its decisions look like ... turning with every breeze.
>
> *(Latour, 2013: 362)*

The logic of law, in sum, derives from the social networks shaping it. Paraphrasing Latour, we may say that legal truth without its network is like an electric wire without power, gas without a pipeline, or a telephone conversation without a connection to a telephone line.

These observations lead us back to the views examined above. We have seen, on the one hand, law as part of the repressive and ideological superstructure of the state, determined in the last instance by the economic base and by the attempt to reproduce the status quo. We have seen, on the other hand, the view positing the universality and independence of the legal realm. It is now worth trying to 'twin' the two views and ascertain whether they can very well coexist or, even, provide supplementary elasticity favourable to the crimes of the powerful.

We can admire the objectivity of law, its capacity to make all powers bow before it, and at the same time be indignant that it is 'so supple, so obsequious, that it has the regrettable capacity to cloak the nakedness of power relations' (ibid.: 362). This constant seesawing may be deemed to be all the more awkward in that it is hardly reconcilable with the stability and permanency of the principles the law is expected to guarantee.

> At various historical moments it has been entrusted with the task of bearing morality, religion, science, politics, the State, as if its fine spider webs on their own could keep humans from quarrelling, going for the jugular, tearing each other's guts out; as if it were law and law alone that had made us civilized and even made us human.
>
> *(Ibid.: 362)*

But it is exactly the varied expectations of human beings in terms of justification for their acts that simultaneously require elasticity and permanency of the law. The remaining section of this chapter may clarify this point.

Having it both ways: knights and bullies

Economic approaches, discussed above, are not only found in law. The theory of justice elaborated by Rawls (1972) is replete with variables such as utility, interest, contract, and, in general, relies heavily on agreements among calculating beings. Such agreements need not become laws, but simply techniques facilitating smooth interactions among people, against a background in which the law itself is expected to fade away. The meaning of law, in other words, is destined to coincide with that of administration, a technique of government transcending generally shared values. If legal principles are not found in immutable texts, they are linked with contingent objectives that individuals and groups set for themselves. The crimes of the powerful may find immediate rationalization in this view of the law, which belongs to pragmatists justifying them as well as to radical analysts fighting them. But, paradoxically, opposite views may lead to similar immediate rationalizations.

Advocates of *strict legality* may be described as formalists, in that they derive rules of conduct from the logic of written texts, without attributing any role to the values, the ideological leanings or the very culture of those who administer law. 'The law as seen from a formalist perspective is a compendium of texts, like the Bible, and the task of the judge or other legal analyst is to discern and apply the internal logic of the compendium' (Posner, 2013: 3). The legal apparatus limits its task to interpreting, and is indifferent to the consequences of its interpretations. On the contrary, the *realist* is sensitive to the outcomes of judicial rulings, and considers systemic as well as case-specific consequences. Now, whether we believe that the law is nothing but a set of techniques for the perpetuation of power, or that its universal values should be imposed upon all, powerful offenders find a degree of legitimation in both beliefs. The former confirms that they will go unpunished because the laws are on their side, while the second helps them claim their right to ignore them or change them pragmatically. Judges who are cognitive misers and regard innovation as costly will adhere to established texts, which are favourable to powerful offenders. They will act as lexicographers, finding answers in books and codes. Cognitive adventurous judges, on the other hand, will 'treat law as a branch of rhetoric, or literature – or (without acknowledgement, of course) politics' (ibid.: 82). They will therefore alter previous interpretations and rulings. Powerful offenders, in brief, will win in both cases.

Classical thinkers such as Holmes (1881) may be identified as one of the main inspirers of this dual justification of the crimes of the powerful. For Holmes, political struggle amounts to natural selection, where the strongest always wins. The law, in turn, will always reflect the relative strength of the competing forces in a society. And if change has to take place, this has to be easy and quick, with the law following the trajectory of power, its accumulation and polarization: 'the more powerful interests must be more or less reflected in legislation, which, like every other device of men or beast, must tend in the long run to aid the survival of the fittest' (Posner, 2013: 156–157). Conservatives manifest their judicial passivity by taking inspiration from original texts, while imaginative innovators rewrite norms: both can condone the harm produced by powerful offenders. Plato and Thrasymachus, finally, find an unexpected synthesis.

To conclude in a literary fashion, let us revisit Miguel de Cervantes (2003) and his explorations of the meaning of justice (Byrne, 2012). Don Quixote and Sancho Panza personify the debate on history and jurisprudence, and express bewilderment at the use powerful people make of laws. There is no sign of humanity or divinity in the practice of the law witnessed by our two heroes: people are sent to the galleys, while brutal officers and repugnant slave masters are protected by the law. But, as has been argued earlier, power both uses and defies its own laws, having the right to suspend rights but also to establish new ones for itself. Sancho Panza comes across large groups of richly dressed characters, describing those adorned in rich corals, golden rings, 'each one worth an arm and a leg'. Others, he tells us, wear strands of pearls, diamonds, rubies and brocades of the richest sort.

> Don Diego de Miranda whose velvet clothing is inlaid with gold thread, the duchess who rides on a silver saddle, the duke and duchess's palace with walls adorned in rich, sumptuous fabric of gold-threaded brocade, the nymph dressed in one thousand veils of silver cloth, each one glittering with infinite eaves of filigreed silver-inlaid gold, and the sixteen-year-old girl dressed in red silk stockings, and white taffeta garters with flecks of gold and seed pearls, green, gold-threaded breeches.
>
> *(Ibid.: 107)*

All these characters violate the sumptuary laws, which legislate to an extra-ordinary specific degree the use by powerful people of certain cloths, fabrics and adornments. These laws are created by those who regularly violate them. And although some powerful people have a form of 'natural shame', particularly those of 'good lineage', most are vulgar, lawless bullies.

5

DOMINATION, HEGEMONY AND VIOLENCE

Politics often denotes an activity about which many people may feel a combination of cynicism, scepticism and mistrust. A 'dirty' word, it is frequently associated with hypocrisy, egoism and manipulation; it is held in high scorn because it suspends all requirements of truth (Held, 1991; Latour, 2013). On the one hand, politics is about power, namely the ability of social groups to maintain or modify existing arrangements and established models of resource allocation. On the other hand, it is directly linked to definitions of the state, its capacity to create consensus and its adeptness at promoting meaningful relations with citizens, among citizens and with other states. The journey through political theory proposed here, however, will also lead to the appreciation of how this specific area of knowledge ignores, explains, justifies or at times even encourages the crimes of the powerful.

In Chapter 2 the crimes of the powerful have been associated with actors endowed with exorbitantly exceeding amounts of material and symbolic resources when compared with those possessed by their victims. Addressing the variable inequality, it has been argued that individuals and groups are granted a range of choices and potential actions they can carry out. Asymmetric distributions of choices, therefore of freedom, trigger a dynamic whereby the privileged can control the effects of their criminality and attribute criminal definitions to others while repelling those that others attribute to them. Traversing political theory proves a worthy exercise for unveiling the workings of this dynamic.

The polis of the elite

Aristotle's small independent city-state, or polis, is not a mere aggregation of individuals, but an organic whole, an organized entity. The polis is, at the same time, an artefact and a natural association, because humans are political animals by nature. And 'naturally' they pursue *eudaimonia*, that is, a general condition of well-being which is an end in itself, something that human beings seek for its own sake. This self-sufficient goal may be achieved through reason, guiding action and making life worthwhile (Aristotle, 1934, 1995). 'The good life is one in which we perform this function well, i.e. in accordance with the appropriate standards of excellence or virtue' (Stalley, 1995: xii). Politics, ultimately, is the prime activity directed at the most sovereign of all goods, namely the creation of virtuous citizens. Only a limited proportion of citizens, however, will be able to achieve virtue, although the existence of all is necessary for the polis to prosper. The majority, in other words, has to function so that the minority can devote itself to leisure and contemplation, a minority organized like a club, a collective enterprise sharing values and pooling resources for their own benefit. This is why Aristotle conceives of the polis as large enough to be self-sufficient, but small enough to allow all its members to know each other and interact meaningfully. But his conception of the polis as a common undertaking 'depends on the presence of slaves and resident foreigners who are not members and do not share its privileges' (ibid.: xix).

The foundations provided by Aristotle to political thought imply that the elite is the guardian of law as well as morality, encapsulated in the single word *nomos*, a set of rules binding 'political animals' together, forging customs, guiding practices and ultimately establishing what is legitimate and what is not. Power and crime, from this perspective, are connected with the ability of the elite to control, amend and constantly shape the *nomos* justifying its actions. Confirming what is stated above regarding the capacity of the elite to repel imputations of criminality while attributing them to others, Aristotle, when discussing the constitution of Sparta, criticizes it because it allows even 'very poor men, whose lack of means renders them open to bribery, to attain office' (Aristotle, 1995: 70).

Violations of the law by powerful groups are addressed by Aristotle when he examines the 'causes of factional conflict and constitutional change'. The elite, with its 'passion for inequality' and its sense of superiority, feels that it has a right to hold advantages over others and manifests a growing appetite for them. Its illicit acts are the result of a state of mind, while 'the objects which are at stake are profit and honour' (ibid.: 182). The promulgation of new rules by the elite, which is part of its political power, will allow it to decriminalize its own conduct.

Echoes of these arguments are found, here and there, scattered throughout the previous chapters.

The polis of God

In the Christian tradition we may not find a similar 'passion for inequality' but a supine acceptance of it. Politics epitomizes the relationship between the ideal divine world and the reality of human conditions: how can people of faith operate successfully but justly in an unjust world? The world of politics, in Augustine (2003), is characterized by selfish interest, lack of concern for the general welfare, and the coexistence of good and evil. Those elected for salvation and those chosen for damnation are also thoroughly intermingled, although they form two classes of persons, to whom Augustine refers collectively and allegorically as cities: the City of God and the earthly city. In the latter we find the unregenerate progeny of Adam and Eve, who are justifiably damned because of Adam's Fall. They are aliens to God's love, as evidenced by their rebellious disposition inherited from the Fall, and distinguish themselves for their lust for material goods and for domination over others. They are the founding members of the political state, which we may assume is dominated by vulgarity, abuse of power and greed. Lack of justice makes politicians gangs of criminals because, Augustine warns, no state can possess true justice, and the legitimacy of any earthly political regime may be understood only in relative terms. What is legal or illegal varies according to how much power approaches, without ever reaching, true justice.

Political states, imperfect as they are, nevertheless serve a divine purpose. They maintain order and prevent destructive conflicts: they are, therefore, divine gifts, and rulers have the right to establish any law that does not conflict with the law of God. Citizens, in turn, have the duty to obey their political leaders regardless of whether the leader is wicked or righteous, although, Augustine adds, when the imperatives of obedience to God and obedience to civil authority conflict, citizens must choose to obey God and willingly accept the punishment that follows disobedience. Politics promotes a 'temporary blend' of the world imbued with grace and the world deprived of it, and this 'blend' explains crimes of greed committed by the powerful. Power, however, is justified in committing crime when, simultaneously, it pursues the highest grace and the lowest goods. In this way, salvation is made certain even for those responsible for despicable acts: faith liberates everyone from the need to perform virtuous deeds; righteousness overrides morality and the law.

Spinoza's (2007) pantheism echoes this distorted realism: because politics is not for perfect people, he remarks, we have to accept imperfection in the form of human passion, and power cannot avoid imitating humans, their greed and cruelty. *Imitatio affectum* is a learning process involving those in power, who express the same violence governing human interactions (Evangelista, 2013). Are we faced with a theological justification of the crimes of the powerful?

Power as contract

From secular thought we learn that mutual violence among human beings and the concomitant violence emanating from power may be averted through the constitution of a social contract. Contractual theories of politics spare citizens a life of insecurity and brutishness while making power exempt from the imputation of criminality. What is right or wrong is not inscribed in nature or in the collective wisdom, let alone in jurisprudence, but is the effect of decisions taken by an artificial political body.

Thomas Hobbes (1987: 184) starts his analysis of the 'contract' with the assertion that nature has made human beings equal, and therefore equally disposed to desire 'the things that all would like to enjoy'. But things being scarce, competition and animosity develop, leading each to attempt to subdue or destroy the other. Without a common authority, an artificial power 'to keep them all in awe', human beings are in a constant condition of war, 'and such war is of every man against every man' (ibid.: 188). This original violence characterizing human interactions in the absence of an artificial power, although dysfunctional, is not immoral or unjust, because the very notions of justice and injustice, of right and wrong, can hardly take shape where there is no common power. This is because notions of right and wrong 'relate to men in society, not in solitude' (ibid.). Violence is reduced when human beings abandon their right to use it, transferring such a right to another person. And when this is achieved, humans will be obliged not to hinder those to whom such right is granted, because 'such hindrance is injustice, and injury; the right being before renounced, or transferred' (ibid.: 191). Rebellion against sovereignty is tantamount to rebellion against reason. By contrast, nothing done by the sovereign is injurious, because all is done with consent, by virtue of an 'antecedent covenant'.

Hobbesian analysis contains the most radical formulation of power and crime, in that it manages to operate a drastic conceptual separation: no logical association between power and crime is therefore permissible, as the former is always legitimate and, even when causing harm, can never be deemed to be criminal. The concept of criminality reappears, however, in other contractual theories. In Rousseau (1964), for instance, vice does not belong to human beings but to ill-governed human beings. In his social contract we encounter a set of institutions, agencies and underlying philosophies capable of making humans evil, particularly when such institutions and agencies do not represent citizens. For Rousseau, only people possess political authority, and this is inalienable, it cannot be yielded to anybody, be that a monarch or a representative: 'The individual who gives up his sovereignty renounces his quality of man. A people renouncing the exercise of sovereignty through a pact of subjugation annuls itself through that pact' (ibid.: 135).

In Rousseau we can read several formulations of the relationship between power and crime, with some suggesting absolute coincidence between the two and others indicating specific circumstances under which that coincidence manifests itself. First, crime is the result of the contract per se, a pact leading to a situation where there are no longer people and their sovereigns or their leaders, but only one master and many slaves. Second, power and crime become closely associated when arbitrary governments and administrations refuse to subordinate decisions to the general will. Third, power is criminal when it expects to be rigidly obeyed, treating those who obey it like beasts. Fourth, power is criminal when it appeals to the right of the strongest rather than to notions of collective well-being and governmental duty. Fifth, power and crime are intimately associated when strength is used in order to create consensus, whereby citizens yield out of necessity or prudence rather than out of will.

In his organic view of civil society, however, a surprising justification of the crimes of the powerful is detectable if the general will as the foundation of power is examined from a different perspective. Rousseau views stable and democratic societies as inspired by a 'civil religion', namely by a set of intense feelings of mutual obligation, belonging and duty. Citizens bound by such feelings experience their collective will and desires as affection towards a specific social and political order. If early on in human history people had no kings but gods, and needed to believe that their kings were indeed gods, in modern times sentiments of obligation and belonging must be as strong as the religious sentiments they replace. In this way, the social and political order is granted a form of sanctity, thus requesting love for its institutions and norms. Dissent from this civil religion must be followed by banishment, as the unsociable fail to appreciate justice and can always plot to subvert it.

> Civic love, then, is incompatible with active critical thought about the political order, and with a sense of the separateness of the individual from the group. The test for sincerity is unanimity.
> (Nussbaum, 2013: 45)

Unanimity, one should add, applies to the national as well as to the international sphere, so that 'unsociable' countries and peoples may also be included among those deserving banishment or punishment, as they fail to appreciate the superiority of a specific civil religion and, with it, of a sacred political order. The powerful, in brief, are justified in criminally defending the status quo from dissent. We shall see later how this type of justification keeps returning when power and crime are interlocked in war, and how those wielding it unwittingly revive Rousseau's concept of civil religion.

Between reason and passion

In a distinctive strand of political theory, consideration is given to the way in which conducts take shape and become widely accepted. Political authority, according to Montaigne (1993), is neither based on reason nor on natural law. All political agents follow a human necessity and make decisions in contingent, ever-changing circumstances, so that a political order is a synthesis of immanent needs, human passion and vice. Whenever this synthesis is reached, we have a just political order, whose stability and duration will be guaranteed by the norms of conduct forged through self-interested, obtuse practices. In Montaigne, these norms amount to strings or chains constraining people who are unable to govern themselves and to control their individual passions. Human beings, therefore, accept a political order as far as the customary constraints they create for themselves are not recognized as such, and as far as the tyranny of norms of conduct neutralizes their freedom of choice. Norms of political conduct may be mean or even despicable; nevertheless, if they remain unaltered they confer vitality and strength to systems. Change in the form of deviance from norms and customs leads to decay, releasing claims of limitless freedom, greed and tumultuous adventure. This, in Montaigne, is a precise allusion to audacious forms of political power, which are physiological to systems, a power that is characterized by chaotic agitation, sectarian interest, degeneracy and human stupidity.

Montaigne draws the contours of politics as a modern realm of human activity, namely activity through which conflict about resource allocation takes place. Politics, in sum, is not understood as rational debate and peaceful conciliation of interests, but as intimidation, threat and violence (Heywood, 1994). The crimes of the powerful, from this perspective, consist of political practices which invent new norms by violating old ones, in a succession of adventurous exploits aimed at conserving or augmenting privilege. We are far from Descartes' rationalism whereby politics unites intimate knowledge and public exercise of power, a sphere of human action where authorities propagate reason and teach respect for the well-being of the collectivity (Tronti, 1982). We are also far removed from Leibniz's universal justice, which annuls evil by making political power the outcome of divine love and perfection. We are, on the contrary, very close to Pascal's (1998) notion that power reflects the pure will of the sovereign and strength is a key aspect of public life. This is, on the one hand, the strength allowing all conducts enacted by the powerful to be seen as acceptable and, on the other hand, the strength to display the privileges gained as merit and their general approval as a mark of social order.

The variable strength returns in Voltaire (1994), who does not condemn it as criminal, but glorifies it as a means to defeat the dispersed forces challenging centralized authority. By contrast, in Vico (1999) power and force are combined in a miscellany aimed at governing social conflicts and competing interests. The criminal element, in his formulation, may be detected in the claim that states need to adopt specific techniques of government and varying degrees of arbitrariness, and that the ideal political power is a unitary apparatus which makes imposture an acceptable ruling tool. Power, then, must be criminal in order to function as such.

The enigma faced by classical political theory revolves around what exactly power should command and why people should obey. Let us see how Montesquieu (1973) attempts to resolve this enigma. He imagines an outsider, a Persian, walking the streets of Paris: what he sees are agitated individuals, animated conversers, traders, lawyers, decaying aristocrats, charlatans and priests, all engaged in the aggressive pursuit of their interests. The outsider is bewildered by the ability of those in power to govern such a mass of individuals and to establish invisible bonds of solidarity among them all. The king must be a true wizard, in that he exercises his power upon the very 'spirit' of his subjects, making them think like himself: indeed, the whole nation seems to be concentrated in Versailles and the entire city of Paris is metaphorically gathered within the golden perimeter of the royal court. Behind the scenes, power coordinates and directs all surrounding energies and the invisible hand of the monarchy moves the numerous, faithful political actors. A king possessing only one head is unfortunate, not only, of course, in the sense that the threat of the guillotine is always looming, but also in the sense that several heads, dispersed within civil society, are more likely to succeed in creating consensus. The Persian, therefore, understands that the king derives his riches from the loyalty of his subjects, an inexhaustible goldmine, and that even when engaging in unnecessary wars he can mobilize support and resources among the masses. In short,

Montesquieu appears to advocate a notion of power as the ability to forge subjects who are prepared to condone all its manifestations, be they benevolent or malicious. The crimes of the powerful, from his perspective, are among the governing acts necessary to preserve national unity.

Tocqueville (2003) examines the relationship between masters and servants in a similar light. The former come to think of the latter as inferior and secondary parts of themselves. The servants, on their part, see themselves in almost the same way, adopting an identity which is an appendage to that of their masters. In extreme cases they lose their own sense of self-interest and become detached from themselves, transporting their own being into that of their masters, where they create an imaginary personality for themselves. The servant, therefore,

> takes pleasure in identifying himself with the wealth of those he obeys; he glories in their fame, exalts himself through their nobility, and constantly feeds on borrowed grandeur to which he often attaches more value than those who possess it fully and in truth.
> *(Boltanski and Thévenot, 2006: 91)*

The crimes of the powerful, in this case, become acceptable thanks to the love elicited by the elite and in general by privileged, successful people.

Political theory centres its analysis on reason as frequently as it does on passion. Those in power, Hume (2011a) suggests, are mainly guided by passion, which in a never-ending process creates new objects that they passionately desire. This process may generate powerful usurpers, but with time those commonly deemed to be usurpers give rise to a new political class, and ultimately to a social system. Once established as wealthy characters, the usurpers have to find ways of making their wealth morally acceptable. This will require that non-wealthy people feel a sort of satisfaction in the riches of others, a feeling that may be ascribed to three different causes:

> First, to the objects they possess; such as houses, gardens, equipages; which, being agreeable in themselves, necessarily produce a senti-ment of pleasure in every one. Secondly, to the expectation of advantage from the rich and powerful by our sharing their

possessions. Thirdly, to sympathy, which makes us partake of the satisfaction of every one.

(Ibid.: 311)

In brief, the pleasure that the wealthy and powerful receive from their condition causes pleasure and esteem in others, which in turn creates yet more pleasure for the beholder of possessions and power. This 'secondary satisfaction' has a multiplying effect, persuading the powerful to find new ways of ameliorating their condition. The crimes of the powerful, in Hume, are the conducts of the usurpers mentioned above, who create a succession of items they passionately want to possess while triggering general admiration for their possessions.

Clearly, this description offers the image of a stable system, unshaken even by the constant stretching of ethical boundaries. But how can disorder emerge within such apparent stability? Can powerful individuals go so far as violating the very rules that guarantee their position of power? Passion, Hume argues, leads them to see an irresistible light in the items they can acquire, irrespective of their intrinsic value. In order to posses those items, they are prepared to infringe the rules of justice and the stability of the systems in which they live. In this way, powerful individuals are said to act in contradiction to their own interests, preferring trivial advantages to the maintenance of social order. While doing so, namely while 'committing acts of injustice', they push others into imitative acts, for: why should anyone 'impose severe restraints on oneself amidst the licentiousness of others?' (Hume, 2011b: 464). In this view, the crimes of the powerful, in an imitative process, have the potential to spread corruption across society, 'trickling down', as it were, in the form of acts of injustice and greed. Note that cooperation and imitation as variables for the analysis of the crimes of the powerful have also been highlighted in previous chapters.

But none of these concerns unsettles Adam Smith's (1976a, 1976b, 1978) mind, who links the sources of authority with utility as well as with 'personal qualifications, age, fortune, and birth'. At first sight, therefore, he combines what Weber's (1991) analysis would indicate as charismatic authority, on the one hand, and traditional authority, on the other. Smith, however, places particular emphasis on 'fortune' or wealth as a source of authority, thus separating a material status (being wealthy) from the way in which that status is acquired. As in Hume, wealth is interpreted as a form of power that elicits admiration, in that the poor hope to get their subsistence from those who may be generous enough to share it. The optimistic expectation that this may happen leads to the neglect of the ways in which 'fortune' is actually accumulated, leaving therefore the wealthy in the condition to negotiate the degree of virtuosity of their acts (Ruggiero, 2013). Persons endowed with wealth, in other words, may constantly move the threshold beyond which their conduct is to be deemed immoral. Smith is well aware of this dynamic, for example, when he notes that wealth represents an important source of authority, but also an important object of dispute. In a situation where larger and larger resources can be acquired, he argues, there are advantages to be gained by committing acts of injustice, because 'that situation tends to give full rein to avarice and ambition'. Hence the necessity to establish a 'civil government'. But he concedes that 'civil government, so far as it is instituted for the security of property, is in reality instituted for the defense of the rich against the poor, or of those who have some property against those who have none at all' (Smith, 1978: 12). If among what Smith describes as 'acts of injustice' we include criminal conduct by powerful individuals and groups, we may infer, following his logic, that such conduct can always be decriminalized through appropriate interventions by government. His definitions of crime, however, clarify another aspect of his thought on the subject matter.

In his *Lectures on Jurisprudence*, the author draws an initial distinction between damage produced by 'willful injury' or *malice propense* of the offender, and damage caused by 'faulty negligence, or *culpa*' (ibid.: 103). After providing a list of what we would now describe as white-collar crimes or crimes of the powerful, he remarks that their detection is very difficult, and that the large profit made is the cause of the great temptation to commit them. He briefly discusses some examples of financial crime, arguing that they do not cause 'willful injury', but are normally caused by pure 'faulty negligence'. The same formula he applies to 'the crimes which the sovereign may be guilty of against the subjects'. In brief, on the one hand, governments can always intervene to neutralize the criminality of the powerful, while on the other, this type of criminality remains ambiguous, a clouded concept that, in fact, may not require governmental intervention at all.

Imperatives and superstructure

In German idealism, political power is entrusted with an ethical mission, and ethical behaviour in general is firmly rooted in reason, which requires respect for the moral law. We will discuss in Chapter 7 the ethical issues around power and crime. Here, in the domain of politics, let us note that Kant (1996, 2007) absorbs previous conceptualizations of power within his fully idealistic framework of analysis. Conducts should follow rules while assessing whether those rules possess universal validity. Similarly, politicians enact laws while expressing the will that they should become universal laws. As a clarifying example, Kant remarks that asking for a loan with the awareness of one's inability to repay it is immoral. This conduct, in effect, cannot become a universal behaviour because, if everybody made false promises, promising itself would be impossible and purposeless. From a Kantian perspective, we may argue that political actors are expected to behave morally for the intrinsic value of morality, not for some concrete beneficial consequences they would enjoy. Kant is an enemy of utilitarianism and consequentialism, namely of judgements of conduct based on their effect. Moral concepts are a priori and originate in reason: they come to us in the form of a sense of duty; they are, therefore, categorical imperatives. A trader who is honest because he fears the consequences of dishonesty, or a person who is naturally inclined to be kind, are not virtuous. Virtue derives from an explicit will to be moral. And the essence of morality resides in the concept of law because, although everything in nature obeys some law or other, only a rational being has the capacity to *voluntarily* act according to the law. This objective principle which constrains the will is a command of the reason and its formulation is imperative. The constraint is not instrumental: you do this if you want to achieve that; it is categorical, in that a certain act is necessary and is a goal in itself. From this perspective, when the powerful commit crime, they signal ignorance of moral concepts and an inability to obey commands of the reason.

It is perhaps with a mind to political actors following moral impera-tives that Kant (1991) formulates his proposal for perpetual peace. In his philosophical manifesto, he stresses that perpetual peace 'means an end to all hostilities, a solution that nullifies all existing reasons for a future war' (ibid.: 94). No independently existing state may be acquired by another and made into a commodity, and armies should gradually be abolished, because they constantly threaten other states with war by the very fact that they are always prepared for it. However, while spiritually recoiling from the horror of war, Kant is led by his practical reason to appreciate its functions. On the one hand, therefore, he points to the ills suffered by humanity due to the incessant preparations in view of future wars, which require enormous waste of economic and cultural resources. On the other hand, he argues that without such pressure and permanent urgency, societies would equally suffer.

> In other words, it is the constant horizon of war that maintains state and social, community and cultural cohesion, and it is the same horizon that ensures a degree of freedom, in spite of restrictive laws.
>
> *(Derrida, 2011: 375)*

In brief, cultural achievement by the human species still finds in war an indispensable means of perfecting it, despite the 'commodification' of countries and persons every war entails. We have to presume that 'cultural achievement' through war, despite the commodification of the other it entails, is still part of rational adherence to the moral law and that, if we want to find allusions to 'power as crime', we have to look elsewhere.

Kant (1998) articulates his doctrine of 'radical evil' alongside his philosophy of moral law: there is an invisible enemy inside human beings pushing them towards competitive self-love, envy, addiction to power and avarice, all corrupting their moral dispositions. This innate tendency, in his view, makes people 'behave badly despite the best social teaching' (Nussbaum, 2013: 167). The crimes of the powerful, according to this formulation, are some among the innumerable manifestations of this radical evil; they are part of the reality of human nature.

Reality, however, is not a composition of separate units: nothing is completely real except the whole. We are now in Hegel's territory, where we find that every component of the real is devoid of a specific function and is regularly contradicted by the character and function of other components. An eye has no value without a body. By the same token, truths and lies are not distinct moral entities, as nothing is completely true or completely false. Using this argument in his political theory, Hegel (1952) sees the state as an accomplished moral reality containing the spirituality of all of its members. The state becomes in this way an earthly 'divine Idea', the personification of freedom and collective will, and citizens can embrace spirituality and morality only when recognizing themselves in the state. This embrace marks a relationship, like that between an eye and its body: when part of a whole, citizens may be acknowledged as precise human entities, whereas when located outside they turn into useless beings, like an eye by itself. Moreover, there is no tension between morality and politics, because states are not subject to the ordinary moral laws.

There may be, Hegel warns, bad states, but they have an ephemeral existence and do not contain reality as a whole. This is the only concession to the possibility that states may commit crimes and that powerful individuals and groups, in the social, political or economic arena, may deviate from spirituality and morality. But if we follow Hegel in his argument, we are compelled to conclude that even the separate criminal parts of the state are, ultimately, included in a whole and the whole is the only existing true entity. Perhaps it is for this reason that, while advocating cruel severity against conventional law-breakers, he fails to mention punishments that are suitable for powerful offenders (Ruggiero, 2010). The latter, in his philosophical construction, do not exist as singularities, therefore they are logical impossibilities. Following his classification, we are led to locate the crimes of the powerful among the naive or non-malicious wrongs committed by those who have no intention of violating the law and share with law-abiding citizens an appreciation of what constitutes acceptable conduct. Powerful offenders, in other words, may deny the validity and moral supremacy of a certain law in a specific situation, but they do not deny the universal character of law in general. Hegel uses the following metaphor: if I say that a rose is not red, I still recognize that it has a colour. I do not deny the universal principle that roses are colourful, but only the particular contingence that the rose in front of me is red. We may conclude that the crimes of the powerful are the effect of moral and legal daltonism.

Political authority is not adept at encouraging morality, nor does it incorporate the spirituality of citizens; it is merely the organized power of one class oppressing another. We are, of course, in Marxist territory now, where we find politics among the components of a superstructure, a corollary of the economic base which provides the core foundation to a social system (Marx, 1976a, 1976b). Political power, therefore, arises out of the social relationships prevailing in a specific productive system and reflects those relationships, which are characterized by antagonism and exploitation. To end both, for example, through revolutionary change, would mean to end politics as a tool of domination, but would also entail its appropriation, which is necessary for that change to be enacted. Politics may be 'ideology', but may at the same time be a revolutionary instrument for social emancipation, namely a counter-ideology accompanying structural material change. In the Marxist tradition, ideology is a system of representation, with its own logic and rigour, offering images, myths, ideas, concepts, narratives and discourses which help social groups make sense of the context in which they live. It functions as a repertoire of symbolic and material tools enabling them to interpret the conditions of their existence (Althusser, 1969). From a Marxist perspective, as we have already suggested, powerful groups operating in the economic or political sphere are criminal by definition, in that they have a constant and growing interest in perpetuating exploitation and social inequality. The ideology allowing them to do so is nothing more than an artefact that neutralizes all imputations of criminality, a set of beliefs that are transmitted to the sphere of the law and turned into impunity. The powerful, in this sense, strive to escape processes of stigmatization and labelling mechanisms, aiming to make their conducts formally acceptable and legitimate. For this reason (see Chapter 2, this volume), scholars with a Marxist background argue that an understanding of the crimes of the powerful may only be grasped if research is prepared to look at harmful conducts irrespective of whether or not they are formally criminalized.

Ideology vs. science?

The usefulness of the concept of ideology, however, is questioned by some theorists because those invoking and formulating it appear to oppose it to the idea of truth or science (Lloyd, 2014). The base-superstructure model posited by Marxism, in other words, is critiqued for drawing too neat a line between a material world which is supposed to be scientifically observable, and a phantasmal world populated by illusions and artificial, abstract constructions. It is suggested, rather, that the analysis should look at how truth is produced through practices and discourses that in themselves are neither true nor false (Foucault, 1980). In brief, it is argued that systems of power do not misrepresent truth but create and reinforce it, and often do so at the margin or periphery of society, where truth is initially conceived before being appropriated or utilized by different institutions or organizations for different purposes (Foucault, 1970, 1972). The argument below may clarify this point.

Normally, innovation occurs at the margins, in unexplored areas where norms are both respected and violated, and where new norms may be created. Here, the acceptance of new conducts is negotiated and their normative strength probed. At the margins, in other words, a grey area is found where behaviours await the outcomes of an ethical conflict, which will determine whether practices become routine or whether they are to be banned. We have seen it before: the conduct of powerful actors is pragmatic, in the sense that it ignores pre-existing principles and requires departure from precedents; it also neglects the potential social injustice it may cause. The argument made in previous pages is worth reiterating: the crimes of the powerful may be foundational, namely they may be inspired by an 'experimental' logic and driven by a consequentialist philosophy; they possess the 'founding force' of transforming old practices and establishing the legitimacy of new ones.

Anti-humanism

Classical Christian thought and modern thought, from the Enlightenment to Marxism, contain normative elements of moralistic and humanistic inspiration. They are finalistic in that they assume that a spontaneous evolution, aided by subjective efforts, leads to change in an inevitable historical, more or less violent process. Critics of this view, by contrast, equate social change with the development of biological species which can assume diverse genetic forms, irrespective of well-determined preconditions or mono-causal processes. In large measure, this development is said to take place randomly. Luhmann's (1975) anti-humanism and anti-historicism provide an example of this line of theorizing, positing that social reality is forged by intermingling correlations of systems and environments whose outcome is open to infinite possibilities. 'No hidden hand will secretively guide history: social evolution is propelled by probability and indeterminacy' (Zolo, 2010: xiv). There is no providence in history. As we shall see in a moment, this analysis places power and its crimes in a different framework.

Material needs, in turn, may have exhausted their capacity to shape a social structure, because they are increasingly dependent on contingency, mutability and manipulation. Luhmann's analysis of systems does not conceive of individuals and groups led by needs and values, but sees actors and protagonists taking on roles and adapting to settings from which they derive their expectations. From this perspective, individuals only possess a 'selective interest' in relation to the problems they encounter in the social system. Similarly, power is selective and its aim consists of reducing the social complexity it faces. Echoes of Simmel's (1971b) work are found here, particularly his notion that a blasé attitude is crucial for selecting the large amount of stimulations we encounter in metropolitan life. In Luhmann, however, systems survive and achieve stability when they manage to respond to a large variety of social demands, and their incessant effort to reduce complexity is a condition of their security, safety and stability. Ultimately, power is compelled to reduce uncertainty and, at the same time, to reduce the social reactions to its acts.

For power, decisions are important, but just as important are the decisions that are not made, the proposals that are never considered, the innovative ideas that are somehow always out of the question. 'Ruling a country means controlling the political agenda, defining what is thinkable and unthinkable, and this work is always done behind the façade of democratic politics' (Walzer, 2004: 24). Selective and reductive activities turn into impunity when crimes of the powerful are committed; this is because citizens interact with the sources of power only sporadically and in extremely limited spheres of social life. They, therefore, are the recipients of injunctions, of binding decisions transmitted to them, but the complexity of their condition does not allow them to orient themselves politically and ethically. By providing such orientation to citizens, in brief, power reduces the autonomy of their judgement, thus making its crimes invisible. A typical simplification of the social complexity experienced by citizens consists, in democracies, of the right to vote, through which the electorate is given the impression of contributing to the formation of decisions and of running the public life. In reality, the electoral choice perpetuates systems which eject social conflict and, by partially and selectively exercising their power, conceal the unorthodox practices of the powerful. In sum, by engaging in an 'economy of consent', powerful groups make themselves free from the interference of political dissent and from the assessment of their conduct.

This argument may contradict the notion presented in earlier chapters that powerful offenders need cooperation and imitation to make their actions acceptable. It may, on the other hand, suggest that such offenders enjoy a particular versatility, allowing them to select the ways in which their behaviour comes to be accepted.

Politics, violence, death

A vivid example of the selectivity of power and their crimes comes to light when democratic states limit the freedoms of their citizens in the name of protecting their lives during periods of actual or presumed emergency. In such situations, power enacts measures designed to immunize the population against risk, but these measures destroy the very democratic principles that are purportedly being preserved, and 'strategies of self-preservation become a form of mortification, shelter becomes its own kind of life-threatening exposure' (Santner, 2011: 7).

A strand of analysis in political theory focuses on the shift from the power of deduction to the power of organization. The end of monarchies in Europe, it is contended, marks the decline of the right on the part of the powerful to seize things, time, bodies and, ultimately, life itself (Foucault, 1990). Supplementing Foucault's analysis discussed in previous pages, it is worthwhile focusing on his concept of 'organization', which includes new strategies to reinforce, control, monitor, optimize and indeed organize: in sum, the power to generate forces, make them grow, order them, rather than impel them. 'The old power of death that symbolized sovereign power was now carefully supplanted by the administration of bodies and the calculated management of life' (ibid.: 140).

Power takes charge of life, accesses the body, does not limit itself to bringing death, but distributes the living while ranking them in terms of value and utility.

> If one can apply the term bio-history to the pressures through which the movements of life and the processes of history interfere with one another, one would have to speak of bio-power to designate what brought life and its mechanisms into the realm of explicit calculations, and made knowledge-power an agent of transformation of human life.
>
> *(Ibid.: 143)*

Bio-power, however, amounts to 'fostering life' but also to disallowing it, to the point of causing death. It can take, therefore, a thanato-political direction, so that the culmination of a politics of life generates a lethal power that contradicts its very productive impulse. The power of life is exercised against life itself, in two parallel or simultaneous processes. 'Why does bio-politics continually threaten to be reversed into thanato-politics?' (Esposito, 2008: 39).

We have now entered what is perhaps the most significant arena in which the crimes of the powerful take place, namely the destruction of life. Contemporary analysis, in this respect, finds supporting arguments in a set of concepts which may well be regarded as classical within political theory (Schmitt, 1976, 1985). Sovereign power brings the entitlement to declare a state of exception, to suspend the law, to suspend rights in the name of protecting the state and its population from sudden or excessive risk (Santner, 2011). In states of emergency citizens are dealt with as bare bodies, as barely worthy of living (Agamben, 1998). We are well beyond the continuation of politics with other means as postulated by von Clausewitz.

According to a more general account, all significant notions we find in modern theories of the state are secularized theological notions, not only because of their historical development, but also because of their systematic structure (Schmitt, 1985; Gottfried, 1990). Liberalists, with their belief in a self-regulating universe, echo eighteenth-century deists, who believed in an impersonal divinity whose predictable conduct was beneficial to human beings and coherent with nature. Radical democrats, in turn, embrace a political theology of pantheism, proclaiming the popular will to be the will of God. There is a form of pantheism even in Marxism and in many versions of historical materialism which, though presented as scientific, in fact display religious types of faith.

Politics entails crime, violence and war, being the realm of conflict, where everyone chooses their friends and enemies (Schmitt, 1976). And war is indeed an essential part of politics: when political theory encounters international relations, a most fruitful analysis of the crimes of the powerful can be carried out. It is to the examination of this encounter that the final section of this chapter is devoted.

War aliments disproportion and paroxysm, which spread across all human conflicts, social interactions and, last but not least, institutional conducts. Despite attempts to publicly sanitize its manifestations, war contains a silent incitement to illegal excesses. An extreme form of the crimes of the powerful, war induces the adoption of the lowest forms of survival: killing grants the sensation of immortality, as it allows one to survive (Ruggiero, 2006). War means mass victimization, violation of human rights and a wide range of state crimes. War zones become enormous markets managed by organized criminal groups and corporations alike (Whyte, 2012). They offer a context, a behavioural framework within which everybody may act as they please: torture turns into patriotic behaviour, while rape may become an act of heroism (Ruggiero, 2013). Those who are recruited are offered a salary, but with it they are provided with a non-written licence to loot, and are promised the emotion to kill without feeling any sense of guilt. Examples of brutality spread, in an imitative, learning process, making ruthlessness acceptable and, in a vicious circle, the 'deviants' are those who do not conform to the unwritten rules of brutality, not those who are brutal (Ward, 2005). Therefore, on the one hand, war is criminogenic and, on the other hand, so-called 'war crimes' are the norm and include predatory and violent acts perpetrated by the police, the armies and paramilitary forces. In many circumstances, it is hard indeed to distinguish between police forces, soldiers, mercenaries and criminals: they all become agents of social control and crimes are encouraged as essential components of the conflict in which they are engaged. The direct involvement of private companies, security agencies and firms supplying military services and paramilitary consultancy suggests the creation of a complex apparatus whose contours are vague and in which missionary militarism, predatory enterprise and corruption mingle in an unprecedented fusion. Recent events show that war manifests itself as a form of economic crime or crime of the powerful, and that its very illegality transcends the economic sphere, being the result of unauthorized action adopted against the will of international agencies (Sands, 2006). Moreover, war is illegal in the very means utilized: torture, kidnapping, prohibited weapons. In this way, war crimes and the crimes of the powerful overlap.

Faced with this gigantic variety and seriousness of criminal activity, we are forced to expand our definition of power and its crimes, suggesting that the core aspect is not simply that power makes decisions while powerless people are forced to comply, but that power can make criminal, irreversible decisions, whose consequences are prolonged indefinitely and whose effects are devastating. Such decisions do not enjoy the support of majorities, nor do those making them elicit admiration or imitation, as Hume, Montesquieu and Tocqueville would have it. International affairs and foreign policy are still an astonishing private affair: 'the records indicate not exactly a conspiracy, but key decisions being taken by a very small number of people' (Mann, 2011: 54). Deliberative democracy and the theory of communicative action may well prompt that decisions should be made by affected persons capable of subjecting them to critical debate, in rational discussions among equals, and after considering alternative possibilities (Habermas, 1989, 1996). The reality is that foreign policy is run by elites in private settings, an amalgam of groups of interest and their lobbyists.

Attempts have been made to establish when some enemies 'lack the moral right not to be killed' (Haque, 2014), namely of enforcing the right of powerful groups to bring death at their will. This would require a type of ideological hegemony that even Gramsci (1971) would find hard to formulate: how could domination through death capture the mind and the political sensibility of majorities? In Gramsci, domination aims at subjugating or even liquidating rival groups, but it is leadership that allows the exercise of power, as moral and intellectual values are widely spread, shared and ultimately internalized by majorities. Currently, large majorities of citizens all over the world are either apathetic about, or overtly opposed to, warfare activity and interests. Veblen noted this long before our times, asserting that common people, making the core of the industrial labour force, were averse to any armed conflict except for defensive purposes. 'In the more civilized communities which have reached an advanced industrial development, the spirit of warlike aggression may be said to be obsolescent among the common people'

(Veblen, 1924: 152). In order to make war acceptable, now more than at the times of Veblen, one solution is to depict it as a defensive fight, another is denying that a war is taking place at all, for example, by hiding it from public view. Both strategies are utilized today. Wars of aggression are staged in remote locations, without the mobilization of citizens' consciousness or even their awareness. As Dal Lago (2012) remarks, since 1991 Western countries led by the US have fought in Iraq, Bosnia, Somalia, Serbia, Afghanistan, Iraq again, Libya, Pakistan, and so on. Yet, we may feel that we have never been at war, a feeling of indifference unprecedented in history. Yet another strategy making war acceptable and, indeed, possible is finding complicity and partnership among specific sectors of society. Veblen (1924: 153) argued that the elite could find their traditional, bellicose frame of mind being replicated among the 'lower-class delinquents', 'those individuals who are endowed with an archaic temperament of the predatory type'. In the current times, this temperament is regularly displayed by powerful offenders, who possess the predatory abilities and the distinctive clannishness necessary for making war a business. Many criminologists would point out that conventional property crime is the price we pay for relative deprivation. Would they be prepared to see this extreme form of crime of the powerful, namely the killing of thousands of people across the world, as the price to keep international relative deprivation as it is?

Conclusion

Political analysis may focus on rules, their consistency and their performance, namely on whether their faithful enactment results in expected rewards. Powerful individuals and groups, against this background, offend when they perceive that playing by the existing rules of the game turns out to be unrewarding (Rosenfeld and Messner, 2013). Instead, in this chapter the crimes of the powerful have been described as a 'state of mind' (Aristotle), as the result of the coexistence of good and evil (Augustine), as the outcome of human imperfection (Spinoza), as acceptable conducts within specific forms of social contract (Hobbes), and as legitimate tools against dissent (Rousseau). They have also been linked with the implicit violence or criminality of political power (Montaigne, Pascal, Vico), assimilated to ordinary acts of government (Montesquieu), and associated with usurpers generating admiration (Hume, Tocqueville). Traversing a variety of political theories, we have found that the crimes of the powerful, in fact, are too ambiguous to be treated as crime (Smith), that they are expressions of human 'radical evil' (Kant), that they are non-malicious wrongs (Hegel), that they are ingrained in capitalist exploitation (Marx), that they originate at the margins of social systems (Foucault), and that they take place when social reactions are selected and reduced (Luhmann). Finally, we have found their supreme manifestations in contemporary wars, which are the result of decisions made by bellicose elites for the preservation or intensification of international inequality.

The avalanche of interpretations we have encountered in political theory vindicates the opinion of Socrates who, retorting to Protagoras' claim that he teaches the art of politics, argues that politics cannot be assimilated to other arts and, therefore, it is not teachable. Discussing how to build a house or a ship, he says, the opinions expressed by architects or engineers are received without any discussion. But if the subject is how to run a city, nobody can claim to know better than others.

6

INGLORIOUS HUMAN ACTIVITIES

Understanding the crimes of the powerful from the perspective of economic thought requires the enumeration of some preliminary notions: above all, the notion that activities previously despised can slowly become honourable. With a sense of wonder, this is expressed by Max Weber (1976) in the question: how could money-making pursuits, love of lucre and avarice triumph above innumerable higher values? Hunger for money and possessions was among the principal sins, along with lust for power and sexual intemperance. The pursuit of glory was also condemned, as was love of praise: both were attacked as vain and sinful. In a long process, changes in the collective sensibility, particularly in the religious sphere, managed to Christianize the activities of merchant bankers and usurers, and, at the same time, to impose the precept of fraternity upon economic actors. Philosophers, simultaneously, paved the way for the acceptance of human frailty, with Hobbes, but also Spinoza, warning that 'men' had to be taken as they actually were, not as we would like them to be, with Vico admonishing that only some dreamer could inhabit the perfect Plato's Republic, and Rousseau clarifying that his search for ideal governments was based on the real nature of human beings (Hirschman, 1977).

Evil passions, on the other hand, may serve higher purposes of which humans are unaware and even the most obstinate desire for gain can prove harmless, if not beneficial. Commerce, in this way, became a deterrent of hostility, requiring cooperation, agreement and mutually satisfying exchange.

> In an age in which men were searching for ways of limiting the damage and horrors they are wont to inflict on each other, commercial and economic activities were therefore looked upon more kindly.
>
> *(Ibid.: 59)*

From the late seventeenth century on, the gentleness of commerce was contrasted to the harshness of traditional interactions. Montesquieu (1989) expounded the doctrine of *doux commerce*, which polishes and softens human beings, distancing them from the rude and barbarous. Making money became a calm passion, and no innovation in the material life of individuals could erase their innate feelings of solidarity: Hume (2011a: 811) stressed that even self-love could never be divorced from 'such dispositions as benevolence and generosity; such affections as love, friendship, compassion, gratitude'.

It should be obvious that these thoughts addressed the main source of potentially destructive passions, those harboured by the powerful, who were in a position to cause harm on a large scale, and whose lust for glory, gain and excesses needed to be bridled, at least in the imagination of society at large. The imaginary curbing of this lust was provided by the 'science' of economics, which found propitious terrain for its development long before it could hubristically claim its scientific status. Ferocity, avarice and ambition, the three vices loathed by Giambattista Vico (1999), were turned by divine forces into civil happiness with the help of reason and empathy, which were inscribed in commercial interactions. A civilizing artifice was identified as the most fruitful device to harness power, so that its acts could be transformed into constructive deeds: concupiscence could be managed and arranged to form an excellent social order, human frailty and greed turned into their opposite, namely general empowerment and generosity. Simulta-neously, money achieved legitimacy despite being an obstacle to salva-tion, merchants and their financiers were appreciated for facilitating commercial exchange with distant peoples, the greedy were removed from the front line of the potentially damned, and even usurers found their place in the Christian conscience, becoming redeemable sinners: Purgatory would 'wash' their souls while they waited patiently to be received into Paradise (Lefèvre, 1902; Le Goff, 1987).

A criminological analysis of economics as a field of knowledge, whose theoretical trajectory accompanied these developments, has been rehearsed elsewhere, and to repeat it here would amount to self-plagiarism. Every school of thought forming this 'dismal science', it has been argued, rationalizes, justifies or even encourages some form of social harm produced by economic initiative. John Locke, the Mercantilists, the Physiocrats, Malthus, Smith, Ricardo, Marx, Marshall, Keynes and Hayek have all been charged with varying degrees of responsibility for overlooking the destructive implications of their doctrines and ignoring the human cost of their fascination with economic growth: in other words, of neglecting 'the crimes of the economy' (Ruggiero, 2013).

The history of economic thought traverses innumerable stages leading to models of humanity devoid of such things as goodwill and moral sentiments. The concerns of Thomas More (1997) remained unaltered for centuries. More perceived a 'conspiracy' on the part of the wealthy, which through 'all means and crafts' try to 'keep safely without fear of losing what they have unjustly gathered together'. These 'means and crafts' are turned into economic laws, whereby the only legitimate thing the non-wealthy can do is endeavour to imitate the wealthy. Centuries later, as we have already seen, Max Weber (1978) argued that markets are antithetic to all other communities, because the latter, not the former, presuppose brotherhood among people. More recently, Galbraith (1987) has described economic history as a constant attempt to explain why most people are poor and a few are rich, and to persuade us all that it is fair that things remain as they are. Finally, it has been suggested that practitioners of economics are not allowed friendliness; they are required to describe human motivations as pure and simple, and to keep their economic models away from ethics (Sen, 1987; Jacobs, 1992). In the following pages we shall probe how some categories elaborated by the 'science' dealing with the economy, this inglorious human activity, may be used for the analysis of the crimes of the powerful.

Goods and 'bads'

Apologists of economics as a scientific discipline claim that their interpretive approach is a comprehensive one, applicable to all forms of human
conduct, be it aimed at the acquisition of material goods, at emotional
ends or at pure physical pleasure. Rich and poor persons, men or
women, adults or children, brilliant or stupid people, patients or thera-
pists, businessmen or politicians, teachers or students: are all guided by
economic calculus (Becker, 1968, 1976). According to the economic
approach, a person decides to marry when the utility expected from
marriage exceeds that expected from remaining single or from an
additional search for a more suitable companion. Similarly, a married
person terminates his or her marriage when the utility anticipated from
becoming single or marrying someone else exceeds the loss in utility
from separation, including losses due to the division of joint assets and
legal fees. Since many persons are looking for companions, a market in
marriages may be said to exist.

Crime is too important a human activity to be left to the contemplation of moralists, and its treatment has to identify the optimal levels of
expenditures that minimize the loss it generates. So goes economic
thinking. The optimal expenditure, we are told, is to be understood as
the ideal amount of enforcement, which depends, among other things,
on the cost of detection, apprehension and criminal conviction of
offenders, the cost of punishment, and the responses of offenders to
changes in enforcement. We have seen in the previous chapter how
this argument, from the perspective of 'legal economism', ends up
condoning powerful offenders, first, because it is costly to prosecute
them, and second, because their incarceration would prevent them
from producing wealth. However, the advantage in using an economic
approach to crime is found in the fact that it 'can dispense with special
theories of anomie, psychological inadequacies, or inheritance of special
traits and simply extend the economist's usual analysis of choice'
(Becker, 1968: 170). Lest readers be repelled by the apparent novelty of
an economic framework for the analysis of crime, Becker reminds us
that 'two important contributors to criminology during the eighteenth
and nineteenth centuries, Beccaria and Bentham, explicitly applied an
economic calculus' (ibid.: 209).

Economists note that the basic premise of sociological work on crime is that criminals are somehow different from non-criminals, and the major research consists of the ways in which criminals differ (Rubin, 1980). Assuming a rationality to all human behaviour, Rubin argues, potential criminals should also be acknowledged as being endowed with principles guiding the rationality of their actions. The choice of action for criminals depends on the value of alternative uses of time, a choice that also engages law enforcers. In other words, all actors involved in the crime sector of the economy 'are consciously or subconsciously weighing the costs and benefits of their actions and making explicit choices among alternatives' (Andreano and Siegfried, 1980: 4). Those involved in illegal activity, be they powerful actors or not, rationally maximize their own self-interest subject to the constraints they face in the marketplace. 'Thus the decision to become a criminal is in principle no different from the decision to become a bricklayer or a carpenter, or, indeed, an economist' (Rubin, 1980: 13).

According to this view, therefore, powerful offenders simply try to maximize their own self-interest, and their choice to commit crime is determined by a favourable weighing of the costs and benefits implied by that choice. In addition, the crimes of the powerful should be examined in relation to the rules of the occupational choice of offenders. These will weigh prospects, returns and costs of violations, and compare them with those of legitimate activities. 'The costs of injuries to a professional athlete are comparable to the costs to the offender of apprehension, defence, and conviction' (Stigler, 1970: 530). Powerful offenders may have to consider which location offers maximum potential income, and therefore, like salespersons, move from area to area. They may consider whether infrequent large-scale crimes yield more returns than frequent small-scale ones, or choose between acting as Pareto's foxes or lions.

Among the crimes of the powerful examined by economists are the specific activities we commonly attribute to organized crime. What market characteristics determine whether a criminal activity becomes organized? As Schelling (1967) notes, the car industry is characterized by large firms, whereas machine-tool production is not. If the economic principles operating in the upperworld also apply to the activities of the underworld, explanations should be found as to why, for example, gambling, extortion and contraband require large firms and a higher degree of organization. The first explanation rests on overall costs and some element of technology that make small firms more costly than large firms. Schelling identifies the lower limit to the size of a firm in the need to keep equipment and skilled personnel fully employed. The second explanation concerns the prospect of establishing monopolistic conditions. Monopolies allow for the rise of prices at which goods and services may be sold. On the other hand, they often result in the overall reduction of output due to the absence of competing firms. But the increase in profit margin will compensate for this. Cartels or mergers can lead to monopolies, as can intimidation. The three options are equally available to firms.

Schelling elucidates a crucial aspect of organized crime as a form of crime of the powerful. This regards the 'preferability' of structured large-scale illicit activities as opposed to dispersed disorganized ones. The author observes that the larger the firm, and especially the larger its market share, the more will formerly 'external' costs become internalized. External costs are those falling on competitors, customers and others outside the firm itself. Violence, for example, could be regarded as one such external cost. Thus, members of organized crime may have a collective interest in restricting violence so as to avoid the disapproval of the public and attention from the police. Ideally, their task would be to reduce violence to a minimum. On the other hand, individual (professional or unskilled) criminals have little or no incentive to reduce the violence connected with their crime. In this respect, Schelling suggests an analogy with the whaling industry, which has a collective interest in not killing all whales, while individual whalers may not consider the future of the industry as a whole when trying to maximize their own catch.

A large organization can afford to impose discipline, holding down violence if the business is crime, holding down the slaughter of females if the business is whaling. In this light, even episodes of 'accommodation' that organized crime sometimes reaches with institutional agencies or individual members of such agencies may be regarded as attempts to restrain dangerous practices and limit violence while delineating spheres of influence.

Schelling's observations about 'compromising with organized crime' include the awareness that corruption of public officials entails a price for society to pay. This is exemplified by frustration at the criminal justice system and a general lowering of standards of morality. Successive analyses, to which I now turn, tend to only emphasize the social 'preferability' of organized crime as opposed to disorganized crime while omitting the evaluation of the moral costs involved.

Buchanan (1980) bases his 'defense of organized crime' on the distinction between goods and 'bads'. Monopoly in the sale of ordinary goods and services, he contends, is socially inefficient because it restricts output or supply. It also permits vendors to increase prices and therefore concentrate profits. This widely shared belief suggests that efforts should be made to limit monopolies and favour competition instead. However, 'if monopoly in the supply of "goods" is socially undesirable, monopoly in the supply of "bads" should be socially desirable, precisely because of the output restriction' (ibid.: 395). The validity of this argument, in Buchanan's analysis, is exemplified by the sex industry. In spite of legal prohibitions, for many customers sex workers are 'goods' in the strict economic sense. Monopoly organizations providing these goods are preferable to competitive ones because they restrict the total output. On the other hand, a competitive situation will result in firms imposing 'external diseconomies' upon each other. In sum, the overall social costs of a number of firms competing in the provision of sex services would inevitably grow. More sex workers would be available, a variety of appealing settings and markets would be set up for the sale of these 'goods', and the diseconomies associated with hostile or violent competition would follow. The replacement of competition by monopoly would have the effect of internalizing such diseconomies. Buchanan concludes his analysis by stressing that organized criminal groups should be persuaded to operate in less socially damaging illicit markets, and that their self-interest can be made to serve social purposes under the appropriate institutional arrangements. Official agencies should therefore discourage competition among illicit firms and translate the self-interest of organized crime into a reduction of the social damage it causes. 'It is not from the public-spiritedness of the leaders of the Cosa Nostra that we should expect to get a reduction in the crime rate but from their regard for their own self-interests' (ibid.: 407).

This skilful paraphrase of Adam Smith's celebrated argument that it is not thanks to the generosity of the butcher and the baker, but to their self-interest, that we enjoy our meals opens up some connected possibilities for the analysis of the crimes of the powerful. First, when such crimes occur within the economic sphere, accommodation can be reached with offenders who may be asked to act as 'regulators' of their own business sector, and therefore to reduce the external diseconomies they generate. In this case, the crimes of the powerful are the cost incurred by that economic sector as a whole to police itself. Powerful offenders can therefore easily claim that their criminality is a cost-reducing practice, provided that its social cost does not exceed that of the potential criminal practices they avert. In this sense, society might 'contract out' some of the regulatory functions to criminals themselves, 'encouraging them to stick to less damaging kinds of crime' (Reynolds, 1980: 43–44).

Second, powerful groups may assert their right to engage in criminality once they demonstrate that groups operating in other economic sectors are more criminal than they are. For example, members of the pharmaceutical industry, notorious for its endemic illegality, can point out that those operating in the industry of armaments are more criminal and more unethical than they are. The former, at least, may claim to produce goods which are expected to heal people, while the latter produce 'bads' which are only designed to annihilate them. For this reason, one economic sector presenting itself as less socially damaging than others may require that its crimes be treated as minor offences, while also posing as a living example that highly harmful industrial sectors may be abandoned without opportunities for profits (and crime) being prejudiced. Ultimately, powerful offenders may be regarded as obstacles hampering competitors who intend to commit crime. In this sense, we may conclude that their criminality, in fact, amounts to crime-prevention activity.

Accommodation with conventional criminal groups, as urged in economic analysis, includes the provision to such groups of money-laundering channels for their illicit proceeds. A typical offence perpetrated by financial operators, this provision also locates the crimes of the powerful in the realm of crime-prevention activities, as it helps criminal groups position themselves with monopolistic force in the illicit markets in which they operate. In brief, financial institutions laundering profits from crime play an important role in maintaining social order and reducing the damaging effects of criminal activity. Similarly, corrupt politicians, judges and law enforcers who are complicit with criminal organizations may be said to ward off the social harm caused by dispersed, disorganized criminal activity. A final example of this analysis pertains to the arena of political and administrative corruption. Here, elites involved in corrupt exchange may argue that their 'higher immorality' staves off the cumulative immorality of ordinary or disadvantaged people: by monopolizing corruption, they prevent it from spreading throughout society. Less dispersed, less 'socialized', and with corrupt income concentrated among limited elites, corruption under certain circumstances appears to entail lower costs (Ruggiero, 2000). *Crime as crime prevention* also applies in other areas. For instance, American and British soldiers bringing democracy with bombs can claim that the deaths they cause will teach a backward system to cherish the life of its members. In addition, rape involving coalition soldiers who 'bring democracy' could be regarded as a strategy to reduce sexual violence in the places invaded and teach those violent societies respect for women.

On justification

One of the most magnificent achievements of economic theory is not so much the explanation of why, when and how the crimes of the powerful occur as in what ways such crimes may be justified. Let us now carry out this theoretical investigation while focusing on the following conceptual variables: equality, inclinations, needs, toleration and liberty.

The work conducted by Sykes and Matza (1957) around the 'techniques of neutralization' has been discussed earlier. Sociological analysis of justification, however, proposes a specific reading of organizations and businesses, where resources and arrangements based on personal ties are said to play a crucial role in determining behaviour (Boltanski and Thévenot, 2006). The crimes of the powerful, following this line of analysis, may be seen as the result of proximity among actors, mutual trust, imitation, and the desire to perpetuate bonds, values and group interests. We may note that such arguments do not distance themselves from the criminological domain, where all of this may be expressed with the notions of subcultures and learning processes. Proper philosophical and political justification requires that partial concerns and factional gains be depicted as beneficial to the collectivity; therefore it entails an agreed-upon definition of the common good and the identification of higher common principles. In this sense, justification is a form of compromise, and 'a compromise, in order to be acceptable, must be based on the quest for a common good of a higher order than the ones the compromise attempts to reconcile' (ibid.: 20).

One strategy allowing for the configuration of a higher order consists of grounding it in the alleged universal appreciation of individualism. By denying the reality of collective phenomena, for instance, the mere interest of individuals comes to be recognized. If we regard the crimes of the powerful as extensions of individual interests, justifications are to be found in the very history of liberalism. We have seen at the beginning of this chapter some religious elements intertwined with this tradition of thought. What needs to be added is that, by linking liberalism with the Christian revolution and its legacy in the modern age, a sacred aura is conferred upon free enterprise and its social effects. Christianity, we are told, freed a world suffocated by hierarchy, where rank was deemed natural and reason belonged to born elites (Siedentop, 2013). It built a world of equal individuals 'sharing a common fate and endowed with equal moral status' (Collins, 2014: 7). Individual conscience developed, as did communities, giving rise to free associations of moral agents defined by St Paul as the 'body of Christ'. Enemies of liberalism and individualism, therefore, became enemies of Christianity.

While powerful offenders may justify their acts by claiming the saintly origin of their predatory instinct, they may at the same time claim that their rectitude is testified by the intimate, individual relationship they establish with the divinity they worship. Before Max Weber associated religious belief and self-discipline with the entrepreneurial spirit, philosophers formulated theories of morality revolving around individual rectitude, theories that ignored collective forms of life while encouraging solipsism. Individualism, in Plato, is characterized by *homo erectus*, namely a person who abandons the cave in which she is held and the uncomfortable position she is forced to assume, and walks in straight paces towards virtue. His theoretical model is 'vertical' and excludes deviations or inclinations. According to this model, therefore, leaning towards vice is a logical impossibility for those who have acquired independence in the form of erect posture. During the eighteenth century, the century of Immanuel Kant, depictions of individualism as independence abound, with Kant himself abhorring children for their 'leaning' on others and their passive attitude towards the mechanics of instincts. In his moral writings the others never appear, the only protagonist being the ego and its reason functioning in solitude (Arendt, 2006). Inclinations, on the other hand, are dangerous for autonomous individuals, because they allude not only to deviant conducts, but also to offers of care and solidarity to those in need (Cavarero, 2013). Rather than leaning towards others with acts of generosity, the 'erect' individual is allowed to act politically; that is, to take initiatives, operate in new areas, be they economic or moral; in brief, to experiment with unique conducts. Acting is the faculty to initiate, the art of giving life to something new: the crimes of the powerful, from this perspective, are tantamount to novel discoveries, unprecedented forays into the static moral world made of continuity and habits.

Inclinations as care of the other entail solidarity and mutual responsibility, associated with reproduction and opposed to the total commodification of life. Against morbid individualism and infinite accumulation, groups may incline towards the defence of nature, ecological justice between genera-tions, political participation and control of economic initiative. 'Such claims, along with the counter-claims they inevitably incite, are the very stuff of social struggle in capitalist societies' (Fraser, 2014: 68). The crimes of the powerful are indeed counter-claims, namely forceful upsettings of rules, challenges to notions of legality, which aim at neutralizing the legitimacy of collective claims.

Needs and tolerance

Justifications of the crimes of the powerful may follow another trajectory: one based around the notion of need. The individuals described above, having achieved independence and rectitude, may advocate the crucial importance of needs defined by the *telos* to which they refer. To say that they need something is merely shorthand for the complete state-ment that they need something in order to acquire something else. The Marxist tradition distinguishes at least three different categories of needs: individual natural needs, or the means of biotic survival; social needs, or the means to an existence that is fulfilled in some ethical sense; and economic needs, the means required for the individual to serve the logic of capital (Heller, 1976). The crimes of the powerful adopt the third *telos*; that is, a logic of appropriating resources before they are wasted. This echoes John Locke's views around economic initiative, which is required to establish private ownership wherever fruits and game risk to rot and wherever rules allow such waste. Surprisingly, however, the crimes of the powerful also follow what may be termed a 'Pareto logic', in the sense that even wealth illegally appropriated may be regarded as loss if no one appropriates it. From this perspective, powerful individuals and groups who abstain from crime cause a 'Pareto-inferior change', which refers to any change leading to at least one player experiencing a fall in utility. The crimes of the powerful, on the contrary, aim at causing 'Pareto-superior change'; that is, utility for all social players. Effectiveness and efficacy are key variables: adequate economic power is not confined to doing something, but must do things without any waste.

From an economic point of view, tolerance for the crimes of the powerful may be generated by this notion of 'utility' that we encounter when powerful actors pursuing their interest find resort to coercion unnecessary. As we have stressed more than once, successful criminals may present themselves as philanthropists, in the sense that their deeds and their outcomes may appear to benefit others rather than the perpetrators. These philanthropic powerful offenders, in brief, manage to repel the criminal label from their activity and to persuade others that their goals correspond to those of the collectivity. For example, criminal entrepreneurs may often claim that their crimes (for example, producing or exporting prohibited or harmful goods) contribute to keeping and creating jobs (Ruggiero, 2007). It is in these cases that we are faced with what may be termed an ethical paradox of toleration.

The paradox lies in the fact that tolerating other people's acts may be opposed to the imperatives of our ethical code. Believing that a certain kind of conduct is wrong can turn into the feeling that the conduct in question should be prevented. Such feeling, however, is avoided if toleration of that conduct is justified by adhering to higher principles which supersede our ethical code (Mendus, 1988). Economics does just that. In the example given above the higher principles embedded in job creation may lead to condoning the crimes of the powerful and recognizing some moral value in them. Even crimes associated with tyrannical systems may find toleration, as in Xenophon's dialogue between Hiero the tyrant and Simonides the poet that I will now discuss.

Hiero has been a private man before becoming a tyrant and is asked by Simonides to explain how the pains and joys of the two conditions differ. Hiero claims that power brings fewer pleasures and greater grief than the condition of an ordinary person of moderate means. Those who are politically or economically powerful have to strive to maintain their status and their wealth; they are constantly fearful of being deprived of what they possess and, as a consequence, they become powerless. Praise and respect do not balance this fear, because these are only bestowed upon them for the sake of flattery. Wealth itself ceases to generate pleasure, as growing amounts of it find the powerful insensitive to what they are already inured. 'So, in the duration of pleasure too, one who is served many dishes fares worse than those who live in a moderate way' (Strauss, 2013: 5). It would be interesting to enquire whether Alfred Marshall took inspiration from Xenophon for the formulation of his celebrated theory of marginal utility: 'the marginal utility of a thing to anyone diminishes with every increase in the amount of it he already has' (Marshall, 1961: 79). Applying this principle to the accumulation of power, money and resources, we are led to conclude that there are natural limits to social privileges and that the abuse of one's position is held in check by spontaneous self-restraining mechanisms. 'The richer a man becomes the less is the marginal utility of money to him' (ibid.: 81). Xenophon's main focus, however, is fear that the disadvantaged may challenge the unjust distribution of wealth or even plot tyrannicide, which will lead to the erection of statues honouring those who commit it. Fear is only tempered by the realization that inequality will constantly increase provided something is left for the needy, because 'the one who lacks something takes his fill with delight whenever it comes to sight before him' (Strauss, 2013: 6).

Another core concern of the powerful operating in markets, however, is the existence of other powerful individuals and groups who may possess more, and this turns into bitter competition. For, as the ordinary individual desires a house or a field, the powerful desire cities, extensive territory, harbours or citadels, 'which are things much harder and more dangerous to win than the objects desired by private men' (ibid.: 11). This is why, in Xenophon, crime is an option, as plundering temples and human beings is the only guarantee that economic power is maintained and augmented. If crime, on the other hand, tarnishes the honourability of the powerful, this does not change the situation substantially, the powerful normally being less honoured than feared. Power, therefore, may comfortably rule without or against the laws. Hiero in fact considers that, in order to become powerful, some unpopular or even criminal measures have to be taken, but he also admits that the conservation of power itself, once achieved, requires incessant 'innovation' in a cumulative, virtually infinite process. From a Hegelian perspective, such a process corresponds to history, which offers a concrete social and political reality while providing an understanding of how to change it. The powerful are impelled to 'go beyond', to deny reality and overcome its restraining force: negation is realized 'by action, struggle and work so that a new political reality is created' (Kojève, 2013: 174). This exercise of 'negation' includes violating rules and decriminalizing conducts.

Codes and secrecy

Let us briefly return to Hegel. His trust in smooth historical evolution is based on the belief that pre-existing moral principles guiding human interactions would temper the belligerence of economic actors; in brief, that the economic sphere could not alter the higher ideals of coexistence. He could not predict that market economies may turn into market societies, namely that an artificial set of tools for the production and exchange of goods may be translated into values seeping into every aspect of human endeavour (Sandel, 2013). Markets do not pass judgement on the preferences they satisfy. 'They don't ask whether some ways of valuing goods are higher, or worthier, than others. They don't distinguish between admirable preferences and base ones' (ibid.: 14). Markets do not trade in morality, they thrive on efficiency and incentives. The former makes sure that goods and services are allocated in a way that maximizes their value, while the latter orient choices and signal their viability. The crimes of the powerful, as has already been argued, constitute implicit assertions that the resources illegally appropriated will see their value maximized; they signal that criminal conduct in the economy is efficient and provides incentives to imitation. In markets, 'signalling' helps overcome information asymmetries: in the form of expensive advertising, for example, it communicates to potential customers that the goods on offer are of such high quality that they deserve the most costly kind of promotional campaign. Powerful offenders, in their turn, may signal to their peers their own impunity, thus acting as catalysts for further crimes. Adopting illegal practices, in other words, may turn into an incentive facilitating colleagues to do the same. Once those practices are sufficiently widespread, mutual information concerning those adopting them will create a network of complicity, mixed with blackmailing opportunities which are likely to perpetuate illicit conducts. Examples pertaining to corrupt political and economic elites prove that networks of powerful offenders are held together by the mutual threat of revelation, as the crimes of each component of the network are known to the others. 'This indicates that not only had they played the game successfully before but that they would probably be afraid to violate the pacts lest the knowledge of their deeds be used against them' (Gambetta, 2009: 61).

Secrecy characterizes many operations in contemporary global markets, with companies being constituted by multiple layers of concealment. A company may be based in a tax haven, be controlled by a sister company in a Western European country, possess large interests in another company in Asia and be managed by one located in the US. Secrecy describes not only the financial aspects of operations, identifiable as the concealment of profits and the evasion of taxes, but also the very productive processes in which companies engage. Resources, practices, peoples, monies, entire productive operations are 'moved from one national territory to another, and they are wholly or partly hidden from the view of the public and/or public authorities' (Urry, 2014: 9). Economic analysis of organized crime, as discussed above, considers how groups choose which location offers maximum potential income, and how criminals, like salespersons, move from area to area. This analysis also applies to legitimate, powerful economic actors who, like conventional criminals, act undercover, delete the traces of their movements and their profits, and at times of their very activities (Brittain-Catlin, 2005). True, secrecy and power have been and are intertwined, particularly with respect to the means and modalities through which power is exercised, as the example of the 'means' we call money clearly demonstrates.

As a peculiar means of exchange, money lends itself ideally to robbery (Simmel, 1990), also because *pecunia non olet*: who can tell its true origin? When money exchange was finally purified from guilt, sin and crime, human relationships and monetary interests finally came to coincide. Money became the absolute means, the unifying point of innumerable sequences of purposes, taking on some traits that we find in the notion of God. The essence of the notion of God is that all diversities and contradictions in the world achieve a unity in Him, because He is the *coincidentia oppositorum*. The original opposition to monetary matters of old clerics and a range of diverse believers, perhaps, was due to their appreciation of the similarity between the highest economic and the highest cosmic unity. There was an awareness of the dangerous competition between monetary and religious interest. The money form, which went relatively undisturbed through the 'robbery' stage of economic development, soon moved on to the 'bribery' stage. This is when the polarization of wealth started to accelerate, slowly bringing monetary iniquity to the appalling levels seen in the present time. More than any other form of value, money makes possible the secrecy, invisibility and silence of exchange. As Simmel remarks, by compressing money into a piece of paper, by letting it glide into a person's hand, one can make someone a wealthy person. Formless and abstract, one can invest it in remote locations, and thereby remove it from the gaze of neighbours. Anonymous and colourless, money does not reveal its source, it does not require a certificate of birth. Odourless, secretive, mobile, swift and silent: is this why we say it 'rolls'?

If the notion of secrecy perfectly applies to the means facilitating economic exchange, its application to the logic, philosophy and values inspiring economic initiative in general is, however, more problematic. Let us try to explain why.

Conventional criminal groups need secret codes of communication to signal their credentials to partners, their power to victims or clients, and their reliability to potential legitimate or illegitimate allies. At the same time they have to hide their operations from law enforcers. In legitimate markets, by contrast, secrecy describes the nature of certain operations, particularly when the market logic invades spheres of life traditionally governed by non-market norms. Marketing body organs, selling hazardous waste or exchanging polluting agents for money, for instance, do require secret communicative conduits between the parties involved, but such conduits play a crucial role only in the initial phases of market invasion. In other words, market practices may require 'innovative' modalities based on secrecy, but the logic guiding those practices is perfectly transparent. The problem is not hiding that logic, but making it as visible as possible in an attempt to make it also acceptable. Offshoring must be followed by in-shoring; that is to say, a process whereby the illegal practices previously hidden are displayed and justified, while consensus is sought in relation to the broad philosophy guiding them. This process is triggered by the corrosive properties of markets themselves, which are far from secret, and which taint the goods they make available and, as economists would say, 'crowd out non-market norms'. Communities accepting the building of a nuclear waste facility within their territory in exchange for money will see their civic sense being crowded out. So will communities embracing market norms in relation to non-marketable goods and services. A market society, in this sense, amounts to a degraded aggregation of individuals whose moral and civic obligations to one another have been dampened or obliterated. The following example provided by Sandel (2013) may clarify this point. Introducing a fine for parents who are late picking up their children from school increases rather than decreases the number of parents being late. The parents are likely to treat the fine as a fee they are willing to pay, and the monetary payment they are prepared to make ends up eroding their moral obligation to show up on time. 'Introducing money into a non market setting can change people's attitudes and crowd out moral and civic commitments' (ibid.: 119).

Markets, in brief, deteriorate the spirit of altruism and undermine gift relationships. All of this is extremely visible. Economists, however, may well resort to a counter-argument, for example, by claiming that altruism is a commodity that needs to be invested sparingly. Generosity, solidarity and civic duty are part of a limited repertoire of conducts and values that cannot be depleted with constant use. Ultimately, we should keep such repertoire intact and limit ourselves to tap into it when dealing with relatives, friends or with ourselves. Markets, which rely on self-interest, spare us from using up the limited supply of virtue available: the scarce resources of altruistic motivation cannot be squandered recklessly (Robertson, 1978). Little attention is given to the Aristotelian observation that virtue is something we cultivate with practice: we become just by doing just things, temperate by performing temperate acts, brave by acting bravely (Aristotle, 1934). By positing that people's wants will be satisfied by selfishness, orthodox economics presents a miraculous mechanism that could be termed 'self-altruism', a natural arrangement serving the interests of all: we are depicted as greedy animals but we are assured that a divine entity will turn our animalism into collective harmony. Political economy teaches us that furious competition is 'naturally' transformed into a general welfare that guarantees a peaceful society. On the other hand, the more we are alienated from nature, the more natural arrangements are deemed crucial for the common good, even though our ability to destroy nature altogether constantly grows.

More than through secrecy, therefore, it is through the hegemonic discourse of economics that power and its crime come to be justified and ultimately accepted as beneficial to all. Economics teaches us facts, laws, necessities, obligations, forces and values, all stemming from nature, while spreading a metalanguage, a mutual understanding geared to the obsessive necessity to measure, calculate and attribute value (Latour, 2013).

> The Economy is not the basis for the world finally revealed to everyone […] but a cancer where metastases have gradually begun to infect the entire Earth, starting from various sources in the old West. In this narrative, the cancer has succeeded in dissolving all the other values in the cold calculation of interest alone.
>
> *(Ibid.: 384)*

Economics as 'science' is implausible also because no science has ever been accused of using indisputable facts to harden hearts and destroy lives. The scientific truth claimed by economics, in fact, is meant to demean opinions, avoid debates, identify necessities and make judgements indisputable.

Economic practices are 'just' as far as they are capable of realizing generally accepted principles. Such principles constitute the ultimate reality of a given society, determining actions, obligations, expectations and justifications. By the same token, the crimes of the powerful need to assert underlying values characterizing the 'spirit' of the context in which they take place. Achievement, success and wealth, consequently, have to become generally accepted values justifying conducts. This is the Kantian effort in which powerful offenders are engaged, namely the display of their deeds as practical realizations of universal values and ideals. It is worth reiterating that secrecy, therefore, is counterproductive, as it conceals the very practices that have to be visible and clear if they are to be justified and legitimized.

Self-determination and juvenile fury

An additional aspect of legitimacy is associated with the extent to which the powerful, through their acts, manage to assert the fundamental principle of self-determination. This principle has to become inseparable from the judgement of how a society tends to the interests and needs of its members.

> In modernity, the demand for justice can only be shown to be legitimate by making some kind of reference to the autonomy of the individual; it is neither the will of the community nor the natural order, but individual freedom that forms the normative foundation of all conceptions of justice.
>
> *(Honneth, 2014: 17)*

Hence the need for economic principles to become universal: the appeal to freedom is one first component of the search for consensus leading to the construction of a universal set of values presumably acceptable to all. We should act, says Kant (1996), following motivations that everybody else would share with us. Powerful offenders, in sum, look for complicity, namely co-offenders even among those who are prevented from seriously offending due to their very powerlessness.

Returning to the argument made in previous chapters, if powerful offenders possess a founding force and a legislative impetus, in the sense that they aim at altering legality and introducing new norms decriminalizing their acts, they also strive to find 'co-authors' of morally valid norms. From an opposite perspective, if the official rules governing conduct in markets cannot be met with universal approval, no legal order can prevent us from rejecting them and creating new ones. The crimes of the powerful, in this way, become forms of self-legislation.

Markets do not encourage relationships among equals; nor can they claim, therefore, to be spheres of human action in which freedom predominates. They do not rest on shared obligations interweaving individuals in a way that one's freedom is the condition for the freedom of another. Moreover, as we have seen, economics as a 'science' claims to be independent from pre-market norms and moral rules bringing mutual obligations among subjects. Without an antecedent sense of solidarity, which requires subjects to do more than merely respect market rules, 'the opportunity offered by the market could be used to cheat, to pile on wealth and exploit others' (Honneth, 2014: 182). The crimes of the powerful are the result of this alleged lack of an antecedent sense of solidarity making all economic conducts acceptable. On the other hand, economic systems claim and request to be free from government influence, although without such influence they would not exist. It is exactly in the relationships between economic actors and actors operating in other spheres that supplementary tools for the analysis of the crimes of the powerful may be found.

The social structure tends to erect barriers between political and economic power, so that the one cannot be transformed into the other. However, it may well happen that the conditions within which barriers are erected are themselves changed by the economy. Every social context, in reality, conceals networks of individuals and groups belonging to different spheres which shape its constitution and determine the actions that characterize it. Networks are associations formed of diverse individuals who, despite the heterogeneous interests guiding them, compose a homogeneous whole and guarantee a certain continuity of action (Latour, 2013). Take the following example. We visit a laboratory and see people dressed in white coats handling test tubes. Suddenly a lawyer comes in to deal with patents, and then a priest arrives to discuss ethical issues, followed by a technician who has to repair an instrument. Later, a politician with campaigning purposes appears, and later still a businessman interested in buying what is being produced. The laboratory, in brief, is not isolated in its own scientific sphere, and in order to understand its function we have to ignore the boundaries designating it as a lab and follow its connections instead.

> There is no such thing as the domain of Science, or Law, or Religion, or The Economy, but there are indeed networks that

associate – according to segments that are always new, and that only empirical investigation can discover – elements of practice that are borrowed from all the old domains and redistributed in a different way each time.

(Ibid.: 31)

The crimes of the powerful are facilitated by such connections and networks, which promote constant movement from one occupational group to the other and cause the sedimentation of partnerships, alliances, solidarity and complicity among representatives of formally different spheres. Powerful offenders, in sum, cohabit a social space where lawyers, politicians, entrepreneurs and other elitist professionals amalgamate their values, forge their ethical allegiances and continue to hit with juvenile fury. This fury is the result of a pecuniary language that translates every aspiration into predatory desire, of the moral bankruptcy of economic thought. Economics as utopia, or rather as dystopia, offers the crimes of the powerful innumerable analytical opportunities to be conceived, enacted and justified.

In a previous chapter, the term 'ethos of entitlement' has been used. It is worth working on this term by isolating the variable ethos, an extremely promising one. We may associate ethos with the principles guiding market economies; that is, with the maximization of profits or with the related justification of self-love provided by Adam Smith. Ethos, however, can be more precisely referred to the domain of ethics as drawn by the classics of Western philosophy, to the distinction between right and wrong postulated by Plato, Pascal, Hume, Kant, Hegel and many others who compose the history of Western thought.

Chapter 7 describes a journey through this thought in an attempt to locate the crimes of the powerful within our very philosophical tradition. As I will suggest, the crimes of the powerful are both within and without this tradition, while the elite is engaged in a permanent attempt to read that tradition in a way that may justify the practices it adopts.

7

THE ETHICS OF POWER

Powerful offenders seek justification for their conduct through a selective interpretation of classical Western philosophy and by elliptically adhering to certain canonical ethical principles. This interpretive process is led by the purpose of expanding their social opportunities, including opportunities for further offences, while making the latter acceptable to their peers and others. The process entails the implicit claim that offences, in fact, comply with the very norms being violated.

Virtue and passion

In Plato and Aristotle, justice is mainly an individual virtue, which nevertheless only finds complete realization within a human community (Plato, 1937, 1970; Aristotle, 1934). Injustice, on the other hand, is a vice, and unjust people are said to be unhappy and live miserably. One may object that contemporary powerful offenders, while unjust, are likely to live well and happily, but a classical objection to the Platonic view of justice comes from classical philosophy itself (Gouldner, 1967). Glauco, for instance, believes that right and wrong are determined by a social contract, namely by conventional collective agreements, and that the distinction between the two is merely artificial. A just conduct, therefore, may be the result of fear of the consequences which the violation of a contract entails. Because of the artificial nature of the distinction, moreover, one is perfectly entitled to pretend to act justly while committing all sorts of injustices, also because the gods are not involved in this conventional human contract, and appropriate sacrifices and propitiatory ceremonies will suffice to ensure the beneficial divine assistance (De Pascale, 2010). Deceit, in brief, pays even with the gods.

The crimes of the powerful sit perfectly at ease within this philosophical reasoning, as powerful offenders can claim that the norms they violate are mere conventional prescriptions, and that, therefore, their conduct cannot be judged as intrinsically unethical. Other classical notions, however, are met with implicit rejection by powerful offenders.

Justice, as we have seen, is an individual virtue, a personal disposition, but is also referred to the collectivity as a whole. Take the Aristotelian distinction. Distributive justice, in his argument, implies the sharing of riches, honours and all the other divisible items among those enjoying the status of citizens. Corrective or regulatory justice, on the other hand, governs social relationships, and intervenes when equity is to be restored. For example, in the face of unacceptable conduct, it weighs the harm produced and re-establishes the previous conditions, neutralizing that harm (Aristotle, 1934). Powerful offenders could not be further removed from both types of justice, as their offending does not lead to 'sharing' the 'honours and all the other divisible items' with citizens, but rather to their increased polarization. Nor does corrective justice affect them, as proven by the wide range of modalities they constantly devise to escape it. It could be added that, frequently, they also deviate radically from Plato's concept of the Republic, which 'belongs to the people', is not a random agglomerate of individuals, but 'a collective association brought together by the common good'. 'The law does not consist of what is beneficial to the powerful' (Plato, 1937: 134).

It is in relation to this last statement that powerful offenders might develop their defence. We have discussed in Chapter 4 the antithetic views of law held by Plato and Thrasymachus. The former contests Plato's concept of norms as necessary tools to govern and avoid *anomia*, arguing that law is a therapy imposed upon subordinates for the interest of those in authority. The crimes of the powerful are embedded in this dilemma, namely in the process whereby rules of morality – and of law – are socially constructed and enacted. In this respect, we have concluded that powerful groups structure their own alternative moral reasoning by adhering to Plato, claiming that rules are beneficial to all, as well as to Thrasymachus, implying that rules serve the interest of those in authority.

Powerful groups and individuals, however, are as concerned as anyone else about how their behaviour affects others. Their evaluation of right and wrong, in this respect, may follow one of the competing logics, available to everyone, which guide moral decision-making. They may follow a consequentialist type of reasoning, thus focusing on the outcome of their moral choice, or elaborate deontological arguments, therefore focusing on the morality of the means adopted and the normative constraints established, irrespective of outcomes. From a consequentialist perspective, 'noble wrongdoing' is acceptable when aimed at collective beneficial outcomes which could not be achieved through rightful conduct (Mendus, 2009). On the other hand, deontological arguments do not apply to powerful offenders, who do not believe that the means they adopt should reflect conventional morality nor that normative constraints are just. By following a consequentialist logic, however, they seem to endorse an argument brilliantly elaborated by David Hume (2008), which is worth summarizing.

Hume poses the question whether it is by means of our ideas or our 'impressions' that we distinguish between vice and virtue. Reason in his view is 'perfectly inert, and can never either prevent or produce any action or affection' (ibid.: 399). It is true, Hume continues, that reason can influence our conduct, but only in the sense that it can excite a passion and teach us how to pursue it. The crimes of the powerful, similarly, are not simply determined by reason, but also by the discovery of a cause–effect mechanism whereby certain acts may be used to pursue passion, for example, in the form of gains. No passion may be termed unreasonable, according to Hume, unless it chooses the wrong means to achieve its ends. Here, Hume seems to postulate a variant of what in criminology are termed learning theories, namely that professional subcultures lead to the realization that certain means will lead one to exercise one's passions and, at the same time, to the discovery of yet newer potential objects of passion. In conclusion, reason can never motivate actions of the will and can never oppose passion in the direction of the will: 'Tis not contrary to reason to prefer the destruction of the whole world to the scratching of my finger' (ibid.: 416). Powerful offenders may well appropriate this principle and justify their conduct with a universal, human need to follow an increasing variety of passions and learn how to pursue them in constantly new fashions.

The concept of normalization briefly addressed in a previous chapter indicates that it is a specific occupational community that designates, in the last analysis, which act committed by its members is criminal and which is not. This concept echoes Hume's argument around the origin of our sense of disapprobation. Where does this sense derive from in the face, for instance, of a murder? Not from reason, reiterates Hume, because however we examine the fact 'murder' we do not find something we are able to associate with vice. 'In whichever way you take it, you find only certain passions, motives, volitions and thoughts; the vice entirely escapes you' (ibid.: 469). You need to 'turn your reflection into your own breast', and there you will find a sentiment of disapprobation arising towards that action. Right and wrong, therefore, are determined by feelings; they lie in us, not in external objects or actions. By describing something as vicious, we only reveal our own nature and our reaction to events. 'Vice and virtue, therefore, may be compared to sounds, colours, heat and cold, which are not qualities in objects, but perceptions in the mind' (ibid.: 469). Morality, ultimately, may be felt, not judged.

Powerful offenders find support in this analysis of subjectivity proposed by Hume, according to whom 'morality is not susceptible to demonstration' and moral certainty cannot be established with the help of sciences such as 'geometry or algebra' (ibid.: 404). In this sense, the crimes of the powerful escape objective categories and qualifications, and may only be deemed to be 'crimes' when they arouse a sense of revulsion, a passion linked with feelings of justice and injustice. But these feelings, as we have seen, tend to wither away when the crimes of the powerful become normalized.

Opponents of this line of reasoning are numerous and include Immanuel Kant, whose philosophy has not ceased to exert influence on contemporary thinking. Kant's qualification of 'good' is closely linked to the notion of 'goodwill'; therefore a central element of agency persists in his analysis of morality which seems to echo Hume's emphasis on subjectivity. What radically separates the two, however, is the relevance they respectively attribute to reason. In Kant, all human qualities, for instance, intelligence, wit, judgement, 'and the other talents of the mind', but also courage, resoluteness, and perseverance, are, doubtless, good and desirable. 'But they can become extremely bad and harmful if the will, which is to make use of these gifts of nature, is not good' (Kant, 1994: 123). The Kantian will is shaped by reason rather than by feelings, and 'moderation in emotions and passions, self-control, and calm deliberation' are achieved through logical association of thoughts and practical ideas.

Misology, or hatred for reason, arises from the assumption that the more a person is cultivated the less he or she will enjoy life and pursue happiness. Hence a form of envy for 'the common run of men who are better guided by mere natural instinct and who do not permit their reason much influence on their conduct' (ibid.: 125). For Kant, reason is given to us as a practical faculty, one which is meant to have a crucial influence on the will. 'As nature has elsewhere distributed capacities suitable to the functions they are to perform, reason's proper function must be to produce a will good in itself' (ibid.). The key variable designating goodwill, however, is a sense of duty. So, for instance, in commercial interactions individuals behave in certain ways for the sake of their own advantage, and their selfish purpose is devoid of any sense of duty. For actions to possess a moral worth, instead, they have to be inspired by a principle of volition which transcends 'the objects of the faculty of desire' (ibid.: 128). Moreover, as we have seen, there is in Kant a total coincidence between duty and the law, as 'the moral worth of an action does not lie in the effect which is expected from it … the pre-eminent good can consist only in the conception of the law itself' (ibid.: 129).

Within this analytical framework powerful offenders would find it hard to justify their conduct unless they claim their propensity towards misology, namely a type of unreasonableness that criminologists would associate with lack of self-control (Gottfredson and Hirschi, 1990). On the other hand, a technique of neutralization available to them may include the claim that duty and law do not coincide, thus reiterating Thrasymachus' argument about the artificial nature of norms of conduct. Their own duty, they may assert, is to maintain stability in the system, irrespective of the means used, a stability which is guaranteed through the perpetuation or the accretion of their power. As for the law, this may well be depicted as an obstacle to individual freedom, a cumbersome machinery stifling political and economic initiative.

If speculative reason suggests categories of space, time and cause, Kant's practical reason imposes a central idea: we cannot do to others what we do not want others to do to us. Moral feelings, in this way, are deemed rational, as they make social interaction possible. Surely, powerful offenders are deeply anti-Kantian, as they see no connection between their actions and the effects these have on others, nor between law and duty, and surely they cannot claim 'moderation in emotions and passions, self-control, and calm deliberation'. An option available to them, however, is to seek legitimacy through an opportune, self-serving use of Hegel's arguments on morality, to which we will now turn.

Hegel (1952: 89) labels Kant's analysis an example of empty formalism, which 'reduces the science of morals to the preaching of duty for duty's sake'. Moral value, in his view, is not an abstract entity, but can only be established in contradiction or in correspondence to a principle. For example, if we presuppose that property and human life are to exist and be respected, 'then indeed it is a contradiction to commit theft or murder'. Will and duty, therefore, have to be referred to specific principles and their contents, otherwise they end up lying on formal, hollow values. Hegel's idea, in brief, is that morality is not simple rectitude in the sense of respect for the law, but possesses its own intrinsic value in relation to a specific 'ethical community'. Once such community is taken as a guiding background, the set of norms, duties, sensibilities and common understandings that informs it will indicate what is virtuous behaviour and what is vice. 'It is easy to say what man must do, what are the duties he has to fulfil in order to be virtuous: he has simply to follow the well-known and explicit rules of his own situation' (ibid.: 90). We may conclude, therefore, that powerful offenders, after identifying themselves with the 'actual order' informing their 'own situation', can claim that their 'general mode of conduct' corresponds to common expectations, 'habitual practice and custom' (ibid.).

Profit maximization, amoral calculation and commercial competition have been thoroughly discussed in relation to the crimes of the powerful, particularly in the economic sphere (Slapper and Tombs, 1999). The focus here, however, is on philosophical arguments which are able to rescue powerful offenders, providing them with subtle justifications for their acts. What we have seen so far is a possible use of such arguments which surpasses in effectiveness any technique of neutralization identified by criminologists. Hume, Kant and Hegel, of course, are far from inciting or justifying immoral conduct, although those who adopt such conduct may well purge their conscience by way of arbitrarily interpreting their thoughts. These thoughts, on the other hand, lend themselves to the exercise proposed in the previous pages, where the effort has been made to unravel what is hidden, nuanced, disguised or implicit. Fewer nuances are found, instead, in the thinkers examined below, who make explicit references to how immorality can be readily legitimized. In Pascal and Machiavelli, as I will try to show, powerful offenders may find what they interpret as unambiguous enticements to ethical and normative violations.

From Pascal to Machiavelli

In a broad distinction within ethics, as we have seen, we may identify thinkers who judge an act right or wrong in accordance with whether it produces the best consequences, and thinkers who judge actions against some pre-established rule or principle (Singer, 1994). Blaise Pascal belongs to the former group and clearly describes a collective mechanism turning vice into its opposite. He identifies the 'marvellous principle, so important in our morality, of *directing the intention*' (Pascal, 1967: 102). According to this principle, intentional actions can be stripped of the evil they cause and turned into acceptable acts. In an exemplar case Pascal remarks that we do not tolerate those who are determined to sin just for the sake of sinning: we find them diabolical. But if we put into practice the method of 'directing the intention', we may discover that even the action of sinning can be granted a virtuous character. When unable to prevent actions, we can at least correct the viciousness of their means by establishing the purity of their ends.

> This is how our Fathers have found a way to permit the acts of violence commonly practiced in the defence of honour. For it is only a question of deflecting one's intention from the desire for vengeance, which is criminal, and applying it to the desire to defend one's honour, which according to our Fathers, is lawful.
>
> *(Ibid.: 110)*

Pascal's argument displays some similarity with the political thinking of Niccolò Machiavelli, a founding master of consequentialist arguments that are still widely endorsed.

Machiavelli describes Ferdinand of Aragon as the man who accomplished great things under the cloak of religion, but who in reality had no mercy, faith, humanity or integrity; and who, had he allowed himself to be influenced by such qualities, would have failed to accomplish anything. Telling the story of Agathocles, he concedes that 'It cannot be called talent to slay fellow-citizens, to deceive friends, to be without faith, without mercy, without religion; such methods may gain empire, but not glory' (Machiavelli, 1944: 68). Still, he does not see why Agathocles should be esteemed less than the most notable and heroic of captains. Wisely, Agathocles caused injuries in one stroke, all at one time, thus avoiding the repetitive infliction of harm on a regular basis. In addition, he obtained sovereignty without the assistance of the nobles, who would have been unmanageable allies, but with the support of the people, and 'he who reaches sovereignty by popular favour finds himself alone, and has none around him, or few, who are not prepared to obey him' (ibid.: 74).

After arguing that leaders acting entirely in the name of virtue 'will be destroyed', he encourages the prince to develop skills in 'doing wrong and make use of them or not according to necessity'. 'If everything is considered carefully, it will be found that something which looks like virtue, if followed, would be his ruin; whilst something else, which looks like vice, yet followed brings him security and prosperity' (ibid.: 119). Machiavelli's acumen is then revealed in this analysis of consensus, which under certain circumstances we would today describe as populism. It is not true therefore that building on the people is like building on mud, he remarks, adding some insights as to how even the crimes of the powerful can enjoy some form of popular consensus along with practical and ideological support. For example, the prince who engages in extralegal activity, such as 'pillage, sack, and extortion', is advised to be 'liberal', and to handle that which belongs to others with generous altruism: a fair distribution of the bounty among his followers is highly recommended. Machiavellian powerful offenders, in other words, have to find the way of manipulating the variable 'benefit' so that the outcomes of their illegality will appear to be advantageous to others as well as to themselves. This argument has been presented before, and examples include entrepreneurs who ignore the rules of fair competition, claiming that by doing so they safeguard the jobs of their employees; or states which engage in cruelty against enemies and dissenters explaining that in this way they ensure the security and safety of citizens. In a previous chapter these have been termed philanthropic crimes of the powerful. Such crimes are perfectly consonant with Machiavelli's teaching, according to which the only thing a prince has to avoid is hatred on the part of his subjects, whereas cruelty, by causing fear, increases social cohesion.

Values as illusions

Following the theoretical path of values as social artifices, we encounter a number of authors who at first sight seem antithetical to power and its crimes. Bernard Mandeville (1989), for instance, argues that stealing provokes a negative feeling, but that feeling cannot be rationally justified. The consequences of theft may be bad for the victim but good for the thief as well as for society at large. We have seen how economic thought offers a highly original interpretation of this point. Mandeville, after affirming that thieves are 'pernicious to human society and every government ought to take all imaginable care to destroy them', suggests that without criminals many jobs would be lost (ibid.: 118). This vaguely Marxist point not only refers to how crime contributes to the development of professional careers in the criminal justice arena, but also alludes to the very material nature of property offending. A rich but stingy man, who has no relatives to inherit his wealth, does not contribute to the circulation of capital and, therefore, to the promotion of collective well-being. The money stolen from him, on the contrary, will turn into consumptions and investments, 'as if an Archbishop had left the same sum to the public' (ibid.: 119). Fiscal policies are often inadequate for an efficient and proper redistribution of wealth; therefore thieves may be said to achieve what politicians and administrators are unable to accomplish. In brief, if we adopt a consequentialist viewpoint, it is impossible to assess the degree of morality of stealing. This is a perfect justification for corruption and all economically motivated crimes of the powerful.

This is not to say that powerful offenders are constantly seeking justifications to offend. Most people devote some time to pondering whether their conduct is fair, good and legitimate, in a permanent questioning aimed at the acquisition of axiological beliefs. Such beliefs regulate our social life and constitute the basis of our identity. Powerful criminals do the same, but may be more inclined than others to forge their beliefs from the assumption that values are mere illusions. In this respect, a powerful philosophical tradition seems to be on their side. When Nietzsche (1968) questions the 'value of values', he feels the necessity to uncover the conditions and the circumstances that led to their supine acceptance. Values are stripped away and reveal themselves as masks, diseases, lies or misunderstandings. The 'value of values' is taken as a given, says Nietzsche, as truth which transcends any questioning: there is no hesitation in stating that 'good' is superior to 'bad'. But could it be the other way round? 'Good' may incorporate symptoms of regression, an obstacle to human spiritual growth: morality, therefore, may be the danger of dangers. Nietzsche's invective targets the aristocracy and other powerful groups, whose prominent position in society designates them as 'good' people. Therefore it is these 'good' people who describe themselves and their actions as valuable, it is their presumed superiority that allows the formulation of morality and determines the right to distinguish between good and bad and to precisely name them. Morality derives, in this sense, from the right to define things, principles, values, and from the power to label people, their nature and actions. In fact, the power to name, for Nietzsche, is associated with the very power to create a language, a manifestation of social strength determining the quality, features, relevance and value of things, events and human beings. Used by Nietzsche as a polemical argument against evolutionist theories, according to which instincts are controlled in the name of utility and progress, this notion that values are artifices or illusions may be readily embraced by powerful offenders. Their crimes, for instance, may be presented as challenges against conformism and authoritarian morality. The privileged can claim to be fighting privilege through crime. The analysis devoted by Nietzsche (1955) to the origins of the herd morality offers yet more opportunities to defend innovative, deviant behaviour. What the author perhaps meant as an attack against the ability of power to create dull and tame subjects may be turned into an apologia of self-responsibility and autonomous initiative. Powerful offenders can claim that their independent intellect is mistrusted or feared, that their distancing themselves from mediocrity is seen as evil, and that they refuse to gain respect if this implies behaving like lambs or sheep.

All relativist theories of values, beyond their differences, have in common the viewpoint of seeing values as illusions (Boudon, 2013). Learning approaches, however, can also support the crimes of the powerful, as individuals end up believing that a behaviour is fair when their peers believe it to be so. Morality as collective consciousness determines individual consciousness, and therefore values are the effect of socialization. A belief is held by a given individual to be true, in a first stage, because it is collective; in a second stage, it becomes collective because it is true. By the same token, harmful conduct by a powerful individual may be legitimate because it reflects collective conduct, and then it becomes collective because it is legitimate.

Powerful offenders, in brief, advocate a sceptical theory of values, according to which axiological beliefs and absolute principles cannot be grounded. Such offenders may be distinguished in two categories: those endorsing *decisionist* and those endorsing *causalist* theories.

> Decisionist theories start from the viewpoint that axiological beliefs are based on principles freely endorsed by the subjects. Causalist theories start from the viewpoint that they are implanted in the minds of people under the effect of psychic, social, or biological mechanisms operating without the subjects being aware of them, but which can be inferred with the help of scientific procedures.
>
> *(Ibid.: 27)*

Both categories of offenders will feel comfortable with their acts, the former by appealing to freedom of choice and autonomy, the latter by presenting themselves and their deeds as the outcome of social and historical dynamics.

As another tradition of thought would suggest, axiological beliefs also have affective causes (Pareto, 1935). Values, from this perspective, are artificial or distorted expressions of feelings: a thing is good and a conduct is fair because instinctively they appear to be so. However, because individuals refuse to perceive themselves and their acts as determined by their instincts, they disguise their beliefs and values under what Pareto calls a logical varnish. They construct arguments (Pareto's *derivations*) to rationally demonstrate what cannot be demonstrated, namely that beliefs have no logical source but are the result of affective causes. In this way, the justification of one's feelings needs an available theory which sustains them. In an example provided by Boudon (2013), the poor will easily endorse theories associating poverty with the existence of unjust and dysfunctional social systems, while the rich will support theories linking their status with personal merit. These *derivations*, what we commonly term rationalizations, are arguments used to justify one's beliefs: rather than the causes of those beliefs, they are their effect. By the same token, the justifications used by powerful offenders for their acts are not what facilitate those acts, but their effects.

While remaining 'illusions', however, values may be the result of collective decisions taken through free discussion, whereby something becomes 'good' when an assembly of equals reaches the conclusion that it is 'good'. This procedural approach to the analysis of values is contested by theories which see little trace in societies of 'free discussions' and 'assemblies of equals'. Revolving around concepts of conflict, the Marxist system of thought, for instance, expresses its own, different sceptical view of values. We have analysed aspects of it already. In contrast to mainstream philosophy, which 'descends from heaven to earth', a materialist analysis 'ascends from earth to heaven' (Marx and Engels, 1963: 13). In other words, Marxist analysis does not set out from what people say, imagine or conceive in order to arrive at people as living beings. It sets out from active individuals and their real-life interactions to understand the 'phantoms formed in their brain, the sublimates of their material life-process' (ibid.: 14). Morality, religion, metaphysics, and their corresponding forms of consciousness are not deemed independent: human beings, developing their material existence, give shape to and alter their thinking and the products of their thinking. 'Life is not determined by consciousness, but consciousness by life' (ibid.).

> What else does the history of ideas prove, than that intellectual production changes in character in proportion as material production is changed? The ruling ideas of each age have ever been the ideas of its ruling class.
>
> *(Ibid.: 24)*

A tautological defence of the crimes of the powerful, indeed, could hold that the ruling ideas, values and conducts are those of the ruling class, but there are reasons to suspect that powerful offenders would be reluctant to use Marxist arguments as their justification. How could powerful offenders state that their conduct is 'good' because it serves their class interests? Other views of morality, values and power may be more appropriate for the task.

In explaining social acquiescence, it has been suggested that power is not only exercised through 'decision-making and non decision-making', but also through the determination of the thoughts, wishes and desires of the dominated (Lukes, 1974: 23). This suggestion is still in debt to the Marxist conceptualization of 'false consciousness' as opposed to 'real interests', which can explain the relative lack of responses to the crimes of the powerful: the dominated are prevented from the correct use of reason and from reaching the truth through the very relations of domination in which they are held. Competing with this patronizing view, another analytical route would hold that power and truth are mutually constitutive, so that knowledge is no longer contested and becomes part of the natural order of things.

> Thus, once the social knowledge that sustains particular relations of domination becomes processed through the mill of truth production by experts, consensus can be created between dominated and subaltern. Hence, when confronted with expert knowledge, which includes social science, the dominated will consent to their domination.
>
> *(Clegg et al., 2014: 2)*

In brief, the crimes of the powerful 'disappear' in the process of truth production enacted by knowledge experts. Ethics becomes situational, contextually grounded, and therefore malleable and adaptable to situated conducts.

Values as socio-biological processes

Neo-Darwinian principles of evolution may be applied to the genealogy of morals, whereby values are a necessary outcome of natural selection.

In effect, human beings and their societies could not survive and reproduce themselves without ethical and social norms: they would be discarded in the evolutionary process. However, even this perspective offers numerous possibilities for the justification of harmful acts. First, evolution entails that conducts once deemed appropriate may be superseded by new conducts which make human beings fitter to survive in a hostile environment. In this sense, deviance from conformity may in the long run prove instrumental for evolution. Initially disapproved of, the new conducts will generate a new, more amicable environment. Second, evolutionism implies that human behaviours and values are not written or grounded in nature, as nature itself is constantly altered by human action. As John Stuart Mill (1969) argued, we should not believe that any thoughts, feelings or actions that we judge 'natural' are in themselves 'good'. On the contrary, it is irrational and immoral to believe that we ought to follow nature or, in other words, ought to make the spontaneous course of things the model of our actions. All action, he remarks, consists of altering, and all useful action in improving, the spontaneous course of nature.

> The duty of man is to cooperate with the beneficent powers, not by imitating but by perpetually striving to amend the course of nature – and bringing that part of it over which we can exercise control, more nearly into conformity with a high standard of justice and goodness.
>
> *(Ibid.: 402)*

Powerful offenders, following the ethics of John Stuart Mill, may justify any offence perpetrated against nature or the environment, which are there to be 'amended' and 'controlled'.

Habit, opportunities and trust

Powerful offenders, in the argument presented thus far, can find justification for their conduct through a selective interpretation of classical philosophy, or by claiming an idiosyncratic adhesion to common ethical principles. This interpretive process is led by the purpose of expanding their social opportunities while making their conduct acceptable as inherited custom. Let us explicate this point.

Opportunities define the set of choices available to actors, who can expand their own and/or attempt to restrict those of others. Opportunities shape preferences, which in their turn shape the pursuit of outcomes through interaction (Hedström and Bearman, 2012). The crimes of the powerful constitute interactions aimed at expanding the opportunities of the offenders while eroding the possibility of collective control and institutional constraint. Being elastic rather than fixed (Petersen, 2012), opportunities need not deliver a constant amount of social advantage, but may be used as a form of investment granting increasing privileges and, simultaneously, neutralizing those social forces which pursue equality. The more unequal the distribution of opportunities, the more hopeless the efforts addressed towards equality, in an expansionist dynamic which involves power in general along with powerful offenders. The concept of normalization fails to capture this expansionist logic, as it implies a stationary condition rather than a constantly 'evolutionary' one. Powerful offenders, through their illegal conduct, set ethical precedents which are liable to be superseded by yet new illegal conducts, in a process involving the permanent evolution of habit.

Moral sense or conscience is said to mark the most important difference between human beings and the lower animals. 'This sense has a rightful supremacy over every other principle of human action; it is summed up in that short but imperious word "ought", so full of high significance' (Singer, 1994: 44). The most noble of all attributes of human beings, this moral sense is acquired and developed through images of past actions and motives; it is strengthened by habit and ultimately by the perception that such past actions enjoy the positive judgement of the community. There is no divine origin in ethics, but a form of 'community super-ego' left by persons and actions which become exemplary in the imagination of its members. Powerful offenders develop their own collective super-ego informing their practices, their views, expectations and interactions with others. Let us spend a few more words on this point.

Freud (1962) posits that the 'cultural super-ego' strongly influences societal development and that it has an origin similar to that of an individual super-ego. It takes its strength from the awe left by the personalities of great leaders, 'men of overwhelming force of mind or men in whom one of the human impulsions has found its strongest and purest, and therefore its most one-sided, expression' (ibid.: 88). These figures may be initially mocked and maltreated, 'and even despatched in a cruel fashion', but later they 'set up ideal demands, disobedience to which is visited with fear of conscience'. The cultural super-ego, in brief, is aggressive and makes its reproaches noisily heard, particularly when it imposes what human interactions must be like. This imposition, says Freud, is comprised under the heading of ethics.

> Ethics is thus to be regarded as a therapeutic attempt – as an endeavour to achieve, by means of a command of the super-ego, something which has so far not been achieved by means of any other cultural activities.
>
> *(Ibid.: 90)*

Note two important aspects in this analysis. First, the deviant qualities attributed by Freud to great leaders, who are initially condemned and afterwards set up ideal demands. This echoes interpretations of the history of powerful individuals such as major entrepreneurs, who 'innovate' in economic as well as in criminological terms (Merton, 1968). Second, the overwhelming nature and qualities of these great figures may lead to a process whereby the qualities and nature of ordinary individuals are devalued, therefore making their victimization amount to negligible events. In this sense, the crimes of the powerful victimizing ordinary people may de facto re-introduce a form of *wergild*, namely a classification of the value of individuals on the basis of their social status (Simmel, 1990). Hence harming a person of little value brings little or no aversion.

The cultural or community super-ego generates custom and habit. While creating custom and habit, however, powerful offenders have to deal with the variable trust. This may be achieved through competence or reliability, for example, conveying images of integrity, honesty, and the commitment to do no harm. In this case, trust is cognitive-based, in the sense that it stems from past experience that informs us of the likelihood of an individual or group to act ethically and live up to their legal obligations (Cook and Gerbasi, 2012). Of course, powerful offenders cannot be accorded cognitive trust, as past experiences make them untrustworthy. This is compounded by the fact that, normally, it is not easy to grant trust in power-asymmetric relationships. The only option for powerful offenders is, therefore, to seek 'affective trust', namely the confidence individuals place in others on the basis of feelings generated by interactions with them. This affective trust, previously discussed from another perspective, amounts to offenders convincing other groups and individuals that their interests are the same as their own and that all benefit from illegality.

Implicit in the creation of affective trust is a notion of hegemony and consensus, which presides over the formation of internalized forms of cooperation and acceptance. Power always needs an amalgam of consensus and coercion, aiming at building trust and repelling imputation of criminality, in brief at constructing images of 'trusted criminals' (Friedrichs, 2004). This process may be smoothed by the fact that, paradoxically, trust in individuals may decline while trust in the institutions and ideologies they represent may not. Simultaneously, trust networks, of cognitive as well as of an affective type, 'can emerge to facilitate social and economic exchange under uncertainty, but can also emerge to support corruption and other forms of illegal activity' (ibid.: 232). The crimes of the powerful, in this way, become organized and regularized, and, due to repeat dealings through social networks, they become commonplace if left unchallenged (Cartier-Bresson, 1997).

The privatization of morality

In order to tentatively complete the picture, we will now look at theories which from the concept of the 'impartial spectator' have developed a number of notions encapsulated in the phrase 'the veil of ignorance'. I am alluding to Adam Smith (1976b) and John Rawls (1972) respectively. The impartial spectator is an ideal guardian of correct behaviour, and is present in all human beings as a 'person within'. According to Smith, therefore, individuals endeavour to examine their own conduct and pass sentence over it, and in so doing they divide themselves into two persons: the examiner and the actor.

> The first is the spectator, whose sentiments with regard to my own conduct I endeavour to enter into, by placing myself in his situation, and by considering how it would appear to me, when seen from that particular point of view. The second is the agent, the person who I properly call myself, and of whose conduct,

under the character of a spectator, I was endeavouring to form some opinion. The first is the judge; the second the person judged of.

(Smith, 1976b: 32)

Like an invisible hand, the judge ensures that conducts comply with ethical principles and do not harm others, so that the self-centredness of the *homo oeconomicus* is tempered by the altruism of the *homo naturalis*. Humans are capable of empathy, claims Smith, and our minds make certain actions the spontaneous object of approbation and admiration. The process allowing us to distinguish between objects of approval or disapproval, according to Smith, depends largely on our capacity to engage in 'other-regarding' activities, and involves a repertoire of abilities and propensities which include sympathy, imagination, reason and reflection. This 'interactionist' argument is translated by Smith into a basic principle, according to which human beings possess a patrimony of feelings which permit them to experience joy or sorrow when faced with their fellows' feelings of pleasure or pain. Our 'acts of reflection and imagination' produce expressions of sympathy for other individuals, and such acts consist in taking the place of others and forming 'an opinion with regard to their mental state'.

Nature, when she formed man for society, endowed him with an original desire to please, and an original aversion to offend his brethren. She taught him to feel pleasure in their favourable, and pain in their unfavourable regard. She rendered their approbation most flattering ... for its own sake; and their disapprobation most mortifying and most offensive.

(Ibid.: 9)

Unethical conduct by the powerful, within Smith's system of thought, is due to the fact that our judgement with regard to others is always likely to be imperfect, at least in the sense that we can have 'no immediate experience of what other men feel' (ibid.: 5). Powerful offenders, therefore, are simply unaware of the harm they cause. On the other hand, the definition of the crimes of the powerful as crimes depends on two aspects under which we may judge an action.

Judgement is expressed 'first, in relation to the cause or object which excites it; secondly, in relation to the end which it proposes, or to the effect which it tends to produce' (ibid.). We therefore perceive a conduct as laudable when we share the motives behind it and when we appreciate its beneficiary effects. The crimes of the powerful, according to this formulation, are to be condoned when the intentions inspiring them are laudable. With this we return to Pascal's argument around 'redirecting the intention', whereby sin can be given a virtuous character if we establish the purity of its ends. So, invading a country may be justified through the intention of bringing democracy, ignoring safety regulations can turn into job opportunities, both because the workers injured will have to be replaced and because flouting the safety rules allows for the investment of the money saved, and finally evading taxes can be 'redirected' as increasing the circulation of wealth. The crimes of the powerful, in this way, present themselves as instrumentally rational, in that they objectively represent good ways of reaching the offenders' goals.

In the theory of justice elaborated by John Rawls (1972), the impartial spectator takes the form of the veil of ignorance, which describes a purely hypothetical situation generating common ethical principles. Rawls assumes that a society is a more or less self-sufficient association of individuals who recognize certain rules of conduct as binding. Such a society displays an identity of interests, since cooperation makes life better for all:

> A set of principles is required for choosing among the various social arrangements which determine the division of advantages and for underwriting an agreement on the proper distributive shares. These principles are the principles of social justice.
>
> *(Ibid.: 4)*

Ethics, therefore, comes to be the object of an original agreement and consists of principles that free and rational persons would accept in an initial position of equality. The principles, chosen behind a veil of ignorance, are to regulate people's claims on one another and include the following. First, each person is to have an equal right to the most extensive basic liberty compatible with a similar liberty for others. Second, 'social and economic inequalities are to be arranged so that they are to everyone's advantage and attached to positions and offices open to all' (ibid.: 60). Ethics so constructed is hypothetical indeed, not least because societies as they are do not allow people to perceive themselves as members of a large community, but rather as peers in a circumscribed group. Identity, therefore, is exclusionary, as those who do not belong to that group are perceived as outsiders. Thus, the impartial spectator and the veil of ignorance may find application among similar and equal actors, not among members of a society as a whole. Smith's ethical judge and Rawls' original agreement may possess a binding force within the elite, not outside of it. Moreover, ignoring the dysfunctional effects of growing inequality turns into an encouragement to selfishness and greed, both opposed to cooperation and identity of interests attributed by Rawls to his imaginary society.

It is true that, among the millions of people who have seen the tragedy *Antigone*, it is hard to find a single spectator who sympathizes with Creon. But does this suggest the existence of universal values? Given the widening gap between powerful and powerless individuals, establishing a common ground of truth is problematic (Elliott, 2014). What is it that binds us together in such unjust conditions? Realistically, there is little expectation that societies are capable of identifying foundational ethical codes, while ambivalence and personalization seem to be more viable options. Individuals, including powerful offenders, must decide for themselves on how to cope with ethics, as well as how to respond to human suffering, vulnerability and frailty (Bauman, 1993, 1995). The crimes of the powerful, in this sense, multiply along with the privatization of ethics.

Conclusion

An ethical interpretation of the crimes of the powerful shows the vagueness of ethics itself and illustrates the efforts by offenders to claim philosophical affiliation to this or that aspect of classical thinking (Ruggiero, 2012). We have seen how an ambiguous reading of Hume, Kant, Hegel, Pascal, Machiavelli and others may lead to justifications for offending that are potentially much more effective than ex-post techniques of neutralization invoked in criminology. We have also seen the centrality of consensus, legitimacy and hegemony, as powerful offenders attempt to mobilize the complicity or acceptance by other actors, implying that their acts are beneficial to others as well as to themselves. By redirecting their intention, as Pascal would have it, they try, in other words, to sanctify their choices and establish the purity of their goals. This process may lead offences to become part of custom and habit, in an evolutionary, expansionary tendency resulting in new and increasingly harmful illicit conducts.

Every justification of authority is based on the fragility of human beings, from Hobbes to Kant. The former abolishes society and communities, including relationships within them, replacing these with pure power relationships, namely between individuals and sovereign. The latter regards human beings as made of crooked wood, incapable of morality unless constrained by laws. Power, therefore, being the result of human fragility, reflects this fragility, being itself like unmanageable crooked wood (Esposito, 2006). It would be a mistake, however, to claim that the crimes of the powerful may also be deemed to be the outcome of such fragility. In this chapter, an attempt has been made to prove that common ethical principles may add strength to already strong actors and groups. Such groups possess a subjective set of dispositions, a lasting pattern of thought, perception and behaviour which at times overlaps with some aspects of classical philosophical thought, in a way that makes their deviance appear, in fact, as a mode of adhering to that noble tradition of thought. Their *habitus*, acquired through internalization of culture and embodied in a set of practical skills (Vaughan, 2012; Bourdieu, 1984, 1990), leads to an enhancement of their position in society: it is a habitus that incorporates licit as well as illicit procedures and justifications. Ultimately, the crimes of the powerful contribute to the reproduction of the power structure in society while seeking ethical neutralization by claiming consonance with the very norms being violated.

8

BALZAC

Power as crime

Fiction is not a mere product of the imagination. The beings of fiction do exist and impose themselves upon us. Don Juan exists inasmuch as we discuss his exploits with the same passion with which we permeate our judgement of concrete events (Latour, 2013). By the same token Vautrin, Rastignac, Eugénie Grandet and Père Goriot exist and it is for us to read these characters and their undertakings criminologically, in order to complete, or perhaps even modify, our understanding of wrongdoing. Of course, interpretations may diverge, but if this is so it is because the work we interpret possesses many folds and engenders a variety of subjective reactions. Fictional characters populate our world and our mind, but they need our solicitude, in the sense that we need to 'take them in', and 'if we don't appreciate them, they risk disappearing altogether' (ibid.: 242). They have this peculiarity, then: they become objectively existing beings when we encounter them and reprise them through our subjectivity. In brief, we complement with our creative work that performed by their creator (Ruggiero, 2003). Fiction, therefore, is a communicative event bringing people together and eliciting in them the need to weigh, discuss and compare values. This final chapter is a journey through some of the many novels written by Honoré de Balzac, through the mythic constitution of his world, his epic which summons up the same recurrent circle of figures: his 'human comedy' will offer surprising insights into power and crime.

Ruthlessness

Balzac draws circles around social groups: the nobility, the clergy, manual workers, poets, artists, scientists, criminals, and so on. He then condenses such groups into one character, so that a hundred different bankers form the Baron de Nucingen and an infinity of usurers form Gobseck. There are no mixed figures in Balzac's human comedy, and this makes his world simple but intense. The different individuals cohabit the same social space more than they would in the real world and interact assiduously and vehemently as they would never do in Balzac's contemporary France (Zweig, 2010). Their identity, therefore, is shaped by relationships with people who are extraneous to their milieu and is built thanks to intersecting rather than concentric circles.

> The first lesson Balzac's young people have to learn is ruthlessness. They know that their numbers are excessive, and that they must therefore gobble one another up 'like spiders in a pot', as Vautrin observes.
>
> *(Ibid.: 13)*

Competitive environments require the toughening of energies, the conversion of intelligence into cunning and of beauty into vice. Balzac's heroes are avid, and all marketable goods propel their greed, including power. Obstacles to one's success must be thumped and rivals poisoned, if necessary.

Following the appreciation of Engels, we can learn from Balzac more than from any historian about the birth of the bourgeoisie in France, but in his characters we also see distinct expressions of universal truths: good and evil, love in Goriot, gold in Grandet. The latter is a miser who grows into a maniac, caring for gold more than for Eugénie, his daughter, robbing her of her inheritance from her mother, 'grasping on his death-bed at the precious metal of a crucifix' (Crawford, 1955: 7). Avarice takes on a new meaning in Balzac's time when, with the decline of the restraining force of the Church and the sudden openings within a rigid social order, dreams of accumulation compound the 'natural' hoarding instincts. Intrigue spreads from the Court of Versailles in a process of dissemination affecting ascending social groups, all eager to follow in the footsteps of the elite in the pursuit of money, hence of power. Money and power are the central protagonists of *La Comédie Humaine*, which is populated by penniless aristocrats, adventurers, dodgy lawyers, improbable careerists, speculators, bankers, financiers, cynical usurers, and misers of every conceivable kind.

> Balzac always declares his moral aim: he is concerned to show what damage these people do to themselves, to the State and to the fabric of society. ... Money-making is a sordid business, and he spares us no detail of the sordidness and the callousness it engenders in human beings.
>
> *(Ibid.: 10–11)*

Monsieur Grandet radiates a cold metallic glitter from his eyes. His fortune follows the breaking up of the aristocratic estates and the expropriation of land after the Revolution. His subsequent business prospers when he starts selling wine to the Republican army and when he learns that money breeds money and financial investments are not penalized, like crops, by the vagaries of the weather. His wife's grand-father and his own grandmother had been misers too, and they had kept their money in their stockings so that they could handle and gloat over it. Grandet shares this physical love for money but, as a man of the new age, is capable of moving it around productively. Wealth, however, does not translate into a decorous lifestyle or even into material well-being, Grandet's house being disfigured by defensive walls, with a rickety, worm-eaten staircase leading to a dingy parlour, permanently occupied by Madame Grandet and Eugénie engaged in tedious needlework. Houses such as this, Balzac warns, have built the history of France, making the environment gloomy and human beings joyless:

> These houses may combine the cloister's silence with the arid desolation of the waste and the sepulchral melancholy of ruins. Life makes so little stir in them that a stranger believes

them to be uninhabited until he suddenly meets the cold listless gaze of some motionless human being, whose face, austere as a monk's, peers from above the window-sill at the sound of a stranger's footfall.

(Balzac, 1955: 33)

On one particular evening in the middle of November 1819, while celebrating Eugénie's twenty-third birthday, the Grandets resolve that it is time to arrange the marriage of the young woman. Families vying for the heiress's wealth arrive after supper and start a hypocritical display of friendliness, and in the middle of the comedy a dazzling young stranger from Paris appears. It is Charles, Eugénie's cousin, who quickly becomes the object of the young woman's desire. Soon Monsieur Grandet makes it clear that Charles could never aspire to become Eugénie's husband, not least because his father's bankruptcy and suicide make him a romantic but penniless dandy. Readers of *Eugénie Grandet* start savouring the disintegration of a family, a metaphor for the dissolution of society itself, with groups and individuals harbouring mutual resentment in the pursuit of their egoistic ambitions.

Grandet is still called 'honest Grandet' by certain old people, though their number is noticeably declining. We learn that he hoarded his wealth by greasing the palm of 'the rough-hewn Republican who was in charge of the sale of the public estates' and that he bought for the price of a crust of bread 'the finest vineyards in the neighborhood, an old abbey and some small farms' (ibid.: 37). The worthy Grandet then becomes Mayor, carries out his public duties soberly and discreetly, and fills his wallet more discreetly still. The Mayor's fortune is estimated at a figure proportionate to the obsequiousness shown to him.

In matters of finance, Monsieur Grandet combines the characteristics of the tiger and the boa constrictor. Like a tiger he waits for his prey, lurking concealed until the moment comes to attack and hold the victim at his mercy. Then the jaws of his purse open to engulf a plenitude of coins, and finally he lies down again peacefully, 'like the gorged python, to digest; impassible, emotionless, methodical' (ibid.: 41). To get the better of others implies the right to despise one's victims, 'those weaklings of the earth who [are] unable to save themselves from being devoured'. The miser lets the 'lamb grow fat, then he pens, kills, cooks, eats, and despises it. Misers thrive on money and contempt' (ibid.: 131).

Balzac seems inspired by physiognomic criminology when he detects malice in Grandet's nose and in his face a dangerous craftiness, a calculated rectitude, the selfishness of a man who concentrates all his emotions on saving money. And he spends very little indeed, as his tenant farmers pay their rent partly in kind, bringing him bread, meat, eggs, butter, corn, flour and wood, and in return receive his thanks. At home, he counts the lumps of sugar his guests melt in their tea in case the precious substance is recklessly wasted.

Having Charles entrusted to his care, Grandet studies the way in which even his brother's bankruptcy may be turned into a chance to make money. A bankrupt, he muses, is a thief who the law takes under its protection: it is better to encounter a highwayman than a bankrupt. However, as lawyers advise him, the creditors of Charles' deceased father can be appeased without spending money. His lawyer friends explain that the commercial tribunal to whose jurisdiction he is subject has the power to name liquidators who will wind up his brother's business. Liquidation is not the same thing as bankruptcy and the liquidator, normally a neutral agent, will be instead a reliable person, a close business or political partner. As for the creditors, they will be promised that he will pay in instalments: 'you can lead dogs a long way with a piece of bacon in front of their noses' (ibid.: 142). The two families, eager to welcome Eugénie and her money among themselves, vie in offering their deviant support in this enterprise. In brief, Grandet shows himself to be an excellent brother, and the whole town talks admiringly about him, while in fact his generosity does not cost him anything. He sells all the remaining properties owned by his brother, pays a portion of his debts and makes some profit, while the liquidators establish that a derisory amount of money is due to the creditors.

Charles, in his turn, appears to be virtuous, but he is quickly imbibing 'all the principles of egoism'. 'The seeds of this destructive political economy lay dormant in his heart, and could not fail to germinate as soon as he ceased to be an idle spectator and became an actor in the drama of real life' (ibid.: 157). After planning to seek his fortune in the East Indies, he entices Eugénie into handing him her gold and leaves forever.

Petty and grand figures

It is true that Balzac does not find petty thieves interesting, namely the hungry and fearful figures who sneak a loaf of bread from the bakery. On the contrary, his grand figures are thieves on a large scale, professional miscreants who steal, not because they are needy, but because they are filled with the desire to grapple everything to themselves (Zweig, 2010). On the other hand, a large-scale thief, as we have seen, elicits respect, mobilizes cooperation and enjoys unsolicited complicity, as those surrounding him hope to reap some material advantage from his dishonesty. The whole town, we are told, is led to admire Grandet, a powerful individual who, irrespective of the means utilized, is in the potential position to benefit others, thus turning his own advantages into general well-being. Similar arguments, put in sociological terms, have emerged in previous chapters. In this sense, the encouragement of Vautrin, whom we will encounter later, incorporates a sinister truth: one has to use people like horses, harness them to one's chariot and whip them towards one's goal. Power and crime, in Balzac, are linked in a theory of energetics, a mechanics of passions, whereby individuals follow their illusions and dissipate their inner force, no matter the objective they pursue. Power and crime are condensed in monomaniacs focused on intense appetites, who cling to their life illusion with every nerve and muscle, concentrating all their thoughts upon it: whatever the illusion they must embrace it wholeheartedly (ibid.).

Balzac's grand figures know everything there is to know about the intricacies of lawsuits, the tactics to be adopted in commercial battles, the tricks to manoeuvre the stock market. Speculators and dishonest journalists are among his characters, all immersed in a volatile economic system, seen as a vast, institutionalized gaming table, guided mainly by the principle of risk (Prendergast, 1978). For this reason reproach is constantly hurled at Balzac, with critics arguing that novelists cannot limit themselves to dissecting worldly hypocrisies and ignominies: too many corrupt types darken literature and authors should avoid being exclusively devoted to the portrayal of moral ugliness (Bertault, 1963). The author's personal experience may be the origin of this exclusive devotion.

In the summer of 1828 he is lying low, in a city full of creditors hunting him. In *La Peaux de Chagrin* Balzac describes bank officials as objects of indifference to him, those embodiments of the commercial conscience, clad in grey and wearing the silver badge of their master's livery (Balzac, 2013). Now, when he sees them pass in the streets of Paris, he hates them because he is in debt: 'To be in debt means that you no longer belong to yourself. Other men could call me to account for my life' (Robb, 1994: 141). Bankers are greedy, but so are aristocratic and bourgeois ladies such as Madame Cibot, who in *The Poor Relations* is dizzy while conceiving the idea of 'worming herself into the testament of the worthy Pons', in imitation of those servant-mistresses whose annuities excite so much cupidity in the quarter of the Marais. She already sees herself living in the suburbs of Paris, strutting about in a country house, where she will end her days being served as a queen (Balzac, 1898). While helping Monsieur Pons in his house, she pretends to get injured and goes straight to a doctor who fraudulently certifies to the severity of her wound. Before even planning how to exploit the mendacious certificate, 'this frightful Lady Macbeth of the streets' is suddenly illuminated by an infernal light: the doctor is her accomplice, having accepted an honorarium for her 'pretended malady', and his reputation for healing his patients so promptly will grow with his monetary requests in the area. How could she benefit from the advantages she has brought to him?

In *Lost Illusions* misers return, as do complex legal and commercial undertakings (Balzac, 2013). We see Old Sechard swindling his own son and witness the moral worthlessness of journalists. We also encounter Sixte du Châtelet, who constitutes a considerable addition to Balzac's gallery of the aristocracy in transition, of the Bonaparte *parvenus* whom perhaps he understands even better than the old nobility, for they are already in his time becoming adulterated and corrupt. In the novel *Le Notaire* young lawyers see how every fortune is brought about by the proverbial oily wheels and face the horrible wrangling of heirs while the bodies of their relatives are not yet cold (ibid.). What is important to note in all these novels is how greed and illicit commercial and financial practices involve all classes, in a new participatory enthusiasm stemming from the decline of the old order. Sure, Balzac is a conservative political observer, but what he condemns is the dehumanized system of connections, the spectacle of 'high' and 'low' being united in a symbolic alliance whose nodal point is money. In the new order money is the source of division and conflict in an individualistic society, a force circulating throughout the social organism, providing the points of contact among its otherwise divided parts. Buying and selling, exploitation and theft are seen to implicate everyone from top to bottom of the social structure, making the very distinction between top and bottom meaningless (Prendergast, 1978). A lady sells herself in order to receive diamonds, which she then sells to a usurer, who sells illusions to the poor, who have nothing to sell but, again, themselves. Petty and grand figures participate with solemn religiosity in the same sordid rituals. *Le Père Goriot* offers a vivid example of these rituals.

Fatherly love

Goriot's fortune buys his daughters access into high society, a purchase which symbolizes the odd and problematic relationship between bourgeoisie and aristocracy in the early nineteenth century. But his very business success is far from epitomizing the shift from hereditary privilege to privilege acquired through merit. The origin of his own wealth is dubious and his existence is, in a sense, hidden from sight. While he guarantees his offspring the luxury of exclusive parlours and the display of social brilliance, he is relegated to a mediocre guesthouse run by Madame Vauquer. Goriot's fortune derives from the squalid manipulation of the black market in flour during the famine of the Revolutionary period. Victorine Taillefer is another boarder of the guesthouse, whose sickly pallor makes her appear as an anaemic girl, although her unvarying expression of sadness is just consistent with the general wretchedness of the place. But her face is young, her movements elastic, and something in her light-brown hair and dark-grey eyes makes her pretty. She lacks two things that create women a second time: pretty dresses and love letters. Her father provides for her but all his wealth is destined to enrich Victorine's brother only, sole designated heir to his estate.

Eugène de Rastignac is the third guest, a thoroughly southern type with a fair complexion, blue eyes and black hair. In his figure, manner and his whole bearing it is easy to see that he either comes from a noble family, or that, from his earliest childhood, he has been gently bred. A little care for his wardrobe would make him a young, stylish man. But his carelessness shows in his shabby coat and waistcoat, an untidily knotted black cravat, and boots that have been resoled. Monsieur Vautrin completes the prime layer of Madame Vaquer's boarders, and his great dream is to trade in human beings as the owner of a slave plantation. Forty years old, with dyed whiskers, he has broad shoulders, a well-developed chest, muscular arms and strong, square-fisted hands. His face is marked by premature wrinkles and his gentle manners fail to hide a perceptible harshness in his character: a certain resolute look, sometimes seen on his face, inspires fear in spite of his easy, good-natured appearance. He knows all about ships, the sea, France, foreign countries, men, business, law, great houses and prisons. He lends money to Madame Vauquer or to the boarders and leads a very regular life, going out after breakfast, returning in time for dinner, and disappearing for the rest of the evening, letting himself in at about midnight with a latchkey, a privilege that Madame Vauquer accords to no other boarder.

Vautrin takes pleasure in deriding the upper classes, accusing them of incompetence, and in mocking law and order, 'as if there were some mystery carefully hidden away in his life' (Balzac, 1966: 42). He vents his anger against frantic extravagance, which leads people to the money-lender's office and those already in deep debt to sell themselves or to tear out their mothers' hearts to find something to pay for their splendour. Eugène de Rastignac will not tear his mother's heart out, he simply writes to his sisters and cunningly takes their savings, an act that only later, in a moment of rueful lucidity, he describes as theft. Those surrounding him teach him that if he is determined to succeed he has to make cold-blooded calculations, that he has to strike ruthlessly and then he will be feared. If he has a heart he has to carefully lock it away like a treasure: the moment someone suspects he has one he will be lost.

Eugène then starts thinking of Goriot's daughters and their ostentatious splendour, the luxury of the *parvenus*, the riotous extravagance of courtesans. After one of them becomes his lover, his dark thoughts gather and his ideas widen, while his conscience grows more elastic. He finally sees the world as it is: he sees how the rich live beyond the injunctions of the law and the judgement of public opinion, and finds himself agreeing with Vautrin that success is virtue, it is the *ultima ratio mundi*. This is when Vautrin attempts to buy the soul, and probably also the body, of Rastignac. The latter realizes that fortunate people have at least 100,000 'livres' a year and a lodger at Maison Vanquer is not exactly Fortune's favourite. Vautrin tells him that he has to stop to peep through holes in curtains, that he must go behind the scenes and watch the whole show. He then starts expounding his philosophy.

Vautrin depicts himself as someone who does just what pleases him, someone who is good-natured to those who are good to him and those whose hearts speak to his. But people who annoy him had better expect the ire of an ugly devil, as he does not shy away from murder if necessary. He can kill 'properly', as an artist, although not in a duel, which is childish, utter nonsense and folly. 'When one of two living men must be got out of the way, none but an idiot would leave chance to decide which it is to be; and in a duel it is a toss-up – heads or tails – and there you are!' (ibid.: 58). He shows Rastignac his scars and claims that, after studying the world very closely, he sees only two alternatives: stupid obedience or revolt, and he obeys nobody. Ambition produces scars, of course, but on the other hand one cannot live in a small room without dreaming about a mansion. 'What sort of men do the women run after? Men of ambition. Men of ambition have stronger frames, their blood is richer in iron, their hearts are warmer than those of ordinary men' (ibid.: 62).

Vautrin then describes Eugène's future, who, being a law student, can at most expect to learn how to browse the penal code and send poor devils to the galleys, so that the rich can sleep in peace. There is no fun in that: 'bark at thieves, plead the cause of the rich, send men of heart to the guillotine, that is your work!' A pirate on the high seas is happier. How about marrying a rich woman? This is not fun either, it is like hanging a stone around your neck, crawling like a serpent before your wife, licking her mother's feet. 'You are at the crossway of the roads of life, my boy; choose your way' (ibid.: 72). But Eugène has already chosen, as he has started visiting wealthy women and perhaps has even learned that a man makes his way 'by brilliant genius or by skillful corruption'. Corruption is a great power in the world, and honesty is the common enemy. An honest man, after all, is just someone who plunders without sharing the booty.

> Life is no cleaner than a kitchen; it reeks like a kitchen; and if you mean to cook your dinner, you must expect to soil your hands; the real art is in getting them clean again, and therein lies the whole morality of our epoch ... I do not think that the rich

are any worse than the poor; man is much the same, high or low, or wherever he is. In a million of these human cattle there may be half a score of bold spirits who rise above the rest, above the laws; I am one of them.

(Ibid.: 76)

Rastignac eagerly interrupts Vautrin's speech and asks what he should do. 'Next to nothing' is the reply: you hunt millions, you set your snares, use lures and nets; there are many ways of hunting. And everyone who comes back from the chase with his game-bag well filled meets with a warm welcome in good society. Mademoiselle Victorine is his prey, but her brother is designated as the sole heir to the family wealth. And if it should please God to take that youth away, the banker her father, Monsieur Taillefer, would have only the girl left: so, 'turn him off into the dark!' Eugène is paralysed and becomes unconscious of his surroundings, falling into deep thought. For a while he hesitates, but intends to act nobly and owe his fortune to nothing but his own exertions. It may be the slowest of all roads to success, but he will lay his head on the pillow at night untroubled by evil thoughts. He then chooses not to think but be guided by his heart.

The world of Paris, nevertheless, appears to him to be like an ocean of mud: whoever sets foot in that black sludge, he believes, sinks into it up to the chin. He is lost in the disorienting maze of Parisian corruption, greed and power worship (Ellison, 2000). When for the first time he sees Goriot's room, he cannot control his amazement at the contrast between the den in which the father lives and the luxury that his daughters enjoy. The window has no curtains, the walls are damp, the wallpaper is peeling, the wretched bed is covered by a blanket made out of large pieces of Mme Vauquer's old dresses. Goriot gives everything he has to his daughters, who in turn forcefully demand it, and as long as

they are happy, and smartly dressed, and have soft carpets under their feet, what does it matter what clothes I wear or where I lie down at night? I shall never feel cold so long as they are warm; I shall never feel dull if they are laughing. I have no troubles but theirs.

(Balzac, 1966: 147)

He even loves his daughters for the pain they cause him. But when Goriot becomes seriously ill, Eugène witnesses the indifference of the two young women, with Delphine who is unable to visit her father because of a previous commitment: a ball, where she would go even if she had to step over the old man's corpse to get there. This is when Eugène ponders on obedience, struggle and revolt: obedience, he says, is dull, revolt impossible, struggle hazardous. On the other hand, the crimes of Parisian high society seem to him paltry, while Vautrin, he starts thinking, is great.

He does not reproach Delphine for her selfishness, but tries to convince himself that Goriot is not so seriously ill after all; in brief, he ends up collecting a quantity of duplicitous justifications for her conduct. She does not know how ill her father is; the kind old man himself would make her go to the ball rather than have her beside his bed. Eugène does not wish to see too clearly; he is ready to sacrifice his conscience to his mistress.

Later, Vautrin is arrested: he is a criminal on the run, an ex-convict who hides the letters T and F tattooed on his body: *Travaux Forcés* (forced labour) and Eugène, thanks to his love affair with Delphine, enters the high society he dreams of. And when Goriot dies, after having comfortably finished his dinner, he goes to find a priest and prepares for the wake beside the bed of the poor man. The other residents of the lodging house keep him company.

> Before nine o'clock that evening the body was laid out on the bare sacking of the bedstead in the desolate room; a lighted candle stood on either side, and the priest watched at the foot.
>
> *(Ibid.: 251)*

Rastignac makes enquiries about the expenses for the funeral, and writes a note to the husbands of both Goriot's daughters, a Count and a Baron, asking the two men 'to authorize their man of business to defray the charges of laying their father-in-law in the grave' (ibid.). He sends a servant to deliver the note and then goes to bed, exhausted, and sleeps. Next day he takes charge of the remaining bureaucratic issues, the death certification and the registrar, and by twelve o'clock the formalities are completed. No word comes from the Count nor from the Baron, and

Rastignac himself is forced to pay for the priest and the funeral. He has already given Sylvie ten francs for sewing the old man into a sheet and making him ready for the grave. After the funeral, attended by himself, Cristophe and two gravediggers, Eugène reaches the highest point of the cemetery, looks out over Paris and the windings of the Seine while the lamps begin to shine on either side of the river. His eyes turn almost eagerly to the space between the column of the Place Vendôme and the cupola of the Invalides: there lies the shining world that he has wished to reach. He glances over that humming hive, seeming to draw a foretaste of its honey, and says magniloquently: 'Henceforth there is war between us' (ibid.: 254). And by way of throwing down the glove to Society, Rastignac goes to dine with his lover.

A criminal criminologist

Power possesses an intimate criminal nature, it is ontologically corrupt in Balzac's descriptions. Those who inherit a fortune wield their social and financial power thanks to the illegitimate accumulation of wealth of their parents and ancestors. Those who experience a decline in their fortunes search for ways of catching up with the powerful by imitating them in dishonesty and illegality. Those who only inherit social disadvantage follow suit, reinventing themselves as businesspeople, wheeler–dealers, accepting risk while rejecting even the thought of failure. Balzac depicts a perfectly interconnected society, where separation or exclusion are counterbalanced by a rampant spirit characterizing all groups, apparently all fighting one another, but in fact all engaged in mutual mimicry. The boundaries between licit and illicit conducts grow blurred as *La Comédie Humaine* unfolds, with characters who leap from one context to the next, at times changing their name, but still holding and often exacerbating the counter-values they adopt. Vautrin, in this respect, represents the apotheosis of 'power as crime', as he combines the deceitful qualities of the greedy with the efficiency of the clerk, the giddy entrepreneurship of the innovator with the respectful solemnity of the institutional actor.

In *Splendeurs et misères des courtisanes*, Vautrin is the supposed Spanish priest Don Carlos Herrera, whose real name turns out to be Jacques Collin (Balzac, 1970). We have seen him in *Le Père Goriot*, a guest at

Madame Vauquer's boarding-house, hinting at murder as a viable path to success. We see him in a play, called indeed *Vautrin*, which has a short, unsuccessful run in 1840 at the Porte Saint Martin theatre. He likes reminding people that there are no such things as principles, there are only events; there are no laws, there are only circumstances: those who are wiser than their fellows accept events and circumstances in order to turn them to their own ends.

The real-life figure inspiring Balzac is Eugène François Vidocq, a great name in criminological history. Vidocq is an ex-convict who becomes the founder of the French *Sûreté* and thus the ancestor of criminal investigation departments throughout the world. Also regarded as the first private detective, as a teenager he is fearless, rowdy and cunning, talented and lazy. A fighter and a thief, he manages to reach a comfortable material condition, and his victims include his own parents, while his combatant spirit finds expression in the French army fighting Austria. After striking a superior officer he becomes a deserter, but adopting a false identity he is enlisted again, until he is finally identified and forced to resign. His love affairs are often followed by duels with competitors and he is imprisoned for a year at the age of 18. Once released he supports himself through fraud and forgery and, after several periods of incarceration, he resolves to cross the line, offering his services as an informant to the police. He is now 34 years old and works in a prison as a spy, collecting information about unsolved crimes. He is adored by thieves and esteemed by the most determined bandits, thus learning about planned offences, in which at times he takes part with the purpose of exposing his partners (Vidocq, 1928; Savant, 1973). Following the success of the private detective firm he establishes, the authorities acknowledge his skills and incorporate his services under the *Préfecture de Police* (Emsley and Shpayer-Makov, 2006; Stead, 1954). Vidocq, as would any member of the Positive School of criminology, records the physical characteristics of criminals and suspects, and develops a rudimentary understanding of fingerprinting, a tool of criminalistics that only in 1914 becomes accepted in France (Morton, 2004). This *criminal criminologist* could not epitomize more vividly Balzac's view of power.

Balzac is accused of possessing a diseased imagination leading him to depict in seductive undertones the most loathsome individuals. In response, Balzac claims to have met Vidocq and heard from him that 'all the criminals he had arrested went from one to five weeks before recovering the ability to salivate ... he had never seen a man spit on the way to the guillotine' (Morton, 2004: 322). Echoing this observation, which Balzac turns somewhat upside-down, in *Le Père Goriot* Vautrin reveals his pathological nature, when arrested, by spitting a torrent of saliva. A similar upturning is found in respect of homosexuality, which Vidocq despises while Vautrin reveals in his feelings towards Rastignac.

Vautrin, however, is not a solitary devil, as he intermingles with a variety of characters who operate in the social system at large. All connect and disjoint, reassemble and retract, providing a closely knitted social whole: bankers, prostitutes, fraudsters and aristocrats do not stand far apart, but conjure up a totality made of interweaving strands of power and crime. The interests shared by all of these characters reflect an all-pervasive moral disease, a universal complicity in corruption and decay. 'High and low, base interest and calculation interact with each other; a class-divided society finds its common factor in amoral anarchy that runs from top to bottom throughout the whole social structure' (Prendergast, 1978: 81).

The ball of spectres

The long descriptions of the environment, the houses, the furniture, the different objects, in Balzac, do not just provide the backdrop against which events unfold and people interact: the link between human beings and things is conceived as a necessity, and there are no boundaries between the concrete entities described and the moral meanings conveyed. Balzac has a mighty passion for things, for material objects, but his is a transfigured materialism: inanimate objects glow with a haunting life in his telling of the world, even if what they communicate is terrifying because it confirms the vanity of human cravings (James, 1984). A countess's bedroom reveals traces of evanescent pleasure: a bearskin rug upon which gleam two white satin slippers flung down carelessly, stockings twined around an armchair, a half-spread fan, open drawers showing flowers, diamonds and gloves. Usurer Gobseck, for whom life is a machine fuelled by money, is a phantasm, the very power of gold made flesh. He ends by succumbing to the madness of greed he has so cunningly exploited, as he in turn lies in a house overflowing with stockpiled delicacies, masses of rotten food of all sorts, fish sprouting mould, worms and insects crawling everywhere (O'Brien, 2014).

The links between objects and human beings allude to, and emphasize, a rigid notion of private property, the accumulation of objects and wealth as the result of a past history. The present is subordinated to the past. While melding with their possessions, the characters of the *Comédie Humaine* 'are trapped in past decades or centuries' (Moretti, 2001: 716). In this sense, these characters are conservative because for them the present is the last stage of the past rather than the beginning of the future.

There is something else to be learned if other aspects of Balzac's work are singled out. Eugène Rastignac feels a deep sense of indignation when, just after hearing the death-rattle in Goriot's throat, he finds himself facing the vanity and cruelty of the man's daughter, surrounded by golden embroideries and the precious garments of her friends. The ball she attends, which she prioritizes over tending her father in his death-bed, is a sumptuous display of wealth, luxury and status, and the objects in view seem to take on their own independent life. The lamps of 500 carriages light up the darkness about the Hôtel de Beauséant, a gendarme in all the glory of his uniform stands on either side of the resplendent gateway, while the great world flocks in, filling the glorious room already close to overflowing. The attire of the most beautiful women in Paris is dazzling, while the most distinguished men proudly deploy their decorations, stars and ribbons, as if showing less their military honour than their bank account. The music of the orchestra vibrates and the waves of notes lend more splendour to the golden ceiling of the palace. It is a society adorning itself with things that speak, move and dance by themselves. In that ball we can see not only a ghostly dance that repels the 'spectre haunting Europe', but also an assemblage of commodities endowed with invincible force and frightening power. Lamps and golden ceilings are not just things, and their properties do not merely respond to human needs. They are on a stage as commodities, symbolic entities acting and interacting among one another, presenting themselves as marked by their specific market value. The ball is a *coup de théâtre*, in which the ordinary is transfigured and metamorphosed into a super-natural thing. Commodities assume ghostly silhouettes, invade the stage with their spectral moves, come alive and address other commodities, their ghostly fellows (Derrida, 2006). In brief, Balzac's characters are not trapped in past decades or centuries, but prefigure the insatiability of consumerism, and many of his fictional characters anticipate an image of man as Faustian man, voracious and ambitious, perpetually driven beyond his own limits by the lure of the infinite (Eagleton, 2009).

A constellation of interests

In Balzac's analysis, power is exercised upon individuals who do not resist or oppose it. In social theory this aspect of social power is rendered as the capacity of one group to make another desist from engaging in any opposition (Poggi, 2001). More than domination, therefore, Balzac anatomizes hegemony, a form of cultural prominence incorporating and attracting others rather than rejecting them. Balzac's power does not rule by force alone: it transforms dependence into acceptance. The accumulation of money, in the works discussed here, is the common goal mobilizing all groups and individuals, particularly, and paradoxically, those who are devoid of status. In this sense his philosophy of money echoes that mentioned in a previous chapter. Georg Simmel (1990), drawing on historians and economists, remarks that the emancipated Roman slaves are predisposed towards monetary transactions because they lack any chance of achieving citizen status. Already in Athens, at the very inception of pure monetary transactions in the fourth century, the wealthiest banker, Pasion, starts his career as a slave. In Turkey the Armenians, a despised and persecuted people, are frequently merchants and money-lenders, as, under similar circumstances, are the Moors in Spain. There is no need to emphasize, says Simmel, that the Jews are the best example of the correlation between the central role of money interests and social deprivation. The issue is that, while it is easy to deny despised groups access to status, it is extremely hard to exclude them from the acquisition of money, because all possible paths constantly lead to it.

There is a difference, however, between entrepreneurs and experts in money transactions: the former acquire material goods such as land, productive tools and machineries, while the latter, as Balzac's misers, accumulate an indeterminate, inert, abstract means of exchange. Material goods cannot be easily expropriated, whereas money can. Therefore, those marginalized groups who are allowed to make some money continue to be despised, because the dynamics guiding monetary exchange can always expropriate them of their means. As we have seen, the 'democratic' aspect of money soon becomes evident, as this peculiar means of exchange lends itself ideally to robbery. Balzac's rich and would-be rich prove the motto *pecunia non olet* veritable. In Roman as well as in modern law, money that has been stolen cannot be taken away from a third person who has acquired it in good faith.

In Balzac, money rolls in every direction, and those who pursue its accumulation 'hold no belief in a life beyond the grave'; the present is all that counts for them. Incapable of delaying gratification, they seem the ideal objects of the study of 'control theory' which attributes to impulsive, physical actors the potential for committing any type of offence. Whether impulsive or calculating, however, Balzac's characters 'undermine the belief in a future life upon which the fabric of society has been built'.

> The grave holds few terrors for us now, is little feared as a transition stage upon man's journey. That future which once awaited us beyond the Requiem has been transported into the present.
>
> *(Balzac, 1955: 126)*

The 'paradise of luxury, vanity and pleasure' described by Balzac turns hearts into stones and 'mortifies the flesh for the sake of fleeting enjoyment of earthly treasure'. Monetary ambition is 'stamped on our age and seen everywhere', and even legislators are no longer required to exercise their power in making equitable laws, but their power of producing money. 'When this doctrine has been handed down from the bourgeoisie to the people, what will become of our country?' (ibid.: 127).

Balzac lays bare a constellation of interests rather than a kind of domination based on authority, showing how the stigma against new, insatiable wealth is collectively overcome. His protagonists, however, do not justify their greed by proving innovative, energetic, honest and self-restrained. In this sense, they are far removed from the Weberian entrepreneur, whose religiosity translates into the conviction of right-eousness accompanied by moderation, spirituality and hard work. Work is not the legitimation of the social power exerted by Balzac's characters, who do not show diligence, assiduity, exertion, or effort. Bourgeois work, historians and sociologists tell us, is a calm passion: steady, methodical, cumulative, and thus stronger than the turbulent (yet weak) passions of the old aristocracy (Hirschman, 1977). And while the old aristocracy 'shamelessly idealized itself in a whole gallery of intrepid knights' (Moretti, 2013), Balzac's money-hunters produce no such myths of themselves.

> As capitalism brought a relative well-being to the lives of large working class masses in the West, commodities became the new principle of legitimation; consensus was built on things, not men – let alone principles. It was the dawn of today: capitalism triumphant, and bourgeois culture dead.
>
> *(Ibid.: 21–22)*

This may also be said of Balzac's bourgeoisie, which unites irrationality and calculus in a single ethos, adventure and careful planning in a unique strategy. This bourgeoisie shows a close resemblance to Sombart's (1915) entrepreneur, who combines the soul of a respectable individual with the spirit of a reckless pirate, bringing to a synthesis the greed of gold, the desire for adventure, the love of exploration, calculation, careful policy, reasonableness and economy. We are always in a phase of primitive accumulation, or accumulation by dispossession, and Balzac's money-hunters bring their picaresque characteristics into the process, arriving to success less by working and praying than through invention and fraud. On the other hand, these anti-heroes may well be obsessed by power and money and may perhaps exist for the mere sake of them, but their acts are equally guided by both irrationality and cold assessment of costs and benefits. One may associate, as Moretti (2013) does, fog with the nascent English bourgeoisie, in that the new class achieves power while losing intellectual vision. 'The bourgeois feels suddenly ashamed of himself. He reveals himself to be much better at exercising power within the economic sphere than at establishing a political presence and formulating a general culture' (ibid.: 13). Not so Balzac's bourgeois, who achieves power and money while persuading all that no one is necessarily bound to fail. Rastignac and Vautrin are two faces of the same medal, as the spoilt courtesans are the alter ego of the humble maids. Balzac's characters appear in real life even more frequently after the death of the novelist: 'Balzac seems less to have observed the society of his age than to have contributed to the formation of an age. Thirty years later, reality arrived on the terrain that his intuition had already crossed in a single bound' (Benjamin, 1999: 760).

Fiction may be accused of steering away from logical argument opting for mythological narrative. With Protagoras, however, we can attempt to resolve the dilemma by saying that there is no difference between the two, both being able to support a demonstration, both being expressions of a functioning intellect (Curi, 2013). Balzac proves that power and crime may be grasped with elegance and passion without the hubris of established academic disciplines and fields of knowledge fascinated by their own alleged scientific status.

9

CONCLUSION

Power and crime are connected in innumerable, creative and serendipitous fashions. We can find such connections when travelling through
areas of knowledge where crime is not necessarily the main concern.
In addition to explanations and analyses provided by criminological
theory and research, we have found a variety of insights in social theory,
legal studies, politics, economics and ethics. As this book has progressed,
and as the analytical possibilities grew, the conclusion could be reached
that studying the relationship between power and crime amounts to
studying the virtual coincidence of the two. Hence the choice to present a concluding chapter in which this coincidence, through the work of
Honoré de Balzac, takes extraordinary literal form.

Religion and politics have often claimed that the existence of the
powerful is justified by the protective role they exercise over the powerless. Hence the view that the elite is able to reproduce itself pre-
dominantly through acts of generosity, renunciation and selflessness.
Throughout the chapters comprising this book we have seen that the
powerful display exactly opposite qualities, while in the areas of study we
have visited we have found suggestions as to how and why they
nevertheless manage to thrive. The crimes of the powerful, ultimately,
have emerged from the previous pages as *performative acts*, namely as

conducts which become assertive, truthful, ethical and therefore acceptable in the precise moment at which they are enacted (Austin, 1962). Like 'utterances', they transmit and produce power by communicating meaning (Berlin, 1973). Their acceptance, or their success, depends on how that meaning is transmitted to an audience. Performative success is achieved when powerful criminals manage to connect to spectators without mediation. 'Audiences are themselves in the action. They are pulled in; they identify' (Alexander, 2001: 181). Power is, of course, the ability to make somebody do something whether they like it or not, but in the different notions adopted in the previous pages we have seen that power, when engaged in crime, needs to iterate codes, narratives and values that become acceptable and reproducible.

Glaucus may persuade us that anyone who is in the condition to commit an injustice without having to pay for the consequences would not hesitate to do so. The best way to avoid consequences, however, consists in wearing a ring that makes those who wear it invisible (Plato, 1937). Powerful offenders, as we have discussed at length, do not need such a ring, as visibility more than secrecy can provide absolution from, if not imitation of, their conduct. The power of seeing, in their case, is accompanied by the power to be seen. Powerful offenders, in this sense, are 'trans-individual' subjects, namely subjects who shape themselves while shaping the society around them. They distinguish themselves from others within their group, but at the same time they claim their belonging to that group, potentially creating a collective subject (Simondon, 1989). Every crime contributes to this act of creation, which never reaches a final stage because there are always untapped potentials, additional possibilities for metamorphosis and further dynamic processes.

Veblen (1924) equates the swaggering delinquent with the powerful and punctilious gentleman, attributing to both an arrested spiritual development. In his view, they mark an immature phase, as compared with the stage of development attained by the average adult in the modern industrial community. That different social groups may form a homogeneous whole sounds worrying, particularly when these groups tolerate, justify or imitate one another's behaviour. This book has described power as diffuse, as a sort of pandemic disease promoting consensus, participation and emulation, in a mimetic process which neutralizes potentials for resistance. This cataclysmic picture is, of course, incomplete, as it lacks an appreciation of oppositional subjectivities inclined to pursue social justice. True, such subjectivities may be denied the resources to develop their own autonomous identities, therefore reflecting the current social pathological developments (Honneth, 2007). The powerful have certainly narrowed the ability of the underprivileged to articulate their experiences of injustice. The latter, due to their experiences of disrespect, may have been impaired in their capacity to be recognized as subjects deserving esteem, credibility and agency. It is with intense trepidation that we should all await and contribute to such recognition to be achieved.

REFERENCES

Adler, L. (2005), *Dans les pas de Hannah Arendt*, Paris: Gallimard.

Agamben G. (1998), *Homo Sacer. Sovereign Power and Bare Life*, Stanford, CA: Stanford University Press.

Albertson, K. and Fox, C. (2012), *Crime and Economics. An Introduction*, Abingdon: Routledge.

Alexander, J.C. (2001), 'Performance and Power', in Seidman, S. and Alexander, J.C. (eds), *The New Social Theory Reader*, London: Routledge.

Althusser, L. (1969), *For Marx*, London: Allen Lane.

——(1971), *Lenin and Philosophy*, London: Monthly Review Press.

Andreano, R. and Siegfried, J. (eds) (1980), *The Economics of Crime*, New York: John Wiley.

Appiah, K.A. (2008), *Experiments in Ethics*, Cambridge, MA: Harvard University Press.

Arendt, H. (1973), *The Origins of Totalitarianism*, San Diego, CA: Harcourt Brace.

——(2006), *Alcune questioni di filosofia morale*, Turin: Einaudi.

Aristotle (1934), *Nicomachean Ethics*, Cambridge, MA: Harvard University Press.

——(1995), *Politics*, Oxford: Oxford University Press.

——(1996), *Poetics*, Oxford: Oxford University Press.

Aron, R. (1964), 'Macht, power, puissance: prose démocratique ou poésie démoniaque?', *European Journal of Sociology*, 5(1): 27–51.

Arthur, C.J. (1978), 'Introduction', in Pashukanis, E.B., *Law and Marxism: A General Theory*, London: Ink Links.

Aubert, V. (1956), 'White-Collar Crime and Social Structure', *American Journal of Sociology*, 58: 263–271.

Augustine (2003), *City of God*, Harmondsworth: Penguin.

Austin, J.L. (1962), *Sense and Sensibilia*, Oxford: Clarendon Press.

Balzac, H. de (1898), *The Poor Relations. Second Episode: Cousin Pons*, Philadelphia, PA: George Barrie & Son.

——(1955), *Eugénie Grandet*, London: Penguin.

——(1966), *Le Père Goriot*, Paris: Garnier-Flammarion.

——(1970), *A Harlot High and Low (Splendeurs et misères des courtisanes)*, Harmondsworth: Penguin.

——(2013), *The Human Comedy: Selected Stories*, New York: New York Review of Books.

Banakar, R. and Travers, M. (eds) (2013), *Law and Social Theory*, Oxford: Hart.

Bankowski, Z. (1983), 'Anarchism, Marxism and the Critique of Law', in Sugarman, D. (ed.), *Legality, Ideology and the State*, London: Academic Press.

Bauman, Z. (1990), *Thinking Sociologically*, Oxford: Blackwell.

——(1993), *Postmodern Ethics*, Oxford: Blackwell.

——(1995), *Life in Fragments: Essays in Postmodern Morality*, Oxford: Blackwell.

Becker, G. (1968), 'Crime and Punishment: An Economic Approach', *Journal of Political Economy*, 76: 169–217.

——(1976), *The Economic Approach to Human Behaviour*, Chicago, IL: University of Chicago Press.

Benjamin, W. (1996), 'Critique of Violence', in *Selected Writings*, Cambridge, MA: Harvard University Press.

——(1999), *The Arcades Project*, Cambridge, MA: Harvard University Press.

Berlin, I. (1973), *Essays on J.L. Austin*, Oxford: Oxford University Press.

Bertault, P. (1963), *Balzac and the Human Comedy*, New York: New York University Press.

Boltanski, L. and Thévenot, L. (2006), *On Justification*, Princeton, NJ: Princeton University Press.

Boudon, R. (2013), *The Origin of Values. Sociology and Philosophy of Beliefs*, New Brunswick, NJ: Transaction.

Bourdieu, P. (1984), *Distinction*, Cambridge, MA: Harvard University Press.

——(1990), *The Logic of Practice*, Stanford, CA: Stanford University Press.

——(2013), *Sur l'état: cours au Collège de France*, Paris: Seuil.

Box, S. (1983), *Power, Crime and Mystification*, London: Tavistock.

Braudel, F. (1982), *The Wheels of Commerce*, London: St James' Place.

Brittain-Catlin, W. (2005), *Offshore: The Dark Side of the Global Economy*, New York: Picador.

Buchanan, J. (1980), 'A Defence of Organized Crime?', in Andreano, R. and Siegfried, J. (eds), *The Economics of Crime*, New York: John Wiley.

Bull, M. (2013), *Inventing Falsehood, Making Truth. Vico and Neapolitan Paintings*, Princeton, NJ: Princeton University Press.

Burns, T. (1963), 'Industry in a New Age', *New Society*, 31 January: 17–20.

Byrne, S. (2012), *Law and History in Cervantes' Don Quixote*, Toronto: University of Toronto Press.

Cain, M. and Hunt, A. (1979), *Marx and Engels on Law*, London: Academic Press.

Cartier-Bresson, J. (1997), 'Corruption Networks, Transaction Security and Illegal Social Exchange', *Political Studies*, 45: 463–476.

Cassano, F. (1983), *La certezza infondata*, Bari: Dedalo.

Cavarero, L. (2013), *Inclinazioni. Critica della rettitudine*, Milan: Raffaello Cortina.

Cervantes, M. de (2003), *Don Quixote*, Harmondsworth: Penguin.

Chambliss, W. and Mankoff, M. (1976), 'Preface', in Chambliss, W. and Mankoff, M. (eds), *Whose Law? What Order? A Conflict Approach to Criminology*, New York: John Wiley.

Chambliss, W., Michalowski, R. and Kramer, R. (eds) (2010), *State Crime in the Global Age*, Cullompton: Willan.

Clarke, M. (1990), *Business Crime: Its Nature and Control*, Cambridge: Cambridge University Press.

Clegg, S., Flyvbjerg, B. and Haugaard, M. (2014), 'Reflections on Phronetic Social Science', *Journal of Political Power*, DOI: 10.1080/2158379X.2014.929259 (accessed 23 June 2014).

Clinard, M.B. and Yeager, P.C. (1980), *Corporate Crime*, New York: Macmillan.

Cohen, S. (1993), 'Human Rights and Crimes of the State: The Culture of Denial', *Australia and New Zealand Journal of Criminology*, 26: 97–115.

Coleman, J. (1990), *Foundations of Social Theory*, Cambridge: Belknap.

Collins, J. (2014), 'Equality of Souls', *Times Literary Supplement*, 11 April: 7–8.

Comte, A. (1953), *Cours de philosophie positive* (vol. VI), Paris: Gallimard.

Conklin, J.E. (1977), *Illegal But Not Criminal: Business Crime in America*, Englewood Cliffs, NJ: Prentice-Hall.

Cook, K.S. and Gerbasi, A. (2012), 'Trust', in Hedström, P. and Bearman, P. (eds), *The Oxford Handbook of Analytical Sociology*, Oxford: Oxford University Press.

Crawford, M.A. (1955), 'Introduction', in H. de Balzac, *Eugénie Grandet*, Harmondsworth: Penguin.

Croall, H. (1992), *White Collar Crime*, Buckingham and Philadelphia, PA: Open University Press.

Curi, U. (2013), *Passione*, Milan: Raffaello Cortina.

Dal Lago, A. (1994), *Il conflitto della modernità. Il pensiero di Georg Simmel*, Bologna: Il Mulino.

——(2012), *Carnefici e spettatori. La nostra indifferenza verso la crudeltà*, Milan: Raffaello Cortina.

Dalton, M. (1959), *Men Who Manage*, London: Wiley.

De Pascale, C. (2010), *Giustizia*, Bologna: Il Mulino.

Derrida, J. (1992), 'Force of Law: The Mystical Foundation of Authority', in Cornell, D., Rosenfeld, M. and Gray Carlson, D. (eds), *Deconstruction and the Possibility of Justice*, London: Routledge.

——(2006), *Spectres of Marx*, London: Routledge.

——(2011), *The Beast & the Sovereign* (vol. II), Chicago, IL: University of Chicago Press.

Douglas, J.D. and Johnson, J.M. (eds) (1977), *Official Deviance*, Chicago, IL: Lippincott.

Drayfus, H. and Rabinow, P. (1983), *Michel Foucault: Beyond Structuralism and Hermeneutics*, Chicago, IL: University of Chicago Press.

Durkheim, E. (1960), *The Division of Labour in Society*, Glencoe: The Free Press.
——(1985), 'Qui a voulu la guerre?', in Lukes, S. (ed.), *Emile Durkheim. His Life and Work*, Stanford, CA: Stanford University Press.
——(1996), *Professional Ethics and Civic Morals*, London: Routledge.
Dworkin, R. (2006), *Justice in Robe*, Cambridge, MA: Harvard University Press.
Eagleton, T. (2009), *Trouble with Strangers. A Study of Ethics*, Oxford: Wiley-Blackwell.
Elliott, A. (2014), *Contemporary Social Theory: An Introduction*, second edition, London: Routledge.
Ellison, D.R. (2000), 'Moral Complexity in Le Père Goriot: Balzac between Kant and Nietzsche', in Ginsburg, M.P. (ed.), *Approaches to Teaching Balzac's Old Goriot*, New York: The Modern Language Association of America.
Emsley, C. and Shpayer-Makov, H. (2006), *Police Detectives in History: 1750–1950*, Aldershot: Ashgate.
Engels, F. (1943), *Anti-Dühring*, London: Lawrence & Wishart.
Ermann, M.D. and Lundman, R.J. (1982), *Corporate Deviance*, New York: Holt, Rinehart and Winston.
——(eds) (1978), *Corporate and Governmental Deviance*, New York: Oxford University Press.
Esposito, R. (2006), *Communitas. Origine e destino della comunità*, Turin: Einaudi.
——(2008), *Bios: Biopolitics and Philosophy*, Minneapolis: University of Minnesota Press.
Etzioni, A. (1964), *Modern Organizations*, Englewood Cliffs, NJ: Prentice Hall.
Evangelista, R. (2013), 'Natura e società. L'individuo in Locke e Spinoza', *La Società degli Individui*, 48: 113–122.
Felson, M. (2002), *Crime and Everyday Life*, third edition, Thousand Oaks, CA: Sage.
Ferrajoli, L. (2013), *La democrazia attraverso i diritti*, Rome/Bari: Laterza.
Fine, R. (2013), 'Marxism and the Social Theory of Law', in Banakar, R. and Travers, M. (eds), *Law and Social Theory*, Oxford: Hart.
Foucault, M. (1970), *The Order of Things. The Archaeology of Human Sciences*, London: Routledge.
——(1972), *The Archeology of Knowledge*, London: Routledge.
——(1977), *Discipline and Punish*, London: Allen Lane.
——(1980), 'Truth and Power', in Gordon, C. (ed.), *Michel Foucault: Power/Knowledge*, London: Harvester Press.
——(1986), 'Disciplinary Power and Subjection', in Lukes, S. (ed.), *Power*, Oxford: Blackwell.
——(1990), *The History of Sexuality* (vol. 1), New York: Vintage.
Fraser, N. (2014), 'Behind Marx's Hidden Abode', *New Left Review*, 86: 55–72.
Freud, S. (1962), *Civilization and its Discontents*, New York: W.W. Norton.
Friedrichs, D.O. (2004), *Trusted Criminals: White Collar Crime in Contemporary Society*, Belmont, CA: Thomson/Wadsworth.
Galbraith, J.K. (1987), *A History of Economics: The Past as the Present*, London: Penguin.
Gambetta, D. (2009), *Codes of the Underworld. How Criminals Communicate*, Princeton, NJ, and Oxford: Princeton University Press.

Geis, G. and Meier, R. (eds) (1977), *White-Collar Crime: Offences in Business, Politics and the Professions*, New York: Free Press.

Geis, G. and Jesilow, P. (eds) (1993), *White-Collar Crime*, Special Issue of The Annals of the *American Academy of Political and Social Science*, 525, January.

Giddens, A. (1986), *The Constitution of Society: Outline of the Theory of Structuration*, Cambridge: Polity Press.

Gottfredson, M. and Hirschi, T. (1990), *A General Theory of Crime*, Stanford, CA: Stanford University Press.

Gottfried, P.E. (1990), *Carl Schmitt: Politics and Theory*, New York: Greenwood Press.

Gouldner, A.W. (1954), *Patterns of Industrial Bureaucracy*, New York: The Free Press.

——(1967), *Enter Plato: Classical Greece and the Origins of Social Theory*, London: Routledge and Kegan Paul.

Gramsci, A. (1971), *Selections from the Prison Notebooks*, Chicago, IL: International Publishing Corporation.

Green, G.S. (1990), *Occupational Crime*, Chicago, IL: Nelson-Hall.

Green, P. and Ward, T. (2004), *State Crime: Governments, Violence and Corruption*, London: Pluto.

Habermas, J. (1984), *The Theory of Communicative Action*, Boston, MA: Beacon Press.

——(1989), *Structural Transformation of the Public Sphere*, Boston, MA: MIT Press.

——(1996), *Between Facts and Norms: Contributions to a Discourse Theory of Law and Democracy*, Boston, MA: MIT Press.

Haque, A.A. (2014), 'Law and Morality at War', *Criminal Law and Philosophy*, 8: 79–97.

Harrington, A. (2005), *Modern Social Theory. An Introduction*, Oxford: Oxford University Press.

Hart, H.L.A. (1961), *The Concept of Law*, Oxford: Clarendon Press.

——(1977), 'Positivism and the Separation of Law and Morals', in Dworkin, R.M. (ed.), *The Philosophy of Law*, Oxford: Oxford University Press.

Hedström, P. and Bearman, P. (eds) (2012), *The Oxford Handbook of Analytical Sociology*, Oxford: Oxford University Press.

Hegel, F. (1952), *Philosophy of Right*, Oxford: Clarendon Press.

Held, D. (ed.) (1991), *Political Theory Today*, Cambridge: Polity Press.

Heller, A. (1976), *The Theory of Need in Marx*, London: Allison and Busby.

Heywood, A. (1994), *Political Theory: An Introduction*, London: Macmillan.

Hirschman, A.O. (1977), *The Passions and the Interests*, Princeton, NJ: Princeton University Press.

Hobbes, T. (1987), *Leviathan*, Harmondsworth: Penguin.

Holmes, O.W. (1881), *The Common Law*, Boston, MA: Little, Brown & Co.

Honneth, A. (2007), *Disrespect. The Normative Foundations of Critical Theory*, Cambridge: Polity Press.

——(2014), *Freedom's Right. The Social Foundations of Democratic Life*, Cambridge: Polity Press.

Hume, D. (2008), *An Enquiry Concerning Human Understanding*, Oxford: Oxford University Press.
——(2011a), 'Of Morals', in Hume, D., *The Essential Philosophical Works*, London: Wordsworth.
——(2011b), 'Of Our Esteem for the Rich and Powerful', in Hume, D., *The Essential Philosophical Works*, London: Wordsworth.
Inglis, D. with Thorpe, C. (2012), *An Invitation to Social Theory*, Cambridge: Polity Press.
Jacobs, J. (1992), *Systems of Survival: A Dialogue on the Moral Foundations of Commerce and Politics*, New York: Random House.
James, H. (1984), *Literary Criticism: French Writers*, Washington, DC: Library of America.
Kant, I. (1991), *Political Writings*, Cambridge: Cambridge University Press.
——(1994), 'Pure Practical Reason and the Moral Law', in Singer, P. (ed.), *Ethics*, Oxford: Oxford University Press.
——(1996), *The Metaphysics of Morals*, Cambridge: Cambridge University Press.
——(1998), *Religion within the Boundaries of Mere Reason*, Cambridge: Cambridge University Press.
——(2007), *Critique of Pure Reason*, Harmondsworth: Penguin.
Keane, C. (1995), 'Loosely Coupled Systems and Unlawful Behaviour: Organization Theory and Corporate Crime', in Pearce, F. and Snider, L. (eds), *Corporate Crime. Contemporary Debates*, Toronto: Toronto University Press.
Kelsen, H. (1945), *General Theory of Law and State*, Cambridge, MA: Harvard University Press.
Kojève, A. (2013), 'Tyranny and Wisdom', in Strauss, L., *On Tyranny*, Chicago, IL: University of Chicago Press.
Korsch, K. (1978), 'Appendix: An Assessment', in Pashukanis, E.B., *Law and Marxism: A General Theory*, London: Ink Links.
Landesco, J. (1973 [1929]), *Organized Crime in Chicago: Part III of the Illinois Crime Survey*, Chicago, IL: University of Chicago Press.
Latour, B. (2013), *An Inquiry into Modes of Existence. An Anthropology of the Moderns*, Cambridge, MA: Harvard University Press.
Laufer, W.S. (2006), *Corporate Bodies and Guilty Minds*, Chicago, IL: University of Chicago Press.
Le Goff, J. (1987), *La borsa e la vita. Dall'usuraio al banchiere*, Rome/Bari: Laterza.
——(2003), *A la recherche du Moyen Age*, Paris: Louis Audibert.
Lefèvre, G. (1902), *Le traité 'De Usura' de Robert de Courçon*, Lille: Université de Lille.
Levi, M. (1987), *Regulating Fraud. White-Collar Crime and the Criminal Process*, London: Tavistock.
Lloyd, M. (2014), 'The End of Ideology', in Geoghegan, V. and Wilford, R. (eds), *Political Ideologies. An Introduction*, fourth edition, London: Routledge.
Luhmann, N. (1975), *Macht*, Stuttgart: Ferdinand Enke Verlag.
——(1985), *A Sociological Theory of Law*, London: Routledge.
Lukes, S. (1974), *Power: A Radical View*, London: Macmillan.

———(ed.) (1986), *Power*, Oxford: Blackwell.

Machiavelli, N. (1944), *The Prince*, London: J.M. Dent & Sons.

Mandeville, B. (1989), *The Fable of the Bees*, Harmondsworth: Penguin.

Mann, M. (1986), *The Sources of Power: A History of Power from the Beginning to A.D. 1760* (vol. 1), Cambridge: Cambridge University Press.

———(2011), *Power in the 21st Century*, Cambridge: Polity Press.

March, J.G. (1990), 'The Technology of Foolishness', in Pugh, D.S. (ed.), *Organisation Theory. Selected Readings*, Harmondsworth: Penguin.

Marshall, A. (1961), *Principles of Economics* (vol. 1), London: Macmillan.

Marx, K. (1960), *India, Cina, Russia*, Milano: Il Saggiatore.

———(1976a), *Capital*, Harmondsworth: Penguin.

———(1976b), *The Communist Manifesto*, Harmondsworth: Penguin.

———(1992), *Early Writings*, Harmondsworth: Penguin.

Marx, K. and Engels, F. (1963), *The German Ideology*, New York: International Publishers.

Melossi, D. and Pavarini, M. (1977), *Carcere e fabbrica*, Bologna: Il Mulino.

Mendus, S. (ed.) (1988), *Justifying Toleration*, Cambridge: Cambridge University Press.

———(2009), *Politics and Morality*, Cambridge: Polity Press.

Merton, R. (1968), *Social Theory and Social Structure*, New York: The Free Press.

———(1976), *Sociological Ambivalence and Other Essays*, New York: The New Press.

Michalowski, R.M. and Kramer, R.C. (2007), 'State-Corporate Crime and Criminological Inquiry', in Pontell, H.N. and Geis, G. (eds), *International Handbook of White-Collar and Corporate Crime*, New York: Springer.

Mill, J.S. (1969), *Essays on Ethics, Religion and Society*, Toronto: University of Toronto Press.

Montaigne, M. de (1993), *The Complete Essays*, Oxford: Oxford University Press.

Montesquieu (1973), *Persian Letters*, Harmondsworth: Penguin.

———(1989), *The Spirit of the Laws*, Cambridge: Cambridge University Press.

More, T. (1997), *Utopia*, London: Wordsworth.

Moretti, F. (2001), *Il Romanzo* (vol. 1), Turin: Einaudi.

———(2013), *The Bourgeois. Between History and Literature*, London and New York: Verso.

Morton, J. (2004), *The First Detective. The Life and Revolutionary Times of Eugène-François Vidocq: Criminal, Spy and Private Eye*, London: Ebury.

Mosca, G. (1939), *The Ruling Class*, New York: McGraw-Hill.

Mouzelis, N.P. (1967), *Organization and Bureaucracy. An Analysis of Modern Theories*, London: Routledge & Kegan Paul.

Nelken, D. (1994), 'White Collar Crime', in Maguire, M., Morgan, R. and Reiner, R. (eds), *The Oxford Handbook of Criminology*, Oxford: Oxford University Press.

Neumann, F. (1957), *The Democratic and Authoritarian State*, London: Macmillan.

Nietzsche, F. (1955), *Beyond Good and Evil*, Chicago, IL: Henry Regnery.

———(1968), *The Genealogy of Morals*, New York: Random House.

Nussbaum, M.C. (2013), *Political Emotions. Why Love Matters for Justice*, Cambridge, MA: Harvard University Press.

O'Brien, G. (2014), 'Balzac on the Brink', *New York Review of Books*, 20 February: 30–32.

Pareto, V. (1935), *The Mind and Society*, New York: Harcourt Brace.

——(1966), *Sociological Writings*, London: Paul Mall Press.

Parsons, T. (1960), *Structure and Process in Modern Societies*, New York: Free Press.

——(1964), *Essays in Sociological Theory*, Toronto: Collier-Macmillan.

——(1982), *On Institutions and Social Evolution*, Chicago, IL: University of Chicago Press.

Pascal, B. (1967), *Provincial Letters*, Harmondsworth: Penguin.

——(1998), *Pensées*, Harmondsworth: Penguin.

Pashukanis, E.B. (1978), *Law and Marxism: A General Theory*, London: Ink Links.

Passas, N. (2009), 'Anomie and Corporate Deviance', in Whyte, D. (ed.), *Crimes of the Powerful: A Reader*, Maidenhead: Open University Press.

Pearce, F. (1976), *Crimes of the Powerful. Marxism, Crime and Deviance*, London: Pluto.

Perrow, C. (1961), 'The Analysis of Goals in Complex Organizations', *American Sociological Review*, 26: 854–866.

——(1970), *Organizational Analysis: A Sociological View*, London: Tavistock.

Petersen, T. (2012), 'Opportunities', in Hedström, P. and Bearman, P. (eds), *The Oxford Handbook of Analytical Sociology*, Oxford: Oxford University Press.

Piquero, N.L. and Piquero, A.R. (2006), 'Control Balance and Exploitative Corporate Crime', *Criminology*, 44(2): 397–430.

Plato (1937), *The Republic*, London: William Heinemann.

——(1970), *The Laws*, Harmondsworth: Penguin.

Poggi, G. (2001), *Forms of Power*, Cambridge: Polity Press.

Posner, E.A. (2000), *Law and Social Norms*, Cambridge, MA: Harvard University Press.

Posner, R.A. (1972), *Economic Analysis of Law*, Boston, MA: Little, Brown.

——(2013), *Reflections on Judging*, Cambridge, MA: Harvard University Press.

Prendergast, C. (1978), *Balzac: Fiction and Melodrama*, London: Edward Arnold.

Punch, M. (1996), *Dirty Business*, London: Sage.

Putnam, R. (2000), *Bowling Alone: The Collapse and Revival of American Community*, London: Simon & Schuster.

Quinney, R. (1964), 'The Study of White-Collar Crime: Toward a Reorientation in Theory and Research', *Journal of Criminal Law, Criminology and Police Science*, 55: 208–214.

——(1970), *The Problem of Crime*, New York: Dodd, Mead.

Rawls, J. (1972), *A Theory of Justice*, Oxford: Clarendon Press.

Reynolds, M.O. (1980), 'The Economics of Criminal Activity', in Andreano, R. and Siegfried, J. (eds), *The Economics of Crime*, New York: John Wiley.

Robb, G. (1994), *Balzac: A Biography*, London: Picador.

Robertson, D.H. (1978), *Economic Commentaries*, Westport, CT: Greenwood Press.

Roebuck, J. and Weeber, S.C. (1978), *Political Crime in the United States*, New York: Praeger.

Rorty, R. (1991), 'The Banality of Pragmatism and the Poetry of Justice', in Brint, M. and Weaver, W. (eds), *Pragmatism in Law and Society*, Boulder, CO: Westview Press.

Rosenfeld, R. and Messner, S.F. (2013), *Crime and the Economy*, London: Sage.

Ross, J.I. (ed.) (2000), *Controlling State Crime*, New Brunswick, NJ: Transaction.

Roth, G. (1978), 'Introduction', in M. Weber, *Economy and Society: An Outline of Interpretive Sociology*, Berkeley: University of California Press.

Rothe, D.L. and Ross, J.I. (eds) (2009), 'State Crime', special issue of *Critical Criminology*, 17.

Rousseau, J.-J. (1964), *Le contrat social*, Paris: Gallimard.

Rubin, P.H. (1980), 'The Economics of Crime', in Andreano, R. and Siegfried, J. (eds), *The Economics of Crime*, New York: John Wiley.

Ruggiero, V. (1992), 'Heroin Use and the Formal Economy', *British Journal of Criminology*, 32: 273–291.

——(1996), *Organised and Corporate Crime in Europe*, Aldershot: Dartmouth.

——(2000), *Crime and Markets*, Oxford: Oxford University Press.

——(2003), *Crime in Literature: Sociology of Deviance and Fiction*, London: Verso.

——(2006), *Understanding Political Violence*, London and New York: Open University Press/McGraw-Hill.

——(2007), 'It's the Economy, Stupid! Classifying Power Crimes', *International Journal of the Sociology of Law*, 35: 163–177.

——(2010), *Penal Abolitionism*, Oxford: Oxford University Press.

——(2012), 'Giustizia, moralità e impresa secondo il metodo mafioso', *Studi sulla Questione Criminale*, 7: 9–20.

——(2013), *The Crimes of the Economy. A Criminological Analysis of Economic Thought*, London: Routledge.

Ruggiero, V. and Welch, M. (eds) (2009), *Power Crime*, special issues of *Crime, Law and Social Change*, 51(3–4): 297–450.

Rusche, G. and Kirchheimer, O. (1968), *Punishment and Social Structure*, New York: Russell & Russell.

Sabuktay, A. (2009), 'Locating Extra-Legal Activities of the Modern State in Legal-Political Theory: Weber, Habermas, Kelsen, Schmitt and Turk', *Crime, Law and Social Change*, 51: 511–530.

Sampson, R. (2006), 'Collective Efficacy Theory: Lessons Learned and Directions for Future Inquiry', in Cullen, F., Wright, J.P. and Blevins, K. (eds), *The Status of Criminological Theory*, New Brunswick, NJ: Transaction.

Sandel, M.J. (2013), *What Money Can't Buy. The Moral Limits of Markets*, London: Penguin.

Sands, P. (2006), *Lawless World: Making and Breaking Global Rules*, Harmondsworth: Penguin.

Santner, E.L. (2011), *The Royal Remains. The People's Two Bodies and the Endgames of Sovereignty*, Chicago, IL: University of Chicago Press.

Savant, J. (1973), *La vie aventureuse de Vidocq*, Paris: Hachette.

Schelling, T.C. (1967), 'Economic Analysis of Organized Crime', in *The President's Commission on Law Enforcement and the Administration of Justice, Task Force Report: Organized Crime*, Washington, DC: Government Printing Office.

Schmitt, C. (1976), *The Concept of the Political*, New Brunswick, NJ: Rutgers University Press.

——(1985), *Political Theology: Four Chapters on the Concept of Sovereignty*, Cambridge, MA: MIT Press.

——(2006), *Political Theology: Four Chapters of the Concept of Sovereignty*, Chicago, IL: University of Chicago Press.

——(2014), *Dictatorship*, Cambridge: Polity Press.

Schrager, L.S. and Short, J.F. (1977), 'Toward a Sociology of Organizational Crime', *Social Problems*, 25: 407–419.

Sen, A. (1987), *On Ethics and Economics*, Oxford: Blackwell.

Shover, N. (2007), 'Generative Worlds of White-Collar Crime', in Pontell, H.N. and Geis, G. (eds), *International Handbook of White-Collar and Corporate Crime*, New York: Springer.

Siedentop, L. (2013), *Inventing the Individual. The Origin of Western Liberalism*, London: Allen Lane.

Simmel, G. (1950), *Sociology*, New York: The Free Press.

——(1971a), 'Domination', in *On Individuality and Social Forms*, Chicago, IL: University of Chicago Press.

——(1971b), 'The Metropolis and Mental Life', in *On Individuality and Social Forms*, Chicago, IL: University of Chicago Press.

——(1971c), 'Prostitution', in *On Individuality and Social Forms*, Chicago, IL: University of Chicago Press.

——(1990), *The Philosophy of Money*, London: Routledge.

Simon, D.R. and Eitzen, D.S. (1982), *Elite Deviance*, Boston, MA: Allyn & Bacon.

Simondon, G. (1989), *L'individuation psychique et collective*, Paris: Aubier.

Singer, P. (ed.) (1994), *Ethics*, Oxford: Oxford University Press.

Skeel, D. (2005), *Icarus in the Boardroom*, Oxford: Oxford University Press.

Slapper, G. and Tombs, S. (1999), *Corporate Crime*, Harlow: Pearson Education.

Smith, A. (1976a), *An Inquiry into the Nature and Causes of the Wealth of Nations*, Oxford: Clarendon Press.

——(1976b), *The Theory of Moral Sentiments*, Oxford: Clarendon Press.

——(1978), *Lectures on Jurisprudence*, Oxford: Clarendon Press.

Sombart, W. (1915), *The Quintessence of Capitalism*, London: Fisher Unwin.

Spencer, H. (1969), *The Principles of Sociology*, London: Macmillan.

Spinoza, B. (2007), *Ethics*, London: Wordsworth.

Stalley, R.F. (1995), 'Introduction', in Aristotle, *Politics*, Oxford: Oxford University Press.

Stead, J.P. (1954), *Vidocq: A Biography*, London: Staples.

Stigler, G. (1970), 'The Optimum Enforcement of Law', *Journal of Political Economy*, 78: 526–536.

Strauss, L. (2013), *On Tyranny*, Chicago, IL: University of Chicago Press.

Supiot, A. (2007), *Homo Juridicus. On the Anthropological Function of the Law*, London and New York: Verso.

Sutherland, E. (1945), 'Is "White Collar Crime" Crime?', *American Sociological Review*, 10: 132–139.

——(1983), *White Collar Crime: The Uncut Version*, New Haven, CT: Yale University Press.

Sykes, G. and Matza, D. (1957), 'Techniques of Neutralization: A Theory of Delinquency', *American Sociological Review*, 22: 664–670.

Tappan, P. (1947), 'Who Is the Criminal?', *American Sociological Review*, 12: 96–102.

Taylor, I., Walton, P. and Young, J. (1973), *The New Criminology*, London: Routledge & Kegan Paul.

Thompson, E.P. (1977), *Whigs and Hunters: The Origin of the Black Act*, Harmondsworth: Penguin.

Tilly, C. (1985), 'War Making and State Making as Organized Crime', in Evans, P.B., Rueschemeer, D. and Skocpol, T. (eds), *Bringing the State Back In*, Cambridge: Cambridge University Press.

——(2005), *Trust and Rule*, Cambridge: Cambridge University Press.

Tittle, C. (1995), *Control Balance*, Boulder, CO: Westview Press.

Tocqueville, A. de (2003), *Democracy in America*, Harmondsworth: Penguin.

Tronti, M. (ed.) (1982), *Il politico 2. Da Hobbes a Smith* (vol. 1), Milan: Feltrinelli.

Turk, A.T. (2000), 'Foreword', in Ross, J.I. (ed.), *Controlling State Crime*, New Brunswick, NJ: Transaction.

Tyerman, C. (2006), *God's War: A New History of the Crusades*, Cambridge, MA: Harvard University Press.

Urry, J. (2014), *Offshoring*, Cambridge: Polity Press.

Vaughan, D. (1983), *Controlling Unlawful Organizational Behavior*, Chicago, IL: University of Chicago Press.

——(2007), 'Beyond Macro- and Micro-Levels of Analysis, Organizations, and the Cultural Fix', in Pontell, H.N. and Geis, G. (eds), *International Handbook of White-Collar and Corporate Crime*, New York: Springer.

——(2012), 'Analytic Ethnography', in Hedström, P. and Bearman, P. (eds), *The Oxford Handbook of Analytical Sociology*, Oxford: Oxford University Press.

Veblen, T. (1924), *The Theory of the Leisure Class: An Economic Study of Institutions*, London: Allen & Unwin.

Vico, G. (1999), *New Science: Principles of the New Science Concerning the Common Nature of Nations*, Harmondsworth: Penguin.

Vidocq, E.F. (1928), *Mémoires de Vidocq*, Paris: Hachette.

Vinx, L. (2007), *Hans Kelsen's Pure Theory of Law. Legality and Legitimacy*, Oxford: Oxford University Press.

Voltaire (1994), *Political Writings*, Cambridge: Cambridge University Press.

Waldron, J. (2006), 'How Judges Should Judge', *The New York Review of Books*, 10 August: 54–59.

Walzer, M. (2004), *Politics and Passion*, New Haven, CT: Yale University Press.

Ward, T. (2005), 'State Crime in the Heart of Darkness', *British Journal of Criminology*, 54(4): 434–445.

Weber, M. (1976), *The Protestant Ethic and the Spirit of Capitalism*, London: Allen & Unwin.

——(1978), *Economy and Society: An Outline of Interpretive Sociology*, Berkeley: University of California Press.

——(1991), *Essays in Sociology*, ed. Gertz, H. and Mills, C.W., London: Routledge.

Whyte, D. (ed.) (2009), *Crimes of the Powerful: A Reader*, Maidenhead: Open University Press.

——(2012), 'Between Crime and Doxa: Researching the Worlds of State-Corporate Elites', *State Crime*, 1: 89–108.

Williams, B. (2007), 'Relativism, History, and the Existence of Values', in Raz, J. (ed.), *The Practice of Value*, Oxford: Oxford University Press.

Wright Mills, C. (1956), *The Power Elite*, New York: Oxford University Press.

——(1959), *The Causes of World War Three*, London: Secker and Warburg.

Yeager, P.C. (1995), 'Management, Morality, and Law: Organizational Forms and Ethical Deliberations', in Pearce, F. and Snider, L. (eds), *Corporate Crime. Contemporary Debates*, Toronto: Toronto University Press.

——(2007), 'Understanding Corporate Lawbreaking: From Profit Seeking to Law Finding', in Pontell, H.N. and Geis, G. (eds), *International Handbook of White-Collar and Corporate Crime*, New York: Springer.

Zedner, L. (2005), 'Securing Liberty in the Face of Terror: Reflections from Criminal Justice', *Journal of Law and Society*, 4: 507–533.

Zolo, D. (2010), 'Complessità, potere, democrazia', in Luhmann, N., *Potere e complessità sociale*, Milan: Il Saggiatore.

Zweig, S. (2010), *Balzac, Dickens, Dostoevsky: Master Builders of the Spirit*, New Brunswick, NJ: Transaction.

INDEX

Forbidden GAME

MADISON FOX

Forbidden GAME

Editor: Katie Krasne
Proofreading by: Caroline Palmier—Love & Edits
Cover Designer: Cat at TRC Designs
Formatting: Alyssa at Uplifting Author Services
Interior Art: Alina Alilyushka

To Cat.
For telling me to never let anyone dull my sparkle.

For everyone dreaming of a hot British billionaire with golden retriever vibes…

May Parker Covington be the man of your dreams.

15 songs • 44 min 47sec • by MADISON FOX

FORBIDDEN GAME

1:11   0:47

        ⊕

Reading Playlist

Name of the song	Time	Artist
Hollywood Perfect	**2:43**	**Unknown Brain**
adonis	2:32	STIM
PEW PEW	3:19	Slushii, Tokyo Machine
Stuck On You	2:48	Stellar
Ocean Eyes	3:58	Highland, Salvo
Just Getting Started	2:27	Jim Yosef, Shiah Maisel
Out Of The Blue	3:18	Punctual
Blue Sugar	2:39	Ren Zotto
ORIGINAL STEPPA	2:06	OddKidOut, Heckler, Scrufizzer
Freefalling	2:33	Facading
Till I Met You	3:15	Said The Sky, good problem
Anchor	3:28	Abandoned, Ashley Drake
UNDEFEATED	2:53	XG, VALORANT
Cherry Bomb	3:30	NCT 127
Meant To Be	2:47	Rave New World

GAMING GLOSSARY

Any% – any percent; a commonly used speedrun term. Refers to the idea that, so long as you reach the end credit scene, your speedrun counts; it doesn't matter the percent completion of the game.

Battle royale – a game where there are hundreds of players who must eliminate each other while avoiding being trapped outside a shrinking "safe zone." The winner is the last player or team alive.

Bunny hopping – a technique used in video games to increase speed. The player jumps and moves forward at the same time.

Carry – when one person ends up being responsible for winning on behalf of their team or another player, normally because the team/other player is new, low-ranking, or just bad or lazy in comparison.

Clip/clipping – a type of glitch in a video game, commonly used by speedrunners. It is when two objects intersect, and it allows one to pass through the other, defying game physics.

Cozy games – a genre of games that are designed to be relaxing and feel good. Typically, they are nonviolent.

DLC – downloadable content. Refers to extra content that can be downloaded for the game that is separate from the main storyline.

Esports – electronic sports; a type of video game competition.

Easter eggs – hidden messages or features in a game.

Exploits – commonly mistaken as a glitch, exploits are when a weakness in the game mechanics are used to a player's advantage.

Fury Kill – when a player kills four enemies in rapid succession. A term coined from *Modern Warfare 3.*

Gamertag – a player's in-game screen name. Players often go by their gamertag instead of their real names.

Glitch – a temporary error in the game system.

Glitching – when a player uses an error in the game to give them an unfair advantage. Examples include running through walls (see: clipping) or going out-of-bounds.

Good game – what players say to each other after finishing a match/game, sometimes abbreviated as "GG."

K/D – "kill-to-death" ratio. This is used to measure performance in a video game.

Lag – a delay between the input of an action and when the action is completed. Commonly, when you are lagging, your character will glitch.

Lobby – an in-game waiting room.

Main – refers to a character/class you play most often or specialize in.

Merk/Merked – kill/killed.

MMO – massively multiplayer online. An online game in which many players play together on the same server.

Mod – a modification that is player made to a game. Not by the game developer.

Noob – refers to someone who is new at a game or lacks skill.

OP – overpowered.

Platinuming – getting one hundred percent completion in a game, not only in the main storyline but by also obtaining every achievement and trophy the game offers; a PlayStation origin term.

PvP – player versus player. A game where people play against each other (no computer-controlled opponents).

RP – role-playing. The act of playing an in-game character within the backstory you've assigned to them.

RPG – role-playing game. You create a character that you then level up through experience points.

Sandbox – refers to a game that is an open-ended world with non-linear gameplay. It allows freedom for the player to explore however they wish.

Sequence Break – A type of skip where a player will bypass the story progression by obtaining items or completing actions outside of the normal linear process. Commonly used in speedruns.

Skip/Skipping – in a speedrun, a skip is when you bypass something like a boss fight, main quest, or mandatory cutscene that is part of the natural story progression in order to complete it faster. A form of glitching.

Speedrun – the act of completing a game as fast as possible.

Swatting – the act of calling emergency services with a fake scenario to dispatch a large number of officers (typically, a SWAT team) to an address. In streaming, people will swat streamers while they are live streaming as a form of cyber harassment.

Troll – a person who posts content online with the aim of harassing, irritating, and/or provoking others.

VOD – video on demand. In streaming, this refers to storing a stream on another platform for people to watch after the stream has ended.

Chapter ONE

SYDNEY

"Why are you naked?"

The blond Adonis before me is lounging in bed, wearing nothing more than a pair of blue Burberry briefs. His laptop is open while he simultaneously plays a video game on his ninety-inch TV.

Parker Covington's toned body is on full display without a care in the world.

Which isn't an uncommon situation. I've never met a man who wears less clothing in his own apartment than Parker. And yet, he has a closet that is three times the size of my own and filled to the brim with custom designer clothing.

"The real question is, why aren't you?" He winks.

I roll my eyes with a sigh. "We have to be at your photo shoot in thirty minutes. Which means we needed to leave," I check my watch, "five minutes ago, and you're not dressed."

"I have a shoot?" Parker runs a hand through his platinum hair.

"I sent you a calendar invite last week. I even texted you a reminder this morning."

I have to fight not to grind my teeth. Working for three famous video game streamers created a little bit of stress.

"I never accept your calendar invites, love," he purrs in his posh London accent.

Make that a *lot* of stress.

Each of the three men I work for is difficult in their own way. Aleksander is the most popular, a natural leader, but he hates going to events and likes pissing people off. Jackson is the most well-spoken and levelheaded, but people are terrified of him because he looks like a giant grump. And Parker? Parker should be my golden goose. He is charismatic, funny, and attractive. He jumps at every opportunity I give him. But he lives in his own world and is as unpredictable as the rain in Seattle.

I walk forward and shut the laptop, looking him directly in those baby blues.

"Get dressed, or I will drag you to this photo shoot as you are."

"You act like that would be a punishment." He grins. "But fine, just give me a second."

Parker shifts off his California king and nudges past me, his hot skin brushing against my arm and sending sparks of electricity up it.

Unfortunately for me, all the men in The System look like they should belong on a teen drama, not streaming video games in dark rooms for hours on end each week. My radar for hot men has gotten all bent out of shape, thanks to them.

It's taken five years of working for The System for me to become somewhat immune to their sculpted bodies and flirtatious jokes.

Especially when it comes to Parker.

Especially after *That Night*.

My cheeks heat at the memory I fight every day to forget.

My professionalism is my armor, and I need to keep it on at all times, otherwise I'll be vulnerable to his attacks.

"All right, let's bounce."

Parker fluffs the collar of his white shirt and checks himself out in the mirror approvingly. I have no doubt in my mind that his entire outfit probably costs more than my biweekly paycheck.

I shoot off a quick message to our driver that we are on our way down before grabbing Parker by the elbow to usher him out of his room.

The System's penthouse apartment is stunning. Custom black tiles and pristine white walls. An open layout living room and kitchen that leads to a massive wrap-around balcony. I've slowly added a few plants over the years, but the space is minimalistic, decorated mainly with limited edition gaming memorabilia, neon signs, and an iconic The System poster.

I live on the fourteenth floor, and while it's a gorgeous apartment, it's nothing compared to theirs.

"Don't forget your mask," I remind Parker, punching the button for the elevator.

I startle when he waves the blue LED mask in my periphery.

"As if I would. It's only been three months. We haven't gotten that used to life without them yet." Parker tucks the mask under his arm while he toes on a pair of loafers.

Three months.

It's only been three months since Aleks, Parker, and Jackson took off their masks and revealed their identities to the world.

For years, these three men rose to the top of the video game world as the most popular faceless streamers—wearing matching LED masks as part of their brand so no one knew what they looked like.

Then, another streamer tried to blackmail them…and they decided they were sick of hiding. They were ready to step out of their own shadows. Level up their careers.

It was a mild PR nightmare for me, though.

I didn't sleep for a week after the reveal went live. My phone never left my hand, not even when I remembered to shower.

Sure, I've spent the last five years eating, breathing, and sleeping everything that is The System, but the way their fame has skyrocketed since the reveal is unlike anything I expected. With their faces out in the world, my job has become eight times harder, making sure that they don't get into trouble and that no one leaks private information.

Hell, just last week I had to stop a story from one of Jackson's exes from high school trying to get her five minutes of fame by telling one of the major news networks that he screwed her in the locker room after a swim meet.

The elevator arrives and we step in. I press the button

for G2 and prepare for my ears to pop during the descent. We live in the tallest apartment building in California. It was only built a few years ago and has sixty floors.

"We're going to be late," I tell Parker as we rocket down to the private parking garage.

"You know, if I drove, we could get there on time."

My pulse races just at the mere mention of him driving, anticipating the fear and the adrenaline. The man has a tendency to drive forty miles over the speed limit.

How he has never gotten a speeding ticket blows my mind.

If I wasn't too chicken to get my own license renewed, I would drive us places, but the idea of being behind the wheel again sends spiders across my skin.

"Francis is perfectly capable of driving us," I tell him as the doors open. "Besides, I informed the company that we were stuck in traffic and would be a little late."

The one good thing about living in Cali is that you can always use traffic as an excuse. No one bats an eye.

Our personal driver, Francis, opens the door to a white BMW. Parker holds his hand out to help me into the backseat, and I graciously accept it. No matter how sarcastic or boyish he can be, Parker Covington is, to his core, a gentleman.

Once we are settled, Francis begins our forty-minute drive to the studio. Parker mutters under his breath a few times at the slow pace, but I let my head loll against the headrest and shut my eyes. The exhaustion over the past few months has been unrelenting.

My phone buzzes in my pocket, and I let out a deep huff.

The world never stops spinning long enough for me to breathe more than one peaceful breath. I pull my phone from my purse and swipe it open without looking at the caller ID.

"This is Sydney Lake."

"Sydney, how are we doing?" Justin Rivera's taunting voice filters through the speaker, and I instantly feel the tingles of a migraine forming.

Justin calling is rarely a good sign. As one of the lead reporters for *Gamer Weekly*, he always has his pulse on the latest news, good and bad.

Although, in my case, it is normally bad.

My brain begins to whirl, filtering through the past forty-eight hours and questioning if there is anything my men have done that could have landed them in hot water.

Aleks and his girlfriend, Stevie, are in New York for a gallery showing, which I would have attended if I didn't need to monitor Parker and this shoot. Jackson hasn't left the apartment and has been grinding out stream hours to make up for the week he took off for his mother's birthday earlier this month. Other than attending a penthouse party Friday night, Parker has had a relatively quiet weekend for once.

My eyes slip to the man in the seat beside me.

Did something happen at the party that I missed?

Feeling my eyes on him, Parker tilts his head toward me and shoots me a grin. I sigh and stare out the window.

"I was doing relatively well until you called."

"Now is that the way to talk to someone who is nice enough to give you the heads up about a breaking story?"

Bad news. It's always bad news.

"I would be a lot nicer if you would allow me to stop the story from running."

"And ruin my integrity as a reporter? Never."

There's no stopping the audible scoff from escaping my lips.

Justin might always warn me about a story, but he only does so to taunt me. No amount of money offered ever stops it from printing. The only benefit is that sometimes he tells me with enough time to craft a counter statement. Sometimes being the key word. It's all dependent on his mood.

I tuck my phone between my shoulder and ear so I can pull my tablet from my handbag. I swipe it open and begin filtering through my recent media alerts for the boys.

Nothing sticks out other than some paparazzi photos of Aleks and Stevie showing a little too much PDA at the gallery opening. My eyes narrow in on his tattooed hand dangerously close to dipping under her dress.

I swear, if they got caught having sex in public—again—I am going to murder both of them.

"Spit it out, Rivera."

"Apparently, Parker Covington is about to be disinherited."

What?

The phone slips from my shoulder onto the seat, and my fingers freeze on the screen before me. A strange sourness swirls in my stomach. The word replays in my brain a few times before I whip my head around to Parker. His brows furrow at the death glare I'm giving him. Parker opens his mouth to speak, but I hold my finger up to shush him while I snatch my phone up with my other hand.

"What's the proof?"

"An internal source from Covington Hotels."

"Oh, really? An unnamed source?"

"I have no issue telling you their name. It's not a secret. Martin Jones."

"And when is this going live?"

"Three Eastern."

"That's in twenty minutes," I grind out.

"Care to comment?"

I hang up the call, not even deigning to give Justin a response.

"Who pissed in your Cheerios?" Parker asks.

"Martin Jones."

Parker pauses the game he's been playing on his phone and frowns at me. "Martin Jones? What does that knobhead want?"

Mother of God. Please let there not be a whiff of truth about this.

"Seems he's telling people you're about to be disinherited." My eyes narrow in on his features, cataloging exactly how he reacts. Parker has a stellar poker face and is a world-class charmer unless he is caught completely off guard. That's the only way to catch him in a lie.

His eyes widen slightly, and his brows lift a fraction.

Crap.

I let out a groan.

"Wait, it's not what you think. I'm not being disinherited." He holds his hands in front of his body, defending himself.

My fingers quickly type this man's name into the search engine.

"You're not listening to me." Parker snatches the tablet from my hands.

"I am." I reach out to grab it back, but he tucks it under his ass. "Parker, stop being a child. The story drops in less than fifteen minutes. I need to notify the rest of the team, and you need to alert your family that this is going to be everywhere."

A wave of panic rolls over his sea-blue eyes before hardening with determination.

"I'm not being disinherited."

I huff and sit back in my seat, crossing my arms. "All right, then why is this man saying otherwise?"

"Martin is one of the board members for Covington Hotels. His son has also been working there the past two years and making his way through the company." He begins to play with the two cartilage hoops in his ear, a nervous habit. "They don't like the fact that I'm blocking their way because I'm supposed to take over the CEO role from my father eventually. They've been trying to discredit me and force my hand. Turns out, I'm quite the threat." He grins at me, but when I continue to scowl, he drops it.

"So, what you're trying to tell me is that they're spreading the lie of your disinheritance in the hopes that you *will* be disinherited. Like some sort of twisted manifestation bs?"

It's an unhinged explanation, but a lot of the people around Parker tended to be a little unhinged.

"Probably." He picks up his bright blue phone and begins tapping away.

Parker is trying to hide it, but I can detect some unease leaking through the wall of confidence he normally wears.

I lean over and tug my tablet out from under his ass.

"I'll get a denial statement out and work with some of the papers to get our side pushed as soon as possible. I don't have to remind you not to interact with anything you see online, do I?"

"And risk you putting me in technological isolation again? No. I've learnt my lesson."

"That's what you said last time."

Last time being a month ago when he went out clubbing and photos were plastered all over social media of girls taking body shots off him, to which he responded online as being a "team player."

My fingers fly as I tap out an email to a few news stations and bloggers informing them that we deny the allegations.

"Mister Covington and Miss Lake, we are pulling up to our destination."

Francis' warm voice temporarily breaks through the puzzle I'm trying to sort in my mind. The story is set to go live in just a few minutes, and I don't need this to distract from the shoot. It's a major collaboration on the line.

I toss my phone and tablet into my handbag before pulling out some mints and popping one in my mouth. I hold one out to Parker.

"Do not breathe a word about this once we get inside. You're English, not Parker, for the next few hours."

He plucks the mint from my hand and crunches it between his teeth with an eye roll.

"Stop freaking out, Syd. The shoot is going to go perfectly. The camera loves me; I'm hot." He pulls his signature cocky grin before slipping his LED mask over his head and turning it on. The bright blue light shines back at me, and my nerves calm just a little.

When Parker becomes English, it's a lot easier to deal with him.

The car rolls to a stop, and I hop out while Francis opens the door on Parker's side. My eyes scan the area for any waiting paparazzi, but nothing obvious stands out.

The second we step inside the building, I feel my phone vibrate once, and after a few more steps, it vibrates again. By the time we make our way into the studio, my handbag is vibrating like a massage chair on steroids.

Once I make sure Parker is settled with the makeup crew and that he isn't at risk of wandering off, I pull my cellphone out.

It's burning up from the sheer number of notifications blasting across the scene.

The story is live, and his fans are losing their marbles.

I park myself on a nearby stool and swipe my phone open to descend into the cacophony of alerts.

My eyes instantly catch on a viral post, and ice shoots through my veins when I see why.

Aleksander Knight, leader of The System and all-around pain-in-my-ass, has decided to comment "RIP Bro" with a skull-face emoji.

I resist the urge to groan. Instead, I shoot a message to my assistant and inform her to login to Aleks' account to delete the comment. It won't stop any of the screenshots that have already been taken, but at least it will douse the flame.

I pull up Aleks' contact and call him.

The call goes directly to voicemail.

Frustration bubbles under my skin as I type in his girl-friend's phone number instead.

The call connects after the fifth ring, but all I hear is a bunch of bickering on the other side.

"Give it back!" Stevie shouts.

"No! She's just going to yell at me," Aleks growls.

"I'm going to yell at you."

"It's hot when you do it."

The arguing continues for another minute until there is a loud male grunt, and then Stevie's voice filters clearly through the speaker.

"Hey, Sydney. Sorry about that."

"It's fine. Just inform your boyfriend that's his second strike this month. One more and I'm putting him in tech isolation and adding another ten hours to his streaming quota."

"Got it," she sighs.

"And remember, no talking to—"

"The paparazzi, I know, I know," she cuts me off. "We've got dinner reservations tonight, but I promise to make him behave."

"All right, I'll see you when you get back."

"Buh-bye!"

I sigh deeply. I should have known he would pull something like that.

My headache begins seeping in again. I close my eyes and tilt my head back for a second before pulling myself together.

My phone buzzes and dread courses through my blood. I open my eyes to see a text from Justin and groan.

JUSTIN

Care to comment yet?

I give my knuckles a crack before firing off my crafted statement.

Today is not going to be my day.

Chapter TWO

PARKER

Every day, I wonder why we had to hire such an attractive publicist.

Sydney Lake is the biggest distraction known to man. Even in this room filled with people running back and forth and shouting directions, she stands out like a golden star.

Her cherry-red lips purse as her delicate fingers flick deftly over the tablet teetering on her knee. She's a fraction too short for the stool, her heels dangling in the air.

The benefit to wearing my mask during this shoot is that no one can tell that I've spent the last ten minutes watching her screw her nose up at her phone before huffing so heavily that her curtain bangs lift off her forehead.

"That's it. Like that. Perfect, English, you're perfect, a natural."

GAME

I can imagine Sydney rolling her eyes at the photographer's words. She's barely even spared me a glance since the shoot started.

I should be a little more insulted that she isn't paying attention to me, but it's nothing different. Ever since That Night, Sydney has been the picture of professionalism. She treats the lads and me equally and keeps our friendship at arm's length.

"Yes, the camera loves you!"

This time, I see Sydney roll her eyes at the photographer, and a small laugh rumbles in my chest.

While the camera might love me, these lights do not.

I'm unbearably hot right now, and sweat is beading around the edges of the mask. One of the advantages of revealing our identities was to prevent situations like this, and yet other than the first hour of the shoot, I've been stuck in the mask breathing in hot air. But they wanted EnglishCoffee, not Parker Covington, so who am I to complain?

"All right, English. Just a few more and we're done."

Thank God.

While I'm stoked for the Wyreless collaboration—they're one of the top gaming software companies, and they are creating a limited edition The System line, complete with headphones, gaming chairs, and even laptops—it's been hard to get my head in the game with all the rumors floating in the background.

It's a load of bullshit. My Covington inheritance isn't going anywhere. Martin and his son are just trying to stir up more drama around me. Even if they smeared my name in the mud, it's not like either of them would be next in line

15

for CEO anyway.

It's so stupid. This is a far reach, even for them.

So why are they?

My head aches as I try to put together the puzzle pieces without even knowing the final picture.

"Can I have you hold onto the mic for the next couple of shots, like you're speaking into the headphones?"

I position the mic down and do as the photographer instructs.

I have to give Wyreless credit for creating headphones that actually fit comfortably with our masks on, but I guess that's the point of a collab.

The lights flash a few more times before he calls out, "That's a wrap. Great job, English."

I give a small bow and thank everyone before stepping off set and ripping my mask off.

Fresh air enters my lungs, and my shoulders relax. One of the makeup artists holds out a damp towel, and I accept it with a wink, pressing it into my hot skin.

The relief is instant.

There's no way Aleks is going to be able to sit through this. He'll throw a fit and walk out. I'd bet my Ferrari on it.

"Come on, hotshot. I need to get you home." Sydney holds out my phone and a bottle of water.

I unscrew the cap and chug the cold liquid. My phone screen lights up with a million notifications, and the rock in my gut begins to harden, but I ignore it, stashing my phone in my front pocket.

"I had Francis park around back. It seems there are a few reporters out front."

"Always looking out for me." I grin, slinging my arm

around her shoulders as she weaves us around the set.

She pushes out of my grip with a grunt. "Stop, you're covering me in your sweat."

"That's what she said."

"Seriously, Parker." She gives me a blank stare from beneath her bangs.

Sydney acts as unaffected by me as ever, but that doesn't stop me from trying. Every once in a while, I catch her off guard and I see that glint in her eye—the one she denies.

"Seriously. People on the internet would pay good money to be covered in my sweat. You could even bottle it up, sell it on eBay. Eau de Parker."

She just huffs and picks up her pace, her heels clacking on the ground as she makes a beeline for the backstage door.

"I bet it would even go to auction. The bids would go into the thousands. All for something I'm giving you for free," I call out to her, admiring the way her pert ass sways in her short pencil skirt.

She's adorable when she's frustrated with me, which is her default emotion.

Once upon a time, I broke through her walls. But since then, she's reinforced her castle with steel, and no matter how hard I try, I can't seem to break through.

At least, not yet.

It only takes a few strides for me to catch up to her as she pushes the door open. The early fall air breezes past us instantly, and I have to squint my eyes against the afternoon light after so many hours indoors.

The white BMW is parked just a few feet away, but a

reporter pops out from seemingly nowhere to intercept us. His cameraman begins firing off bursts of photos. The shuttering clicks echo in the back of my mind as the reporter starts peppering me with variations of the same question.

"Fucking hell," I mutter under my breath, allowing myself a second of annoyance before slipping an easy smile on my face for the camera.

Sydney wraps her small hand around my wrist and begins marching us to the car, but the reporter just follows.

"Is it true that your family is disinheriting you because of your gaming career? How does that make you feel?"

"I'm still very much a Covington, and my family is supportive of my career," I promise the stoutly man.

"Parker," Sydney hisses, pushing me toward the door Francis is holding open. "Get in the car."

"Don't believe the rumors, mate," I call back with a dazzling smile before hopping onto my seat.

The door slams a hairsbreadth away from my nose and, not a minute later, a very disgruntled publicist slips onto the seat beside me.

"You know what I'm going to tell you."

"I didn't say anything bad." I shrug.

"You weren't supposed to say anything at all." Sydney rubs the spot between her brows with an audible sigh.

"It'll be fine, Syd." I reach over and give her knee a squeeze. Her skin is warm beneath the thin tights, and I let my hand linger for a second longer than necessary before pulling away.

She doesn't even bat a lash.

I fish my phone out of my pocket and reluctantly scan the notifications. There are hundreds crowding my screen, all a result of the stories that are circulating, but it's the one from my dad that hardens the rock in my gut.

DAD
Call me.

I didn't want to worry Sydney earlier, but there is no way my family didn't know that this story was dropping. Syd thinks she has enough contacts to get ahead of any breaking news involving us, but she has nothing on the team the Covingtons employ. Nothing against her, it's merely the simple math of British aristocracy.

But what this means is that someone in my family didn't see an issue with it…which is *not* a good sign.

I'm trying to wrack my brain for what the reasoning could be, but nothing makes sense.

I bypass my dad's message and settle for texting my older sisters instead.

PARKER
What am I walking into?

PAIGEY
Give dad a call :)

PARKER
Not helpful

PHOEBE
Call dad

Now

I stifle a groan. All right, that just made things worse.

The cards are slowly stacking up against me, one by one, but I don't even know what game I'm playing.

Fuck.

My finger hovers over the dial button before tapping down. It barely rings once before my dad's deep baritone filters through the speaker.

"Took you long enough. You are aware it is almost one in the morning."

Shit. I forgot they went back to Kensington this week.

"In my defense, I was in a photo shoot the last few hours."

"I hope it went well. You'll have to send us the pictures when you can. You know your mother will find some way to frame them."

"It did, and I will."

There's a long pause of silence, and it does nothing to calm the growing worry in my gut. My dad is never silent. No one in our family ever is. We are always in constant communication, updating each other on our lives. Family always comes first for us, and there is no one we trust more than each other. Which is why this entire situation has my insides shriveling.

"Your grandfather is in town," he finally says.

"He's in London?"

"No, California."

I don't even know the last time my grandfather left the estate in Buckinghamshire, let alone England.

"And what's he doing in California?" My tone does nothing to hide the impending dread swirling through my blood.

"Getting dinner with you tonight; his assistant should have emailed you the details."

"He flew all the way to California just to have dinner with me." I see Sydney's attention perk up out the corner of my eye. I give her a wink before subtly turning the volume down on my phone. "Any chance you can give me a hint of what to expect?"

"Unfortunately, I can't. Your grandfather has only afforded me the barest of details, but I know the board isn't too happy."

"Wonderful." The sarcasm drips from my tongue.

"Be smart, Parker, and keep your head about you. That's the best advice I can give you."

"Thanks, Dad."

"I'll talk to you tomorrow."

"Love you."

"Love you, too."

The line goes dead, and so does my hope.

I'm beginning to think that coming to dinner was a very bad idea.

The restaurant is empty. Other than the employees, there's not a single other patron inside this establishment. It's a Saturday night downtown at one of the most renowned seafood restaurants, The Bay. It shouldn't be empty. Which can only mean that my grandfather has taken it upon himself to rent out the entire place.

This is *so* not going to be a good conversation.

I should have faked sick…pretended I caught food poisoning or something.

I reach up and absently spin my hoop piercings while tapping my foot against the hardwood floors.

I spent the entire ride over here trying to figure out how tonight was going to go down. My bike couldn't go fast enough to combat the barrage of ideas pounding through my head, each one worse than the next. Something tells me this dinner has everything to do with that damn rumor.

Reaching forward, I grasp the delicate stem of the flute in front of me and down the remaining champagne inside. The crisp bubbles travel through my system and mingle with the butterflies in my gut, popping around them.

A gust of wind signals the arrival of my grandfather, and I promptly stand up as he walks through the door.

Philip Covington is a formidable man. The eighty-year-old looks not a day over sixty with a full head of silver hair and deeply corded muscles.

He shucks off his coat, and one of the hostesses snaps it up instantly before another one steps in to take his hat. My grandfather's eyes scan the restaurant briefly before landing on me. He gives me a dip of his head before strolling over.

A thin, wiry man reveals himself from behind my grandfather's figure. Frank, his right hand, is carrying a worrisome briefcase in his hand.

A wrinkly smile breaks out across my grandfather's face, and the storm brewing within me calms a touch.

"Come here, boy." He encases me in a giant hug, patting my back, and I grip him tightly in return. "It's been far too long. You never come home."

"I'll be back in a few months for the holidays," I remind him as he releases me. My grandfather gestures for me to take a seat while Frank pulls out a chair for him to sit on.

"Christmas is the only time of the year I know I'll see you. You need to make an effort to come back more often. Your nana misses you."

"And here I thought it was you missing me." I give him a wry grin, and he scoffs.

"I love you, boy, but you're a troublemaker. Having you home promises something uncouth on the horizon. Your nana might be forgiving, but I still remember that time your bum was on display in the Venus Fountain."

"I was seventeen."

"You were seventeen," he deadpans.

One drunken night with the lads in Chelsea, and I'm still paying for it eight years later.

A waitress comes out to deposit an assortment of fresh oysters and caviar on the table before refilling my champagne glass and pouring one for my grandfather. Grandfather takes a small spoon of the deep black caviar before depositing it onto the back of his hand, letting it warm briefly, and then tipping it to his lips. He hums in approval before taking a sip of champagne.

I repeat the same motions, picking up one of the mother-of-pearl spoons. The slight saltiness of the caviar pearls melts onto my tongue with a mild undercurrent of richness.

We make small talk, exchanging stories about what we've been up to lately while polishing off the appetizers. All the while, the true purpose of our dinner looms in the background like an ex-girlfriend at a bar.

It's not until the waitress removes our empty plates that Frank clears his throat and my grandfather sighs. His expression turns weary for a minute before steeling. He turns from jovial grandfather into the hardball founder of the Covington Hotel conglomerate in mere seconds.

"We have to talk about your future, Parker."

His words are like a vice to my lungs, squeezing them tight.

Fuck.

This is the exact conversation I didn't want to have.

Grandfather laces his hands and places them on the table in front of himself. "I'm sure you saw some of the tabloid stories today."

"I did."

"And your thoughts?"

"That they were just that, stories." I make sure to keep my tone neutral and light.

He hums, taking a sip of champagne.

"I'm afraid they're not. Alas, I'm not pleased with how the information was leaked, and that is another issue I'm dealing with. Nonetheless, we must have a conversation regarding your inheritance."

I feel like throwing up.

"I don't understand. Why?"

"Because the circumstances have changed."

"Changed, how?"

"Your career is no longer anonymous."

"There are no rules to my inheritance. There's no stipulation that my career must stay anonymous. That choice is and was entirely up to me."

"True. However, you did not consult me before you

decided to make your career so…public." He frowns, and I can't help but avert my gaze briefly.

Guilt prickles my neck. It always does when I think back to three months ago.

I was so excited to come clean, to tell the world that EnglishCoffee was Parker Covington. That the rich party boy who everyone thought was neglecting his familial duties is actually one of the most successful video game streamers of this generation. That I am one of the top speedrunners and have people who look up to me as the goal of what to achieve.

I was the one who came up with the idea to reveal our identities to the world, and I was the one who convinced Aleks and Jackson that it was the best course of action. Even though, deep down, it was for my own benefit.

I know I can be the best, but I couldn't do that if I kept to the shadows as a faceless gamer. There were so many opportunities slipping by because of the masks we wore.

"There were circumstances that made it necessary," I tell my grandfather, fully knowing he was aware of the blackmail situation. "Plus, it has created additional opportunities that will lead to higher success. Our income has almost doubled in the past twelve weeks, and we don't expect a plateau anytime soon based on the trajectory." I try speaking to his business eye, focusing on the profitability over anything else.

"That is true. However, your decision caused some wrinkles within the company. Stakeholders are worried that you are forfeiting your place as heir, and there is a power play stirring that I am not entirely happy with. Martin Jones is barking at my heels again like a damn yippy dog."

A part of me wants to ask why they even care. What difference does it make whether I step into the family business or not?

But that's just me being childish because I know the answer. I was raised in this family, and I've been part of the business since I was a child. I know that, despite the iron fist my father and grandfather rule Covington Hotels with, there are some people under them who wish to rise to a greater role. A role that will always be barred from them because of me.

"So, what do you need from me?"

"Ideally, I would need you to confirm your place as heir and start work at the company within the year."

The nausea increases, and the champagne turns sour.

"But I don't want that."

"I know," he sighs.

"If you need a Covington heir, why not just make it Phoebe? She's already been with the company for six years, and she's done wonders. I've heard the rumors about her taking on the CFO position before the next fiscal year ends. It wouldn't be hard to transition her to CEO one day."

"I've considered it. Your sister, for as whip smart as she may be, is a bit, how should I put this," he rolls his wrist, "brisk."

I snort in response.

My two sisters are night and day in personality. Paige is the middle child and sweet as flowers. Unless you get her in the court room; then she'll pull out the trusted Covington iron fist to win for her clients. Phoebe, however, is an acquired taste. She's blunt and crass to a fault, but her loyalty is like no other. If you need something to get done, Phoebe will find a way, no matter the cost. Even I don't question her methods, lest it be the day I get questioned by MI6. People are scared of her more than they like her.

"A CEO doesn't need to be likeable."

"True, but you are preferred among the stakeholders. You are a natural charmer and negotiator."

"The stakeholders are a bunch of old dudes who just don't want a woman as CEO."

"Parker," he warns.

"I'm just speaking facts." I shrug. "You know she would be the better fit; you just don't want to stir the water with those stakeholders."

"Well, those very stakeholders are holding a vote soon."

My grandfather gestures to Frank, who opens his briefcase on a nearby table before passing a stack of papers over. Grandfather leafs through them briefly before laying them in piles before me. My eyes snag on the numbers before me, adding them up and connecting the various documents together to form a story.

"While your profession is profitable, Covington Hotels is a multi-billion-dollar company. You would make more with us than your projected trajectory as a streamer." He taps on one of the papers before me.

"It's not about the money. I already have that."

"Parker, it's always about the money. And that's exactly what the stakeholders want to take away from you."

Realization dawns on me.

"They want me to forfeit my shares."

"Correct."

"That's ridiculous!"

"To them, what's ridiculous is a man with majority ownership over the business running around playing video games instead of having involvement in said business."

"But I'm a Covington."

"You are, which is why I agree with them."

Betrayal slides along my skin like a deadly kiss.

"You can't be serious."

"Parker, your career is not exactly one of prestige."

"I'm one of the top video game streamers in the world."

"It's still just playing games. It's not as though you're not the head chef at a five-star Michelin restaurant or an Emmy award-winning actor. What do you have to show for it other than followers on the internet?"

The dismissal stings and burns.

"But Dad—"

"Your father coddled you. He let you pursue this career too far, allowing you to come all the way to America." He shakes his head. "You have the mind for this business, Parker. I don't want to see you waste it."

"But I don't want it."

"Then you have to be prepared to sacrifice something in return. You either join the company or you forfeit your shares, and with them, a portion of your inheritance."

A portion? My shares were worth billions.

Billions.

I'd be a Covington but in name only. I'd lose my power, my safety.

I've been able to pursue my gaming career because I have the Covington name to fall back on. I have my inheritance, my family, the hotels, all as a net to catch me in case I slip up.

They are trying to take away my contingency plan.

I struggle to swallow. My throat is dry as a bone at the impending doom. With a steady hand, I grasp my champagne flute and take a large gulp. Grandfather polishes off his seabass and turns to whisper something to Frank.

My phone vibrates, and I discreetly slip it off the edge of the table and into the palm of my hand before swiping it open.

Hope pounds in my chest as I zero in on the small words.

SYDNEY

Just got confirmation. You're in the bracket for the speedruns at DCS. I'll work with Mathias on your training schedule and qualifying events. You have twelve weeks.

You're welcome. I worked my magic.

And work her magic she did.

Bloody hell.

This could be it.

DCS, the Divizion Championship Series, is an annual gaming tournament run by Divizion, one of the top video game companies worldwide. It's not as big as the annual *Gods League* World Championship, but it is the largest game-diverse championship. The prize pool is three million, and last year they had twenty-five million unique viewers watching it online. It occurs every December, and on top of the esports tournaments they run, they have the largest speedrun tournament in the world.

Across three separate speedruns, you need to have the lowest collective time to win—but to even qualify for the series, I'd need to win three out of five mini tournaments held across the country beforehand. I've never been able to participate before because I can't speedrun while wearing the mask.

The aim of a speedrun is to complete a game as quickly as possible, and you need to be at your sharpest in order to make sure your reflexes are quick enough to not mess up. Even a second's worth of hesitation can cause you to lose drastically, and the visibility is pretty shit through the blue LED of my mask.

Ever since we revealed our identities, I have been begging Sydney to get me on the roster. She told me she would try, but that I shouldn't get my hopes up because we were late in the season. Clearly, whatever strings she pulled worked.

If I win the speedrun tournament, I'll be recognized as the best speedrunner in the States, and potentially the world.

I'll be able to prove to my grandfather and the board that my career is successful, that I'm not just *playing games*.

PARKER
Ur an angel. Thank u

SYDNEY
I know.

My grandfather clears his throat, and I snap my head up to meet his quizzical stare. In my distraction, the waitress has cleared our plates, and a lone pot of tea has been left to brew on the center of the table.

"So, what shall it be, Parker?"

I grin at my grandfather as I pull up the event page for DCS and slide my phone across the table to him. He adjusts the frames of his glasses while squinting down at the screen.

"What am I looking at?"

"My counter offer."

He raises a brow before settling back in his seat. "All right, let's hear it," he says, gesturing for me to go on.

I puff out my chest and lean forward. "It's the annual gaming championship held by Divizion—who are arguably the top gaming company in the last decade. Part of their event is a speedrun tournament. The winner is recognized as one of the best speedrun players in the world, on top of a major cash prize. It's like getting a Michelin."

"Interesting. And you believe you can win?"

Do I?

It won't be easy. As confident as I am in myself, I know there are gaps in my gameplay.

But I have to try.

I give a sharp nod. "Without a doubt."

Grandfather taps his fingers rhythmically against the table while I wring mine nervously under the tablecloth.

Frank produces a tablet from God-knows-where and begins swiping across the screen, showing something to grandfather. Grandfather nods his head at the slides in front of him, rapping his knuckles on the smooth glass every minute or so, muttering words under his breath.

"All right, Parker, I'll entertain your idea. If you win

this championship, if you prove that there is worth to your career, I'll veto the board. But if you fail, I will do nothing to help you. You will forfeit your shares and ties to the Covington conglomerate by year end."

Nerves spin and swirl in my gut, but I nod like a damn bobblehead.

"Understood."

"Wonderful. Frank, can you organize that and get the car from valet?"

"Yes, sir." Frank flips the tablet case closed, gathers the documents scattered across our table, and places them all in the briefcase before swiveling on his wingtips and power walking away.

Grandfather sits up and pours us both a cup of peppermint tea. The minty liquid cools my tongue while warming the center of my chest. A sense of peaceful determination settles over me.

For the first time since I sat down, it doesn't feel like the world is hanging by a thread.

For a second, I let the mask slip and entertain the devilish smirk that tugs at the corner of my lips.

Three months might not be enough time for the average person, but I'm not average.

I'm Parker Covington, and I don't lose.

Chapter THREE

SYDNEY

A small scream escapes my lips.

The engine of the Porsche revs loudly, reverberating through my body, as Parker steps on the gas, narrowly avoiding the car merging into our lane. You would think we were running late with the miles he keeps racking up on the speedometer. But no. We are actually going to be early to our boxing class for once.

As much as it terrifies me, I can't even get too mad because Parker maneuvers the car with the finesse of a seasoned Formula 1 driver. He's probably the safest risky driver I've met—a complete contradiction.

The Porsche glides around a sharp corner, and I white-knuckle the bright blue seatbelt across my chest as my body sways to the right.

Just a few more minutes, I tell myself.

I stare down at my workout leggings and begin playing connect the dots with the glossy black stars printed on them to pass the time. The loud bass music playing steadily thrums against my skin, and my heart rate slows to match the beat.

Finally, the car pulls wide, and I look up to see Parker swing into a parking spot right out front of our boxing studio. I release the death grip I have on the seatbelt and flex my hand a few times to relieve the tightness.

"Ready to crush it today?" Parker gives me a lopsided grin before ducking out of the car.

I sigh before cracking the door open and getting out of the car while Parker pops the hood to grab our gloves, his grin still in place.

Maybe I can get him to channel some of this energy into a game later. He is going to have to seriously increase his hours to prepare for the championship.

I spent hours last night booking flights and accommodations for five smaller tournaments over the next twelve weeks so he can get a feel for playing on a stage while also accumulating the three speedrun wins he needs to cement his place at the championship.

As confident as Parker may be in himself, there is a large difference between completing a speedrun alone in the safety of your room versus a high profile, public competition with thousands of people watching you from the stands.

It's like giving a work presentation virtually versus in person; there is something about the physical aspect that adds an extra layer of pressure. The last thing I want is for him to get performance anxiety.

I snort at the idea of Parker Covington ever having performance anxiety.

"Oi, you coming or not?" Parker calls from the open door to the studio.

My cheeks flush, and I shake off the thought, jogging to catch up to him. He keeps the door propped open, and I slip under his arm and into the cool confines of Jax's Boxing House.

The smell of fresh sweat, antiseptic wipes, and worn leather envelops me.

I've been coming here almost weekly with Parker for a little less than a year now. It all started after a bet gone wrong, which was my own fault. Anyone who knows Parker knows not to bet with him. But I was caught up in the haze of the latest reality show I was watching; my internet had gone out during the finale, and I didn't have the patience or time to fix it, so I went up to the boys' apartment.

Parker had just finished a stream and was sprawled out on the couch playing on his Switch.

He wasn't even paying attention, hadn't seen an episode in his entire life, and yet he had the audacity to say that my favorite couple was not going to win and that instead the couple that I hated would come out on top. It was ludicrous. Especially since that other couple had broken up four times that season, and *my* couple had become exclusive just two episodes prior.

So, when Parker offered up a bet, I wasn't exactly in my most professional mindset. I'd turned off for the day... and I agreed. Suffice it to say, I lost the bet, my couple broke up two weeks after the finale, *and* I got roped into a month of boxing lessons with Parker.

The only positive was that I didn't hate it. It was a lot of fun, even though I was miles behind anyone else in the gym. When the month was up and I had my first Sunday free, I found myself out in front of the boxing studio anyway.

"How's my star pupil doing?" Jax claps me on the shoulder.

I crane my neck up at the buff person before me. I swear, everyone in this gym has a solid five inches on my height. At five foot five, I'm only a little shorter than the average woman, and yet everyone here seems to defy the rules of logic.

"She's ready to kick butt." I smile.

"Perfect, because I have a surprise if you do well today."

The smile slips off my face. I deal with enough surprises with The System; the last thing I want is to deal with them outside of work.

"Don't look so worried. Let's warm up first."

I trail behind Jax as they lead me farther into the gym, toward the back corner where I normally train.

Parker has already slipped off, and my eyes track him as he hops onto a treadmill. His strong calves flex and his arms pump as he gains speed.

I shake myself and grab a jump rope to begin my warmup routine, alternating between sets of thirty and dynamic stretching. Once I've worked up a light sweat, I start some rough shadowboxing and lose myself in the repetition.

My brain is always working at a mile a minute; it feels like it never shuts off, except here.

I'll never admit it to Parker, but losing that bet was one of the best things to happen to me in a long time. I'm well aware that my work has taken over my life, to such an extent that I struggle to ever switch off. I can't help it. In the silence, my brain just drifts back to the boys, to what they are doing, to what they *might* be doing.

When I first started working for The System, they had a tendency to end up in the worst possible situations every time they left the house in their masks.

Aleksander was fighting in clubs, mouthing off to anyone who got close. Jackson would disappear, only to get photographed leaving the houses or apartments of very high-profile women at all hours, requiring copious NDAs. Parker was spraying champagne, dancing on tables, and climbing fences into restricted areas—including the rooftop pool at the Kelton Hotel Vegas, where he threw an extremely illegal party with thirty models.

They were losing sponsorships left, right, and center—not that they needed them with how much their monthly streaming income was. But after Parker wound up on a stripper pole with Aleks throwing money at him, I found that it was just easier to have them stop attending events and promo parties unless it was absolutely necessary. To have them just be Blade, English, and Shield while they were streaming or filming, and then leaving them to be Aleks, Parker, and Jackson in their free time.

It was their bored resentment at events that fueled half the situations they found themselves in, trapped in their masks. I sympathized with them, even though it was a headache.

It solved a lot of issues, and I only had to send security when they went to major award ceremonies. My stress levels decreased by half after that first year, but even now, they are still higher than your average publicist.

I try to decompress during the week when they aren't streaming by watching reality shows and listening to unsolved crime podcasts, anything that will transport me into the drama of someone else's life. I even have a standing date every Tuesday with Lee and Deer, two female streamers who are good friends of the guys, to watch the latest episode of this haunted house investigation YouTube channel while we gossip.

However, my reprieve was short-lived because now that The System's identities are known, I have to keep tabs on them at all times, not just when they are their masked personas. It is five years ago all over again…maybe even worse.

My stress levels are skyrocketing, and I am barely sleeping.

Which is why I need these boxing lessons.

In these last six months, these two hours of kickboxing have given me a small slice of sanity. Jax might work me to the point of my muscles wanting to melt off my bones, but that single-minded focus in making sure my form is correct, that my punch is sharp, that my kick is high enough, is all worth it.

Jax pulls me out of my warm-ups to begin our training. We switch it up every week, sometimes focusing more on kickboxing and other times more traditional boxing. I definitely have a preference toward kickboxing because I always get a bolt of satisfaction when my foot connects with the pad. The instant gratification is addicting.

We go at it for almost an hour and a half before stopping. My lungs feel like they are expanding out of my chest, and I know my cheeks are flushed a bright pink. My quads feel like jelly, but it's my biceps that are really screaming at me from the countless uppercut combos Jax had me perfect. I swear they pushed me way harder today.

I peel off my gloves, tossing them on a nearby bench before grabbing my towel to dab the back of my neck. A quick peek at the floor-to-ceiling mirrors lining the right side of the gym confirms what I already know. My bangs are slick with sweat and sticking to my forehead at thirteen different angles. I attempt to fix them, rubbing the towel against my hairline vigorously.

I toss the towel back on the bench with a huff before trudging to the fountain to fill up my water bottle.

As I squirt the cold water into my mouth, my eyes drift across the gym to the men battling it out in the main boxing ring.

Parker's platinum hair flops around as his body bounces back and forth. Pure mischief glints in those icy blues as he grins around his mouthguard.

He lands a quick three-punch combo, clipping his opponent's jaw with the final jab and sending him staggering back. Sweat glistens across his pale skin, shining like ice. My eyes are drawn to his contracting muscles, and I watch as they flex with each extension of his arm.

Try as I might, I can't deny that Parker is attractive. It's just a fact.

My stomach lurches for a moment when Parker's opponent finds an opening with his right cross, and I watch in slow motion as the glove connects with his abdomen. His blond brows furrow with pain, and his lip curls back ever so slightly before he shakes it off with a curved grin. He says something to the guy. I can't hear from this far away, but his opponent's eyes narrow and Parker bounces back a few steps, putting a little distance between them.

It only takes a few more moments until Parker slips past his defenses and clocks him with a left hook just below his ribs. He pulls his opponent close and continues to land punch after punch until a whistle is called.

The two split apart, breathing heavily. Parker claps the guy on his back with a bright smile, and the stocky man gives him a tense grin. He probably has a solid thirty pounds of muscle on Parker, but if there's anything I've learned, it's that you can't underestimate Parker.

He's a pretty boy with a lot of power.

Parker lifts the bottom of his T-shirt with one hand to wipe the sweat from his forehead. My eyes linger for a second on the pale V of his hips, which is a second longer than necessary. He doesn't have the same defined arms as Aleks or the thickly corded quads Jackson sports. Parker is more model fit, the causal kind that almost comes off effortlessly attractive.

It's annoying.

He's annoying.

I reinforce my mental barriers, the very ones that have helped me survive five years working with The System without losing my head.

I spot Jax walking out of their office with a frame in hand.

"Ready for your surprise?"

"Not really." I press my lips together tightly.

They just chuckle as they walk past me. I let out a deep breath before following them to the front of the gym.

They stop right by the wall that separates the small lobby from the rest of the gym. My chest tightens as they lift the frame onto the empty nail on the wall.

My own face smiles back at me with the words "Rookie of the Season" painted in gold on the bottom of the frame.

"Really?" My voice comes out with a slight squeak, but I can't even be embarrassed by it.

"Really." Jax smiles, the skin around their eyes crinkling with pride. "You've improved a lot these last few months, Sydney. You even managed to get that right cross past me last week."

"Jax is right. Your spinning back kick almost puts mine to shame." My head whips around at the introduction of Parker's voice to find him peeling off his gloves. "Soon you'll be able to spar with me. What a privilege that'll be for you." He grins down at me before tossing his arm around my shoulders.

My body heats uncomfortably under its weight.

Sparring with Parker sounds like an awful idea.

"Thank you both."

"You more than deserve it." Jax gives me a pat on the shoulder before passing by us. "I'll see you next week, champ."

I take another look up at the photo on the wall. Pride warms my chest while the perfectionist within me drinks in the accomplishment.

"Not a bad surprise, right?" Parker gives me a squeeze, and I roll my eyes at him before slipping out of his grip.

"Don't get any ideas," I warn him, heading back into

the gym so I can stretch.

Parker trails behind me like a lost puppy, chittering away.

"Come on, love. Don't be so modest."

I plop onto the floor and spread my legs before leaning forward and stretching out my inner thighs. Relief tingles through my overworked muscles as I go about my cool down routine. Parker flings his blue gloves next to mine on the bench before joining me.

He sits just a fraction too close, his long legs only inches away from my own. I try to scoot away without making it obvious.

If it weren't for the fact that I've seen how precise he is while playing games, driving, or even boxing, I'd think he had depth perception issues. He just seriously lacks any personal boundaries.

Parker starts to mimic my movements, and I feel his eyes acutely on my body.

I press up into a downward dog and begin walking out my calf muscles. I focus on the way they are screaming at me to distract myself from the looming blond in my presence. Parker doesn't always join me for my final stretches, but when he does, he glues himself to my side.

I hate it.

I hate it because it makes me feel a way I don't want to feel.

I'm so lost in the repetition of left heel down, right heel down, repeat, that I don't even register the words until a fraction too late.

"Nice ass, sweetheart. Pop it a bit higher, why don't you?"

My elbows falter in shock, and I lose my balance. My forearms hit the mat, and milliseconds later, my knees follow suit. Confusion and embarrassment momentarily run through my brain as the words repeat themselves. I'm not even sure if they were meant for me, but the pit in my gut says otherwise.

"You wanna repeat that, mate?"

I pull myself out of the trance and tilt my head up.

Parker is no longer next to me; instead, he is standing inches away from a hulking guy in a muscle tee that barely covers his artificially bronzed chest. There are two similarly dressed, jacked-up men behind him. I've never seen them here before.

"Yeah, I said nice ass. It was a compliment," the main guy sneers.

"Sounded a little more slimy than that," Parker counters.

I see someone whip out their cellphone and it instantly triggers my publicist persona. I'm on my feet and tugging on Parker's arm in record time.

"Enough, let's just go."

Parker's eyes blaze like the hottest fires in hell as he looks down at me. I see the fierce determination, and my heart softens for a split second before turning back to ice.

"Cellphone." I say the word through a gritted smile.

His eyes flick around before landing on the girl by the speed bags, his sharp jaw ticking with annoyance. His chest huffs with a sigh, and I relax as I watch the reluctant resignation pass through him.

Parker swoops down to pick up our gloves before tucking me protectively under his arm and stalking away.

"Pussy."

The word floats through the air, and I feel Parker freeze. I open my mouth to stop him, but he's already pushing the gloves into my hands and spinning from me. He doesn't make a move to walk back to the guy; instead, he smiles, running his tongue over the top of his teeth.

"What's your name?" His tone is calm, playful even.

The guy looks at him in confusion.

"Your name. You have one, don't you?" Parker tilts his head and shoves his hands into his pockets.

The guy eyes him warily, eyes bouncing from Parker to me to his friends. "Boyd." He puffs out his chest, gaining his confidence back. "Boyd Frent."

Parker purses his lips, nodding his head a few times. Then, without saying another word, he turns around and replaces his arm across my shoulders.

I follow his lead in a trance. My mind is still whirling by the time he pushes the door open and the fall breeze whips around us.

I don't bother fighting against Parker as he ushers us toward his car. The bright blue Porsche sticks out among the white Teslas. He opens the door for me and doesn't move until I'm settled safely within.

Parker slips into the driver's side before reaching over and grabbing the gloves that I am still absentmindedly clutching to my chest. He tosses them into the backseat and then starts the engine.

"You all right?" he asks, his right hand coming down to squeeze my knee briefly. The movement causes electricity to crackle up my thigh.

"I'm fine." Honestly, I'm more concerned about him.

It's not like I wasn't catcalled on the street just last week. "Are you okay?"

"Oh, I'm brilliant." He shoots me a bright smile, bringing his hand back to the steering wheel as he peels out of the parking lot.

"Really? Then what was that whole thing back there?"

"Just a bit of friendly conversation."

"Sure. And I'm the Queen of England."

"Sensitive subject, Sydney." He throws me his hurt puppy dog eyes.

"Just don't do anything stupid," I huff.

"Never," he replies.

The smile tugging across his face tells a different story. There's a serpentine quality to it.

Against my better judgment, I push the uneasy feeling aside. I pop the glove box and pull our cellphones out. Our one rule is that we never bring them into the gym with us. It's another one of the reasons why I'm able to decompress there…normally.

Today, I'm not feeling as relaxed as I usually am when I leave the gym.

Both of our phones are littered with notifications, but that's nothing new.

I place Parker's phone on the center console before unlocking my own and scanning for any pressing updates. There isn't anything glaringly obvious, and I silently thank God that the world, once again, didn't burn down during my boxing lessons.

Parker snatches his phone up immediately and begins typing something. My heart lurches, and I snap it out of his hand.

"Don't text and drive." My panic is thinly veiled.

Guilt flashes in his eyes as he regrips the steering wheel with both hands. "Sorry, Syd. Sorry, I forgot."

I will my heart rate to calm down. Driving safety is my one nonnegotiable. There are enough idiots on the road that you can't trust, that you can't control, that you can't stop. The only thing you can control is how you drive. Even a moment of distraction can end everything—has ended everything.

I let the pain wash over me and follow my old therapist's advice to tap my fingers against one another rhythmically. It's practiced at this point and keeps me grounded in the present. Years have passed, but there are still moments that trigger me.

One of the only reasons I reluctantly get in the car with Parker is that, despite his speed limit aversion, he's an extremely safe driver and has certificates to prove it.

Except right now.

"Syd, I'm really sorry."

There's nothing but pure regret in his tone, and I let out a sigh. Even I can't stay mad at him for long. My heart has a soft spot for him no matter how hard I try to harden it.

"It's fine. What were you doing anyway?"

His lips thin, and my senses go on high alert. I hold up his phone and key in the code. An unsent text message sits on the screen to a contact name I don't recognize. The words Parker typed, however, I do recognize.

BOYD FRENT.

"I literally just told you not to do anything stupid." I click the phone off and toss it back onto the center console.

"Dealing with Boyd is not stupid. In fact, it's very

smart."

"Oh yeah? And how exactly do you plan to *deal* with Boyd? Get his body chopped up into tiny pieces and thrown into the bay? Or maybe you'll feed him to the pigs. They are one of the most effective methods of body disposal."

"First, you really need to tone down those crime podcasts. Secondly, no. The Covingtons are not in the murder business. However," he shoots me a quick grin before turning his attention back to the road, "we have a lovely network of blacklisting."

"Parker, that's ridiculous. You can't possibly blacklist him from every gym."

"What's ridiculous is someone thinking they can disrespect what's mine with their filthy words."

My brows twitch together, and I stare at him out of the corner of my eye. Confusion laces its way through my system until it hits those bubbles sitting in my lower stomach.

"Mine?"

He swallows, and his knuckles tighten on the wheel. "Yeah, you're my publicist."

Right…

That's what I thought.

And yet those little bubbles burst, leaving an empty feeling inside me.

I shake off the feeling, refusing to look at it closer, knowing that it can only bring me trouble.

Parker reaches forward and turns up the volume of the British EDM rap music blasting through the car. I'm a country music girl, but I've become well acclimated to the music preferences the guys have. It's all some variation of heavy bass music.

I let the music thump around me as I stare out the window at the passing ocean. Sunshine glints off the water, and it makes me think of the man next to me.

My life has always been bubbling rivers, rolling hills, and quiet storms. Parker is a crashing wave, a flash of lightning, that first pile of leaves in the autumn you can't help but stomp in.

He is a golden ray piercing through my cloudy sky.

The sunshine to my ice.

I've always been attracted to the sun, but I can't afford to let it scorch me.

And there is not a doubt in my mind that Parker's heat would burn me alive.

Chapter FOUR

PARKER

I pull out my pistol and shoot three enemies before slipping into the elevator. My fingers flick over the keyboard in quick succession, tapping out commands at a breakneck pace as I prepare for the upcoming skip.

My eyes flick ever so briefly to the timer perched to the right of my monitor.

Two hours, fourteen minutes, and thirty-six seconds.

I smirk.

I'm sitting forty-six seconds faster in comparison to yesterday's run, but I can't get ahead of myself. If I don't time my next move perfectly, I won't be able to clip my character between the elevator floor and the map below, which will cost me precious seconds.

I watch the elevator move on the screen and keep my left middle finger poised on the W key while my left pinky hovers over the SHIFT key and my right pointer waits on the mouse. My mind is silent in anticipation. A small flash of orange appears in the upper right corner—my signal— and I hit each key in succession.

SHIFT. W. CLICK.

My heart stops for a solid second as I wait to see whether I was quick enough.

My character falls through the bottom of the elevator and lands in the basement of the building I was sent to infiltrate. I let out a small sigh of relief at the successful sequence break before zeroing back in on the task on hand, my left hand moving quickly to rush my character to pick up a package sitting in the back corner.

This room is where the bomb is being kept, and that clip just allowed me to bypass the entire maze of enemies and locked doors I would've needed to beat to get here— something that would've taken an average player an hour or so to get through. If I'd messed up that move, I would've needed to reset to my last save, which would easily add on those forty-six seconds I've managed to shave off the run so far.

That's the thing about speedrunning, every move counts. If you mess up even once, it could ruin everything.

Speedrunning doesn't really make a lot of money out- side of streaming, but it's always been my favorite subsect of the gaming space. Some people just enjoy beating their own times, but I love the challenge of finding new ways to complete the game faster. Not everyone is able to find a new skip or exploit, a way to glitch through the game, but if you are someone who does, your mark is permanent— your name becomes known in history.

That's how I got addicted to speedrunning.

In the gaming community, I wasn't Parker Covington, heir to a multibillion dollar hotel conglomerate and tabloid-pronounced party boy. I was EnglishCoffee, the speedrunner who completed the fastest run of *Understory* at the age of sixteen, beating the previous record holder by an entire eight minutes. I'm still the record holder. I found a skip that lets players clip out-of-bounds and circumvent a major boss fight, and it is still used by gamers all over the world. The knowledge of that makes me feel like a badass.

Creating EnglishCoffee and rising through the ranks of the gaming and streaming community is an accomplishment that I can only credit myself for. I've spent hours platinuming games, learning their ins and outs, because I love that moment when I see the little trophy that ranks me in the top percent of players worldwide.

That isn't to say I don't like being Parker Covington. Both halves of my life are fucking amazing. I was flying to Paris at fifteen to party in the most exclusive clubs with literal royalty. When I was nineteen, I was invited to an exclusive rave in Monaco before watching the Formula 1 qualifiers from the paddock the next day.

I've never been one to settle.

Why not have the best of both worlds?

Just because other people can't handle it doesn't mean I can't.

Sure, it gets exhausting, but there is always a little pain that comes with fame.

I'm close to finishing the game now. Around fifteen minutes, based on my previous run times. I just need to fast travel to the final city, defeat the boss, and I'm done.

It's the one battle I can't avoid during the gameplay since it is quite literally needed to trigger the end scene.

My focus tunnels as I fight to keep my time. The tips of my fingers dance across my keyboard, and my right wrist twitches side to side as it controls my mouse.

I can feel my heart accelerating in my chest. I really don't want to repeat this speedrun again tomorrow. I need to get my time right, now.

The final boss's health dips into the red, and I watch as my next blow defeats him.

I quickly maneuver my left thumb to button mash the SPACE key. I skip through the final cutscene with ease, and the second the end credits load, I hit the timer to stop it.

Two hours, forty-three minutes, and three seconds.

My head drops to my chest, and I smile.

Thank fuck.

I quit the game and then set about turning off my screen recording and my webcam recording before popping both clips into a shared folder for our team to go over. My speedruns are pretty easy to edit because, well, there is no editing, but I don't upload every speedrun to my channel. Some are more performative, I'll chat during them and make them entertaining for subscribers to watch as VODs. Others are runs just for me, to analyze and learn from. Today was one of those.

I push away from my desk and stand up, letting my chair roll behind me. Stretching, my shoulders make an audible clicking noise as they loosen up. These next few weeks are going to be brutal on my body. I'll need to be careful on my wrist.

I send a quick text to Sydney letting her know that I finished my practice hours for the day and update her on my new run time. As much as I'm obsessed with her, I'm also deathly scared of her. She was camped out in our apartment most of last week to keep an eye on me, making sure that I was sticking to my new practice schedule.

If I wasn't a little bit of a masochist, her overbearing nature wouldn't be such a turn on. Instead, I found it a treat every time I left my streaming room to find her either perched at our kitchen counter working or lounging away on our couch. Her stormy eyes would narrow in on me, and I relished the attention as she logged my hours, run times, and stats.

After five days of successfully following her schedule to a T, she deemed me trustworthy enough to work on my own and went back to her own apartment. If I wasn't serious about winning this tournament, I would've fudged my hours to get her to stay around more. Sydney hasn't been over since Friday, and her cherry scent has long since dissipated.

When I open my door, I'm assaulted by the bright lights from our kitchen. I practically hiss as my eyes squeeze shut before I force them to blink open. I rip open the fridge and pull out an energy drink. Cracking it open, the hissing sound provides a sense of comfort. I drain half of the fizzy caffeinated beverage while shuffling items around the fridge.

Nothing looks good.

I'll order in with the boys instead.

The apartment is silent, so I trudge over to Aleks' streaming room and shove the door open. The room is lit in a deep red glow, but he isn't inside. It's midafternoon, so he could still be sleeping.

I really thought once he got a girlfriend that his hours would get a little more normal, but Aleksander is still as nocturnal as ever.

Shifting down the hall, I pause outside Aleks' bedroom and lean my ear against the frame. When no sounds of pleasurable moans creep through the crack, I deem it safe enough to open.

I scowl when I'm greeted by his empty, rumpled bed.

I spin around, all patience lost as I use my foot to push down the handle to Jackson's streaming room and kick it open.

Aleks and Jackson have rooms in the same hallway, while mine are in the one off the kitchen.

Naturally, mine are the biggest.

The door flings open with force, and I step into the green LED-lit room. Sure enough, Jackson is gaming on his PC while Aleks looms in a chair next to him. My two best friends pause their yelling to look at me for a second and nod before going back to the game in front of them.

"Are you wankers really going to ignore me?" I huff.

"You still have your headphones on, wanker," Aleks mocks back in a shitty British accent while pawing at a bag of crisps.

I quickly shove the headset off my head and leave them to rest around my neck before walking farther into the room and snatching the bag from him.

I barely manage to shove a handful of the honey-bar-beque crisps into my mouth before Aleks grabs them back from me, almost knocking my energy drink out of my hand in the process.

I give his chair a kick, sending it rolling backward, and quickly grab one of the nearby puffy, round seats to claim my spot to Jackson's right. Aleks flicks me his middle finger, and I return the gesture twofold.

"What're you guys playing, anyway?" My eyes scan the screen as I lean forward.

It's a first-person game, that much I can tell. Jackson's character is using a flashlight to search what looks like a very illegal, backwater surgery room. I don't recognize it as anything we've played before, but Jackson tends to play a lot of games from indie developers.

When the music starts to turn creepy, I get a sinking feeling in my stomach.

Jackson also tends to play a lot of horror games.

"What game is it?" I ask again while draining the rest of my energy drink, but the fizziness only upsets the growing unease as the assholes remain quiet. "Fuck this."

I go to push up, but I'm not quick enough. Some fucked-up looking zombie creature flashes onto the screen with a screeching sound, and I just about piss myself. My attempt at leaving turns into me tripping backward over the round seat, and I end up sprawled on the ground with a grunt.

Aleks and Jackson let out a holler of laughter.

I fucking loathe jump-scare horror games and they know it.

"I hate you both." I crush the can that is still gripped in my hand and fling it at Jackson.

He bats it away with ease before extending his hand out to me. "Come on, princess."

"You are aware you died," I point out with a grumble, knocking his hand away and standing up myself.

"Worth it." He shrugs, spinning back to the screen and restarting the game. "It's a new game, by the way. They're still in beta but asked if I would test it out and give them some feedback. It's pretty good. I haven't had any glitches or major bugs so far, and the creatures look super realistic."

The brief image of the zombie creature flashes in my mind, and I suppress a shiver.

"There's something wrong with you people," I grumble.

I'll never understand why people willingly scare themselves. Seriously. Why?

"How'd your run go?" Aleks asks through a mouthful of crisps.

"Shaved off thirty seconds total."

"Ay, nice." He holds his hand out, and I slap it before fist-bumping him.

"Yeah, I was going to celebrate and get us a table at High Wire, but I'm not feeling so hospitable anymore."

"I'm pretty sure Syd would drag you out of the club before you even popped a bottle."

At least it would give me an excuse to see her.

"I could always turn my location off," I supply.

"You tried that last month," Jackson reminds me. "Only gave you three hours, and she added five hours to your streaming quote."

"Ugh, I'm one strike away from a tech lockdown myself," Aleks groans. "I need to do that stupid photo shoot next week to wipe my slate clean."

"The one for Wyreless?" I ask.

"Fuck. I still need to do that one, too." Aleks runs a tattooed hand down his face. "High Wire doesn't sound so bad anymore. Might as well cut my losses early and get drunk."

An ungodly screech comes from Jackson's laptop, and I match it with a yelp of my own. My head automatically jerks to his screen, and I spot a skeletal-looking creature with melting skin gracing his monitor in 4K. Fucking lovely.

"Turn that thing off," I growl.

Jackson laughs but turns his monitor off. "All right, all right." He crosses his arms across his chest, his thick biceps bulging. "Let's not get on Sydney's shit list any more than necessary. Why don't we order in tonight and play a couple of rounds of Smash?"

I grin. "Loser's penalty?"

"The Aprilia?" Aleks smirks.

"We're not betting the Aprilia during a game of Smash." I may bet dumb shit but not that dumb. "Plus, the Aprilia is already in play, remember? Whoever wins the next Hottest Streamer of the Year gets it."

Aleks has been eyeing my motorcycle for the last four years, ever since I had it shipped over. But no matter how many times I put it up as collateral for one of our bets, he has yet to win it.

He thinks it's cursed.

Right now, the Aprilia is sitting as the reward for whoever ranks higher on next year's Hottest Steamer list that *Gamer Weekly* publishes. Aleks seems confident he will win again, but now that he's scored himself a bird, I think the odds tip more in my favor. I really don't want to lose it since it's a vintage model, but I can always buy something else to replace it in my collection come worst case scenario. It would give me an excuse to head out to the track and test drive.

"I don't even want the Aprilia," Jackson sighs. "Why can't we just bet something simple?"

"Because that's no fun."

"Whoever loses pays for dinner," he pushes.

Jackson sucks at bets. Mostly because he is a sore loser. Out of the three of us, he is the most competitive, but he is so competitive that he refuses to play unless he knows he has a good chance of winning. When it comes to Smash, it's a pretty even playing field between the three of us, but Jackson does have a higher likelihood of losing in the long run.

"I'm fine with dinner." Aleks shrugs.

I roll my eyes. "Fine, loser buys dinner."

We all shake hands on it, but when Jackson goes to let go, I grip his hand harder and give him a broad smile. "I'm ordering from Silver Fish, by the way."

Jackson gives me a deadpan expression as Aleks snorts at the name of the top omakase restaurant in California, run by the renowned Chef Takisawa.

"Silver Fish sounds delicious," Aleks muses. "I've really been craving a forty-dollar sushi roll; it will go great with the twenty-dollar miso soup and thirty-dollar edamame."

"Seriously, English." Jackson quirks an eyebrow.

"I thought you loved sushi," I innocently reply.

"I do, but that place is stupid expensive."

"Then I guess you're gonna have to win."

"You're on."

Aleks elbows me, and my character almost goes slipping off the platform, plunging to its death.

"That's fucking cheating!" I yell, smashing my thumb down on the A button repeatedly.

I land a blow on his character, and his hit-score gets dangerously high. I just need to hit him with a special attack, and he will lose his second to last life. He needs to lose this round, or I'm royally screwed.

The game isn't exactly going according to plan.

Somehow, Aleks and I are tied for last place, while Jackson is magically beating both of us by three rounds. If I don't beat Aleks this round, I'm going to be stuck paying for Silver Fish, and I know Jackson is going to order the Hokkaido Bafun Uni roll just out of spite. I have nothing against the roll; it tastes amazing. But it's one hundred and sixty dollars, and Jackson doesn't even like Uni. In fact, he hates it.

Jackson's character engulfs mine before spitting it back out, and I watch as my character goes blasting off the screen to its death.

Fuck. I only have one life left.

"You've been practicing in secret, haven't you?" I accuse him with a waggle of my finger as I wait to respawn.

"It's not in secret, you've just been busy." He shrugs.

"Nope, I agree. It's been in secret." Aleks agrees with

me as his own character falls to its death at the hand of Jackson.

Thank God. We both have one life left now.

"You've also been busy." Jackson is a broken record and a pain in the ass.

I need to kill Aleks.

My knee taps up and down as I focus on dolling out hits to Aleks' character, but it's tough when Jackson is going after me like a dog with a bone. This round is turning into a 2v1 at this point.

A power-up appears on the screen, and I let out a yell when I manage to successfully grab it. I launch my attack, and Aleks' character goes spinning diagonally off screen. He chucks his controller onto the couch with a curse, and it bounces onto the floor.

I let out a maniacal laugh.

My win is short-lived as Jackson knocks my character off the ledge and then hits me again, so I have no chance of saving myself. I die, but coming in second place was all I needed.

"This is bullshit." Aleks folds his arms over his chest.

"You lost fair and square, mate." I shrug.

"You wouldn't be saying that if you were in my position."

True. But I'm not.

I pull up a new text message to Akari, my Silver Fish contact and Chef Takisawa's granddaughter. We went to the same international boarding school in Switzerland for a year when we were fifteen. My order at Silver Fish tends to be the same every time, so I just copy and paste my last text before holding my phone out to Jackson.

"Here, type what you want."

"You can order whatever for me." He shrugs.

"You sure?"

"Yeah, but I'm sort of feeling like sea urchin tonight. Do they still have that Uni roll?" A wolfish grin spreads across Jackson's face.

"Why, yes. Yes, they do." I grin back.

"Come on, guys," Aleks whinges.

"I'll just add some rolls on for you while I'm at it, Aleks. How does the Gold Caviar Surprise sound?"

"Fuck no."

Aleks lobs his body at me, crushing me onto Jackson as he attempts to wrestle my phone out of my hand. Jackson pushes us out from under us, and we go tumbling onto the carpet. Aleks grips my shoulder, and his black nails dig in as he tries to keep me in place while I attempt to wiggle out from under him.

"You're breaking skin, asshole."

"Give me the phone, and I'll let go."

"No."

I manage to get my elbow free and clip him in the ribs. I start to scramble backward, but Aleks lunges for me again. This time, my back lands on the stupid fucking controller he tossed earlier. The plastic bites into me, and I let out a deep grunt.

I lift up my knee to push him off me and gain a split second to flip around and shove the controller away. Then Aleks is back on me, flattening me to the floor.

"Get off of me, you oaf."

"Stop shoving your ass in my face," he complains.

"Your mum thinks my ass is great."

"My mom is dead."

"Why do you always have to ruin that joke?" I let out another huff as I try to keep my phone away from his grimy hands.

"Because it makes people uncomfortable." Aleks reaches around and tickles my left underarm, and my body spasms. I have to fight to keep my hand clenched around my phone.

"Fuck you, Blade."

"Seems like you're trying to."

"Motherfu—"

"Well, this is quite the show."

We both go still at the feminine voice.

Aleks let out a breathless, "Hey, babe," before digging his elbow into my back.

"Stephanie, be a dear and get your sore loser of a boy-friend off me," I plead to the lithe brunette who is leaning against the wall.

"Seems like I might break a nail doing that." She scrunches up her nose while examining her hands. "But don't worry, Parker. I'm rooting for you. You've got this. Kick his ass." She gives me a thumbs up.

"You're going to pay for that later, Stevie," Aleks growls.

"I hope so." She winks.

I take the momentary distraction to twist myself around and land another elbow to Aleks' ribs before kneeing him. He curls in on himself for a millisecond, and I scramble up. I finally manage to stand, but I only take one step before Aleks' hands close around my sweatpants and tug.

"What is with all this grunting?" Sydney rounds the

corner from our private elevator with an annoyed expression.

Aleks pulls my sweatpants down.

Chaos breaks out as cold air runs across my bare ass.

Sydney lets out a screech as she comes face to face with my dick, and Stevie doubles over, clutching her stomach in laughter.

"Stevie, stop staring at Parker's dick!" Aleks yells.

"You're the one who just pantsed him," she cackles.

"Pull your damn pants back up," Sydney shrieks through the hands covering her face. I don't miss the way she can still see through her fingers and is staring at my junk.

I can't help but grin.

"Your ass is super white, dude," Jackson comments.

I reach down and jerk my sweatpants back up. "Sorry, next time I go to Italy, I'll make sure to visit a nude beach so my ass tans."

"You have a nice butt," Stevie supplies.

"Thank you." I grin at her.

"Stephanie," Aleks growls.

"What? I didn't say anything about his penis."

"Why can't you guys ever be normal?" Sydney is beet red beneath her golden blonde bangs. Her embarrassment is adorable. I just want to pull her into my arms.

"You should all feel very privileged right now. Not many people get to see the big P."

"Dude, did you just refer to your dick as 'the big P'?" Jackson judges.

"What? It's not like I gave it an actual name like Parker Jr or Lil' P." I freeze. "Wait. No."

"Lil P," Aleks hollers.

God-fucking-dammit. Why do I always dig my own grave?

"Quit while you still can, dude." Jackson claps his hands around my shoulder.

"Sod off," I grumble. "You still have to buy us Silver Fish." I point my finger at Aleks.

His face instantly sobers into a scowl.

"Oh, I love Silver Fish," Stevie croons.

"How perfect, we were just finishing our order. What do you want, love?" I hand her my phone and shoot her a conspiratorial smile, which she matches pace for pace.

She taps out her order and then offers the phone to Sydney. "You joining us, Syd?"

"They don't really have vegan options, and I still have work to finish before Parker and I leave Friday. I only came up because I needed to give him his new mouse from Wyreless."

She looks at me for a brief second before the redness returns to crawl up her neck and she looks at the floor.

I like how much I'm affecting her right now. That I'm seeing a glimpse of discomfort in her usual poised façade. Every day I break through a little more. She thinks I can't get in because she changed the locks to her heart, but she forgets she gave me the keys once before. Nothing is going to stop me from getting them again.

Sydney shoves the box in my hands before spinning on her kitten heels and giving Stevie a quick hug. She throws the rest of us a fleeting wave.

"I'll see you guys later. Behave."

She's almost out of sight when she pauses and turns

back. Her eyes automatically skip to mine before they shift to Aleks, and she points a finger at him.

"I rescheduled your shoot for Monday. I'll be taking you there personally. Don't think for a second that I won't chain you to your bed Sunday night to make sure of that."

"I'd love to see that." Stevie winks.

Aleks loops his arms around her midsection and pulls her against him, placing a kiss on the top of her head. "Of course, you would, little dove."

"Aleksander," Sydney warns.

"Yeah, yeah, Syd. I promise."

"Good." She resumes her retreat to the elevator, and I follow her. I lean against the wall as she waits briefly for the doors to open. She steps in and eyes me warily while hitting the button for her floor.

"You can chain me up, too, love."

I blow her a kiss as the elevator doors start to close, and she rolls her eyes.

I smirk and return to the chaos behind me.

Brick by brick.

I'll break down those walls.

Chapter FIVE

SYDNEY

This is a serious problem.

My finger refuses to push the call button. I've been staring at my phone for five minutes without moving a muscle. All because I keep seeing Parker's cock flash in my mind every time I go to press it.

We need to leave for the airport in the next few minutes to make our flight. Normally, I would've gone right up to the penthouse and dragged Parker's ass out of the apartment. But I just couldn't bring myself to do it.

Because for some stupid reason, I'm still hung up on seeing him completely naked two days ago.

And hung he was.

Ugh.

I thought I'd made myself immune to the guys. I've seen Parker in just his briefs thousands of times. Jackson is always shirtless for Sunday breakfasts. I've even gotten an eyeful of Aleks' cock before when I walked in on him changing for a shoot. So why is this time any different?

I think I'm spending too much time with him.

There used to be a clearer divide between my personal and professional life. But each year that passes with The System blurs it more and more. And now that their personal and professional lives have become one, it feels like I'm playing a whole new game.

"Miss Lake." Francis' voice breaks me out of my spiral. "Is Mister Covington on his way?"

I shoot a bright smile at our driver. "Yes, he'll be here any second."

I bite the bullet and hit dial, but it's all for naught as the elevator doors slide open to reveal the blond prince within.

Parker pushes off the elevator wall and strolls out, rolling his designer carry-on behind him. He is dressed in a custom pair of electric blue joggers with a matching hoodie, which he has paired with a pair of all-white Balenciaga sneakers and sunglasses.

How does he look so damn good wearing that?

I bet if you put that same outfit on anyone else, they'd look like a giant blue jellybean. But Parker Covington isn't just *anyone else*. You could dress him in a brown take-out bag, and he'd still look ridiculously handsome. With his perfectly high cheekbones and knife-sharp jawline, it's like someone plucked him out of a fantasy novel.

"Earth to Sydney."

I snap to attention as Parker dips to face me, his nose inches away from my own—his perfectly sloped nose.

I'm sure if you went on Pinterest and searched "attractive British model," Parker would pop up.

"You're late." I snap my shields down as I take a healthy step away from him.

"I'm never late, other people—"

"Are simply early," I finish for him.

He says the same overused quote all the time.

I avert my eyes from his piercing gaze, instead opting to watch as Francis takes Parker's roller bag and places it in the trunk alongside my own overnight bag. Mine, however, looks comically small compared to his.

"I'll have you know that not even you can make an airplane wait." I hop into the car, and Parker follows suit, shutting the door behind him. His legs spread, knees almost touching my own.

"You can if it's a private jet," he muses, lifting his sunglasses to the top of his head with a wink.

"Unfortunately for you, we are not taking a private jet." I cross my legs to put some more space between us.

His smile falls. "What do you mean?"

The car rumbles as it starts, and Francis drives us out of the underground parking lot. I lean back against my seat as the sun filters in through the tinted windows.

"I mean your sister took the jet to Vancouver, so I booked us commercial."

"Why couldn't we take JetSuite?"

I swear, next he is going to ask why I couldn't book us a helicopter and say that commercial should have been the last possible resort. Sometimes I forget just how privileged Parker is compared to the rest of the guys—compared to me.

"They were booked. Our flight is only two and half

hours. You'll survive. It's not like you haven't flown commercial before."

He scowls and slumps back in his seat before nodding his head so his sunglasses fall back down on his face. He looks like a sad puppy. A sad, rich puppy.

"Just because I've flown commercial before doesn't mean I like it."

"I booked you first class, and we're flying Imperial."

He perks up at that, like I knew he would. I wouldn't book *the* Parker Covington on just any commercial flight. This isn't my first rodeo. Imperial Airline is the only commercial airline company Parker is okay flying because it is—of course—owned by one of his friends, Weston Hill, so he gets special treatment.

Francis eventually pulls up to the busy airport, and I make quick work navigating Parker and myself through the throng of people moseying around bag drop. If there's one thing I hate, it is inefficient people at the airport. I have everything planned down to the minute so that nothing can go wrong.

We finally make our way through TSA, and I let out a sigh of relief when I see that we are perfectly on time despite Parker's slight delay earlier. We have thirty minutes until boarding. Just enough time to grab a water or a snack before the flight.

I come to an abrupt stop when I reach our gate, and Parker bumps into my back. He looks up from the mobile game he is playing with an apologetic grin.

"Sorry, Syd."

"It's fine," I brush him off, squinting at the screen next to our gate.

The word "DELAYED" is spelled out in bright yellow.

That can't be right. I didn't get any notification of a delay. I double-check the airline app before refreshing my email, but there's nothing there.

"Wait here." I steer Parker to a free seat and sit him down, perching my overnight bag on top of his roller.

I plaster my brightest smile on my face and head over to the employee working at the gate. "Excuse me, miss."

The woman behind counter peers down at me with a brittle smile. "How can I help you?"

"I was just wondering, how long is the flight delayed?"

"I don't have a definite time currently."

"I'm sorry?"

"We are waiting to hear back from air control," she elaborates.

"All right," I drawl. "Do you know why we are delayed?"

"Inclement weather at the destination."

I just frown. This woman seems determined to give me the bare minimum information. I'm sure she's been asked this question a few times already, but really. I'm trying to be civil.

"There's a snowstorm in Denver," she sighs. "We'll make an announcement once we have more information."

It's September. There hasn't been a snowstorm in Colorado in September in years. Literal years. But of course, the one weekend we need to fly there, there's a snowstorm. Just our luck.

I blame climate change.

"Okay, well, I guess I'll just…wait."

The woman gives me a tight smile before returning

back to the computer before her.

I purse my lips and take a deep breath through my nose. I hold it for a few seconds before letting out a loud sigh.

It's fine. Everything will be fine.

Parker has his head down, still distracted by the game he's been playing since the second we made it through TSA. Honestly, I was impressed that he never bumped into anyone on the walk to the gate. Then again, all the guys have multitasking down to a T.

My eyes dip briefly to his crotch, and I all but pinch myself.

"How long until we board?" he asks when I slump into the seat next to him.

I grimace as I try to come up with an answer I don't have. "Uh, there's a slight delay, so we have at least an hour or so."

Parker pauses his game and furrows his brows at me. "That long?"

"Yeah. Roughly."

He shoves his phone in his pocket and stands up, holding his hand out to me. His icy blue eyes spear straight into my soul as I look up at him before taking his hand. He tugs me alongside him while steering our luggage with his other hand. Heat travels through my palm, up my arm, and into my chest.

Sweat beads on my skin.

I must be wearing too many layers.

"Where are we going?" I ask.

"The lounge." He winks back at me.

Parker doesn't even need to look where he's headed because people move out of the way for him automatically.

A few minutes later, he leads us to a set of glazed doors. There is a long line of people who seem to be waiting to enter, but Parker pays them no mind as he strolls right by them.

An employee holds out their hand just as the doors slide open.

"I'm sorry, sir. You need to wait in line. The lounge is currently full."

Parker side-eyes the line of people for a beat before slowly blinking back. He then reaches into his back pocket and slides a card out of his wallet, flashing it at the employee. They squint at the emerald-green card momentarily before their eyes widen and they move aside with a flourish of their hand.

"Apologies," they mutter.

Parker lets out a soft huff before walking past them. When we get to the counter inside, Parker flashes the card again to the three employees behind the counter who are checking people in. The tall woman in the middle immediately straightens her back as she takes Parker's card and swipes it before taking his phone to scan his boarding pass. She returns his phone and the shiny card with a million-watt smile.

"Mr. Covington, welcome to the Imperial Lounge. I see you're flying to Denver today. The flight appears to currently be delayed, and I don't have an estimated hour of departure at this time. Please feel free to use all our amenities, and I'll send someone to find you once there is an update on your flight." She gestures around the corner to an escalator. "If you take a right at the top, you'll see the doors to our Emerald Elite Lounge. We hope you enjoy your stay."

"Thank you, Marigold."

The woman's smile stretches an inch wider, and I worry it might split. He's not a mind reader; her name is printed on her name tag.

Parker takes my hand and guides me up the escalators. My eyes immediately begin to scan our surroundings. There is a large seating area to our left where people are snacking on little plates of tapas and tapping away on their devices. They're all engrossed in their own world, and everything is generally quiet despite it being completely packed. It's a little disconcerting.

I make note of the signs on the wall that explain which way the bathrooms, buffet station, bar, and children's entertainment area are.

Children's entertainment area?

Just how big is this place?

There is another set of glazed doors to our right when we step off the escalator, and Parker just gives the attendant outside a nod before walking through them.

Somehow, this area is more exclusive and even quieter. I count only a handful of patrons milling about: there's a couple having cocktails at the bar, a lone man talking low into his headphones in a round chair, a mother rocking her child in the corner, and a group of businessmen drinking coffees and clacking away at their keyboards in the center cluster of seats.

It feels like my head is swiveling like an owl as my eyes flicker around the room while I simultaneously try to keep up with Parker.

I'm pretty sure I just read a sign pointing out the direction of the private shower suites.

I have no clue what I'm doing here. I can count the number of times I've flown to events with The System on one hand, and each of those times has been on the jet. As extravagant as the Covington jet is—it has two bedrooms, and video game consoles are set up in the main cabin— there is something *more* about this whole experience. It's like booking a room in a hotel and finding out you have the honeymoon package. It's a white-glove experience with no expense wasted.

It doesn't matter how much time I've spent working for Parker over the years, it's different when I'm dumped into the spotlight next to him instead of watching from the sidelines.

I'm afraid I'll breathe wrong and someone will glare at me.

Probably the businessmen.

"I'm a little peckish. How about you?" Parker squeez- es my hand. "It looks like they've just started their lunch service."

I notice that he's stopped us outside a tiny dining area. There are only ten tables, one of which is occupied by a woman and three men. Of course this lounge has its own mini restaurant within it.

"I could go for a snack."

And water. Lots and lots of water.

Parker swipes his emerald card, and the door to the dining area beeps open. I notice that everyone's head pops up at the noise, and they give us a once over.

I inch closer to Parker to avoid their scrutiny as we walk inside. Not that I'm wearing anything out of place.

I'm technically on the clock even though we are travelling, so I'm in a pair of brown pants and a cream knit sweater with a matching woolen jacket and little brown boots. I even put on a little makeup because I have a feeling there might be paparazzi when we get off the plane on the other side.

You go out bare face with The System once and see how unflattering the paparazzi shots can be, and you never make the mistake again. I work so many long hours that the bags under my eyes need severe coverage, otherwise I apparently look like a ghoul.

Distantly, I register a tug on my wrist.

"As much as I love holding your hand, Syd, I kind of need my own back," Parker teases.

I look down and realize that I've still got his fingers entwined with mine in a death grip.

I immediately release my hold and wipe my palm on my pants. My hand feels odd after being attached to Parker's for so long.

He ducks his head and grins before reaching around and pulling a seat out for me.

"Thank you." My voice comes out softer than necessary as I sit down, and he pushes my chair in.

God. I'm off-kilter today.

I need to hit the reset button or something. Whatever is going on with me is not okay. I'm supposed to be the guard dog keeping the sheep in line, not the puppy getting distracted by its own reflection.

A waitress comes around and presents a bottle of champagne to Parker.

"Mr. Covington, welcome back. I have a bottle of the

2008 Bollinger R.D. Extra Brut that Mr. Hill had reserved for you. Would you like me to pour you a glass?"

We haven't even had water yet, and they're pulling out the champagne.

"If Mr. Hill is offering, why not?" Parker couldn't look happier as he stares at the glass bottle the heir of Imperial Airlines has apparently put aside for him.

"Would your girlfriend like some as well?" she asks him.

First, I'm sitting right here, so I'm not sure why she isn't just addressing me directly.

Second, I am not his girlfriend.

"My girlfriend doesn't drink."

Butterflies swarm my stomach.

I take a mental flamethrower and burn them to death.

"I'm not his girlfriend." I give the waitress a tight smile. "Just a water for me, please."

"Oh, come on, love. No need to be shy." Parker pats my hand, and I scowl.

"I'll be right back with water, a champagne glass, and your menus." The woman dips her head before disappearing behind a hidden door.

"It's not funny, Parker," I reprimand him.

"Whatever do you mean?" His look is one of feigned innocence.

He knows exactly what I'm talking about.

"You can't go around saying to random people that I'm your girlfriend. It takes just one person to mention the rumor to a media outlet, and they'll turn it into a circus. The last thing I need is you boys turning me into my own PR nightmare."

"Sounds more like a dream than a nightmare."

He looks directly at me as he says the words, his accent drawing them out. My neck begins to burn, and my palms turn clammy.

Did they turn up the heat in here? I should just take off my coat.

"Regardless, this is a work trip." I contort my arms to get them out of the sleeves and brush his statement off. "Please try to remember that. The public eye cared who you were when you were just Parker Covington; now they know you're EnglishCoffee as well. That's double the fame than you're used to."

"I've never been *just* Parker Covington, love."

My eye twitches.

When he says things like that, I remember how insufferable he is. It helps dim the shine.

His ego really shouldn't be endearing. It should be a turn off. Today, that doesn't seem to be the case.

The waitress finally returns with my glass of water, and I practically pounce for it. I drain the cool liquid like I've been lost in the desert for days.

I immediately feel better. The waitress, however, looks at me with mild concern as she pops the champagne. I make a point of keeping eye contact with her while I crunch on the remaining ice cubes.

She swallows before switching her attention back to Parker, her face lighting up as she pours him a glass.

"Mr. Hill also left some suggestions for food; would you like us to follow that, or would you like to pick something off the menu yourself?"

"Let's go with whatever Weston has cooked up. Just

make sure there is a vegan alternative for my," he slides his gaze to me and grins, "companion."

The last ice cube in my mouth crunches between my molars as I clench my jaw.

I can feel the edges of a headache begin to fester.

"I'll be right back," I clip.

I don't give Parker a chance to respond as I stand up, grab my handbag, and power walk out of the secluded dining area.

My head feels like it is full of clouds, and it takes me a moment to reorient myself.

There's a low buzz of chatter around the lounge; more people have filled the previously unoccupied chairs. I straighten my shoulders, pulling some sense into myself, before donning my mask of cool professionalism.

My eyes slip back to the sign from earlier, and curiosity wins. Well, curiosity and avoidance.

I follow the little arrows directing me to the shower suites.

After a little navigation and winding around hallways, I come to a set of six wooden doors. The first handle doesn't budge, so I move on to the next. It clicks open, and I carefully pull the large frame open before tentatively stepping inside. The heels of my boots clack against the marble titles as I begin to gawk at my surroundings.

My mind spins as I take in the rainfall shower, custom robe, bidet, and what looks to be one of those heated toilets. There's even an assortment of skincare products lined up next to the sink, including a full-service shaving station.

The hotels I stay in don't even have bathrooms that look this nice normally.

I spot a phone on the wall and squint at the placard next to it.

Dial 9 for dry-cleaning services.

Dial 7 for amenity refreshments.

Dial 4 for food/beverage.

Do they expect people to live here? How are there dry-cleaning services?

I lock the door and sit on the stone bench next to the shower.

If they had a bath in here, I would seriously consider taking one.

My head falls back against the cool marble wall, and I let my eyes drift shut for a few seconds. There's something different about the quiet of a bathroom. The silence here speaks differently. It grounds you.

I open my eyes and stare at myself in the large mirror across from me.

I still look pretty decent.

I cross to the sink and slap my handbag onto the counter before reaching in and sifting around for my cherry lip gloss. My fingers close around the hourglass tube. I apply a healthy coat, inhaling the sweet scent. I've been using the same lip gloss since I was in high school. I'm honestly lucky it's never gone out of production. Sure, they've tweaked their formula over the years, but it's mostly stayed the same.

I smack my tinted lips together in the mirror a few times. I take out some of my blotting papers to fix the shine on my cheeks and then give a quick wipe under my eyes to clear up any mascara smudges. After giving a quick fluff to my bangs, I feel a little more put together.

I spin in the mirror, checking that my outfit is still pristine, and give myself a quick nod.

All right. Back to business.

I fling open the large wooden door, but it's a lot lighter than I remember. My arm is nearly wrenched out of its socket as the door goes wide. I grimace as my shoulder twinges but shake it off.

I make a beeline for the dining area, belatedly realizing that I don't have a card to get in. I take a step aside and embarrassment creeps up my cheeks as I pull out my phone to text Parker.

However, the door slides open and the man of the hour smiles at me before I type a single word.

"Glad to see you didn't run away."

"The bathrooms in this place are too much." I swerve around him back to our table and plop down on my seat.

"If you think this is extra, you should see their lounge in Hong Kong. It has a sauna."

After what I saw today, I really don't doubt him. I'd even go so far as to bet that they offered massages, too.

The waitress has dropped off our meal in the time I've been gone. There is a steaming hot bowl of what looks to be an asparagus risotto. I eye it warily. Despite how good it looks; little flags go off in my mind.

"You're sure this is vegan?" I ask him, pushing the creamy rice around with my spoon.

"I double-checked with the waitress; I promise."

Apprehension still rolls in my gut. It would've been easier if I'd just picked something off the menu knowing there was a little vegan symbol next to it. You have no idea how many times someone has said something is vegan without knowing exactly what veganism is. The confusion for vegetarianism is disproportionate.

Still, Parker is one of the few people I trust to look out for me in that way.

I take a tentative bite and the flavors melt on my tongue. The light nutty taste combines with the deep roast of the asparagus. There's a pop of brightness from some lemon, which is cut by the sprinkling of parsley.

Wow. Who knew airport food could be this nice?

"Cracking, isn't it?" Parker smiles at me as he cuts into his quiche.

"Not bad." I smile back, letting some of the tension peel off my back.

After we finish our meal, we make our way out to the seating area. Parker secures us two chairs in the back corner with a view overlooking the runway.

I sink into the leather before grabbing my tablet out of my handbag. If we're going to be stuck here for the foreseeable future, I might as well get some work done. Plus, I don't think I can handle any more conversations with Parker today. Clearly, one of my wires is crossed and I'm not functioning right.

I refuse to slip up.

I've worked too hard to craft the perfect friendly yet professional relationship with the guys. It's a fine line I walk, and I won't let that line become blurred because my brain keeps replaying a certain British man's penis.

After an hour passes with no news from any of the employees about an update to our flight and a lack of an email or app notification from the airline, I grow worried.

"We should've heard something by now," I mutter.

Parker looks up at me from his gaming laptop. His headset is half on, one ear free from the padding. There's something oddly attractive about that look.

"I can go ask for an update?" he offers.

"No, I need to stretch my legs. Just keep playing whatever it is you're playing."

I peel myself off the leather chair and give my back a quick twist. A few bones click with the movement. I can't imagine what I would've felt like if I'd been stuck camping out on the chairs by the gate.

I stride up to the agent assist desk—although podium would be a better word to describe it. The man gives me an overtly kind smile.

"Hi, I was just wondering if there was any update on our flight. We had an indefinite delay." I show him my phone so he can scan the boarding pass, but he waves it off.

"Mr. Covington's companion, correct?"

There's that word again.

"Correct." I maintain a placid smile.

"Unfortunately, it still doesn't look like we—" he pauses as the computer makes a little dinging sound. "Oh, look at that. Serendipitous timing. They just updated your departure time. It looks like it will be ten p.m., but we will come find you for your boarding at nine fifteen p.m."

My insides crystalize. That's in eight hours.

Eight. Hours.

God help me.

Chapter SIX

PARKER

Sydney is pissed.

I watch as she gets on her tiptoes and leans farther forward on the counter that separates her from the hotel clerk. Her voice is hushed but full of derision as she grinds out every word. The poor clerk's eyes grow wide as saucers at her clipped remarks and sweat begins to bead at his temples.

"I don't understand, Stewart. How is it possible that I booked two rooms but only one is available?"

"With so many events this weekend and the snowstorm grounding flights, we ran out of rooms."

"I booked these rooms two weeks ago. Not one day ago, two weeks ago. And you're telling me that one of them was just," Sydney pauses to flick her wrist dramatically, "given away?"

The clerk, Stewart, visibly swallows. I feel a little bad for the lad, having to go toe to toe with Syd. He doesn't look a day over eighteen.

"Again, Ms. Lake, because you checked in so late and we hadn't heard from you all day—"

"Because we also got stuck in the snowstorm," she interrupts with a huff. "We got stuck and now we want our rooms, but you have given one of them away, so what am I supposed to do, Stewart?"

Our plane was stuck in a holding pattern for an extra hour in the air because there wasn't sufficient visibility to land. All in all, it's taken fifteen hours since we left the apartment this morning to reach Denver. It's well past midnight, and I need to be up in a few hours to prep before the tournament.

When the clerk doesn't respond, Syd bolsters on. "I would like to speak with the person in charge, please. This is ridiculous."

Stewart's face turns three shades paler before he splutters out, "The manager is also stuck in the storm and has been unable to come in."

I swear I see a blood vessel pop on Sydney's forehead.

We're getting nowhere.

And as much as I love to see Syd battling it out with one of our rival hotel chains, I also desperately want a hot shower and a good night's sleep. There's nothing a low-level employee can do at this stage, and I would rather step on hot coals than call up Jace Kelton for a favor.

I wasted my last one when I broke in and skinny-dipped in his Vegas rooftop pool a few years back.

"Syd, let's just take the room, and I'll deal with the

compensation later." I give her shoulder a squeeze as I sidle up next to her.

Sydney's narrowed gaze flicks to me before shooting back to the clerk.

"Fine," she grinds out even though it's clear to all of us that everything is not.

Poor Stewart shakes as he holds out the key card for us. "Your suite number is nineteen twenty-three. You can take the west elevators, which are located left of the statue. Breakfast is served starting at six at the buffet and in our restaurant at eight."

Ugh. That hideous white marble polar bear statue. It's almost ten feet tall and placed ostentatiously in the center of the entry hall. How the Keltons ever thought that was a tasteful decision escapes me. Now, the ice sculpture at the Covington Hotel in Norway? *That's* a great design choice.

I gingerly pluck the key card from Stewart before looping my arm around Sydney and steering her away before she melts the boy to death with her glare.

"This is why we always stay at Covington Hotels," I comment under my breath. "We'd never have a manager-less hotel."

"You guys don't even have a hotel in Colorado," she shoots back with a hiss.

"Yet."

"Metaphorical hotels do not help us here."

"Yes, but the hotel you did book is owned by one of our biggest rivals."

"Every hotel is your rival."

"Which is why you could've picked a quaint bed and breakfast." I shrug letting go of our luggage so I can scan our key card for the lift. It beeps and directs us to enter elevator five.

"You would stay in a B and B?"

"Why wouldn't I?" I pull us into the opening lift. It has a glass backing so you can look out onto the rest of the hotel as you shoot up to your floor.

Sydney snorts. "Sure, whatever you say, English. Just remember that."

She tries to shrug out of my hold, but I just pull her closer. Her nose is still red from waiting out in the cold earlier.

She's more exhausted than I thought because she doesn't fight back. In fact, it almost feels like she is leaning into my side. Thank God she is wearing her coat right now. The layer serves as a barrier between me and her soft body.

We finally reach the nineteenth floor and follow the little arrows to our room. Naturally, it is at the very end of an already long hallway.

By the time I see the silver placard denoting "Room 1923," I'm ready to fall to my knees.

I scan the key card, and Sydney dips out from under my arm. The loss of her petite body is immediate. She fit me so perfectly, and not having her cradled against my side feels like a sin.

She strolls into the suite ahead of me, leaving me to follow with our luggage. I can't even admire her perky ass because of that damn wool coat covering it.

Never was an ass man until I met Sydney Lake, but there is no denying the goods she is carrying.

I dump our luggage by the closet in the small lounge area before collapsing onto the cream couch. This isn't the

Kelton's best hotel in the States. The suite is smaller compared to their normal standards, not that the regular person would notice. The upside is that it does have a balcony.

"What the hell is this?" Sydney speaks the words with deathly precision.

I look up and peer around the partial wall that separates the lounge area from the bedroom.

"I believe most people would call that a bed," I toe off my sneakers, "or *le lit* if we were in France."

She spins around, shooting me daggers.

"There's one bed, Parker," she deadpans.

"I see that."

"We can't sleep in one bed."

"I mean; it looks like a king. I doubt you would take up more than a quarter of the bed."

"That is not the point."

I know that's not the point. But I'm worried that if I don't calm her down, she's going to make me sleep on the couch, and I *really* don't want to sleep on the couch. I'm not made for couch sleeping. I would probably call Jace and make him kick some poor sap out of their room before sleeping on the couch.

I also can't deny that there is another part of me—a stiffening part of me—that gets a thrill out of the idea of sharing a bed with Sydney

"I'll just sleep on the couch." She takes off her coat and tosses it onto the nearby desk chair.

I take everything back.

I'd sooner sleep on the couch than make Sydney sleep there.

"You can't sleep on the couch, Syd."

"It looks like a very nice couch."

Of course it does. This is the Kelton, after all. You don't get crappy couches at a five-star hotel.

Instead of arguing with her, I just walk over to where she is pacing and pick her up by the hips. She lets out a squeal of protest before I toss her onto the bed.

"Parker Covington, what do you—oomph!" She bounces a few times before sinking deep into the mattress. "Oh my God." She runs her hands over the duvet. "This is so soft."

The image of her sprawled out on the bed burns itself into the back of my brain, and I tamp down a strangled groan. Instead, I give a noncommittal hum as she distracts herself with the bed, crossing back to grab my luggage.

As much as I like to shit on Jace and tear apart his family's hotels, I can't deny that the one thing they always get right are their beds. They're like sleeping on a cloud of fairy floss.

I grab my toiletries out of my roller bag, and a pair of briefs, before trekking into the bathroom. I'm not masochistic enough to subject myself to a cold shower just to erase the image of Syd from my mind, but I do spend longer than necessary under the spray trying to empty my thoughts of the blonde bombshell on the bed.

By the time I return from the bathroom, Sydney is drifting off to sleep on top of the duvet. Part of me says to just let her be, to allow her to fall asleep. The other part of me, the one that grew up with two older sisters, tells me that she is going to be mad at herself in the morning when she realizes she fell asleep in her makeup.

I can practically hear Paige scolding me.

"Don't be daft, Parker. A girl's skincare routine is sacred."

Sighing, I pick up Syd's overnight bag and drop it on the foot of the bed. I give her shoulder a quick nudge, but she just turns over and snuggles deeper.

She looks like an angel. Her hands are cradled under her cheek, and her chest rises and falls with slow breaths. I'm tempted to crawl behind her and scoop her into my arms.

Instead, I poke her again.

Harder.

"Love, you can't fall asleep yet."

"Why not?" Her voice comes out quiet and crackly.

"Because you're still in your airplane clothes and your makeup."

Her eyes squeeze tight as she lets out a groan. She rolls over, and they pop open. As always, those beautiful silver eyes steal all the breath in my body. With a sigh, she swings off the bed.

I hold her overnight bag out to her, and she takes it with a grumble, trudging into the bathroom and shutting the frosted door behind her. The sound of the shower turning on fills the silence.

My lips dry as I imagine her taking off her clothes just a few meters away.

I let loose a strangled laugh before crawling into my side of the bed.

I double-check that all my alarms are set for the morning before shutting off my lamp. The only light left is the one filtering in from the bathroom, but it's not bright enough to bother me as I close my eyes. I'm knackered, and I need all the sleep I can get to be at my best tomorrow afternoon.

That's the one good thing about gaming competitions; they tend to be later in the day.

I can feel the edges of sleep creeping in when the room brightens and Syd pads out of the bathroom. I squeeze my eyes shut to cancel out the light.

"I'm not sleeping in the same bed as you, Parker."

"It's almost two a.m. Please, just get in the bed."

The bathroom light turns off, and I hear her shuffle around, bumping into the bed in the process.

"It's unprofessional, Parker. Mathias would have my head if he found out."

As much of a hard-ass as our manager might be, Mathias couldn't give a flying fuck about our personal lives. That's why he hired Syd in the first place.

I roll over and reach out, grabbing her arm and pulling her onto the bed. She lands centimeters away from my face. Her dewy skin glistens in the faint moonlight, and it takes what little sanity I have left to not run my thumb over her cheek. Her lips haven't been this close to mine in years. Not since That Night.

"Get in the bed, Sydney." My voice takes on a low growl.

Her lips part slightly before quickly pursing. "Fine." Her gaze flickers over my face. "Just make sure to keep to your side."

She tugs out of my grasp and shifts back to her side of the bed. Grabbing one of her pillows, she positions it in between us and attempts to fluff it a few times. I try not to laugh at the action, but it's kind of cute.

Once she's happy with its placement she scoots so far away that I wouldn't be surprised if she fell off the edge of the bed during the night.

"Good night, Sydney."

She turns her back to me. "Good night, Parker."

Chapter
SEVEN

PARKER

The subtle smell of cherries surrounds me, and a tender warmth cups my body. I dip my head into the soft waves, chasing that comforting scent. My hands curl around the heat source, desperate to keep it near. Something brushes against my dick, and I groan, my grip tightening.

The responding light moan has awareness flooding through my body.

As my eyes flutter open, I wonder if I'm still dreaming. Sydney's back is curled against my chest, her pert ass a hairsbreadth away from my cock. The slightest movement has it grazing my slowly stiffening length.

My entire body freezes.

Everything in this exact moment is a fucking wet dream come true.

I haven't moved an inch all night. I'm not a restless sleeper; in fact, I sleep like the dead when I do. Which is how I know that it was Sydney dearest who somehow made her way from one end of the bed to the other during the night.

A distraught beeping fills the room, and my arms flinch in response.

Sydney's eyes pop open as her body jerks to attention.

Her head swivels and wide eyes meet my own. A range of emotions crash over her before she settles on panic. She scrambles out of my arms, leaving nothing but loss behind.

I blindly reach behind me for my phone, slapping it a few times before successfully shutting off the incessant blaring.

"Where are your clothes?" Sydney's look is one of pure horror.

"I'm wearing briefs." I lift the sheets to show her.

Her stormy gaze travels down my body. It lingers low for a beat too long, and I can't keep the smirk off my face. I've never been ashamed of my body, and the way Sydney's taking her time cataloging every inch of my skin only bolsters my confidence.

"You can take a picture. Keep it for nights when you miss me," I tease.

She sucks in her cheeks, gaze immediately bouncing to my eyes before flicking to the window behind me.

"You were wearing clothes last night."

"I was." I sit up and rest my arms behind my head on the headboard. "Then I had a shower and I took them off."

"I would remember getting into bed with a naked man." She tries to pin me with a glare but fails as her eyes stray to my biceps.

"Again, not technically naked."

"Why would you sleep in just your underwear?" She crosses her arms over her chest, drawing attention to the hard nipples poking through the white silk pajama top.

I refrain the urge to readjust my cock.

"Because I figured you'd take offense if I did sleep naked. Commando is my preferred sleeping attire." I wink.

Her pillowy lips part, and she can't stop her gaze from straying. The bed sheets still cover the lower half of my body, but that doesn't mean I can't tell where she is looking. Her small hands tighten around her biceps.

Fuck. What I wouldn't give to have those delicate fingers wrapped around my cock.

"Whatever. I saw enough of your penis the other night, I don't need to see it again," her button nose wrinkles in feigned distaste. "It wasn't that impressive anyway."

Liar.

But if she wants to play that game…

"Sydney, love. I think you're mistaken. I can show you again, just to be sure." I fling the bedsheet away and ignore the cold air as I toy with the edge of the band around my briefs.

Sydney pitches forward screaming, "Don't you dare!" as she throws her hands out to stop me.

She realizes her mistake too late, though.

I also realize my own mistake, for a totally different reason.

Sydney's hands are on my cock.

Heat flushes her cheeks, and her doe eyes widen dramatically. Blood rushes directly down my length and my balls tighten. I can feel her fingers jolt through the soft fabric, and my dick twitches in response.

My earlier prayer has been answered in a bit of a roundabout way.

Sydney's phone begins to ring on her nightstand, crashing reality back down. Her hands rear back, and her fingers curl into her palms like she just touched a hot plate. Her melted gaze hardens back to its default setting of professional disinterest.

"I have to take this. You should get ready. We've got a long day ahead."

She doesn't even check the caller ID, just swipes accept and jumps out of the bed.

Her steps are smooth as she strides to the balcony and unlocks the door, stepping out into the cold.

The little night shorts she is wearing do nothing but hug the globes of her ass. I afford myself an extra few seconds admiring them before forcing myself out of bed.

My dick is rock hard. There's no hiding it.

Fuck.

I run a hand down my face as I turn the shower blistering hot and step under the scalding spray.

The burning water does nothing to drown out the noise in my brain. The last ten minutes just play on a loop.

Sydney's perfect lips. Her smooth skin. Her round ass. Her soft fingers.

I brace my forearm on the wall as I grip my heavy cock.

I give it a quick pump, and the pleasure is immediate.

"Fuck," I groan under my breath.

My hand starts moving on its own, fisting my dick at a slow rhythm. My eyes close, and all I can see is Sydney.

This wouldn't be the first time I got off thinking of her. But it would be the first time with her so close.

I imagine, what if she walked in? What if she joined me? If she strolled right into this shower, that silky night set becoming drenched in the spray. It would stick to the curves of her small body, hugging her juicy ass and tiny tits. I think of her getting to her knees before me and taking me between those soft lips.

My forehead falls against the wall as my pace quickens. It's no longer my hands fucking my dick but her throat. The vision, the fantasy, blooms in my mind.

"Shit," I mutter deeply, my breath becoming ragged.

My abs clench and my balls tighten right before I come in hot spurts. Pure bliss spreads throughout my body as the last of my come coats my hand. I don't move for a minute. I just stand there as my chest begins to even out and the high lessens. I step back fully under the water and allow it to wash away the evidence.

I feel a lot better.

I feel like I could conquer the world. Which is good because that's exactly what I need to do in a few hours.

Finally, I get out of the shower and dry off a little before wrapping a towel around my waist. I brace my hands against the sink, letting my hair drip onto the marble.

There's a knock on the door followed by, "Hey, can I come in?"

My dick begins to stir again at the sound of Sydney's honey-sweet voice.

Not the fucking time, lad.

I take a deep breath and force the tension to leave my body.

"Sure." My voice comes out with a slight husk.

Bloody hell.

The door pops open, and the steam is immediately sucked out as I get hit with a cool breeze. Sydney dips her head around the frame and her gray gaze narrows on my body, snagging on the towel low on my hips. She lets out a small huff before walking in.

"How do you feel about today?"

I give her a noncommittal shrug. "I feel fine."

"It's your first time on stage," she reminds me.

I roll my eyes at her before applying moisturizer to my face. "Syd, I've attended more red carpets than I can count. I've walked for Prada in Milan and given a speech at a royal wedding in Denmark. This is nothing different."

"If you say so."

When I look up, I see concern flash in her eyes. She skirts behind me and comes to stand on my right, reaching for her toothbrush.

I don't try to keep the conversation going. I don't want to.

I wasn't lying when I said I felt fine. I do. But I also know that if I really start to think about it, I'll get in my head. And that's the last thing I need.

This isn't the championship; this isn't the make-or-break event that has my future on the line. But…it's close. Each of these matches in the upcoming weeks will define how I move forward. I need to win at least three of them. I know I'm one of the best, but I need to prove that I am *the* best. And I've never done anything like this before.

I grab the hairdryer and turn it on high, letting the noise drown out the growing nerves as I style my hair.

I need to get my head in the game.

Chapter EIGHT

SYDNEY

"He's playing well today." A thick British accent pulls me out of the trance I've been in. It's different from Parker's, deeper but just as posh. The man who takes a seat in the empty chair next to me keeps his eyes on the stage ahead.

"Of course he is."

I give the man a once over before dismissing him. I let my gaze travel back to the stage.

Parker is playing a *FrozeLine* team battle right now, and he is in line for MVP. When I'd entered him into the tournaments initially, I'd focused on only getting him into the speedrun matches so he would be able to qualify for the championship, but Parker didn't want to just do that.

He wanted to do it all.

The most popular games on the market for competitions are the ones that are big in esports, like *Gods League, Kill Strike, VERTEX,* and *FrozeLine*. Out of those, Parker's strong suit is *FrozeLine*, which is a first-person shooter MMO. The only issue is that he isn't on an esports team, so I could only get him in individual matches and the occasional team battle—where he would be teamed up at random with other tournament gamers for the match, like now.

"And that's another kill for EnglishCoffee," the male announcer calls over the speaker.

"He could be going for a penta-kill," the female announcer returns.

"Only a few minutes left. Looks like he'll get MVP," the guy next to me muses.

My back straightens as I try to figure out who he might be. I keep my expression neutral, face ahead, as I scan him from the corner of my eye.

He is dressed in a suit, which is out of place in the stadium today. The stubble he sports is purposeful, cut clean around his jaw. If I needed anything else to confirm that this man came from money, when he goes to unbutton his suit jacket, I catch a flash of silver on his wrist. A Chopard watch.

He's not someone I recognize from the gaming world. He's not an owner of any of the esports teams here, nor is he part of the C-suite of any of the game dev companies. I have them all memorized like the letters in the alphabet. There's not a key player I don't know.

The section I'm sitting in is reserved. Not just anyone can get a seat this close to the stage.

My suspicions rise, and I begin to mentally run through

Parker's known acquaintances. If this isn't someone connected to The System or EnglishCoffee, they must be here for Parker Covington.

Oh.

"I didn't think you were a video game enthusiast, Mr. Kelton."

Jace Kelton turns to look at me with a smile. I'm once again reminded that Parker Covington is somehow always surrounded by freakishly attractive people. The top one percent of Parker's world are not only filthy rich; they are gifted with the looks to go with it.

"I'm not," he admits. "But I make it my job to know my rivals inside and out, Ms. Lake." His lips curl around my name with a flirty tone. Unfortunately for him, it has no effect on me. Like I said, being around The System has made me immune to the whims of hot guys.

Well, most of them.

A fire burns through my blood and my palms begin to sweat as I remember this morning. I've come into contact with Parker's dick one too many times this last week. I literally just stared at him while my hand cupped his dick.

Mortification rips through my body again. I'm having second-hand embarrassment at myself.

The story of my life: Attracted and Embarrassed.

It sounds like the name of a trashy reality show.

"And that's game. Victory goes to the blue team,*" the male announcer states.*

Parker's team lets out a series of whoops as they clap each other on the back. The last time I saw him this happy was when he bought his blue Ferrari from a custom dealer in Italy last year. Not that Parker isn't always smiling and joking, but there is pure, uninhibited joy in his eyes right now. It's contagious. It makes me smile back.

Parker starts to put his blue LED mask on, but he gives the crowd a quick scan, his gaze landing on mine. The smile on his face falters briefly when he notices Jace by my side. But ever the showman, Parker just lets his smile shine brighter before winking at the crowd and slipping his mask on.

Now, he could be scowling at Jace and no one would know.

He holds hands and bows with his team. But instead of walking offstage with them, he jumps down and comes up to us, walking through the small mosh pit around the stage. The publicist in me freaks out for a second until I see one of the security guards jump into action to help him through the crowd.

I swear, that boy doesn't think sometimes.

With the help of the security guard, Parker gets through the wave of fans and up to the raised deck where I'm seated.

"You're supposed to be in the greenroom," I scold him. "Your speedrun is in an hour."

"That's plenty of time."

It's not, really. Not when he has two interviews lined up after the speedrun and an invitation to a network party tonight. He needs every second of rest he can get.

"Jace, didn't know you were in town, mate."

Jace eyes Parker, and I don't miss the way his gaze bounces across the mask.

It unsettles him.

I tamp down the laugh that threatens to spill. Even

though everyone knows who The System is now, it hasn't done anything to mitigate the intense aura these men exude when in their gaming personas. They've always held the attention of every room they're in, and people are afraid of their undeniable power. The masks definitely add to that.

When Parker is EnglishCoffee, there is no stopping the self-assured cockiness he bleeds.

"I was just in Vegas. Flew in on the jet this morning when I heard you'd made an appearance at the hotel. It's always a glorious day when a Covington admits defeat and stays at the Kelton."

"Defeat?" Parker laughs. "I just wanted to see what the standard was in Colorado. Considering your hotel botched our reservation, I'd have to say it wouldn't take much for us to raise the bar."

"A minor oversight." The muscle in Jace's jaw ticks. "Early snowstorm threw everyone for a tizzy."

Jace is in a similar position to Parker. His family has numerous hotels across Europe, but unlike the Covingtons, the Keltons have a large market share in the USA. If I remember correctly, he is a year or so older, which isn't saying much considering Parker is only twenty-four.

"Whatever you say."

"You always give me a headache, Covington," Jace sighs.

"It's one of my many charms."

I know Parker is grinning like a madman beneath that mask.

"I look forward to your event later." Jace places his hand on my shoulder. "I even have this beautiful lady to keep me company."

Parker immediately bats Jace's hand away and replaces it with his own as he tugs me toward him. "Thanks, it should be a good speedrun."

Jace studies the movement until Parker tucks his hands back into the pockets of his black pants.

"I'll catch you for a drink later tonight? You owe me a round."

"I have a pretty packed schedule. Everyone wants a piece of the Parker pie."

I beg myself not to roll my eyes at that cringe statement.

"*English* needs to get ready for his run and head back to the greenroom," I remind him. "Make sure you down an energy drink beforehand, okay?"

"You're staying here?"

"Unless you plan on getting in some sort of PR nightmare in the next thirty minutes, yes, I plan on staying here. I'll meet up with you after the run like planned."

Parker looks down at me, and I stare up into the blue LED Xs of his mask.

Is he nervous about the run? Does he need a pep talk or something? It didn't seem like he was worried earlier.

I give his shoulder a light squeeze.

"You've got this. You're going to crush it, trust me. I believe in you."

His hand comes up to rest on my own, and it sends a jolt of electricity through my body.

"Just keep your eyes on me, Syd." The way he says it is strangely intimate. "And Kelton?"

"Yeah?"

"Don't touch what isn't yours," Parker calls out as he

jumps backward off the raised platform.

My heart lurches at the move. He spins around and follows the waiting security guard back through the throng of fans.

"What about you, Ms. Lake?"

"What about me?"

"Care for a drink while we wait?"

"I don't drink."

"Never said it had to be alcoholic." He grins.

I would not be getting rid of this man.

Then again, what is the harm? They are still setting up the stage for the speedrun match. Four players will be going head-to-head.

"Sure," I relent. "I guess there's some time to kill."

"Brilliant."

Jace holds his hand out to me. I sigh and take it, allowing him to lead us through the fans crowding the stands as we walk up to the main deck.

I'll admit, the event is busier than I expected. It's one of the smaller tournaments this season, so I didn't think a lot of people would turn out. We have one in two weeks in Seattle that is a major event, and then the rest should be on the same level as that until we hit the championship.

Because speedrunning isn't as big as the esports-focused games, it's harder to find events for Parker to compete in this close to the end of the season. If we were just focused on *FrozeLine* or even *VERTEX*—another popular esports game that is battle royale which Parker excels at—it would be a different story. The opportunities there are endless.

But the guys aren't focused on becoming pro-esports

gamers, and Mathias has never had an issue with the boys doing as they please. The money they make from streaming and uploading videos is more than enough. Mathias has been pushing for more sponsorships lately because he wants to take advantage of the face reveal, but he still doesn't care much about the guys dipping into the esports arena.

"What can I get you?" Jace asks once we reach the first bar.

"I'll take an iced tea," I tell him, pointing at the bottles in the fridge nestled between the waters and hard seltzers.

Jace orders our drinks while I watch one of the TV screens above the bar. It shows the current match playing on the main stage. Two esports teams are competing in *VERTEX*, and I recognize one of the players as a guy the boys play with occasionally.

"Here." Jace hands me the bottle.

"Thank you." I twist open the lid and take a deep gulp.

I actually haven't had anything to drink in a few hours, now that I think about it. I've been so distracted by watching Parker and monitoring the guys back home that it didn't even occur to me.

"Let's go back to our seats before someone nicks them." Jace puts his hand out again for me to hold onto. I don't bother pointing out that our seats are in the reserved area, so no one can *nick* them, per say.

It takes us longer to get back to our section because some girl got the wings of her cosplay stuck to the tail of another girl's cosplay, and they were making a fuss in the middle of the staircase.

We sit down just as the MC announces the players taking the stage.

None of them have the same energy as Parker.

He stands there in his blue glory, waving at the crowd before taking his seat at his desk. The camera zooms in on him as he tears off his mask and runs his hand through his hair. A chorus of high-pitched cheers breaks out across the crowd, hundreds of women fawning over him.

"Popular one, isn't he?" Jace comments.

I tilt my head in a shrug. "Without a doubt."

"And now for the speedrun of Styx. Players will begin their game in five, four, three, two, one!"

Each gamer starts up their game, the load screen shifting into the opening cut scene.

"I have to say, I was surprised when I learned about his little side career. Thought my cousin was joking when she told me. None of the boys knew about it." Jace takes a large sip of his drink.

Apart from their families, no one knew about The System's real identities. Most of the people who worked for The System didn't even know their identities. Everything was a need-to-know basis. It wasn't until Stevie, Aleks' girlfriend, entered the picture that things began to change.

"And what do you think now?" I ask, keeping my eyes on the screens above the stage.

There are five, four of which mirror the screen of each gamer, while the one in the middle moves between face shots of the gamers and the announcers. Parker's screen is the last one, and I watch as his character runs across a barren field.

"Honestly, it makes sense. He was always busy once he moved to the States, but none of us could figure out why. He wasn't helping out at the hotels enough for that to be the case, and growing up, Parker was never as into the business as the rest of us. I'm not shocked he found a career that's more his speed."

I hum in agreement. I've only known Parker since I began working for The System, but even I know he is the type of person who can't stay still. He needs to be constantly stimulated, and his career is the perfect outlet.

"I'll admit; I'm surprised his family has been so supportive. Despite Parker's reluctance, I still thought he would inherit Covington Hotels. With how focused he is about this whole gaming thing, I'm not so sure anymore."

I say nothing. I really have no clue where Parker's head is on the subject.

Honestly, it's something that I have wondered myself. In the past few years, I haven't worried too much about Parker's role as the Covington heir because it didn't really impact his gaming career. But it was still something that always lingered in the back of my mind. Out of all the guys, he really did lead two separate lives, and now they are being forced to face one another. I'm not sure if they can coexist.

Considering that Parker hasn't brought it up, though, makes me think it's not something I need to be worried about. Mathias also hasn't mentioned anything on the matter either.

But still, there were those rumors.

My stomach sours at the thought of Parker leaving his gaming career behind, of leaving me—I mean us—behind. At the end of the day, he was raised a Covington.

I shake off the thoughts and take a deep gulp of my

iced tea.

Three hours pass by in a blur.

Jace attempts to make more small talk, but I think he eventually realizes that I'm more invested in Parker than chatting with him. Instead, he busies himself with a spreadsheet on his phone while glancing at the game in between.

I've kept my eyes on the screen as much as possible as Parker plays, but I've also been scrolling through my emails and the guys' social media. I've seen Parker run through this game enough times that I don't need to keep avid watch. I keep flipping to my notes app, though, to look at the standard times of the others players. I know them by heart, but it's a force of habit at this point.

So far, everyone is on track with their last public speedrun of the game.

If everything goes right, Parker should be done in the next fifteen minutes. The closest competitor is a solid ten minutes behind his gameplay time. Honestly, I had planned this tournament as an easier win for Parker. The gamers who signed up are well-known, but they aren't *that* wellknown. Not like the matches in the upcoming weeks where he will be up against his biggest rivals in the space.

As chill as Parker has been about everything, I still wanted him to have a higher likelihood of success for his first public speedrun.

I really shouldn't have worried. He's taken everything in stride. The press from the event has been nothing but positive so far. Everyone's been raving about his performance in the team *FrozeLine* matches, and now they are fawning over his solo speedrun.

I watch as the clock keeps ticking up.

Just a few more minutes.

Parker defeats the final boss and quickly implements a skip through the penultimate cut scene before rushing his character through a cemetery so he can finish the game. There's a cheer from the crowd. That skip is one that I know is hard to time correctly, and Parker's success has effectively guaranteed him first place.

I let out a loud whoop when his character finishes digging up a coffin and opens it to reveal the empty interior. The end credits grace the screen, and Parker grins wildly. He pushes away from the desktop and stands up, raising his arms as he walks across the front of the stage.

The crowd cheers his name.

English. English. English. English.

He stops when he makes eye contact with me. I give him two thumbs up, and he returns the gesture with a dramatic bow. One of the workers comes up to escort him offstage, which is my cue. He's going to be pulled into a few interviews now that all his events are over.

As happy as I might be with the way today has gone so far, I'm not about to let it cloud my judgment. Parker is still a loose cannon when it comes to interviews. He has a habit of getting a little too comfortable with the reporters. Something about being in his EnglishCoffee persona makes him more relaxed than usual.

"It was great meeting you, Mr. Kelton, but duty calls."

"Please, call me Jace. It was a pleasure to meet you, Sydney." He smiles before taking my hand and placing a kiss on the back of it.

Any regular woman would be melting at the panty-dropping grin, but it's nothing Parker hasn't done before.

If anything, it feels more robotic coming from Jace.

"And do remind Parker that he owes me a drink. He polished off my bottle of Paradis Imperial during our last poker game."

"I can't promise you anything, Jace, but I'll try. Until next time."

I hop down from our platform and begin weaving my way through the fans crowded around the stage. There's a small hallway I need to get to that only gamers and their teams can access. It effectively bypasses the regular route to the greenroom and brings you right to it.

I finally manage to break through the sea of people and stumble into the hallway. A quick flash of my badge has me passing through the two beefy security guards.

I finally come to the door and breathe a sigh of relief as I step across the threshold. The greenroom isn't relaxing by any means; it's packed with all the top players and their teams, but it's better than being out in gen pop.

Parker's white-blond hair isn't hard to miss. That, and he is one of the tallest people in the room and is wearing his mask.

He's already in conversation with a black-haired journalist.

My hackles rise.

Press isn't supposed to be allowed in here.

I pick up my pace, twisting around the other gamers until I pull up next to Parker.

"Genevieve, talking to my client without me, I see." My smile is thin and tight.

"Sydney, there you are. English and I were just talking about you." She taps his forearm, and my stomach swirls.

"Oh, really? How lovely. But our interview isn't scheduled for another twenty minutes."

"Well, I caught English right after the run, and he invited me in, so I thought, why not get it out of the way." Her smile is as fake as her veneers. "It was great chatting with you, English. Sydney, we'll send you the article once it's live." She gives a wiggle of her fingers before she flounces off.

"Seriously?" My voice is low and harsh as I pull Parker to the side, leading him to the private back room. Technically, it is reserved for the top esports teams, but I got access for Parker, considering his level of notoriety.

"She bombarded me! I couldn't just ignore her without her turning it into a story," he whines. "Plus, it's Genevieve. She's interviewed us a bunch of times. I know how to field her questions."

It's true. Genevieve is one of Justin's top reporters for *Gamer Weekly*. He tends to send her to most of the esports events because her looks get her around the red tape more often than not. If I'm not dealing with Justin, I'm dealing with Genevieve.

Still, it makes me uneasy. With the recent drama of the false disinheritance, Parker's upcoming participation at the Divizion Championship Series, and this being his first live match...there's too much at stake.

I let out a sigh.

"I'm sure it was fine." Or at least, I hope. "Great job, by the way. The run went smoothly."

Parker peels off his mask and grins at me.

My stomach does a little flip.

When Parker wears his mask—when he is English—it

is so much easier to think of him as just my client. When he takes it off and forces me to confront that boyish grin, it makes everything muddied. Lines begin to cross, and my heart gets confused.

"I totally crushed it! Didn't shave off any extra time, but I could have."

"I know. But we don't want you showing your hand this early," I remind him in a hushed tone.

Mathias instructed him to just play as expected, to not do anything flashy. We want to save that for the championship so no one has a chance to counter his improved times. Parker still has eight weeks, but he's already five minutes faster in practice than his current publicly recorded run times.

"What about Jace? Did he have anything to say?"

"He was impressed. Definitely a little jealous of all the fangirls you have."

"He certainly seemed distracted by my girl, that's for sure." Parker grabs a water bottle from the mini fridge and twists it open before guzzling half of it down. I watch his Adam's apple bob with the movement.

I'm so distracted I don't completely comprehend what he just said.

I brush off the comment, pulling out my phone to text the other reporter to see if we can move up the interview.

Once I get confirmation from him, I give Parker a nudge with my elbow, not realizing he is still drinking his water. The liquid goes sloshing.

"Shoot, sorry."

"It's fine." He looks down at me with a bemused expression, using the back of his hand to swipe the water from his lips. It's a simple movement, but it sucks the air from my lungs.

Come on, Sydney. Focus.

"I got your interview moved up. Let's knock it out so we can dip early and relax before the party tonight." I force the words out.

"Sounds good."

He slips his mask back on, and the storm of emotions within me calms to rolling waves.

I really need to get myself under control, or I don't know how I'm going to make it through these next few weeks.

Chapter NINE

PARKER

I stumble into the hotel room a little after midnight. Exhaustion tears at my body as I lie on the ground in the middle of the lounge area.

"I told you we didn't have to stay at the party that long," Sydney muses as she steps over me.

"Tell that to all of the people who kept coming up to me," I groan.

I'll never say no to a party; I love them just as much as the next person. But tonight wasn't a *party* party, despite how Syd makes it sound.

Everyone from the tournament was there, reporters and game developers included. It's not the same as going to a club with Aleks and Jackson or a penthouse party with the lads. I had to be switched on, make sure that I said hello to everyone, and play the role of English. The slight buzz I had from the champagne at the start of the night has worn off, and now I am just tired.

"Come on, party boy, get off the floor."

Sydney holds out her hand, and I take it even though her strength does nothing to help me up. I just crave her contact.

I haven't taken my mask off yet, and the LED bathes her in a soft blue. She looks gorgeous, even though I'm sure she's tired as shit as well. Honestly, I'm glad I didn't have to do this weekend alone. Throughout the craziness of today's event, I knew I could look over at her and ground myself. She was my constant in the chaos.

Syd wiggles her hand out of my own, and it brings me back to the present.

"We have an early flight tomorrow." She bends down to take off her heels.

"If we'd taken the jet, we could've slept in." I peel off my mask and toss it onto my overnight bag before working to undo the buttons on my shirt.

"You're like a dog with a bone, I swear," she chastises, setting her heels carefully next to the couch.

I love when she gets annoyed; it's adorable.

The doorbell to our room goes off, and Sydney peers up at me with confusion.

"Did you order something?"

"I don't know. Did I?" I give her a teasing grin as I run to the door. I take the cart from the employee outside, slipping them a fifty dollar note before rolling the cart into the room.

"What are you up to now, Parker?" Sydney lets out a deep sigh before padding over to me.

"I got us a little gift for all our hard work."

I take the plate covered by the silver cloche and put it on the coffee table before placing two champagne flutes and a bottle next to them.

I flop on the couch and toe off my shoes, kicking them across the room so they land somewhat close to my bag. I should probably be a little gentler, considering they cost me north of a grand.

I pat the cushion next to me, "Come on. Pop a squat."

Sydney climbs onto the couch, tucking her legs under her ass. She stares at my bare chest for a moment before turning her attention to the assortment on the table.

"That's a lot of champagne for one person."

"Ah, see that's where you're wrong, my dear Sydney." I grab the bottle and hold it out to her. "It's nonalcoholic." I pop off the top and pour us both a glass.

I hold mine out to her. "Cheers to a successful weekend."

"Cheers." She gives me a soft smile, clinking her glass to mine. "I know you don't need me to make your ego any bigger than it already is, but you did well today, Parker. You were a natural on stage, and your gameplay was amazing. DCS isn't going to know what hit them."

Pride warms my chest. Sydney's approval always burns brighter than anyone else's. I could win ten games in a row and not feel as accomplished as I do right now. I want to impress her, no matter the cost.

Which is why I remove the silver cloche to reveal the sweet treat underneath.

Sydney's eyes widen, and I watch as excitement dances across her moonlight eyes.

"Are those chocolate-covered berries?"

"Sure are. And before you ask, yes, it's vegan chocolate."

She picks up a fork and stabs a strawberry excitedly before popping the entire thing in her mouth. The little hum of pleasure she makes as she closes her eyes has my dick twitching.

I quickly pick up a fork and stab one of the little round balls, holding it out to her.

She barely ate anything at the party because the asshats didn't think to cater to people's dietary restrictions.

"Here, try this one."

She hesitates for a second, eyeing my fork. "I can feed myself."

"Just trust me on this one, Syd." I give her puppy-dog eyes. "Please."

She purses her mouth, but I see her shoulders relax. "Fine."

Her lips close around the fork, and I inwardly curse myself for this torture I've willingly inflicted upon myself.

I see the second she realizes what she's just bitten into. The corners of her eyes crinkle and a smile stretches across her face before she hurriedly chews to finish the treat.

"Cherries? No way. These are, like, one of my most favorite things in the world," she says as she stabs another one onto her fork and pops it into her mouth, completely distracted. "I can't believe they have them here."

Technically, they don't.

Oddly enough, chocolate covered cherries aren't easy to come by. I know Syd makes her own at home, so I had to pay the chef at the Kelton to make some just for us.

I take a sip of the sparkling drink, letting the bubbles fizzle across my tongue as I watch her happily devour the treats. I could watch her eat these for hours and not get bored. The way her lips form a perfect circle every time is mesmerizing.

"I'd feel bad eating all of these if I didn't know you hated sweets," she comments, demolishing the cherries at a breakneck pace. "You should've gotten something for yourself."

"This is my treat," I murmur, picking up a strawberry and holding it out to her.

Her eyes widen, and I watch a war play out across the dark gray skies of her gaze. For a moment, a split second, I think maybe I've won. Her tongue peeks out through the small gap in her mouth, licking her lower lip ever so slowly before she bites it.

Everything stops. My breath slows and I wait. Wait for her to make the move. Because no matter what I want, I know it has to come from her.

But the fire dies, and I see the storm in her eyes calm. She reaches out and plucks the strawberry from my hand, popping it into her mouth instead.

"I'm gowwing to hafe a shower," she mumbles around the chocolate as she shoots to her feet and basically sprints to the bathroom. The door slams shut, and I throw my head against the back of the couch.

I misread the distance, and my head clashes against the wall instead.

"Fuck," I hiss at the pain. But I don't move, I just close my eyes and take deep breaths, willing the blood in my veins to cool.

So close.

So damn close.

I'm beginning to wonder just how much longer I can last by her side without the glass castle crashing down around us. I'm beginning to wonder if I even care anymore.

This weekend has been torture.

Hell, the last five years have been torture.

But when I saw Jace next to Syd earlier today, it sent a bolt of ice into my chest. The fear was immediate. Jace makes women fall for him without trying. He's observant and knows how to make people feel at ease within seconds of knowing them. It's a talent that has broken more than a few hearts since we were in school.

Seeing Syd share her glowing smile with him sent me into protection mode. I didn't want him looking at her, let alone touching her.

Sydney Lake has been mine from the moment we locked eyes at that restaurant, even if she doesn't know it. She branded me, and I've never forgotten the taste.

The bathroom door blasts open, and I barely blink before Sydney practically dives into the bed.

All right.

If that's how she wants to play it.

I peel off my shirt and trousers, folding them haphazardly and leaving them on my roller bag. I stroll into the bathroom in just my briefs, keeping the door open as I get ready for the night.

If I have to suffer the torture of sleeping next to her without touching her, she can deal with my body.

I catch Syd checking out my ass a few times while

brushing my teeth before our eyes lock and she abruptly turns over and pulls the sheets up to her neck.

I roll my eyes, shutting off the lights and maneuvering through the dark room to the bed. Sydney doesn't budge as the bed dips under my added weight, but I do see her eyelids tighten. I lie on my side, propping my chin on my palm as I look at her. Try as she might, she can't fake asleep.

A few seconds pass before her left eye cracks open slightly. When she sees me, both eyes pop open, dipping briefly to my bare chest then back up to my gaze. Her jaw tightens and she flips over, giving me her back as she curls into a ball.

It's that split second of want that blooms in her gaze which gives me strength.

Sydney might like to think she is an iron castle, that she doesn't let anyone see what's past the gates unless she wants them to, but she forgets that I own the kingdom. I always see the little moments where she stares just a touch too long, where her attention slips lower than she intended it to.

Sydney Lake can say whatever she wants, she can be as professional as she deems, but I know that there is a piece of her that craves me just as much as I crave her. She's Eve and I'm the forbidden fruit. I just need to find a way to convince her to take a bite.

"All right, Syd?" My voice breaks the silence, and I see the way her shoulders pinch.

"I'm fine." It's a short, clipped response.

"You seem a little tense."

"I'm just tired."

"Didn't seem that tired when you were eating your

cherries." The silence returns as she proceeds to ignore me. "In fact, seemed like you were really enjoying them."

"Parker, I'm trying to sleep. We have to be at the airport in six hours."

"Wouldn't be worried about that if we took the jet," I bait.

"Seriously?" She flips over and frowns at me.

"Seriously." I knew that would get her.

We lock eyes, and I hold, waiting to see if she'll cave like always. She holds out longer than I expected, but eventually her gaze slides to the left to stare out the window behind me.

"I'm not in the mood to deal with this, Parker."

"With what?" I push.

"With you."

Her eyes return to mine. There's an undercurrent of pain curling around the steel. This is the closest I've ever gotten her to admitting something. Hidden by the night, with only small slithers of moonlight leaking in through cracks in the blinds and the soft glow of the alarm clock.

I see her step closer to the tree and take a closer look at the forbidden fruit dangling within her reach.

I reach forward, gathering a loose tendril of hair that has slipped out of her bun. I push the golden lock behind her ear, letting my fingertips trace the shell before coming to rest on her chin. Her body shivers at the contact.

I leave my hand between us. An open invitation.

The silence grows until it is thick with the tension bleeding around us.

Her chest rises and falls as her emotions create a whirlwind inside her small body. Those eyes dip to my lips, up to my stare, then back to my lips. I don't stop the urge to bite my lower lip, I embrace it, letting the pain center me.

Her hand comes up to circle my raised wrist, and the world stops spinning.

I know this is the moment. The moment when she decides to take a bite or not. She's plucked the fruit off the tree; the temptation is right there in the palm of her hand.

This is the one shot.

"Parker."

My name slips from her lips ever so quietly, and I hear the reluctance in the tone. The worry. The fear. I see her trying to take a step away from the tree, away from the fruit that calls her name.

I can't.

I can't let her go.

"Fuck it."

I close the distance between us, and Sydney sucks in a breath just as my lips crash into hers.

She tastes exactly as I remember. Like cherries and pure fucking sunshine. I drink it all in, savoring every second like a man finding a stream in the middle of a forest fire.

I'm an astronaut who has been stranded, floating in space, and I've just been brought back down to Earth. Gravity hits me all at once, pulling me toward her. I feel at peace, grounded. I don't stop kissing her, I don't chance it.

My free hand comes around the back of her neck, and I tilt her up to me, deepening the kiss. I stifle the groan building in my throat as I continue to taste every inch of her marshmallow-soft lips.

Now that I've started, I don't know if I can stop. Every

thought in my mind disappears as I single-mindedly focus on the way she feels pressed against me.

She pulls back slightly and murmurs my name against my mouth.

"Parker, I don't think—"

"Don't think," I cut her off. "For five minutes, just don't think." I nip her top lip, and her eyes flutter shut.

"Five minutes."

Sydney's hesitant lips push back against my own, and I refrain from pulling her on top of me. From hauling her sweet body onto my hips so I can feel every inch of her on me.

She said five minutes, and I'm not going to do anything to lose even a single second by doing something that could throw her off.

I'm not a patient man, but I've waited five years for these five minutes.

Because Sydney will always be the exception. I'll move like molasses for her, so long as she keeps teasing those sinful lips against mine.

Her tongue teases against my mouth, and I open to her instantly, letting her in. It's a perfect dance, and my blood roars to attention when a low hum slips out of her.

My briefs do nothing to stop my straining cock, thick with want for the beauty before me. I reach down and give it a rough stroke through the fabric.

God, I need her. I need her so fucking bad.

I groan against her lips, intoxicated by her, fading into the oblivion that is Sydney Lake.

Her hand comes around my shoulder, and I shudder at the feeling of her fingers on my bare skin. My body heats wherever she touches as though it is imprinting the feel of her down to my very soul. Her nails dig into my biceps, and the slight tug is the only signal, the only invitation, I need.

I swing my leg around her, caging her between the bed and my body.

I'm careful not to crush her, using my knees and elbows to hover above her, because I know the second I come down on her, she will feel exactly how much I want her—and I'm not sure if that is going to freak her out or not. But then her soft legs hook behind my own, her ankles cross beneath my ass, and she pulls.

Every sane thought flees from my mind as my body connects with hers. She's wearing that silk night set again, but my bare chest can feel the hardened peaks of her breasts pressing against the fabric.

My hips buck ever so slightly, my heavy length jerking against her heat, and I feel her sharp inhale in response. I lean into her with a bruising kiss, taking as much of her as she will give.

There is no end, there's just the continuous whirlpool of our lips as we meet in crashing waves.

"I think our five minutes are up," she mutters between kisses.

"Are they? I'm not very good at being punctual."

She giggles, and it sounds like fucking tinkling bells, mesmerizing me as I drink the sound directly from her lips.

Then it hits.

She lets out a sigh that speaks a thousand words.

Her lips tug in one final kiss, and I do everything I can to keep her there, sucking her bottom lip into mine until it releases with a pop. My forehead falls against hers, and her hand comes up to rest on my pecs. I have no doubt that she can feel the erratic beating of my heart.

I don't want to open my eyes. I don't want to see what is written on her face. There are too many options, too many possibilities, but every single one of them is a potential blade ready to stab my soul.

"Parker…"

One word and my ribs hollow.

"I know." I try to keep the disappointment out of my voice, try to keep my composure, but it's hard. It's hard because the woman I want, the woman I've always wanted, who has just given me a small slice of heaven, is taking the halo back, sending me back to Earth.

So, I take the coward's way out. I roll off her and lie there, listening to her shift away. I feel the distance as the bed dips and rises from her movement. I squeeze my hands, fisting them so my nails dig into my palms.

The taste of cherry is still on my tongue, so I bite it—hard—until my teeth bring out little drops of blood and the metallic tang chases away the sweetness.

She doesn't say another word, and I lie there listening to her breaths, counting them as they slow down. I don't know how long it takes, but eventually she falls asleep.

I lie awake for hours.

I worry that if I fall asleep, I'll wake up and find out everything was just a dream.

When the remnants of moonlight begin to fade and the first rays of sun start to filter into the room, I pull myself quietly out of the bed. I throw on a jumper and grab my laptop, heading onto the balcony. The icy wind bites into me, but I welcome it as I slump onto the lounge chair.

I open my laptop and lose myself to a game while praying that by the time the sun rises and Sydney wakes up, everything will be okay.

That those five minutes weren't our last five minutes.

That maybe, *just maybe*, Eve will stay in the Garden of Eden.

Chapter TEN

SYDNEY

66 *T*he stalker would leave Barbie dolls altered to look like the woman he was infatuated with at various locations, including the doorstep of her mansion, which had a minimum of six security guards present at all times on the grounds. No one knew how the assailant was getting past not only the guards but also the various security cameras posted around the property.*

"I'm telling you now, it has to be one of the guards." Lee shakes the lollipop in her hand at the giant television mounted above the aquarium in her living room.

"That seems kind of obvious, though." Deer hums. "Do you think the guy is altering the dolls on his own? Or is he getting someone else to make them for him?"

"He has to be making them himself. There would be a trail if he had someone else making them, and they would be a loose end," I chime in.

"What if it's not a guy at all?"

The three of us turn our heads to the brunette with her long legs draped over the edge of the armchair she's made herself comfortable on. The newest addition to our Tuesday Crime Nights, Stevie takes a large sip of the red wine she's nursing as she analyses the latest episode of our favorite true crime show.

"True." Lee tilts her head, black hair swaying. "But I highly doubt it. Most stalkings are committed by men. Plus, the MO reads way too male."

"Mmm, I agree." Deer chews on the straw of her drink, some spiked boba concoction she whipped up. "You can tell it's based on some fantasy he's built up, especially with the way he is focused on the dolls and having them look like her, ya know."

"Damn," Stevie whistles.

Lee, Deer, and I have been meeting for weekly crime nights for almost two years now. We alternate between true crime and haunted house investigations, depending on our moods, but always add in a healthy dose of gossip. We rarely miss a week unless it's a holiday or there's some sort of gaming conflict.

Allison Lee is the top female video game streamer in the United States. Going by the gamertag "LoveLee," she has made waves in the community and come out a queen. I've known her for almost as long as I've known The System because Aleksander took her under his wing when she started breaking out in the streamer space. We became fast friends when we found out that we both had a deep love for disturbing true crime podcasts and documentaries.

It was Lee who started our weekly hangouts when she made friends with Deer, another fellow streamer. Known as "TheCozyDeer," she is one of the most-viewed content creators when it comes cozy video games. She puts out a new video almost every single day. Recently, though, she's been going viral from edits of her horror streams. For someone who bled the color pink and spent hours cultivating cute towns online, Deer plays some unhinged stuff.

Deer didn't hang out with The System much, but since meeting Stevie at the club a few months back, she'd begun going out with them a bit more. Truthfully, considering how long I've known her, there is still a lot I don't know. She likes to keep her gaming life pretty well separated from her personal life, unlike Lee, who is a bit too much of an open book.

The two girls are my sanity, honestly. I am surrounded by testosterone twenty-four seven, and up until recently, I couldn't really be open about my job to anyone else I met. It made making friends a little hard when you couldn't talk about ninety percent of your day-to-day life, so having girlfriends in the same space as the guys helped.

That being said…

I hadn't breathed a word about this past weekend to them.

There is no way I ever could.

Oh my God.

I kissed Parker Covington.

I can't believe I freaking kissed him?

I work for him, for God's sake. Even though it isn't the most conventional publicist relationship, it is still a professional one. Mathias would kill me if he found out. Heck,

I'd do it for him! Everything about what I did went against everything I know. I am becoming my own PR nightmare, let alone a legal nightmare. A romantic relationship with anyone in The System is a direct violation of my contract.

What is wrong with me?

I crossed the line on so many levels, and I just…I don't even have an excuse. It's not like I was drunk, high, or clinically insane at the time. I'd even been lying when I'd told him I was tired that night. My body had been on high alert the second he held that chocolate-covered strawberry out to me. A want swirled deep within my core, and I could do nothing to tamp it down, no matter how hard I tried. Even the cold shower I doused myself in didn't cool the heat crawling across my skin. He ignited me, and the flames aren't going away.

Years.

I'd spent years ignoring my attraction to Parker. I'd placed him squarely in that little box in my brain that said, "Do not touch." I made sure to just treat him like English-Coffee, a mask and nothing more.

Maybe that's where it all went wrong. Ever since the guys came clean about their identities, their gamer personas and real-life ones have been blurring. I don't see him as just English anymore; he is becoming Parker to me, and that…that is dangerous because Parker is someone I have history with.

History that I tried to erase from the books.

If that one night had never happened, I wouldn't be stuck where I am right now.

I need to get myself together. I have to put him back in that little box before it is too late. Sure, we'd made out, but that was nothing.

Liar.

It was everything.

I groan into my tea, but the noise is drowned out by the TV.

"When the victim was set to get married, the chapel was blown up in an act of retaliation. Here are pictures from the scene shortly after."

"I'm not going to lie, it's sort of creepy that this girl has the same hair as me." Deer's pouty lips purse as she runs a manicured hand through her wavy pink hair. I don't know how the little charms on her nails don't get all tangled in her hair.

"Better sleep with one eye open, then, babe," Lee croons, wiggling her fingers creepily in the air.

"Don't be an eejit." She rolls her eyes, her slight Irish accent peeking out with the slang. Normally, it only slips out when she's mad, super drunk, or speaking to her family. "Although, that being said, I am thinking of moving out. The security at my place isn't great; they've had some issues lately."

"Why don't you just look at getting a place in our complex?" I suggest, forcing myself to pay attention. "The guys have great security there."

Stevie snorts. "The rent at your place is stupid high."

"What? No, it's not." I reach forward and pluck a pretzel from the bowl on the coffee table. "It's barely half my biweekly paycheck."

Lee's brows furrow. "That can't be right."

"I swear; I only pay twenty-five hundred." I look around at the three girls, popping the salty pretzel in my mouth. The crunch is loud compared to their silent stares.

Deer pitches forward, over Lee, and slaps her hands on my thighs. "Syd, it's okay, you can tell me. Whose dick did you have to suck for that price? Or vagina. I'm very open."

I choke on my pretzel.

Deer's wide eyes blink up at me from beneath her anime lashes, and Lee lets loose a loud howling laugh between us, tears beading in her eyes.

"Oh, she didn't even have to suck a dick for that deal. It was given freely. Without her knowledge, clearly." Stevie throws us a wolfish grin as she drains the last of her wine.

"What are you talking about?"

"Sydney, your apartment costs ten grand a month." She raises a perfect brow at me before pointing a finger at Deer. "Which you can afford, by the way."

"I know, I'd just rather not." Deer pushes off me and slumps back across the velvet couch.

"Hang on, rewind. My apartment does not cost that much."

I would know if my apartment is actually four times the price I pay.

Stevie flicks her wrist. "Google it."

I let out a huff, standing up and grabbing my phone from the bowl by the door. Lee has a strict "no phone" rule during Crime Night unless absolutely necessary. We all spend way too much time staring at the little rectangle screens during our day-to-day life that it is always a nice break.

I throw the name of the complex into the search engine and click on the website before scrolling down to available apartments. There's only one one-bedroom apartment for rent right now, and it has a similar floorplan to my own. I click on it and wait for the price to load.

My brows pull together at the number on the screen.

I hit the refresh button and let it load again.

When the same number appears, I look up and see Stevie grinning at me over the back of the armchair, her head perched between her hands like a demonic cherub. I toss my phone back into the bowl and stalk over to her.

"Explain."

She spins back around, her glossy lips pulling up in a smirk. She makes a dramatic show of crossing her tan legs and placing her clasped hands on her knees. Her catlike eyes sparkle with mischief. It is no surprise Aleksander fell for her the second he laid eyes on her. She is stunning.

"Parker owns the complex."

My eyes narrow. "The Covingtons don't own residential real estate."

"Which is why I said Parker." She leans forward to fill up her wine glass. "Parker Covington owns your apartment complex, and he gave you the apartment at a reduced price."

"That's not a reduced rate, Stevie! That's basically fraud!" My voice comes out higher than I intended. "It can't be legal."

My head is spinning.

"I mean, if he did it of his own volition, I don't see an issue with it," Deer cuts in with a shrug.

"You really didn't know?" Lee gives me a look of incredulity, and I just shake my head.

"I barely even knew him when I got the place."

The excuse is weak and, honestly, does nothing to help

my case. It just makes it even more confusing.

I'd only been working with The System for a few weeks when Parker had told me that it would be a lot easier if I lived in the same building instead of commuting over an hour—especially since their schedules could change on a whim. It helped that I kind of hated my dingy apartment at the time. It was all I'd been able to afford moving out to California not really understanding how much higher the rent was compared to Missouri, and the idea of living in a glitzy apartment complex seemed like a dream.

I should've known it was too good to be true.

"Hmm, well, he does have a nice butt. Wouldn't blame ya if you were giving him alternative forms of payment. Just saying." Deer sucks loudly on her boba.

"Ew." Lee scrunches her nose. "He's like my little brother. I really don't want to think about his ass or any other part of his body naked."

"Actually, I saw that package the other week and," Stevie purses her lips and raises her brows, "not bad."

Deer squeals and Lee lets out a groan that turns into a laugh.

"Stop, stop, stop. He's my client, I'm not doing," I wave my hands around, "any of that stuff."

Lies.

"Me thinks she doth protest too much," Stevie sings.

Panic rears inside me, and I see Lee's eyes narrow mid-laugh, assessing me.

"How do you even know this?" I ask Stevie, desperately attempting to divert the conversation away.

"Aleks offered me the same deal after the whole black-mail thing since the security there is lightyears ahead of the stuff at my place," she tosses out. "But it seemed like a waste of money to rent a whole second apartment for a few months when I'd just end up with Aleks most of the time anyway."

"The next thing you're going to tell us is that you have a company car when it's really just a car English gave you," Lee jokes.

I, however, blanch.

"No." Lee's eyes round as she clutches my forearm. "Sydney, seriously?" She lets go and clutches her stomach in a fit of laughter. Stevie joins her, cackling.

"Wait, hang on, it's not like that," I protest. "I don't even use the car."

Deer reaches over and pats me on the knee, "Quit while you're ahead, babes."

I bury my face in my hands as my skin turns to ice.

The stupid car sits in the parking garage. It's sat there for five years. I've driven it exactly three times. I haven't touched it since the guys gave me full access to Francis and to their joint rideshare account my second week working for them. I think Parker still takes it out every once in a while to make sure it's running smoothly, but that's it.

The car is one thing…it makes sense in the grand scheme of things. Lots of people had company cars. But the apartment? What is that about? Why not tell me?

God. This is a mess.

"I mean, it is Parker," I say. "He does tend to drop money without a second thought. He literally decided two days ago to fly to Japan this week for the F1 race."

"Boys and their cars. Aleks is raging he didn't get an invite," Stevie adds.

The F1 race was the last thing he talked to me about before we split ways after landing back in California on Sunday. Parker flies out tomorrow night, so I just have to avoid him for one more day.

I've been successful so far.

He has been grinding hours online since he will be gone all weekend again. When I'd stopped by the apartment today to go over some things with Jackson, I didn't have to worry about seeing him, since he was holed up in his streaming room.

Realistically, I can't avoid him forever. I quite literally have to fly with him to Seattle next week, but the more distance I can put between us while I screw my head back on straight, the better. These feelings I have are nothing more than a momentary lapse in judgment.

They have to be.

I'd gotten over them once before. I can do it again.

"I don't know, it still smells fishy," Lee comments as she crunches the last of her lollipop.

"I mean, maybe he just likes you," Deer throws out, picking an invisible piece of lint off her skirt. "I haven't seen you guys interact much, but it seems like the sort of thing he would do. It's a rich-person response."

"Stop. You guys would be so cute." Lee smiles. "I don't think I've seen you go on a date in years."

"That's a little sad." Deer side-eyes.

My stomach bottoms out.

Parker Covington doesn't *like* me.

Sure, he'd kissed me, but that...I don't know what that was. Maybe he just got caught up in the moment, in the proximity. It was late, and we were sharing the same bed.

It was dark.

I mean, come on. This is Parker. He doesn't take anything seriously. There is no way he thinks of our kiss as more than something in the heat of the moment.

I kissed him and I don't like him.

I mean, I like him. But I do not *like* like him.

I just have to keep reminding myself of that.

"I think you're all reading into it waaaay too much." I wave them off, reaching for the TV controller and bumping up the volume. "It's Parker. No one knows why he does anything he does."

"Whatever you say." Stevie smirks at me, and I fight to not let my skin flush.

I'll have to play this carefully for the next few weeks. Stevie is more observant than people give her credit for. I mean, she figured out The System's real identities in just a few weeks when people had been trying to figure it out for years. I have no doubt she might be able to sniff out whatever is going on with Parker and me. I need to bury our tension under ten layers of dirt and then build a house over it.

My phone pings with a very particular alert tone across the room, and Lee levels me with a glare.

"Don't look at me like that." I peel myself off the couch, thankful for the distraction. "You know I have it set so I only get specific notifications during Crime Night."

Which is not a good sign.

"I know. Grab the blondies while you're up."

I roll my eyes.

"Pleeeease," she calls out.

"All right, all right."

She blows me a kiss before snuggling into Deer and turning her attention back to the TV, which is showing an opulent mansion with hundreds of police cars outside it. Stevie gives me a look over her wine glass before also returning to the murder-stalking at hand. Honestly, I'll do anything to keep them from fixating back on Parker.

I pluck the tray of fresh-baked blondies from on top of the stove and grab more of the spiked-boba concoction from the fridge. Maybe if I ply them with enough sugar and alcohol, they'll forget the Parker thing entirely.

I balance the tray on my forearm as I pick up my phone and then almost drop it when I see the name on my screen.

Justin Rivera.

I plop the tray on the table and fill up Deer's cup with the drink before flopping into the corner of the couch, angling away from the girls before unlocking my phone.

JUSTIN ☠ RIVERA
Hello

ME
Yes.

The phone rings and his caller ID pops up. I hit decline. Any call with Justin is on the record, and if he's messaging me this late at night, it won't be anything good.

JUSTIN ☠ RIVERA
Really, Lake?

I have a gift for you.

ME

Return it. I don't want it.

JUSTIN ☠ RIVERA

Are you sure?

ME

No gift from you is free.

JUSTIN ☠ RIVERA

And here I thought you would be interested in some...interesting...photos I have.

Crap.
I bite my thumb.

ME

What do you want?

JUSTIN ☠ RIVERA

Let's discuss the details tomorrow.

ME

I'm pretty busy.

JUSTIN ☠ RIVERA

I guess it can wait...gives me time to gather extra evidence.

Does Monday fit into your schedule better?

Hm. Whatever these photos are, he must be the only one with them if he is willing to give me almost a week.

It's all suspicious.

ME

Monday works.

JUSTIN ☠ RIVERA

Wonderful. La Sienna at 12.

I toss my phone onto the coffee table, too lazy to make the walk back to the bowl.

"Everything all right?" Lee nudges me with her fuzzy-socked foot.

"As much as it can be." I grab a handful of mini pretzels and stuff them into my mouth.

"Ominous," Deer croons.

"If it was Aleks, I apologize in his stead," Stevie salutes.

"Depends, you guys get photographed doing something you shouldn't?"

Stevie swirls her red wine as she thinks, and I pinch the bridge of my nose. Those two, I swear. Aleks is supposed to get into less trouble with a girlfriend, not more.

"We should be in the clear." She gives me a thumbs up. "We made sure to lock the door of the bathroom before fucking."

"Lovely," I cringe. "Bathroom where?"

"The Electric Tyger. We went clubbing to celebrate Parker's win Saturday—in spirit."

Of course, they did.

They were all out clubbing while I was busy sticking

my tongue down Parker's throat, where it certainly did not belong.

"I'm sure it'll all be fine," I sigh, sinking deeper into the couch.

I try to focus on the rest of the podcast episode, but my mind keeps wandering.

What could the photos be of?

Why would Justin want to show me them in person?

How come Parker never told me about the apartment?

What else has Parker done without me knowing?

I am going to drive myself into a wall at this rate.

One thing is certain. I have a week to pull myself together.

Chapter ELEVEN

PARKER

She's avoiding me.

I step on the gas and watch the speedometer tick higher and higher and higher. I swerve between the lines of cars on the freeway. The engine rumbles below me, and I sink into the smooth leather as I let the speed carry me and turn the world outside into a blur.

It's frustrating as hell.

I know for a fact that she went to the apartment a bunch of times last week, and not once did she come in to see me.

She knew I was there; knew I was grinding. I wasn't even streaming, so she could've come into my room without interrupting. But no. She came up to check on Jackson and just left me a new supply of energy drinks from our sponsor.

My chest aches with the pain that has been present all

week. The very same pain I tried to douse with champagne and cars and games.

It isn't going away.

I went to Suzuka and didn't hear a peep from Syd. She normally tracks me like a bloodhound and sends me little reminders to "behave myself" and "not make her job harder." I even made a point of posting a bunch of videos to my stories, at the clubs with the drivers after the grand prix—there was even one of me drinking from an ice luge—and she still didn't say anything.

I'd heard from Aleks nonstop though. He was chafed that I didn't bring him along and wouldn't stop bugging me for photos until I told him I'd bring him to the Vegas race.

The GPS signals my final turn, and I swing into an open parking spot a few doors down from the restaurant. I pull down the visor and touch up my hair before pocketing my phone and lifting the scissor door. Once I'm standing in the warm September sun, I take a second to admire the way my new car shines in the light.

The Lamborghini Revuelto arrived while I was in Japan, and she is a beauty. I'd even gotten it a custom aqua color, which had tacked on a solid chunk of extra change to the already hefty price tag, but I have no regrets. It is hands down the best car I have in the States, reaching sixty miles per hour in under three seconds.

Aleks is going to nut when he sees it.

I shove my hands into my pant pockets as I stroll up to the restaurant, the smell of fresh pizza and pasta permeating the air.

Quiet determination thrums in my blood as I bypass

the host desk entirely and walk right into the belly, scanning the tables.

I spot that recognizable head of blonde hair and smile, proud of myself. The mere sight of her after a week causes desire to curl under my skin. That is until I notice the obviously male figure she is seated in front of.

Thick jealously stirs in my stomach when I see Sydney laughing alongside the guy.

Syd locks eyes with me, and a flash of panic has her gaze darting from me to the man and back. My jaw ticks.

Who the hell is she with?

I'm a few tables away when I recognize the guy.

Fuck.

It's Justin Rivera.

Without drawing attention to myself, I alter my course and slip into an empty chair at a nearby table. It's not close enough to hear their conversation, but at least if Justin looks around, he'll have a hard time seeing me.

This isn't exactly going to plan.

Then again, I didn't really have a concrete plan in the first place.

Sydney has already regained her composure and is chatting away with Justin.

My curiosity bubbles. Syd wouldn't just take a meeting with Justin for no reason. He's one of the few reporters I'm actually wary of. It costs a lot—and I mean *a lot*—of money to stop him from running a story. Most of the time, it's cheaper to deal with the fall out than to prevent it, even for me.

Sydney takes a sip of her drink, her lips closing around the straw, and I have flashbacks to the other night. Those lips closing around my own and sucking on them. Her tongue tangling with mine in pure sweetness.

God dammit. I would give anything to taste her again.

If all I can get are a handful of forbidden kisses and stolen touches, then at least it's something.

Selfishly, I want her to give me more.

I just don't know how to convince her. I don't know how to get her to move forward, to give me more than five minutes.

What I know is that the want I've had for her hasn't lessened since the day we met. In fact, I'm beginning to realize that it's just gotten stronger and I'm falling deeper and deeper for a woman who wants me and wants nothing to do me with me at the same time. A woman who will only grant me a stolen kiss before icing me out.

And that's what I'm most afraid of. I'm scared that she's going to retreat further into her icy shell and I'm going to lose any hope at having her take my hand.

"Sir, excuse me, but you can't sit here. This table is reserved for a party of two arriving shortly." The waitress pulls me out of my memories and gives me an apologetic smile as she points to the "reserved" placard on my table.

Seriously? There are no other open tables.

I flick my eyes over to Sydney and Justin, who are still locked deep in conversation, a silent battle on both their faces. I open the wine menu and point to the most expensive bottle of champagne.

"I'll take this."

The woman's brows turn down in confusion. "Um. I…I said the table was reserved."

"I know, and I said I'd order this four-hundred-dollar

bottle of champagne."

I deliver the line with a very fake, closed-lip smile. The kind that borders the line of asshole and privileged.

She blinks at me like a robot rebooting before snatching up the placard with a smile. "Of course, I'll bring it right out."

The waitress come scurrying back out and brandishes the bottle with a flourish before popping it.

The noise resounds through the restaurant. I curse under my breath, turning my head to the side and shifting my chair so I'm obscured by the waitress. She pours me a glass with a smile. "Is there anything else I can get you?"

"No, thank you," I wave her off, my hand coming up to play with the hoops in my ear nervously.

When she moves away, she reveals the promise of murder in Sydney's gaze from across the restaurant.

Yeah, this really isn't going to plan.

Although, contempt is better than indifference. I'd rather her want to cut off my dick than want nothing to do with it. I'll take the win where I can at this point.

I raise the flute of champagne to my lips, watching them as I sip. It's not bad; the honeysuckle sweetness bubbles on the tongue, but it's definitely overpriced. I could buy three of these directly from my seller for the same cost.

But the price is nothing when it gives me a chance at Sydney.

Whenever Justin takes a sip of his coffee, Syd's gaze strays to me briefly and her anxiety oozes out. It's enough of a sign that whatever conversation she's having with Justin isn't a great one.

It means one of us fucked up.

I run back through everything I did in Japan, but nothing sticks out as overtly problematic, and I mentally pat myself on the back. I don't try to make her life harder, but sometimes life happens and the next thing you know, you're streaking nude through the garden of the Skaugum Estate.

Two glasses of champagne, a complimentary bread bowl, and five rounds of the MMO game I play on my phone later, I finally catch movement at Syd's table again.

She stands up and straightens her skirt before grabbing the matching jacket from the back of her chair and slipping it on. Justin follows suit and brandishes his elbow for Syd to hold onto. She quirks her brow at him but places a dainty hand in the nook. I stop myself from rolling my eyes and instead pick up my menu to hide behind.

"I'm glad we were able to clear everything up," Justin comments as they get nearer.

Sydney snorts. "You would've been delusional to post that rumor, Rivera."

"*Se mezcla un poco la verdad con mucha desinformación*," Justin tsks. "There's always a little truth, little Sydney."

"Yeah, the truth is that he's a pain in my ass."

"Is that on record?"

"You wish."

My shoulders slump back after they pass, and I toss the menu back onto the table before taking a healthy gulp of champagne.

A hand slams down on my table and I jerk, tipping way more champagne down my throat than planned and coughing.

"Seriously?"

I look up into Sydney's furious face.

She aggressively pulls the extra chair at my table back, sending a screeching noise through the restaurant, before dramatically sitting down. She folds her arms across her chest and crosses her legs, the top of her pointed heel grazing my leg in the process. If this were a video game, I would've just unlocked the achievement "pissed-off publicist."

A very hot, very pissed-off publicist.

Yup. There is definitely something wrong with me.

"What are you even doing here, Parker?" Her face is one of unveiled displeasure, but I don't miss the flicker of anxiety underneath.

"Well, I was enjoying an overly expensive glass of champagne." I place the flute back on the table.

Her eyelids lower in annoyance. "You're supposed to be filming gameplay content."

"I'm going to do it later."

"You're streaming later."

"*Later* later, then."

She closes her eyes and brings one hand up to pinch the bridge of her nose. "Seriously, what are you doing here?"

"Looking for you because you've been avoiding me."

"I'm not avoiding you." Her eyes dart down as she smooths out the sleeve of her jacket.

"Rubbish." I scoot my chair to the side and lean forward, resting my forearms on my knees. My face levels with hers, and I raise a brow. "I know you, Sydney, and I know you've done everything you can to avoid being in the same room as me since—"

"This isn't the place," she cuts in with a low hush. Her lips squish together as her eyes flick around the room.

"Fine." I take out my wallet and drop a bunch of notes on the table. "Then let's go somewhere else."

I stand up and hold my hand out to her. She ignores it and strides out of the restaurant ahead of me.

"This is going great," I mutter under my breath before strolling after her.

She's turning to ice, freezing more and more by the second.

Will I be able to thaw her before it's too late?

"Come on, I'll drive us." I press the button on my car keys to open the scissor doors.

"New car?" Her voice holds a little less animosity as she eyes it warily.

"You bet. A '24 Revuelto." I give the roof a tap before swinging onto the custom obsidian leather and running my hands over the steering wheel. God, she's a beauty.

Syd slips into the passenger seat and buckles her seat belt. "You say that like I'm supposed to understand what it means."

"Good car. Expensive car. Go very fast. Very nice," I say in a caveman tone as I start up the engine and begin pulling out of the spot.

She huffs out a little laugh, the corner of her lips twitching up in the smallest of smiles as she rolls her eyes.

Thank God.

Her tiny smile turns into a screech as I hit the main road and switch from the electric mode to sport mode on the car and rev it, increasing my speed by the second.

"Parker Covington, I do *not* need another heart attack

today."

"Come on, Syd, live a little."

"Parker, I'm serious. Slow down. I saw that champagne bottle on your table."

"All right, all right." I ease off the gas pedal, not wanting to upset her. "In my defense, I'm well within the legal
limit. I barely touched the champagne even though I paid
out the ass for it."

"Then why'd you even buy it?" she mutters, looking
out the window to the ocean.

There's something off about her tone, but I don't push
it. Not yet. Pushing Syd to open up normally results in
her doubling down. She's like those sea creatures with the
little tentacles that, when you poke them, close in on themselves.

"Because they wouldn't let me stay in the restaurant
otherwise." I shrug.

"How'd you even know I was there?"

"Phone tracker."

Her head whips to me. "What the hell, Parker?"

"What? You do it to us all the time."

"That's different," she defends.

"Not really." I reach forward and fiddle with the map
on the digital monitor to make sure I'm headed the right
way. "What were you meeting Justin about anyway?"

"Oh. *That*." Her eyes narrow with irritation and her entire mood dips like she was dunked in ice water.

"What? Why are you looking at me like that? I haven't
done anything wrong."

"Except you did." She points an accusatory finger at
me. "*You* joked to that waitress in the airport lounge that I

was your girlfriend, and *she* took a photo of us and sent it to *Gamer Weekly* in an exclusive."

"Oh."

"Yes, 'oh.'" She flops back into her seat, crossing her arms over her chest. "And then he tracked down more pictures of us snapped throughout the airport when we touched down in Colorado with your arm slung all over me. The whole thing didn't look good when pieced together. You're lucky it was an easy story to kill because Justin knows you guys, knows me, knows I wouldn't risk everything to date somcone like you."

Her words lance me like a sharpened blade in my back.

"But he still could have run with it just to mess with us if he felt like it, especially after Aleksander blew off that interview. Everyone has their eyes on you with this upcoming championship. You need to be smarter, Parker."

My gut churns uncomfortably as nausea mixes with anger.

Nah, fuck this.

This isn't what I deserve.

I'm not going to let her disguise her panic with poisoned words.

I press on the indicator and speed the car three lanes to the left before pulling into a mostly empty beach car park. I throw the Lambo into park and switch off the engine.

"What are you doing?" Sydney's head swivels as she looks around us in confusion.

"Having a conversation." I unbuckle my seat belt and face her. "What's going on with you?"

"What're you talking about?" She mimics my movements.

"First, you avoid me. Then, you ice me out. And now? Now, you're just being mean." My voice cracks on the last word.

"I…" Hurt flashes through her eyes before they fill with shame. "I didn't mean to be mean," she says softly.

"Someone like me? I need to be smarter?" I repeat the words back to her. "Might as well just call me a dumb rich boy like the tabloids."

Her head drops, her bangs hiding her eyes, and it hurts me to hurt her. Every part of my body is screaming at me to stop talking. To just brush it under the rug and ignore it, like I do when anyone else says the same shit. I've dealt with people spewing this sort of stuff to me my entire life, and I hate it, but I accept it because I know it's not me. Just like I know *this* is not her. I know it. I'm willing to put myself through the pain, put her through the pain, if it gets us to the truth.

"I thought you knew me better. You're supposed to be my friend, Syd."

"I'm supposed to be your publicist." She looks up at me through her bangs, a slight sheen to her eyes. "I'm supposed to be your publicist, and you're making it hard for me to remember that."

"You've never been *just* my publicist, Sydney. You know that."

"Parker." Her voice is a silent plea for me to stop, to not push.

But just like the other night, I know that if I don't cross the line, if I don't hold my hand out for her to cross into the darkness, she'll always stay on the safe side. I don't care if I have to always be the one putting my heart on the line.

I don't care if I have to take the leap first. Not if it means there's even the smallest chance she'll follow.

"I'm serious. For years I've pretended like there is nothing more to our friendship when there damn well is."

"It was a mistake."

My fists clench at her words. "That's what you said five years ago. Can't make the same mistake twice, Sydney."

"Don't. Don't go there."

"No. We're having this conversation. I let you brush it under the rug last time; I'm not doing that again just because you're afraid of the truth."

"I'm not afraid of anything." Sydney fumbles as she tries to open the door, and it takes her a second before she successfully lifts it and shoots out of the car. Surprisingly, she's careful in closing the door before she stalks off.

I sigh, grabbing my keys and shoving them in my pocket before following her out. Five years ago, I kissed Sydney Lake.

I'd only recently moved to the States for The System, and I ran into her while I was waiting in que for takeaway one night. I was instantly obsessed with the petite blonde; she was so fucking cute and when she laughed, I knew I was a goner. I couldn't stop myself from offering to walk her out to her car, and after her engine sputtered and failed to start, I convinced her to let me drive her home. It didn't matter that it was in the opposite direction, I just wanted to spend more time with her. I'll never forget the shy look she gave me before she pressed her lips to my cheek, or the way her eye widened when I pulled her into a kiss.

Not even eight hours later, Mathias had introduced her as our new publicist.

Aleks had run off our last one, and the gossip columns were already littered with more rumors about the "bad boy of streaming" than he could count. I hadn't bothered getting involved in the hiring process because I had my own external PR team via my family, who were more than equipped to deal with any of the stupid shit I used to pull.

She acted like she'd never met me before and I'd been forced to play along with her little game because I didn't want to rock the boat. But now? Now, I was going to tip the whole ship over.

I come to stand behind her as she crosses her arms and stares out at the ocean.

"Sydney."

"I work for you."

"That's a shit excuse, and you know it."

"It's not an excuse, it's a fact." She turns around, and her eyes blaze into mine.

"Fine, you want to talk facts? We'll talk facts." I perch on the short fence separating the parking lot from the sandy beach. It brings me eye level with her, even if it doesn't feel like the most supportive chunk of wood under my ass. "Fact one, I fancy you. Fact two, we've made out. Twice. Fact three, I want to kiss you right now even though you look like you want to drown me in the ocean." I tap my finger with each statement, and I see her resolve waver each time.

"Fact four, Mathias would fire me for all of that," she adds.

"Fact five, I can fire Mathias," I counter.

"You can't do that." Her tone softens.

I hop off the fence and come up to her, leaving inches

between our chests, and she sucks in a breath. "I like you, Sydney Lake. I've liked you since the moment I met you, and I've spent the last five years pushing those feelings aside because I care about you, because you drew a line in the sand, and I respected that. But I don't want to wait anymore. I'm tired of ignoring this thing between us, of playing this forbidden game."

I lift my hand to cup her jaw. Her eyes shine with a myriad of emotions, and I see her trying to process everything. I see the little wires connecting and buzzing in her mind as she tries to make sense of everything I've said.

Her lips part and her breath hitches, the words stuck in her throat. But the panic takes over and she steps out of my touch, bending down to kick off her heels and grabbing them before making a run onto the beach.

This girl has a worse fight-or-flight response than me.

"Seriously, Sydney? Can you stop walking off?" I call out to her. But she's already meters ahead of me, stalking through the sand.

I look down at my shoes and curse before removing them and rolling up the bottoms of my pants.

The beach is sparingly empty; the nearest people look like little dots in my vision. The wind has picked up, and the afternoon tide pushes and pulls against the sand, rising higher with each crash. Sydney stops right where the coarse pebbly sand turns soft and wet. I come up next to her, letting my feet curl into the cold dampness below.

My confession hangs in the air, but we stand in silence, letting the soft caw of seagulls and the crash of the waves sing around us.

Eventually, she lets out a sigh.

"Why didn't you tell me about the apartment?"

"Pardon?" I turn my head to her, but she continues to stare out into the horizon.

"My apartment. I'm paying a fraction of the rent."

"I told you, I got a deal from the owner."

"*You're* the owner."

Well. Fuck.

How'd she find that out? I'd purchased it through a shell corporation so no one could link it back to me and it would be free of any Covington constraints. I could count on one hand the number of people who knew about it. That's why it had been so easy to convince Syd to move in.

"Right, that." I rub the back of neck.

"Parker." She finally tilts her head to peer up at me with an unamused look, but there's some warmth hidden underneath, and with that comes hope.

"Look, you were staying in that shitty apartment in a dangerous suburb. I wasn't going to let you just live somewhere like that when there was something I could do about it."

Her jaw drops. "It wasn't *that* shitty, and the neighborhood wasn't *that* dangerous."

"Sydney, I literally saw someone get robbed outside your apartment that night I dropped you off."

"Okay, it wasn't the best area. But I'd just moved here and had no money." She averts her gaze.

"I know. That's why I told you there was an open apartment in our complex with a reduced rate, because I knew it was the only way I'd get you to agree. It had already been a chore getting you to trade your deathtrap of a 2005 Volvo for the Tesla, and that only worked because I made

Jackson tell you it was a company car."

"Oh my God," she whines into her hands. "They were right. It's not even a company car. I don't even drive it, Parker!"

"I mean, it is safer having Francis drive you."

"You're insane. Why would you stick your neck out so far for me when you barely knew me?"

"Because from the moment I met you, I knew there was something special about you, Sydney. I told you, I've always liked you. And it might make me a total knobhead, but I wanted to look after you in whatever way I could until you came around."

A gust of wind sends her hair tumbling around her face, and I reach forward to tuck a loose tendril behind her ear, admiring her beauty. There is a light smattering of freckles across the bridge of her button nose, so faint that you can only see them when the sun hits her skin. The cherry scent of her gloss is faint, but it is one I have memorized so keenly that I can recognize it even under the salty ocean spray. It's a blessing and a curse that I know she tastes the same.

Her fawn-like eyes widen, and I lose myself to the silver sea swirling with hesitation inside.

My Eve has taken a bite of the forbidden fruit and has returned to the garden for another taste, but she's still wary of the snake within. Everything inside her screams to follow the rules, to act properly, to follow the straight and narrow.

I understand how she feels. I was raised in a family where the world always had eyes on us. Since before I could tie my own shoes, I learnt how to behave in high society and present myself in public. But I never let that stop me from being me, sometimes to a fault.

Sydney wouldn't even let herself be truthful with herself.

I run my thumb along her jaw and her breath stutters.

"I don't like you," she whispers. "Not like that."

"Are you sure?"

"No."

"I can wait, Sydney. I've waited five years. All I ask is that you stop denying this."

It feels like a lifetime passes before she leans into my touch, and I watch as the storm clears from her eyes.

"Okay."

"Okay?"

"Okay." Her heels drop into the sand as she reaches up to grip the collar of my shirt and closes the distance between us.

Finally, Sydney kisses me.

Chapter TWELVE

SYDNEY

Oh God.

    I'm kissing Parker Covington.

    Again.

I pull him closer, my grip tightening on the soft collar of his shirt. I'm worried that if I let go, I'll lose all my strength, and I don't want to lose this moment. I want to savor it.

Every kiss with Parker has been different, tasted different. This kiss is like the first bite of an apple in the fall; the tart skin gives way to a crisp and juicy sweetness.

I'm confused as all heck right now.

I don't know left from right, but I do know this man in front of me. I know that I want to be kissing him, that deep within me there is a part of me that never forgot our first kiss and held onto it, waiting for this moment. I'm not sure what this means, and the logical side of my brain is screaming at me to stop, to pull back, to really think about what I'm doing right now.

But I'm so tired of thinking.

I rise up on my tiptoes, feeling my toes sink farther into the sand. Absently, I hear Parker's shoes fall as his hand comes to rest on the small of my back, bringing my chest flush against his.

My kiss is hesitant as it explores every inch of his lips, memorizing every line. I let my grip loosen and snake my hands around his neck, slowly turning it into something heady and intoxicating. It's the ocean crashing around us and the salt sticking to our skin. It's the tide crawling closer and closer to our feet, tempting us to swim into the unknown.

Parker nips at my top lip, and I inhale as it sends a flurry of butterflies through my stomach. I could stay in this moment forever, making out with him like some love-struck teenager on their first date.

This might be the worst idea I've ever had.

It might be the best.

I could lose everything.

But he might be my everything.

I might not be ready to open the door to my heart, but I'll crack the window open.

Honestly, I don't know what any of this means. Where this is going to leave us tomorrow or next week or a year from now. There is a sliver of me that worries if I'm being selfish. If I'm ruining everything for just a moment of indulgence.

But, God, indulge I do.

Parker tastes like the sweetest dessert, and his touch slides against my skin like melting chocolate. He tilts my chin up, angling me in the way that he likes, as his tongue dances on my bottom lip sending a shock through me. I open up and let his tongue swoop in, our tastes merging as one. I lose myself to him, and my head turns dizzier with each passing second.

I inch closer to him, seeking more, taking everything he is giving me.

Our feet get stuck in the sand, and we fall to the ground, Parker letting out a playful curse while a giggle escapes my chest.

I feel free.

That weight that is always pressing on my shoulders, that anxiety that is constantly swirling in my stomach, that voice in my head that never quiets…it all slowly fades away with each forbidden kiss.

Since when does sinning feel like salvation?

I take advantage of my momentary lapse in judgment and swing on top of Parker, angling my legs on either side. The sand digs into my knees, and my skirt rides so high up my thighs that I wouldn't be shocked if my ass was on display. But for once, I don't care.

No regrets.

Parker's sea blue eyes widen as I hover above him.

Damn, he's a pretty thing.

Who was I kidding, telling myself I was immune to his good looks?

I'm the biggest liar of them all.

He gives me a devilish smirk as his eyes darken like the ocean behind us. It's all the warning I get before he pulls me into a bruising kiss. My chest presses against his, and I feel his body rise and fall. Our breaths become a tangled mess of heavy sighs and desperate moans.

His tongue darts out and traces a path up my neck, and there is no stopping the unfiltered groan of desire from tumbling out of me as pleasure shoots through my core.

He grabs the shoulders of my jacket, peeling the fabric off my body and tossing it next to us. I shiver momentarily as the sea breeze rolls over my body before his hot hand loops under my blouse and around my waist, burning into my bare skin. His simple touch causes my blood to heat, and a wave of molten desire begins flowing through my body.

I want more of it.

I want his hands everywhere.

His touch moves lower, toying with the waist of my skirt until he runs his hand over my ass, cupping it strongly.

"God, I love your ass," he mutters against my lips before giving my cheek a squeeze. My stomach swoops at the action, and my center heats with a telltale wetness.

His hand snakes lower, settling itself in that fold between my thigh and pussy, his fingertips dangerously close. I battle against the desire swirling within me and the small sliver of sanity I still possess. I reach down and push his hand away. He pulls back, his hand resting on my hip, but he gives me a puppy dog pout.

"Nope, not happening," I chastise, placing a kiss to his neck before diving back to his soft lips.

There was no way I was getting caught having sex on the beach or anything adjacent. That gave me more anxiety than pleasure. I wasn't ready for that. Not yet. I was barely wrapping my head around whatever this was with Parker. Any more would short-circuit my system.

Plus, I'd gotten enough of an eyeful of Parker's dick a few weeks back to know I was not ready for that.

I fight my way through the haze of lust clogging every inch of my lungs.

I give him one last long kiss, dragging his top lip into my mouth with a bite before rolling off him onto the hard sand. Parker reaches out and grabs my hand, bringing it to his mouth and placing a soft kiss on the knuckles before holding it to his chest. Warmth spreads throughout my body, matching the pink horizon bleeding across the sky.

None of this feels real.

"What are you thinking about?"

"You," I answer honestly.

"Mmm," he hums. "I think about myself often, too."

"Seriously." I lift our joined hands and let them fall back against his chest in a soft push. He lets out a laugh, and I feel his chest rumble as a smile spreads across my own face.

Parker is infectious. Even in the darkest hours, he never fails to bring light. He could give the sun a run for its money.

"Do you promise you're not going to go back to avoiding me?"

I turn my head, silently lamenting the sand getting stuck in my hair as I face him.

His face is lit up with the golden sunset, casting a glow on his pale skin and making his cheekbones stand out more than normal. I trace the gentle slope of his nose before stopping on his eyes that are watching the clouds above us.

"I promise."

The corners of his lips twitch up in a smile.

"But…" I say slowly, and his eyes slide to me with the slightest tilt of his head. "Whatever this is, it stays between us."

"I figured." I see a gust of sadness swoop through his gaze before it disappears. "I'm good at keeping secrets." He gives me a playful smile even though I know it masks something deeper.

I feel so selfish because I hate asking him to keep such a large secret when he just got free of his last one. But I need to take the time to figure out what this is before I commit to anything. This isn't something I can be rash about, and Parker deserves more than a false promise.

At the end of the day, I am still his publicist. I'm still Aleks and Jackson's publicist. I have to think of The System first, and they do not need another scandal right now.

Until I know where my heart sits, we need to tread carefully.

"I'm sorry."

"Don't be." He sits up and leans over to place a kiss on my nose. "Come on, I'll drive us home."

He gives my arm a squeeze, and my chest aches when he lets go, already missing his touch.

I need to get myself together; everything is burning too fast.

Parker curses and I push myself up onto my elbows, gritting my jaw against the little specks of sand digging into me. The tide has risen, and all our stuff is slightly drenched.

I groan as he lifts my damp jacket off the sand. This

was one of the nicer sets that I'd splurged on.

The logical part of my brain, the part that is slowly coming back to me, realizes that the matching skirt is also covered in sand under my butt and probably not in much of a better state.

I force myself to stand up and dust said sand off myself before taking the jacket from him.

Parker reaches down and plucks our shoes from the shoreline. They're both in a sorry state. Although, I know for a fact that mine, at the very least, don't cost as much as his.

I see Parker's jaw tick as he surveys his shoes. My heels don't look great, but they might be salvageable.

Or not.

The white leather is dark beige around the heel.

Parker sighs and tosses me an impish grin. "I needed an excuse to buy new shoes."

"I didn't think you needed an excuse for that."

He links his arm in mine and swings me into step with him as we trudge back up the sand to the parking lot. My bare feet prick slightly against the asphalt as we make our way to the car, and Parker stops short with another curse.

"What?"

"Nothing. Just…stay there a second." He unlinks our arms as he lifts the door and reaches behind the driver's seat for something. He pulls out a sweater and walks over to me.

I stare at him in confusion as he bends down and uses it to dry my legs and dust off the sand.

A small snort escapes my lips, and he glares up at me.

"It's not funny, Syd. The car's brand new."

"I'm not laughing," I say through soured lips, stopping another smile from slipping through.

"Turn around."

I do as he asks, letting my grin loose once I'm facing away from him. He begins beating the sweater against my ass, and I let out a yelp, glaring down at him this time.

"Maybe I should just call a rideshare. Pick the car up tomorrow," he ponders.

"Parker, you can't be serious."

"The sand, Syd."

A beeping noise begins filtering out from the car, and I step out from Parker's obsessive cleaning to open my side of the car and pull my phone from my abandoned purse. My eyes widen when I see the time and the reminder blinking up at me.

"Parker, we need to head back, like now," I call out.

Parker comes around and rests his chin on the crook of my shoulder, staring down at my screen. The connection sends a jolt right to my heart.

"It's only five," he comments. "Plenty of time to get back before the stream." He pulls back, putting his hands on my shoulders and guiding me into the passenger seat. He takes the sweater and brushes the remaining sand from my feet.

"Not if we get stuck in traffic," I get out between breaths at the ticklish sensation.

"Nah, we'll be fine. Don't sweat it, love." He takes my heels and jacket from my arms before closing the door and dropping them into the compartment in the hood.

An hour and a half later, we finally pull into the private garage, and I give Parker an "I told you so" as I hop out of the car.

We got stuck in a nasty chunk of traffic, and now he only has thirty minutes until the stream. Plus, he never got around to filming his content for his channel, which I am now going to have to hound him on for tomorrow.

Parker gets out of the car and dusts off his seat with his sweater.

"Next time we go to the beach, I'm taking one of the bikes instead," he mutters.

"Good luck getting me on one of those death traps." I fiddle around with the hood before popping it and grabbing my stuff.

"Stevie loves being Aleks' backpack." Parker shuts his door and comes around, grabbing his shoes from around me before clicking the hood closed.

"That's because Stevie is just as ridiculous as Aleks. She merely hides it better."

My feet are cold on the concrete as we walk to the elevator, and Parker slings his arm around my shoulders. The practiced movement feels different now.

"I'll convince you." He hits the elevator button with his knuckle while popping a kiss on the top of my head.

"In your dreams."

There is no way in hell I would be getting on the back of one of those things. He is lucky enough that I even get in the car with him half the time. I chalk it up to the fact that some part of me trusts him more than I can admit. That he feels safe, even when he is driving a million miles an hour.

An engine rumbles, and I jump out of Parker's hold to see Jackson's Jeep curving around the corner.

I frown as he pulls into his spot, wondering where he

could have been. I don't keep track of the guys like an FBI agent, but I do know their general schedules and whereabouts pretty damn well. I'm mostly surprised because Jackson doesn't normally cut it this close to his scheduled stream times. Out of the three guys, he is always the most punctual.

Parker puffs his cheeks in a pout, and I counter with a raised brow.

"No touchy-touchy," I remind him.

"Oh, come on, Syd. I always do that."

I know he's right. It's the entire reason why Justin was able to pull up over twenty photos of Parker and me between the airport and the hotel, practically attached at the hip. But still, this is Jackson, and I don't trust my poker face to fool him. Not yet. Not when the taste of Parker is still fresh on my tongue.

The elevator door opens just as Jackson steps down from the Jeep. He flings the door closed and shoves his hands in the pockets of his jean jacket as he strolls up to us. He looks up and nods his head, throwing out a deep, "Hey."

I return it with a smile as I step into the elevator, pressing my back against the cool metal.

Parker uses his hand to keep the elevator doors open for Jackson, but I watch as he kicks out his foot at the last minute, tripping Jackson up as he enters. Jackson stumbles for a second before righting himself and throwing a punch to Parker's shoulder.

"Oww." He rubs his shoulder. "Did you have to hit me that hard?"

"Dunno, was hoping maybe it would knock those five

brain cells you possess back into place." Jackson leans against the corner of the elevator, crossing his feet over one another lazily.

"Ass."

Parker punches the button for the penthouse before hitting the button for my floor. While this elevator can access all floors, it can only be called from the garage or the penthouse. I have to use a fob in the regular elevators to access the penthouse when I go up from my place.

"Where the hell have you guys been?" Jackson asks, giving a pointed look at our bare feet.

My eyes dart to Parker, and I finally take in the way his typically styled platinum hair is disheveled from all the sand. His short-sleeved shirt is rumpled within an inch of its life, and his pants are still rolled halfway up his defined calves. Despite his best efforts, sand still coats both of our skin.

He looks like a rough and tumbled sea god.

I don't even bother looking down at myself. I don't want to draw more attention than necessary.

"Parker forced us to take a beach detour after our media meeting." I keep it simple. The less information, the better. Parker going rogue is pretty on brand.

"I gathered." Jackson rolls his dark eyes. "How'd you end up covered in sand? You both look like you ate shit."

"I bet Syd that if I could run across the sand faster than her, I could go out clubbing next week."

I fight to keep my jaw from popping open.

That was an awful lie.

There is no way he will believe that.

Jackson blinks at us before letting out a bark. "You

come up with the weirdest bets, dude."

Then again, most things Parker does are unbelievable.

My chest lightens with relief.

The elevator dings as we reach my floor, and I keep my composure as I exit.

"Have fun with your streams tonight, boys." I turn around and use my heels to point at Parker. "Don't stress your wrist too much before the tournament."

The elevator doors close on Parker rolling his eyes, but I catch the wink he gives me before they finally shut.

I hold my breath as I pad across the carpeted hallway to my apartment door, keying in the code and letting myself in. I make it all the way to my ensuite before I let out a sigh, my heels, handbag, and jacket dropping to the tiles. A glance in the mirror confirms my assumptions.

I look like a mess.

God, I'm lucky Jackson didn't question us further.

There are bits of sand stuck in the plaid fabric of my skirt, and my blouse hangs loosely around my hips, the bottom wrinkly from where Parker tugged it free. My hair looks like it went to war, and I sigh, knowing that I'm going to need to douse it with detangler before getting in the shower.

I lean a hip against my sink as my hand comes up to touch my lips.

They're red and puffy. One might just chalk it up to the cherry-tinted gloss I wear, but I smile in the secret confines of my apartment at the knowledge of the boy who made them this way.

Chapter THIRTEEN

SYDNEY

My eyes flit over my laptop, cataloging the schedule the guys have set for the week.

Most people would think that working as a streamer would be an easy gig, but there's a lot that goes into it. Each guy doesn't *just stream.*

Parker's schedule is the most hectic right now because of the upcoming championship and the fact that he has Covington obligations outside of his stream schedule.

My core zings at the thought of Parker.

His shiny blue eyes and boyish smile.

A smile with plush, kissable lips.

Lips that I can't stop thinking about.

A knock sounds at my door, and I hop off the stool at my kitchen counter. My slippers slap softly on the tiles as I make way to the door and stand on my toes to peer through the peephole. One of the doormen stands outside.

I undo the deadbolt and give him a bright smile.

"Hi, Jericho."

"Hi, Miss Sydney." He holds out two small parcels. "Delivery came for you; one of them is perishable."

Odd. I haven't placed any recent orders.

"Thanks."

"Of course, have a good day."

"You, too."

I take them, and he gives me a nod before turning on his wingtips. I knock the door shut with a pop of my hip before dumping them on the marble counter.

Curiosity bubbles under my skin as I break the smaller of the two packages open. The brown packaging reveals a Styrofoam box, and I smile, realizing what perishable item it must be.

I pop the lid off the box and squeal at the goods within. An assortment of handmade soaps, lotions, and candles greets me. I bypass them, my fingers closing on the hand-written note scrawled on a piece of torn graph paper. Dad's kind words stare back at me, and warmth floods my veins.

Hey, Bug.

Mrs. Feeney got ahead this season and made her first batch early. Thought it would be a nice surprise to send them over.

Don't work too hard.

Miss you and love you,

Dad

I pull my phone out and dial his number, putting it on speaker as I rifle through the treasures before me.

Mrs. Feeney lives at the end of our cul-de-sac, and she

is known around town for the amazing goods she makes. Candles, soaps, lotions, you name it. She has a set line that she makes year-round, but every season she brings out specialties. With fall upon us, it means it is time for her annual pumpkin spice and caramel apple scents.

I crack open one of the candles and melt at the sweet pumpkin scent mixing with spicy cinnamon. I move onto one of the body scrubs and twist off the top to whiff at the sugary caramel smell. The woman is a flavor witch.

I hurriedly unpack everything, smiling at the memories of my hometown.

Mrs. Feeney is also the main culprit behind my cherry flavor love. Her brother owns the largest farm in town, and growing up, she would also pop over to our house with food she made from the extra produce.

Knowing my father was a single dad and not the best chef (despite his efforts), she treated my brother and me like long-lost grandchildren. The farm grew the sweetest cherries known to man, and Mrs. Feeney's cherry pie was heaven wrapped in buttery pastry. While the cherry overload made me obsessed, it made my brother totally hate them.

My chest tightens at the broken memories, but I let them wash away as my dad finally answers on what feels like the millionth ring.

"Hey, Bug."

"Hey, Dad."

"The package arrived safely, I'm guessing?"

I laugh. "It did."

"A nice surprise, I hope?"

"It is. The only kind of surprises I like are the ones

from Mrs. Feeney."

"I know."

I can hear the eye roll my father is no doubt giving.

I carry the lotions, scrubs, and soaps to my bathroom, hanging my phone around my wrist so I can continue chatting with him.

"How are you?"

"Doing well. Went to the old brewery last night with the rest of town to celebrate Maisy Mae's engagement, and I'm off on a fishing trip next weekend with Darrell and Ray."

"Mmm," I hum, stacking the scrubs perfectly on top of one another. "Maisy Mae's marrying Tyrell, right?"

"Sure is. High school sweethearts are a dear thing. You know, Vince is still single."

I snort at the name of my high school boyfriend. "I'm sure that's of his own volition, Dad. Plus, I'm not interested."

I have no doubt in my mind that Vince Thompson will marry someone when he is ready. The girls flock to him like bees to honey. I seem to have a tendency to fall for popular men.

"Does any boy have your interest these days?"

Glass-blue eyes and a lopsided smile flash in my vision. My stomach flips.

I force the image of a certain British man out of my head as I shove a lotion under the sink with more force than necessary.

"I'm a little too busy to date," I dismiss.

"You work too hard," my dad grumbles.

I laugh as I stack the last of the soaps under my sink

and then stand up, padding back to the kitchen.

"You know you can come out here anytime, Bug. Take a little break and use some of that PTO."

"I know, but it's hard right now. The guys have crazy schedules." I grab a magnet from one of the drawers and stick his note to my fridge. It sits there amongst the hundred other notes he's sent me over the years. "You'll see me in like two months. I'll be back for Thanksgiving."

It is the one holiday that is nonnegotiable when it comes to my work with The System. The boys know that, no matter what, I have to go home for it. Still, I do wish I could go home more often.

There are just too many things that could go wrong at a moment's notice with the guys. It gives me more anxiety being far from them.

"I know, Bug. Just make sure you are looking after yourself, okay? All work, no play isn't healthy."

"My life isn't all work."

Even I can taste the lie.

"Doesn't sound like it."

"Dad," I say in a warning tone.

"Don't mean to pester you. I just care and want you to have a little fun in life. Go on trips with your friends. Meet a nice boy. Live life outside your schedule. You know that's all Carson wanted for you, too."

The air in my chest solidifies and drops like stones at the name.

I quickly scoop them out of my stomach and dump them on the ground. I don't want the pain to weigh me down.

I've learned to break through the pull of the memories

after years of therapy and am finally at a stage where I am living my life again—even if it isn't to the fullest, it is still more than the shell I had once been.

But that name is still a trigger.

"Sorry, Bug."

"It's fine, Dad." I collect myself with a deep breath and let the light back into my body. "I'll have you know I went to the beach the other day."

"Oh, really? I'm happy to hear. Who with?"

"Parker."

The second his name leaves my lips I regret it.

"Oh?" My dad says it in that curious way that makes me cringe inside.

"Yeah, we were driving home from a thing, and he made us pull over." I try to keep my tone light so he won't read into it. I am an extremely perceptive person, and I got that way because of my dad. He can read me like a book. "You know Parker, always playing."

"Yes, I do know. Interesting of you to indulge him."

I grit my teeth as I search for a box cutter to open my second package.

"I wouldn't call it an indulgence."

"It's not a bad thing, Bug. You need to loosen up more, have fun, and he seems like a good egg."

"Good egg. Bad egg. He's still my employer." I huff as I give up and just grab a pair of scissors to slice the tape with. "And I don't need to loosen up."

My dad sighs. "You hold your reins tighter than a rider getting on a horse for the first time."

I purse my lips as I run the scissors down the tape. I adore my dad, but he laments my work ethic and has been harping on it for years now.

I open the cardboard package and blink down at the red box inside. The very box that has the word *Valentino* printed in shiny red foil.

I lift the cardboard package to read the name on the label again.

Yup. It's definitely addressed to me.

I take the Valentino box out and then flip the package to see if there is a note or anything, but it's empty.

Slowly, and using both hands, I lift the red lid.

My breath hitches at the sight of the beautiful white patent leather heels within. The gold Valentino logo glistens on the ankle strap as I pick one of them up and hold it in the light.

They're stunning.

They put my current white heels to shame. Which would be expected given the price difference here. Plus, my current pair were still ruined from the beach. I hadn't been able to fix the water damage and was probably going to need to toss them.

Wait.

My heart pounds as I entertain a lofty thought. The corners of my lips tug up in a smile as my chest flutters.

"Bug, you still there?" My dad's voice grounds me.

"Yeah, sorry." I carefully return the pointed heel to the box. "I have to go, Dad. But I'll chat with you later."

"All right." I hear the hesitancy in his voice, but he drops it. "I love you."

"I love you, too. Send me pictures of your fishing trip."

"Will do."

I hang up and continue to stare at the shiny shoes in

front of me.

My mind whirls up the memories from the beach. The warm afternoon sun on my skin. The salt on my tongue. The sand beneath my knees. The stolen kisses on my lips.

The excitement has me feeling like a giddy schoolgirl, and I scold myself.

These shoes are too much.

It's not like anything serious is going on between us. It is just…

I don't know what it is.

Fun?

Fun.

Everyone seems to think I need more fun in my life.

What is Parker Covington if not fun?

Something thick and dark swirls in my stomach at my light dismissal of our connection. But I need to keep it light. If I don't keep some distance between us, it will put me in danger of letting him in. I can't afford that.

I can't afford the pain of loving someone like Parker, someone who brings sunshine into my life. Because when you lose that sunshine, the world becomes so dark. And crawling out of that darkness is dangerous and difficult.

I'm not sure if I can do that again.

I shut the lid on the shoes and tuck them under my arm as I grab my phone and leave my apartment to ride the elevator up to the penthouse.

Silence greets me as I trek into the boys' space, which is expected because they are all gaming right now. When I make it to Parker's streaming room, I open the door slowly so I don't spook him.

Except the room is empty.

I frown into the blue abyss.

I shut the door before weaving my way back to the entrance and to Aleks' streaming room.

When I come face-to-face with another empty cavern of red, dread begins to coil in my gut.

I spin around and open Jackson's streaming room on the opposite side of the hall.

A small slither of relief hits me when I spot the titan leaning back in his gaming chair, black hair tied in a bun at the nape of his neck, skin shining in the green glow of his room.

He chatters away into his mic, and I walk in to see two familiar girls gracing one of his monitors. Jackson, Deer, and Lee are playing the latest co-op scavenger horror game that people are obsessed with. It's done wonders for his views, and Mathias is peeved that Parker won't cave and play with the rest of them.

Deer spots me in the background of Jackson's camera and begins waving frantically. He flicks his gaze to me briefly and reaches up to maneuver his headset off one of his ears.

"What's up, Syd."

"I'm trying to track down Thing One and Thing Two."

"Ah, they went for a ride."

I frown. "That wasn't on the schedule."

Jackson snorts. "Like that would stop them."

Fair.

"There's a bunch of loot out front, Deer." Jackson turns his attention back to the game. "We just need to find an exit."

I stand and watch them for a few minutes, drawn in

by the creepiness. Jackson's character is running around on screen in some sort of derelict basement with a bunch of bursting pipes. The screen is dark, so I can barely make much out.

It's part of my job to always stay up-to-date on whatever new games are coming out and work with the companies on getting early release versions or beta versions for them to play to help increase hype.

The horror game Jackson is obsessed with passed under the radar for a little while before randomly gaining virality. I've been doing some digging, and I'm hoping to land him a collab with the developers for a special skin in one of the upcoming updates.

A terrifying, bloody creature suddenly appears on screen, and I stifle a gasp.

"What's that?" I lean forward to get a better look.

"A Wailing Angel." His voice is a hushed whisper. "If I stop looking at it, it'll kill me."

"Oh. That's not good."

"Nope."

I can see Lee and Deer talking on the monitor, but I can't hear them. A part of me is a little jealous. There are times when I want to play with them, but I'm really not all that good, and the last thing I want to do is embarrass myself.

Plus, I worry that if I start, it'll blur those final strings of professionalism I'm trying to keep tethered.

I pad into the kitchen and grab a can of electrolyte-infused seltzer and bring it back to Jackson's streaming room, placing it on the desk next to him.

He gives me a brief nod.

"Thanks, Syd." He uses one hand to open it, his middle finger flicking the tab open.

"I'll catch you later."

I give the girls a wave in the camera before clicking Jackson's door closed behind me.

I contemplate just heading back to my place but decide to take advantage of the empty living room and killer surround sound system to watch an episode of my favorite reality show. If they aren't back when it ends, I will leave.

Except, forty-five minutes pass and there's still no sign of them.

I check my phone and sigh. I know they'll have to be back in a few hours for their stream, at least, but I won't waste my time waiting around. I have emails to write and calls to make.

That damn red Valentino box burns a hole in my peripheral vision.

I lift the lid again, sighing at the beauties within.

Why?

I shut the lid and tuck the box back under my arm as I shuffle my way to the elevator. It takes a while, but finally the doors begin to slide open. I step forward only to almost crash into a leather-clad chest.

I stifle a gasp as I stumble backward.

Aleks' tattooed hand steadies my shoulder. "Whoa. Hey, Syd."

My eyes dart from him to the man by his side. Parker runs a hand through his platinum hair. He grins when he spots me, eyes lighting up. My stomach swoops.

"Darling Sydney, to what do we owe the pleasure?"

I swallow, regaining my composure as they stack their

helmets in the hall closet. I can't exactly ask Parker about the shoes while Aleks is in the room. It would raise too many questions.

So, I just go with my standard excuse these days.

"I just had some things to go over with you before the tournament this weekend."

Parker's eyes flick to mine before they dip to the red box under my arm. A smug smile tugs at his lips, and I fight to keep a straight face.

"Sure." He angles his head toward the kitchen. "Let me just grab a drink."

"Toss me one while you're at it," Aleks adds, shucking off his leather jacket and tossing it on the couch.

Great, doesn't seem like he is going anywhere soon.

This is a dumb idea.

"You know what? It's fine, we can go over it tomorrow." I spin on my feet, but Parker grabs my arm.

"Hey, pause. Just head to my streaming room, I'll be there in a sec."

I want to argue, but my traitorous mind is too distracted by the feeling of his hand on me. I purse my lips, nodding, before strolling past him.

I slip into his room and start to feel a little more at ease in the blue glow.

I pad over to his set up, resting the box on the corner of the long black desk. My hand reaches out to trace the blue LED mask on display.

God, how quickly things have begun to change.

"Did you like my gift?" Parker takes a loud sip of his energy drink as he kicks the door shut behind him.

I'd been right.

"You didn't need to do this." I hold a hand out to the box.

"Well, the shoes go with the outfit, so." Parker shrugs, flopping into his gaming chair, rolling backward.

"Outfit?"

"Oh, it hasn't arrived yet?" He pulls his phone from his pocket and begins scrolling. "Ah, nine p.m. delivery. How disappointingly slow."

I pluck the phone from his hands and stare down at the order on his phone. It's a matching black and white plaid skirt and blazer set—not too dissimilar to the one I had on the other day, but the price tag is triple what I'd spent.

"Seriously?"

Parker places his can on the desk before standing up and reclaiming his phone. He scrolls a little more before flashing the screen at me with a grin. "It comes in blue, too. But that one's on back order, so it won't arrive till next month. Thought you'd look hot in my color."

I open my mouth to argue, but I'm cut off as his lips press against mine.

It stuns me as he pulls away.

"Do you always complain when people do nice things for you, love?"

"I wasn't complaining. It's just…it's not like I bought you a pair of shoes to replace the ones the ocean damaged," I whisper weakly.

"Oh, those. I already bought a better pair."

"Of course, you did," I laugh.

"There she is."

He gives me a bright smile, and I cave. My walls are crumbling around him more and more as each day passes.

It takes an insurmountable amount of effort to keep them somewhat in place, and I am getting tired of fighting.

"The shoes are beautiful, thank you."

"Maybe you try them on for me, *sans vêtements*." He winks.

"You're hilarious." I roll my eyes, picking up the box.

"Hey, hang on. You're just going to leave?" He places his hand over mine.

Warmth rushes through me, but I try to steel myself.

"I still have work to do."

He takes the box from my hand and places it back on the desk.

"I know your boss; I'm sure he wouldn't mind if you took a little break."

He snakes his arms around my waist. I swallow against the growing heat in my stomach.

This is such a bad idea.

Any of the guys could walk in.

And I still don't know where any of this is heading.

"One minute."

"What?" I blink.

"Just give me one minute."

My lips twitch up in a smile at the mirror of his words to the other night.

"Okay."

The word barely leaves me before he descends. His lips capture mine in a fevered plea. One of his hands comes up to cup the back of my head, and he pulls me into him.

He tastes slightly sweet from the energy drink.

I moan against him, my hands curling around his collarbone to remove any distance between us.

"Yo, dude. Did you steal my GameCube controller?"

Parker's door flings open, light streaming in.

I shove Parker from me, and he goes tumbling back, landing conveniently in his gaming chair. The momentum has him rolling halfway across the room. I snatch the red box and clutch it to my heaving chest as I spin around to face Aleks.

I pray the blue hue of the room hides the redness in my cheeks.

"All right, well. I'll see you boys on Friday for the flight. Don't overpack. Bye."

My body moves like a robot as I push past Aleks and make a beeline for the elevator.

"Ow, the fuck? You didn't have to throw it at me," Aleks' yell filters through the apartment just as the doors open.

I slip inside and hit the button for my floor a billion times, hoping it will make the doors close faster.

It's only when they shut completely that I let my grip loosen on the box. My head tips back against the metal wall.

This boy is going to be the death of me.

Chapter FOURTEEN

PARKER

"**O**h my God, you're English! Can you, like, sign my boobs?"

I blink down at the girl in a *Gods League* cosplay.

Honestly, I'm surprised she wants to ruin the outfit with my signature. It's a really good one. She looks just like the character Lee mains when she plays.

Which is probably why Lee is currently shoving a permanent marker at me while announcing, "He'll totally sign them."

"All right, all right," I laugh back.

I uncap the marker and make some light small talk as I sign her chest. The girl's friend films us, and I'm careful to keep my eyes on my hand and not the giant pair of tits in my face. Fan service is one of my favorite parts of the tournaments. I love meeting people who watch my videos and my streams. There's this addictive rush of dopamine when someone recognizes you, and it makes you feel on top of the world. Although sometimes it gets a little weird.

Like now.

At least this isn't like that time some chick threw her knickers at Aleks.

"Can I get a picture as well?" The girl asks as I finish my signature.

"Sure."

She glues herself to my side, and I smile despite the mask I'm wearing. After the girl and her friend leave, I pull off my mask for some air. I need to blink a few times to clear the blue hue from my vision.

The Seattle tournament is easily double the size of the Denver one. Lee and I have been stopped no less than a hundred times in the last two hours since our *FrozeLine* match. Syd's been keeping an eye on us, but Jackson and Aleks are participating in a charity *Gods League* match, so she's been flitting back and forth around the arena.

"Aren't you going to get in trouble for taking that off?" Lee uses her lollipop to point at my mask.

This girl has an addiction to lollies like no other.

That being said, I would kill for an energy drink right about now. The tournament has been going on for hours, and I had to be here first thing to play my speedrun match. For some reason, they decided to schedule it right at the beginning of the day.

Eleven might not be early for most people, but in our world, it was basically dawn.

"Nah, I've worn it for long enough." I loop my arm

with Lee's and give a nod to her security detail. "Can we head back to our greenroom?" I ask the James Bond-esque man who is the head of her team.

He gives me a nod and helps guide us through the crowd so we don't get stopped by any more fans. Without Lee's security team, I doubt she would ever be able to move an inch. For every person who comes up to me, there's another three fawning over her. It's part of the reason I recommended them to her in the first place. Nothing is more secure than a Covington-approved security detail.

We get back to our greenroom without incident, and I immediately beeline for the mini fridge, grabbing a cold, blue energy drink and cracking it open.

"How's it out there?" Deer calls from the couch. She's lying on her stomach, feet kicking in the air, as she plays a game on her Switch. Her bright pink hair cocoons her face as her matching nails move over the joystick. She's been holed up in here since her panel this morning.

"It's really not that bad. The crowd has calmed a lot since everything is winding down for the night." Lee flops down next to her best friend.

"Mmm," she hums. "No more creeps?"

"No more creeps. Parker here did a lovely job scaring any of them away."

I give them a snort as I sink into the chair across from them. "Oh, yes. Haven't you heard? I am positively terrifying, my dear Deer."

She looks up at me and smirks. "Do you scare them away by throwing wads of cash at them?"

"Nope. I have no doubt it is my devilish good looks that stuns them into submission. It's certainly not the five-person security team."

"One hundred percent." Lee nods with a serious expression before cracking into a fit of laughter. Deer joins in, and the thread of worry I carry loosens. We might be joking, but there is a kernel of truth to it all. Whenever we come to events with Lee, we try to make sure one of us always has an eye on her. And now that Deer has joined the fray, she's under our watch, too.

Gamer girls.

It's all fun until some creep tries to follow them into the bathroom or gets handsy during a meet and greet.

I treat the two of them like my sisters, and I know Aleks and Jackson do the same.

My phone vibrates in my pocket, and I fish it out, smirking at the caller ID while taking a large sip of my energy drink.

Speaking of sisters.

"Paigey, you all right?"

"Sparky! Just finished up a case and thought I'd give you a buzz. Haven't heard your voice in a while. You all right?" My second eldest sister greets back, the familiarity of her accent and my childhood nickname warming me. Paige works as a real estate lawyer for the family and is based out of our main London office, but she's been coming out to the States recently to help with the US expansion.

"I'm at another tournament right now in Seattle. And before you ask, yes, I crushed it. I had the fastest run in my match this morning."

"Two for two, then?"

"Two for two," I confirm.

"That's brilliant!" I hear the smile in her voice. "You know, I had no doubt when Dad told me about the new deal you made with Grandfather."

"'Deal' sounds a lot better than 'ultimatum.'"

"Oh, come off it. You're the one who thought you could just be the heir in name only forever," she tsks.

She would never let that go. And, in hindsight, she is right to do so.

I'd well come to the realization that I'd been skating by and holding on to my inheritance as armor. But it was one thing to decide on my own, rather than being forced to decide, and I really don't like being told what to do.

"I know, I know. There's just a lot riding on all of this now." I lower my voice, eyes flicking to the girls, but they're cooing over some video on Deer's phone.

Honestly, I've been trying to forget the deal with my grandfather as much as possible. Shoving it into the deep, dark recesses of my brain. I know I'm a great gamer, and I would like to think I'm one of the best when it comes to speedruns. But that was when it was all for fun. Now that there is pressure, it's beginning to stress me the fuck out.

Coming face-to-face with Philip Covington is like facing the final boss in a video game: you can't really back down, you just have to full send. There's no time to pause or back out.

"You'll be fine, Parker. It'll work itself out. Trust me. This is what you're meant to be doing."

They're just words, but they comfort me all the same.

Paige and I are only a few years apart, and she was the first one who knew about EnglishCoffee. My sisters have always been my number one advocates though they show it differently. Our mum and dad are supportive, but they were a little hesitant when I moved halfway around the world for a career they didn't really understand. Five years later, and they now send me screenshots whenever they see my face pop up online and take photos with my billboards.

"Thanks, Paigey."

The greenroom door busts open with a bang. Aleks comes catapulting into the room, Jackson hot on his heels. They're hooting and hollering.

"Sounds like I should let you go," Paige muses. "Say hi to the lads for me, and we'll talk soon, okay?"

"Okay, love you."

"Love you."

"Aw, I love you, too." Aleks throws his body on top of me just as I hang up, and I let out a groan.

"What about me?" Jackson grins above us. "Don't you love me?"

"No, mate. Don't you dare," I warn him.

He gives me a shrug before falling like a domino. The crushing weight of my two asshole best friends knocks the air out of me.

"Fuckers," I wheeze. "Get off me." I'm pinned to the beanbag with no way out. I can barely wiggle my fingers.

"Smile," Lee croons, pointing her phone at us.

"Adorable, aren't they?" Deer snickers, joining her.

"Traitors," I grumble.

The door clicks open, more softly this time, and Sydney power walks in a beat later. She's out of breath, her cheeks flushed. Just seeing her makes my dick twitch, even more so in her disheveled state. Which is not a good thing with Aleksander literally on top of me.

"You boys," she huffs, "are so dead."

"Ooooh, you're in trouble," the girls sing.

"What? I didn't do anything!" I struggle to shout.

"Guilty by association, bro." Aleks grins.

"Bullshit."

"Technically, I didn't do anything either," Jackson supplies, slipping off us.

"Again, guilty by association." Aleks waves his hand nonchalantly.

Now that Jackson's weight is gone, I have enough strength to shove Aleks off me. I make sure to put my elbows into it, and he lets out a groan as he lands on the ground.

"What did they do?" Deer asks.

"This one," she points a finger at Aleks, "just flipped off all the reporters and went on his merry way."

That tracked.

"I don't like interviews," Aleks growled.

"I hope you like tech isolation then." Her foot taps against the ground rhythmically, and I grin, noticing that she is wearing the shoes I got her. It makes me want to buy her more stuff. I like seeing her in my things.

"Seriously, Syd?"

"Seriously. Three strikes this month. Effective once we're back in Cali."

Aleks groans. "Come on."

"You dug your own grave, Aleksander." Sydney shrugs.

Aleks walks over to Syd and throws his arms around her. "Come on, Syd. Just this once, please. Think how sad you'll make Stevie if you put me in iso."

My possessiveness rears even though, logically, I know

there is no reason for it. I just don't like the look of any guy too close to Syd.

"Enough." Sydney pinches the bridge of her nose and shrugs him off; the action is basically a reflex when it comes to us. "Let's just pack up and head out of here."

Sydney pads to the corner of the room and begins organizing her stuff. The rest of us follow suit, gathering our assortment of backpacks and duffle bags.

Lee shuffles over and gives Syd's free hand a squeeze. "You sure you're feeling okay? You seemed off earlier."

"Yeah, just a little tired." She smiles, but I see the exhaustion weighing on her.

I know for a fact she didn't get any sleep last night because she ran into some issues with one of our sponsorship contracts and had to work with Mathias to get it sorted. I want to go over there and give her a hug, but I know she'll push me off and get all worried that the others will read into it.

It sucks, but there's really not much I can do, yet. She's still warming up to the whole idea of something more between us. I don't want to push her away before I've held her close. I just need to find some way to get a little more time with just us.

"What's the plan?" Jackson asks. "I'm starving, so I vote food."

"Fuck yes," Aleks agrees.

"I'm down!" Deer chimes in. "There was a great pho place I came across."

"Pho is solid." I shove my mask into my bag and zip it up before hauling it over my shoulder.

I walk over to Syd and take her bag from her, slinging

it onto my other shoulder. She opens her mouth to protest, but I don't give her a chance, walking away with a wink through the door Jackson is holding open.

"I heard there's an exclusive after party, too," Deer adds as we all begin to file out of the greenroom.

"Exclusive?" Lee grins, spinning around and causing her slick black pigtails to whip around her head.

"How fun can a party in Seattle be?" I wrinkle my nose. This city isn't exactly the first destination I think of when it comes to fun. With all the rain, it's like a much shittier version of London.

"Maybe." Aleks stretches his arms over his head, yawning. "I promised Stevie I'd video call her."

"Don't want to upset the missus." Jackson gives Aleks a sympathetic pat on the back before strolling up to Deer and plucking one of her duffels from her hand. The five-foot-nothing Polly Pocket was carrying two bags the size of herself and waddling on her heels.

"Hey. I can carry my own bag," she protests with a frown.

Jackson ignores her, hiking the pink bag under his arm without a hitch in his stride.

"What? Is no one going to help me?" Lee dramatically pouts up at Aleks.

Aleks gives her a pointed side-eye. "Nope."

We make our way through the back corridors to where our transport is parked, the security detail following us the entire time. Even though everyone should be heading home, it doesn't mean some fans aren't hanging around for an extra glimpse.

Our two Escalades are ready and running when we get

outside. The gray sky already has the smell of rain to it, and it further reminds me why I don't like this city. If I wanted rain, I'd go home.

Deer and Lee—plus her security detail—pile into their car while the boys and I get into ours. I keep the door open for Syd, but she waves us off.

"I'm heading back to the hotel for the night. You guys figure out whatever it is you're doing, just don't get into any more trouble, okay? I really don't want to have to bail anyone out of jail."

I frown at her. "You can't go back alone. Just get in the car. We'll drop the guys off, and I'll go with you back to the hotel."

"Dude, you can't bail." Aleks leans forward from the backseat to throw his unwanted two cents into the conversation.

"See." Sydney gestures to Aleks, and it makes me want to strangle him. "I'll be fine, really. I'm exhausted, and I might be coming down with something. I just want to get back and sleep."

My frown deepens as I continue to scrutinize her. I hate that she's brushing me off, but I'm not going to throw a tantrum over it in a Seattle back alley.

Plus, the more I look at her, the more I see the signs of exhaustion stamped onto her body. Sure, the guys and I work a full schedule and don't really have any set vacation days, but that doesn't mean we don't take days off here and there, depending on how we feel. Sydney, however… something tells me that she hadn't had a real day off in a very long time. Something I was going to have to fix.

"Fine, we'll catch you back at the hotel."

I give her hand a secret squeeze as I step into the car.

"I'll see you guys in the morning. We're meeting in the lobby at eight for breakfast before the flight."

"Seriously, Syd? The flight isn't until midday," Aleks complains.

"And you boys are a nightmare to corral, so we're meeting at eight."

"Okay, okay. We'll meet you at eight." I wave off.

She gives me a smile, and I see the hidden message in her eyes, the one meant just for me.

Thank you.

"Bye, boys." She shuts the Escalade door and takes a step back. My heart already aches at the distance between us, and I watch her out the window as we begin to drive off.

I don't know what I'm going to have to do, but some-day soon, I'm going to convince her to never leave my side.

In the meantime, I have an idea.

Chapter
FIFTEEN

PARKER

I knock on the door a few times and wait in the silence that responds.

After the fifth knock, I pull a key card out of my pocket to open it.

"Room service," I sing, kicking the door closed behind me.

Sydney bolts up on her bed, eyes wide. "Parker! What the hell?" She hits pause on the show playing on her laptop before she clutches the silky robe she's wearing close to her chest. "How'd you get in here?"

I wiggle the key card in my hand as I walk in and place the takeaway bag on the small coffee table.

Her eyes flit from the bag to the key card as she takes everything in. "How'd you get a key card to my room?"

"Unlike the Kelton, I have a lot of sway at W Hotels."

"That's an abuse of privilege."

"Comes with the territory."

I sink onto the edge of her bed and begin untying my shoes, trying my hardest to keep from grinning as Syd continues to stare at me. It's not until I unbutton my shirt sleeves and start rolling them up that she snaps out of her daze and quickly moves off the bed.

She shuffles around me at a slight distance.

"What are you doing here, anyway? I thought you went for food?"

"I did. I went for food, and I brought it back. Couldn't have my girl eating alone when she wasn't feeling well, could I?"

"Your what? No. I—I actually feel completely fine. I'm just a little tired." She averts her gaze as it fills with guilt, pulling her robe tighter. "Honestly, I just needed some downtime. I was going to order room service and relax."

I push off the bed and walk past her, purposefully brushing up against her shoulder in the process.

"Why have room service when you can have this delicious pho in the company of a dashing British man?"

I hold up the white plastic bag I brought in with me before placing it back down. I take out the four containers inside and begin setting them up on the little table, opening the ones with the noodles and veggies before carefully cracking open the ones with the soup inside.

The smell of the warm broth immediately fills the air, and Sydney takes a few steps closer.

"You got me pho?"

I hold out a pair of chopsticks toward her. "Vegan, too."

She takes them from my hand and sinks down on the

carpet beside me, crossing her legs. She twists the container around and smiles when she sees the sharpie-written words on the side indicating the vegan broth. I don't tell her, but it's not even the same restaurant the others went to. That one didn't have any vegan options, so I ended up leaving them to rideshare to another restaurant that had a broth she could eat before coming back here.

"You didn't have to do this for me."

"Who said it was for you?" I grin, breaking my chopsticks apart. "It was entirely selfish. I just wanted to spend some time with you while the kids are distracted."

Her cheeks flush and she averts her gaze, pouring her hot soup over her noodles carefully before blowing on it and taking a bite. Her eyes light up as she hums with pleasure.

"Wow, this is good," she says between slurps, the tension leaving her shoulders as she becomes distracted by the taste.

"Better than room service, no?" I pick up a generous heaping of noodles and shovel them into my mouth.

"Maybe." She gives me a cute smile. "Thank you."

"Of course."

The silky robe she's wearing has started to come loose now that she isn't holding it in a death grip. I lean over and kiss her shoulder briefly.

She sucks in a breath and freezes, the carrot poised between her chopsticks falling back into her soup. She swallows a gulp before quickly picking the carrot back up and popping it into her mouth.

Her nerves are radiating off her body like little sparks. I don't think I've ever seen her like this before.

The normally calm and collected Sydney Lake is a fumbling mess.

I lean against the coffee table and watch her. The way her clear gray eyes focus pointedly down on the strands of rice noodles she scoops up, instead of flicking up to me. Her toes tap back and forth against her legs—a habit she doesn't even notice.

Eventually, she lets out a huff and glares at me. Although she looks more like a cub than a lioness.

"Would you quit it?"

"Quit what?" I pop a piece of pork in my mouth and chew it innocently.

"Staring at me."

"Nope. Why? Does it make you uncomfortable?" I grin.

"No," she scoffs. "Why would it make me uncomfortable?" Her chopsticks swirl idly in the remaining broth.

"Dunno. Maybe cause you're picturing my tongue in your mouth?"

She gapes at me, her eyes flicking to my lips.

"Or maybe." I slide closer to her and lower my voice. "You're imagining something else entirely. What a dirty mind you have, Miss Lake. I had no idea."

"Stop messing with me." Lust-fueled panic dances across her eyes, and she shoves me away. Her nudge is a little too strong, though, and my elbow bumps against my soup, sending splatters across my sleeve. Her panic turns to embarrassment before she feigns frustration. "That's your own fault," she mumbles through pursed lips.

"Guess so." I reach up and swiftly undo the buttons of my shirt before stripping it off and tossing it behind us. I stretch my arms behind my head and give my neck a quick crack.

"Oh, you have got to be kidding me right now."

"See something you like?" I smirk.

"You play dirty, Parker Covington." She points a finger at me, and I shoot forward, nipping at it before she squeals and reels away.

"I have to play dirty, love. You've been ignoring me all day."

"Because we were around people."

"I don't see anyone in here now."

"That's because…" she trails off, and peers up at me through the wisps of her bangs. "I don't know what I'm doing." Her voice is soft as her fingers nervously twist in her hands. "I don't know how I'm supposed to act around you anymore. It's freaking me out."

"You're thinking about it too much, Syd." I take one of her hands in mine and link our fingers together.

"All I've done is think of you."

She blanches, realizing what she just said.

"I mean, I—," she tries to backtrack, but it's too late. "Crap."

Her face falls, and I let out a soft laugh.

I'm on cloud-fucking-nine. Syd doesn't even know the effect her words have on me. There are about a million fireworks going off in my chest right now because this blonde bombshell just admitted that she can't stop thinking about me. That I'm living rent-free in her mind.

I've waited for the day when she thinks of me for even a fraction of the time I spend thinking about her.

"Then keeping thinking of me." I let go of her hand

and trail my hand up her arm, across the soft fabric, pausing when I reach the bare skin of her shoulder before cupping the back of her neck. "Think about how good my fingers feel against you. Think about how good they might feel inside you." My thumb glides up her neck, and her lips part as I pull her toward me. "Are you thinking about it?" I whisper against her ear.

She nods absently. "Yes." Her voice is deep and breathy and sexy as all hell.

"Good." I pull back and look in her eyes. "Still freaking out?"

"Only a little." She bites her lip and smiles.

Fuck me. That's hot.

"A little?" I lean closer, keeping us centimeters apart. My heart thumps loudly within my chest, beating against me with every breath I take.

"Yeah. Now kiss me." The corner of her mouth twitches up slightly.

"All you had to do was ask, love."

I drag her lips to mine, stealing her breath for my own.

She sighs into me, and I drink her in, thirsty for every morsel she gives me. My hand tangles in the hair at the base of her neck, angling her up to me, deepening our kiss.

I can't get enough of Sydney.

She could drown me with the taste of her, and I would say thank you until I passed into the afterlife.

I haul her onto the couch behind us, laying her on the soft cushions as I tower above her.

"There's a perfectly good bed a few feet away," she mutters against my lips.

"Too far." I swipe my tongue across her lower lip.

The taste of her cherry lip gloss has me smiling. Always predictable this one.

She gasps into me. "Parker, bed."

I growl, gripping the backs of her thighs and picking her up against me again. Her hot center presses against my dick as I carry her. The movement shifts her against me in a way that has my knees threatening to buckle.

She bounces on the bed, splaying against the crisp white sheets. Her hair tumbles loose from her bun, and her robe spills open, revealing a pale-blue matching lingerie set. The bra is sheer, and I see the hardened peaks of her nipples teasing through. She looks like an ice princess coming undone, melting under my touch.

"Damn."

She smiles at me shyly, her hands coming down to toy with the belt of her robe. "Like what you see, Mr. Covington?"

"Baby, you look like a wet dream."

Her confidence grows with my compliment, her smile tipping seductively as she reaches out a hand and beckons me forward.

"Then be a good boy and come play."

I almost come in my pants.

Pants that I am unbuttoning and tearing off with lightning speed.

I descend on her in record time, caging her between my thighs and rocking against her as I take her lips with mine. Her body is warm beneath my touch, and I can't keep my hands from tracing all over her. There isn't an inch of her I want to miss. She's fucking delectable.

I kiss a path down her body, stopping when I reach

her breast. I swirl my tongue around the sensitive tip, wetting the lace. Her chest lifts slightly as she arches into my touch, urging me on. My hand comes down to squeeze her other breast, running my thumb over her nipple while I lave away at the other.

Her hands thread in my hair, manicured nails scratching against the shortened sides. I drag my lips lower, leaving a hot path down her stomach. Just as I reach her bully button, I feel her tense, abs contracting.

I peer up at her through hooded eyes. "Not yet?"

She shakes her head. "Lingerie stays on."

My head tilts. I can work with that.

"So, this is okay?" I place a kiss on her inner thigh, and her whole body breaks out in a shiver. I place another one a bit higher, and her knee pulls in slightly. My hands dig into the thick curves of her hips.

So responsive.

"God, you're a tease," she breathes.

I just grin at her before I lick a line up the inside of her thigh, stopping just short of the lacy barrier. I repeat the action on the other side, and her strong thighs clench inward. My cock strains in my briefs, the sensitive head pushing against the band.

I'm torturing myself with my face inches away from her sweet cunt.

Relief.

I need some sort of relief from this pain.

I drag myself back up the length of her body, nuzzling her neck and inhaling her cherry-sweet scent and placing a hot kiss just beneath her ear. Sydney's small hands run along my shoulders, scratching down my biceps. She pulls me closer, lips parted as she desperately searches for my kiss.

Her eyes are a stormy haze, and I drink in her taste as we crash in a heady kiss.

My hips roll against hers, dragging my cock against her center, and my eyes almost roll back in my head at the blissful relief the contact creates.

I release a strangled groan against her lips.

If she feels this good now, how fucking amazing is she going to feel with nothing between us?

Will I even survive that?

I keep up the rhythm, my hips churning in waves as our bodies move as one against each other. Sydney gasps and her fingers curl around my ribs, piercing my skin as she lifts her body to be closer to mine.

Whether she notices it or not, she's matching me beat for beat, chasing after my touch.

My thick length knocks into her heat, the tip beading with precum. Her own wetness begins to seep through, and I feel it soaking my briefs. The added lubrication has my balls tightening as the friction between our bodies turns to fucking water, letting us slide against each other.

Sydney's legs lock around the backs of my thighs, and her hands tighten on my hips, pulling me against her at a new angle and keeping me there.

She lets out a low moan.

Fuck.

I might be able to come like this.

It's like I'm in seventh form again, getting off like a fucking prepubescent teen.

But damn, she drives me absolutely mad.

"That feel good, love?"

"Yes, oh my God." Her eyes tighten.

"Fuck, Syd. The things you do to me," I groan.

She moans again in response, her arms sweeping up against my sweaty back. She links her hands between my shoulder blades, and her hips pick up their pace as she lifts them against me, increasing the pressure between us. My dick basically slides against the folds of her pussy, nothing but soaked fabric acting as a barrier between us.

"Fuck, Syd," I repeat. Blood is rushing to my dick, and stars are dotting my eyes. There is barely any rational thought left in my brain right now. All I can focus on is the feeling of her against me. "God. Do you think you can come like this?" I ask her.

"Maybe," she pants. "I think so."

"Fuck." It seems to be the only word my brain can form. "Fuck, okay, what can I do?"

I plant kiss after kiss against her neck and down her jaw.

I'll do literally anything. Anything.

There is no way I'm coming like a fourteen-year-old in his boxers without Sydney joining me for the high.

"Flip over."

I almost miss the words between our tangle of breaths, but I scoop my hands under her shoulders and hold her against me as I roll over. She rips off her robe and looks down at me. Her chest heaves heavily, pert breasts pressing against the little fabric left on her body. Blonde hair cascades around her flushed face. Every inch the melted ice princess.

My hands come down to settle on her ass, and I decide

that I like this position a hell of a lot better. I knead her round cheeks, groaning at the feeling and shifting my hips under her.

I love her ass.

Syd eyes glaze over as she begins rolling her hips, and I have to calm myself down so I don't shoot my load.

I take it back.

I don't love this position, because watching her body rock above me is going to send me to an early death. Although, this wouldn't be a bad way to die.

Her body tips forward and crushes against mine. The lace of her bra is sensitive across my skin, and she plasters herself to my chest and picks up the pace. Her nails dig into my shoulders. She grinds against me like her life depends on it. I curse into the crook of her neck as she sends me closer and closer into a state of oblivion.

"Fuck, yes, baby," I breathe. "Use me. Fucking use me. That's it." I urge her on, sinking the pads of my fingers around her waist to deepen her rough movements.

"Oh God." The words leave her in a strangle, her voice pitching higher and higher as her hips move faster and faster. "Oh God, Oh God, Oh God." The pleas fall from her lips against my skin.

The top half of her body arches up, and she jerks against me in short motions, her clit rubbing frantically against the throbbing tip of my dick.

It's too much.

I'm not going to last.

I'm not going to fucking last.

My abs contract as my balls tighten one last time. The euphoria shoots through me.

"Fuck, babe, I'm coming." My head pushes back against the mattress as hot jets of come coat me.

Her hips stutter, her rhythm faulting, but my grip remains tight on her, guiding the movements.

"No. Keep going. Keep going. I told you to use me."

The sensation is fucking out of this world, and my cock is sensitive as shit, but I keep myself together as she keeps rocking back and forth, the last of my cum pulsing out of my cock.

I'm riding my high as she continues to chase hers.

Little gasps of "yes, yes, yes," fall from her lips, and she sucks in a shaky breath before her lips part in a silent moan, the perfect O forming as her eyes squeeze tight and her hips jerk roughly before she freezes and I feel her cunt pulse against me. Then, she collapses, her skin slapping against mine as she lies on my chest.

Our breathing is ragged, the tempo a total cacophony, but it sounds like music to me.

"Oh my God."

"I know," I agree with her. I lift my hand to move back the damps strands of her bangs that are plastered against her forehead.

She cranes her neck at the motion, her chin digging into me.

"We really did that." She blinks at me as if she doesn't quite believe I'm there.

"We did."

She snorts, resting her cheek against my chest again. "I don't want to move."

"You don't have to."

"Good," she mumbles. "Too tired."

I laugh and continue to lightly stroke her hair, careful not to pull any of the tangles. Post-orgasm Sydney is the most relaxed I've seen her in my life.

Her breathing slows, and she burrows herself further into me.

"I hate to be the party pooper," I start.

She groans.

"But aren't you supposed to pee or something?"

She groans again. "I think that's only sex. I'll be fine."

"If you say so, but—"

"Parker," she groans at me even louder.

"But I'm currently covered in my own jizz, and I need to shower, love."

She lifts her head and stares up at me through narrow eyes. She rolls off me and digs at the sheets until she crawls beneath them. "Have fun, I'm going to sleep." The words are muffled by the pillow she's stuck her face on. I lean over and drop a kiss on her head before slipping out of the bed.

"You could join me," I call back to her as I make for the bathroom.

Her garbled response gets lost, and I just chuckle.

I peel off my briefs, using them to wipe off the remaining cum before tossing them on the floor and rinsing off in the shower quickly. It's only when I step out and dry off that I realize I have nothing with me. There's not a chance in hell I'm putting my underwear back on. My room is the one across from hers, but I don't really want to chance that little excursion in the nude.

With my luck, I'll be halfway across the hall, and Aleks or Jackson will pop out of their rooms.

I hang my damp towel up before going about Syd's hotel room and shutting off each of the lights. The room slowly descends into darkness.

When I pick up my phone from where I abandoned it on the coffee table, I see a bunch of texts blowing up my phone. All of them are from the group chat I have with the guys, minus a stray text from my mum congratulating me on my win earlier.

I send Aleks and Jackson a peace emoji to shut them up and then bump a quick response to my mum before tossing the phone on the nightstand.

Syd is still cocooned on her side, curled into a little ball and breathing softly. I slide under the covers and inch my way over before wrapping my arm around her waist.

"You smell good," she mumbles.

"Thanks, it's eau du English. A pretty limited edition scent; not many people can afford it."

Her chest lifts with a light snort. "Cute."

"Not as cute as you." I dip a kiss to her shoulder.

"You think I'm cute?"

"I think the face you make when you come is *very* cute."

She jerks in my grasp, her head twisting so she can stare up at me through sleepy eyes. "Seriously, Parker?"

"Shhh, love." I pop a kiss on her nose. "Just go back to sleep. It's been a long day."

She huffs but cranes her neck to kiss me back before she returns to her snuggled position. I squeeze her tighter, bringing her back flush to my chest. There's a ninety per-cent chance that my other arm falls asleep from where it's propped under my head, but I'd sooner cut it off than move it.

I inhale Sydney's sweet scent and lose myself to the feeling of her soft flesh pressed against mine as I let the darkness take me away.

When I'm with her, it's like the rest of the world doesn't exist.

Nothing can disturb the peace she brings me.

Chapter
SIXTEEN

PARKER

*B*ANG.

BANG, BANG.

My peaceful dreams are shattered one by one with each incessant knock that resounds through the room.

Who the fuck is pounding on a door this early?

I try to ignore the noise by focusing on the woman in my arms. The one who, miraculously, has not woken up yet.

She must be exhausted to sleep through the sound because I'm a pretty heavy sleeper, and even I can't deny that the force with which that person is hammering on the door across the hall is waking up the entire damn floor.

I crack my eyes as annoyance trickles into my blood.

That was a damn good dream they interrupted.

There's barely any sunlight filtering into the room, just

a small sliver that is beginning to crawl its way across the floor from the crack in the blinds.

The bangs resume but with yelling this time.

Sydney's entire body shoots up, tearing out of my arms. Her first few steps out of the bed are a stumbling mess, and I quickly follow behind her, steadying her as she reaches out an arm.

She blinks around rapidly, trying to clear the grogginess.

"Whoa, there. What are you doing, love?"

"I—" She looks up at me, confusion marring her face. "I thought I heard Aleks."

I raise my free hand to my chest in fake pain. "Are you having dreams about my best mate while I'm cuddling you in bed? That hurts, Syd."

"Ugh, I must still be wired from the tournament."

She sighs, padding back to the bed. Her knees barely land on the mattress when the voice outside becomes clearer.

"Parker, you lazy fuck, wake up."

Sydney's body freezes, head whipping to mine. She stares at me like a deer in headlights. Then her eyes dip down my body and widen even farther before a look of absolute panic takes over.

"Why are you naked?" she whisper-shouts.

"*That's* what you're focused on right now?" I whisper-shout back.

Granted, my dick is currently at half-mast after being plastered against her bum all night. But it's not the first time she's seen it.

She lets out a strangled moan before shuffling quietly to the door. She perches on her tiptoes to stare out the peephole. Her raised shoulders drop slightly at whatever she sees across the hall. She spins back around and opens her mouth to say something before the knocking resumes, a lot louder this time.

Almost like…

"Sydney!"

…It's now directly outside her door.

Syd's face blanches at Aleks' voice. She raises her index finger to her lips and mimes a "shh" motion. I zip my lips and throw away the key before raising my hands innocently and walking farther back into the room.

She cracks the door open slightly and the glow of the hallway leaks in as she peeks her head out.

"Aleksander, someone better be dying, otherwise I have no idea why you thought it was a good idea to assault my door this early in the morning."

"What are you talking about? You said we had to meet in the lobby for breakfast at eight a.m. It's half past."

"What?" Syd's knuckles tighten on the doorframe.

"Yeah. We tried calling you, but it went straight to voice—" his words cut off as Syd slams the door shut. She sprints to the bed and starts flinging the covers around.

"What are you doing?"

"My phone. Where's my phone?" She's frantically running around the room now.

"Sydney?" Aleks calls out.

"Oh my God." Panic starts to take over, and I see her hands begin to shake.

I grab hold of her, trying to steady the nerves coursing through her body. She attempts to wiggle out of my grasp, but it just makes me tighten. I run a hand over her head, smoothing down her hair in slow repeated movements. "Stop. Take a deep breath."

She lets out a shuddering breath, but her chest continues to rise and fall in short puffs.

"Sydney?" Aleks starts knocking on the door again.

If she wouldn't hate me for it, I would rip the door open and tell him go suck a dick.

Instead, I cup her face in my hands. "Hey, it's going to be fine."

Her worry-filled eyes stare back at me. "I forgot to charge my phone. We slept in. I never do that. Aleks is at the door, you're naked, and we're going to be late. The flight—"

"Is literally my private jet. They aren't going to leave me behind, Syd."

"But everyone's downstairs."

"So?"

"So? I told them to be down there early because I knew they would all run late, and instead I'm the lazy one!"

"Babe, no one is ever going to accuse you of being lazy. It's okay. You've got this. It's all going to be perfectly fine. You—" Aleks pounds on the door again. "You just need to get rid of *him*," I sigh, placing a kiss to her forehead.

She closes her eyes and takes a deep breath, holding it for a concerningly long period of time before exhaling. When her eyes reopen, there is nothing but cool determination. I watch as she collects herself and pads back to the door. Her shoulders straighten, and she pops the door open to poke her head out again.

"Sorry. I'm still feeling a little under the weather.

Guess I overslept." Her voice is steady.

"Oh, need us to grab you anything? You didn't seem that great last night either."

"No, it's fine. I'll be down in fifteen. Just entertain yourselves until then."

"No rush, it's Parker's jet fuel we're burning. He can afford it." *Wanker*. "He's still asleep, by the way. No shock, but I think his phone's dead as well."

"I'll deal with it. Don't worry."

"Okay." There's a wariness to Aleks' tone. "See you down there."

Syd shuts the door with a soft click before turning around and sliding down onto her bum. I go over and crouch in front of her, tucking her hair behind her ear.

"That was great, love."

"*That* was a mess," she huffs. The exhaustion of yesterday is back on her face. As much as she likes to claim that she's just a little tired, it's clearly more than that.

"Nah, could've been worse." I take her hands and pull her to her feet. "You know; this wasn't exactly how I thought our first morning after would go."

She gives me a teasing smile. "Really? This isn't what you had in mind?"

"No, my vision included a lot more cuddling and a lot less Aleks."

Sydney laughs until her eyes dip down my body and she chokes. Her skin turns that cherry-red color, but she doesn't seem able to rip her gaze from my dick. The very same dick that is growing harder every second she looks at it.

"Syd. You keep looking at me like that, and I'm not

sure you're going to make it downstairs in ten minutes."

She sucks in a breath, and her eyes rip back up to mine.

"You're the one walking around naked."

"And you're the one who made me come in my briefs."

She makes a choking sound, and somehow, her face gets even redder. A part of me wonders just how far I can push her. She has these little moments of sexual confidence, but more often than not, she retreats back into her shell.

I see the heat behind her eyes. The want that she tries to hide so badly.

Sydney can keep putting up walls, but they're made of glass and I see right through them.

I take a step toward her, and she takes one back.

We repeat the same dance over and over until she bumps up against the bed.

"What are you doing, Parker?"

"Admiring you."

I run a hand down her body, feeling her hot skin beneath the pads of my fingers. I toy with the sides of her panties and twist the lace tight.

Her fingers twitch at her sides, reaching out to touch me before pulling back. She conducts a silent battle in her brain. Without saying any words, I already know what she is thinking. There's a part of her that wants to give in to her attraction to me again, but there is still that little voice that tells her to keep her distance, to retain some shred of professionalism.

It's that little voice that is keeping us apart.

But it's getting smaller and smaller the more time we spend together. Because as her feelings for me get louder, that voice gets softer. I know I'm getting close; I have to be.

Because as much as I like Sydney, sitting in this half-way zone with her is taking a toll on me. I didn't think it would, but it is. I told myself that getting even a slice of her affection would be enough. But it was easier to survive when we were dancing around our attraction since there was nothing more to compare it to. Now that I've held her in my arms and tasted her lips and seen her come, it rips something inside of me when she brings the shields back up.

Syd wins against her silent debate, and her hands come up to rest on my chest. My body sings in relief at the contact.

Little by little. Piece by piece. She's coming around. As much as I complain about how slow this process is, it really is worth it. Anything regarding Sydney is worth it because she's a priceless gem.

My dick twitches, and I ignore the urge to push her back onto the sheet and devour her. Instead, I lean forward and plant a soft kiss on her mouth. She sighs into me, and I melt against those pillow-soft lips.

"I'll see you downstairs, sweetheart."

I give her ass a cheeky slap before forcing myself to step away and collect my clothes from around the room. With a final—very naked—bow, I leave her room.

In hindsight, I probably could have spared the extra few seconds to put on my clothes before darting across the hall.

But I'm Parker Covington, and I really don't give a fuck.

Chapter
SEVENTEEN

SYDNEY

This is karma.

I feel like absolute crap.

My entire body aches, and my lower back specifically feels like someone has taken an axe to it. It is as though they are hacking at the muscles, over and over and over. The pain just won't stop.

And don't even get me started on the headache. It was the first thing to appear two days ago. I thought it was nothing. Just brushed it off and went about my days as normal. A little pain wasn't something to fuss over when there was so much to do.

Now, it's like a truck ran over my brain and squished it. I've taken every pain med under the sun, and it just keeps coming back. My throat hurts a little, but it's nothing compared to everything else.

This is what I get for lying about being sick and hiding a naked man in my room.

I manifested the sickness.

Groaning, I slink out of my bed and drag myself into the kitchen.

Fluids.

I need fluids.

I flick on a light, but the brightness stabs my eyes and causes my brain to pinch.

Nope.

I whack them back off. It's not that dark. The microwave glows the time into my blurry vision.

3:30 p.m.

God. I've been in bed all day.

Cracking open my fridge, I pull out my filtered pitcher and pour a glass of water. The cool liquid instantly soothes my hot body.

Since when was I hot?

I pour myself another glass and somehow make my way back into my bedroom. I slip the glass onto my nightstand and grab my phone instead. A few notifications litter the screen, and I tell myself to reply to Lee's text as I crawl back under the covers. But as I squint at the light, trying to get myself to focus, nothing really makes sense. It's all a glowing fuzz.

I shut my eyes for a few seconds, hoping it will clear my vision.

A hushed voice swims in my head.

Like I'm talking underwater, so it's all muffled.

Except the voice is British.

I'm not British.

Something cool touches my forehead, and I lean into it, begging it to stay.

And it does.

Then I'm lifted into the air, floating on a cloud.

I ride the cloud until it turns stormy and starts to rain, sending droplets pattering across my skin.

It feels good, though, and I turn my face up to the sky before sinking back under, trying to ignore the pain all over me, trying to wash it away.

It feels like eons pass before I finally resurface and break for air.

There's another voice.

Flashes of memories start to come back to me, and I will myself out of the haze.

My eyes crack open, and there's an oddly attractive man in my room. He is bathed in a white light. Or maybe it's a white coat. I should be concerned. Except, I also don't know if he is real...and I'd seem really crazy if I started screaming at something that wasn't there.

Although, if there was no one in the room, there would be no one to see me lose my marbles either.

When the man sticks something under my tongue, some of my senses return to me. Those flashes of memories start coming into focus, and I remember Parker's voice, his hand on my forehead, the cool compress.

I blink rapidly as my eyes try to adjust to the low light of my bedroom.

I stare up at a man with a sharp jaw of stubble and cool green eyes, who is most certainly real, and let out a meek squeak as I try to scramble back. But my body is like jelly, and I don't really make it more than an inch.

"How are you feeling, Ms. Lake?" His voice doesn't really match how he looks; there's a slight Southern twang to it.

"Not great," I answer hesitantly.

He chuckles, capping the thermometer in his hand. "That would add up. You had a high-grade fever; it's only just breaking."

"You're awake." Parker stands in my door frame holding two mugs, and I see relief pool across his features. His face is lined with exhaustion, but his hair is still a perfectly styled wave of white blond on his head.

He's dressed casually, which is an uncommon occurrence for Parker Covington. A tight blue T-shirt and dark gray joggers hang on his sculpted body. Even in my haze, he's hot. When he spins to place the mugs on my armoire, I see the giant "Dior" letters printed across the back of his shoulders. Of course.

Parker perches on the side of my bed and helps me sit up slowly.

"What's going on?"

It's all still disorienting.

"You have the flu," says the man in the white sweater. The more I look at him, the more he has that rugged mountain man parading as a city boy vibe. "Can I ask when your symptoms began?"

"I had a headache three days ago."

"Yes, that's what I feared." He taps his jaw in thought.

"I'm sorry, who are you?"

"Dr. Reston."

"Right." I nod.

Until I start to get a grip on reality and comprehend that there are two men—one of whom I do not know—inside my apartment whom I never let in. At least, I don't think I did. The last few hours are hazy.

Has it even been hours?

What time is it?

Who is this man really?

"Are you sure she's going to be fine?" Parker looks at me with concern, and I realize that I've just been having a conversation with myself while nodding blankly into dead space.

"Are you really doubting me after I flew all the way here, Covington?" Dr. Reston reaches down and zips up the black duffle at his feet. "Just make sure to keep her hydrated with lots of rest. If she's been sick for four days, I can't prescribe her anything, anyway. She's fought through the worst of it. Which, unfortunately, seems to have been worse than most of the cases I've seen this season." He cocks his head at me. "You really should sleep more. Exhaustion makes you immunocompromised."

This doctor has awful bedside manners.

"I'll send you my bill." He hikes the duffle over his board shoulder and claps Parker on the back. "Good luck at your championship."

Dr. Reston leaves the room before I can blink, his heavy footsteps echoing throughout my apartment.

Right.

My apartment.

"God, you scared me, Syd." Parker brushes my sweaty bangs out of my eyes and despite myself, I sink into his touch.

Except, now that I think about it…my bangs aren't sweaty.

They're wet.

Like I took a shower.

I don't remember a shower.

Do I?

My brows furrow and I look down at my body.

Now that there isn't some mountain-man doctor in my bedroom to distract me, everything is starting to come into focus.

The main one being that my clothes are not the clothes I was wearing when I passed out., And the more I shift on my bed, I realize my sheets are also not the same sheets I put on last weekend.

What the heck happened?

"What's going on in that head of yours, Syd?" Parker's voice breaks my spiral.

There are a million questions swimming in my brain, but I settle on the one floating closest to the surface. "How did you get into my apartment?"

"Would you believe me if I told you that you left it unlocked?"

I narrow my eyes at him as I try to think back to when I last got home. It was just after Crime Night, and I was in a world of pain after putting on a smile for hours at Lee's. I definitely locked it.

I *always* lock it…especially after Crime Night.

Wait.

I can't even leave it unlocked.

It has a damn keypad.

As if sensing my growing frustration, Parker pops off my bed and grabs the mugs he abandoned on my armoire. He hands the apple-shaped mug to me, reserving the blueberry-shaped one for himself.

"Well, love, as you now know, I do own this building. Access isn't exactly hard to come by." He takes an innocent sip of his tea.

"Abusing your privilege once again, I see." I take a small taste of my own mug, careful not to burn myself. The flavor is a little strange. I can't tell if I like it or not. Mint is the main note. However, there's a deep bitterness to it, as well as some slightly nutty tones. It makes my throat feel better though.

"You don't like it?"

"It's not that I don't like it…" I trail off. "What exactly is it?" I take another sip and tell myself not to curl my lip at the initial bitterness.

Parker laughs. "It's Yin Qiao San." The man has a habit of saying things to me that he just expects me to understand. "Chinese herbal medicine. I had the doctor send it over when I explained your symptoms."

"Dr. Reston?"

"No, Dr. Zhu. He's the one who does Jackson's cupping and is a lot easier to get a hold of than Reston." He rolls his eyes. "Are you still tired?"

I shake my head. "Not really. I feel a little stuffy though."

Parker hums and holds his hand out to me. I take it, careful not to spill my tea as I get out of bed. Parker rests my hand in the crook of his elbow as he guides me out of my room. My muscles don't feel like noodles anymore, but I don't let go of him.

As we enter the living room, I realize that the sun is setting, sending a bright pink glow over my apartment.

Parker places his mug on my coffee table before he fluffs up a new knitted blanket on my couch and cocoons me in it. I'm wrapped in warmth, sipping on the not-so-bitter-anymore tea, watching as he cracks open my balcony door to let fresh air in before he turns on a pot on the stove.

My apartment has a similar floor plan to the boys', but just on a smaller scale. It's an open concept with the living room, kitchen, and small dining area all nestled within the same twelve-hundred square foot space. I have one bedroom off to the side, whereas they have six. My balcony only fits a two-person table set, while they have an entire outdoor barbeque area as part of their penthouse.

If my rent is ten thousand dollars…I don't even want to imagine what theirs costs.

My eyes track Parker's movements over the top of my mug. There's not a single part of me that is ashamed anymore to admire the way his joggers hug his firm ass. Not after what happened in Seattle.

I swallow at the memory as my stomach swoops briefly. With my body no longer in crushing pain, my mind is free to trace his defined biceps as he stirs something in the pot. There's something soft about seeing Parker dressed so down-to-earth; it's like another barrier has broken between us. Just being in his presence feels intimate.

"What happened?"

Parker looks at me over his shoulder, "Stevie said you were acting strange at Crime Bingo—"

"Crime Night," I correct him.

He rolls his eyes. "Crime Bingo sounds a lot more fun."

"Parker."

"Okay, okay." He starts to ladle what I think is soup out of the pot into two bowls. "Stevie said you were strange at *Crime Night*, which tracked with the way you barely checked in on Tuesday on my run times—which were beast, by the way. You weren't responding to my texts all day Wednesday, and then Lee texted us that night to see if we'd heard from you because she wasn't getting any response either."

Shoot. I do remember her text.

"Wait, what day is it?"

"Thursday." He opens my oven and pulls out an entire baguette, which he proceeds to slice. "Anyway, I grabbed your keycode and came in to check on you. As your landlord, it is technically legal for me to conduct a welfare check." He winks.

Oh God.

If it's Thursday that means I lost an entire day that I don't even remember.

How's that even possible? It was just the flu.

"You were barely responsive and scared the living daylights out of me, you know. You burned through cold compresses faster than I could make them, all while your whole body was shivering like it was freezing. It was worse than heatstroke." Parker comes over and takes my mug from my hand and places it on my round dining table along with the food he's cooked up. "I called up Reston, and he told me to put you in a cold shower and attempt to get you to drink water whenever you woke a little. It took a few hours for him to get here, but finally your fever broke. Honestly, he didn't really do much. Useless expensive fuck."

I vaguely remember the shower, I think. It's kind of scary that I went through all that and my brain didn't even record any of it. I didn't think I was that bad. It was just a little cold…

"Wait a second. A shower? You saw me naked?" Mortification, rage, and something disturbingly close to lust combine in a confusing haze at the realization.

He holds his hands up in defense. "I swear I closed my eyes for like half of it."

"Parker!" His name leaves my lips in a whine as I clutch my arms around my body.

I get it, I really do. But that doesn't necessarily make the whole situation better. Mostly, I hate that my first thought is whether or not he liked what he saw.

I push my thoughts to the side and gesture at the periwinkle nightdress I'm sporting.

"That explains why I'm dressed in this."

I bought it on a whim a few months ago when it went on sale but hadn't worn it yet because the silk seemed too luxurious. Of course, Parker picked the most expensive nightwear I owned. I'm pretty sure I had it tucked in the back of my closet.

"I think you look hot." Parker grins as he proceeds to scoop me up, blanket and all, before depositing me on one of the dining chairs. "Blue suits you."

He slips a finger under one of the straps and runs it across the length. His touch sends goosebumps immediately down my arm. For a second it feels like someone is pressing hard on the center of my chest, and it becomes hard to breathe. But then he sits down, and the distance makes everything lighter again.

"Bon appétit, mademoiselle." I don't miss the glimmer of mischief dancing in his eyes.

I clear my throat and eye the steaming bowl of soup topped with cilantro and the fluffy baguette slices in the center of the table.

"There's no way you made this yourself."

Parker barely remembers to eat the premade food their personal chef makes for them, let alone cook something from scratch for himself. The most I've ever seen him make successfully is beans on toast and two-minute ramen, both of which only require heating skills. And even then, he sometimes burns the toast.

"Depends on your definition of made." He blows on the soup before eating a spoonful. "I heated everything to the exact temperature the chef told me."

That made more sense.

"Chef?" I mimic the same motion, blowing on the steaming soup before tasting a spoonful.

The vegetable soup is like a warm hug. All the spices warm me the second I swallow. I scoop up some of the carrots floating around, and I get excited when I notice that there are even wood ear mushrooms. It is a silly thing to be excited about, but they are my favorite.

"Yeah, I ordered it from Le Forêt. It's their seasonal

mushroom elixir soup."

"No way! I've been dying to go there. I stalk their page religiously."

Le Forêt is a Michelin star vegan restaurant in New York that is known for the way they create dishes based on the health properties of each ingredient. Their menu changes every four months to accommodate for whatever vegetables are in season. They even have a quarterly event with an energy guru, and the waitlist is bonkers.

Wait.

"Le Forêt doesn't have a restaurant in California, do they?"

There's no way I would have missed that.

"No, they don't." He picks up a piece of bread and dunks it in his soup, taking a bite. I try not to get distracted by his sharp jawline and the vein that is sticking out on his neck.

"Then how did you get their soup?" I swallow another bite and stifle a groan at how good it tastes.

"I flew the sous-chef out. She cooked a couple of batches. There's a few frozen in your freezer for the next couple of nights, plus more in the fridge for tomorrow. It should help you feel better and replenish the nutrients you sweated out."

The piece of bread I'd been in the middle of grabbing promptly falls to the table.

"You flew the sous-chef of Le Forêt to California to cook me soup?"

"She made some celery juice, too. She said that would only last till Sunday, though, or else you won't get the health benefits."

"You know that's not what I meant." I point my spoon at him menacingly, or as menacing as I can be after coming back from the brink of death. "Why on earth did you fly her here? Soup from the supermarket would have been fine."

"Supermarket soup would not have sufficed." He looks offended by the mere thought. "I was already flying Reston out, so it didn't cost any more to have Amber on board."

I blink a few times as I process his words.

"You flew the doctor out as well?" It's more a hushed yell than a question.

"Of course. Reston might be a bit of a dick, but he's one of the best private doctors I know. It's just unfortunate he moved to New York last year. He lives to make my life harder, I swear." Parker sips his tea without a care in the world, as though all of this is very normal.

"Parker," I say slowly. "I don't think you understand what I'm trying to say."

My brain might be mush, but even I have enough sense to realize that this entire situation is abnormal.

Last year, Jackson broke his foot skiing, and Parker never mentioned this Reston guy. In fact, I distinctly remember Parker taking selfies with a severely drugged-out Jackson in the private hospital room and attempting to upload them online, and I had to confiscate his phone.

"What I think is that you need to keep eating." He makes a pointed look at the soup I've barely touched because my brain has been too distracted. "You haven't had anything to eat in twenty-four hours. You need fuel, love." His spoon taps against the side of my bowl.

I purse my lips before taking another sip of the heavenly soup.

My stomach warms, but it's not because of the food.

It's because of him.

I'm not used to this.

Normally, it's me checking in on him, making sure that he has something to eat after gaming for eight hours straight with nothing but energy drinks fueling his body. I'm the one who keeps track of where he is and makes sure that he isn't getting into trouble. And I'm the one who normally scolds him to take a second to breathe and look after himself.

It's weird to have him hovering over me like this. To have him caring about me. I don't like to let people see me like this. I don't like to be vulnerable. Because that means you have to let someone in, and that's dangerous because the pain of losing someone you love is irreparable.

But this, right now?

I don't hate it.

I don't hate it, because it's him.

And I don't know what that means.

Sure, we had that moment of attraction five years ago, but attraction can be surface level. It doesn't have to mean anything deeper. And after I drew the line between us, he never tried to push.

I thought he'd lost interest.

Yeah, okay. He has always been touchy and flirty. But that's how Parker is with *everyone*.

I never took his flirting seriously. Why would I?

Parker Covington hasn't been in a serious relationship since the day I met him. Heck, he's the only one of the guys who *hasn't* had a dating scandal—something which he always proudly points out to me. He always says he would rather spend time hanging out on the couch with me than wasting it with the girls at the club.

My stomach drops as realization kicks in.

The apartment. The car. The shoes. The doctor. The soup.

Those are just the tip of the iceberg. When I look beneath the surface, I see all the little things that he's done over time piling up. It's something you wouldn't notice unless you added them all together. I always thought Parker was extra because…Parker *is* extra.

But that's not it.

God dammit.

Parker Covington is smooth. So smooth, even I didn't notice what he was doing.

No one else hangs out with me while I binge-watch reality dating shows. No one else takes weekly boxing sessions with me. No one else drinks mocktails with me just because I don't drink and asks no questions…especially when said person is a champagne aficionado and instead subs it with sparkling apple juice.

Why didn't I realize this sooner?

I take another sip of soup, Parker's hawk eyes still watching me.

Where does this leave me?

Do I want a relationship with him?

A real one?

Do I want to risk that?

The only thing I know is that I don't want to lose my job. Not just because I love working for the guys—even though they are driving me to an early grave—but because

I love my job. And being in a relationship with anyone in The System *is* a direct violation of my contract. There's no gray area there. The wording is literally printed in black and white.

If I start dating the guy I work for, in a community as small as this, I'm going to be blacklisted. Who would trust a publicist who slept with her employer?

Not that I've slept with Parker yet.

Oh God.

Yet?

I contemplate shoving my face into the bowl of soup and screaming.

Now I'm thinking of Parker's dick.

I've seen that monstrous thing way too many times given the fact that I've never touched it.

Do I want to touch it?

The fluttering in my stomach says yes.

Could I like him?

Do I like him?

My spoon clinks against the bottom of the bowl and the sound startles me out of my spiraling thoughts. I blink down at the near empty bowl. I hadn't even realized how lost I had gotten, mindlessly eating the soup while drowning in the mess of my crush-struck brain.

I peer up at Parker who is leaning so far back on the dining chair that it threatens to tip over. He has his phone turned horizontally in his hands, which means he is playing something. Probably the mobile version of *Kill Strike*.

Sensing my stare, Parker flicks his gaze up and rocks his chair forward, so he is once again level with gravity.

"You feeling okay? You zoned out for a bit there." He

clicks off his phone, standing up and grabbing our empty bowls before taking them into the kitchen.

I attempt to unravel myself from the blanket to help, but it's wrapped around me like a friggin' straitjacket.

"Don't bother. You're the sick princess today; just stay where you are. I can load a dishwasher, you know."

"Since when?" The natural quip leaves my mouth before I can stop it. He does have a copious number of stray cups littering his streaming room, so it isn't completely invalid.

"Since I was fifteen." His tone is a little too serious. I can't tell whether he is telling the truth or not. I mean, this is the same guy who still gets his underwear dry cleaned.

I give up on untangling myself and resume my earlier admiration as he bends down to place the bowls on the bottom rack of the dishwasher.

It is a pity he doesn't wear sweatpants more often. The man has a dump truck.

"Admiring the goods?" Parker stares at me upside down from between his legs with a smirk.

Heat crawls up my neck. It's on the tip of my tongue to say something snarky back, to deflect the conversation like I always do. But for the first time, I don't. For the first time, I take my head out of the equation and just listen to my heart.

"Yep." I say with a pop on the 'P.' "Sure am."

He stands straight and gives me a soft smile. "You are feeling better. That's good."

I give him a shrug, averting my gaze again. I can't keep my confidence high around him for long when he looks at me like that. Especially now that I'm looking more closely and can see the genuine relief and care detailed in the fine lines of his face.

Put me in a room full of the press shouting questions and berating me, and I'm a steel wall. Throw me in front of a flirty British man, and the steel warps.

I do feel better compared to an hour ago, but I still feel exhaustion pulling at my bones. Instead of it being like I've been run over by a train, it's more like I was clipped by a bike while walking. The pain is there, but it's more of an inconvenience than something debilitating. I can function and form coherent thoughts, which I couldn't do yesterday.

"All righty, then." Parker comes back over and scoops me up again in one fell swoop and carries me back to the couch.

"I can walk, you know," I squeal, my heart racing. All my earlier thoughts are coming back with his face mere inches from my own. The blanket is thick between us, but somehow his fingers still burn through.

"Nah, I told you, Syd. Today you're under my care."

Instead of just dropping me onto the cushions, he sits down with me in his arms. My ass and feet are on either side of him. My back is supported by his arm as he cradles me to his chest.

I eye the disappearing orange hue outside.

It has to be late afternoon by now.

Parker leans forward, crushing me even closer to his body as he grabs the remote from the coffee table. My heart rate spikes to obscene levels.

Crap.

I am definitely screwed.

He flicks on the TV and starts scrolling until he finds

the reality show I'm currently watching and pops on the latest episode. In my sick haze, I am now three episodes behind, which means I have a tasty three hours' worth of content to drool over.

The classic opening sequence plays out with its signature song, and my body calms in a practiced response. I find myself snuggling deeper into Parker's arms, laying my head on his chest as I watch the couples flirt and squabble on screen.

Sometime during the second episode, my eyes start to flutter shut. I push myself to keep them open, but the screen keeps getting fuzzy and my brain swims. Eventually, I give up and just let my body do what it wants.

When my consciousness starts to return, the first thing I notice is that I'm still held in Parker's protective arms.

Slowly, I open my eyes. The apartment is coated in darkness, and there is a chilly breeze sweeping in through the open balcony door. I blink a few times, adjusting to the darkness. Parker's chest moves in shallow breaths under me, and in the silence, I hear the short puffs of breath leave his lips. It's stupidly comforting.

I'm careful not to rouse him as I tilt my head up to look at his sleeping face.

His lashes look even longer from this angle, and the shadows of his cheekbones are darker in the moonlight. There is the faintest smattering of stubble along his chin and above his upper lip. I try to think of the last time Parker wasn't clean-shaven and fail to come up with an example. Even during their annual twenty-four-hour stream, he was more put together in the last hour than he is right now.

His platinum hair is sticking up in eight different directions, and I have the impulse to run my hands through it to smooth it back into its regular perfection.

My chest aches again, and the emotions swirling inside of me are so strong all I have is the urge to cry. I want to cry over this pretty boy because what I feel for him is inexplicable. I would say it's the exhaustion talking, but I've spent the last two days sleeping. So if anything, it's the clarity of getting enough rest that is making me see things in a new light. It's forcing me to face the reality that I've been stubbornly ignoring within an inch of my life.

I've been gaslighting myself.

God dammit.

I'm not just attracted to Parker.

I like him.

I like this frustratingly handsome man with his panty-melting accent and disregard for money.

More than I can admit. More than I'm willing to acknowledge.

I've spent so long closing myself off to Parker, to the idea of him, that I blocked out the truth that was already there. That's always been there. The truth that's been threading itself together bit by bit over five years until it became strong enough that even I can't deny it.

I like him.

I like him, and I have no idea what I'm going to do about it.

Do I play this forbidden game?

Do I take Parker's hand and step over the line, leaving it blurred in the sand behind me?

I hear my brother's voice in my head. A voice that brings me happiness and pain at the same time.

"You have to live for yourself, Syd. No one else is going to do it for you. We can't be perfect. You can't be perfect. Something is always going to go wrong, so just embrace what you can. No regrets."

My brother lived life by the seat of his pants. He was a force of nature that attracted everyone into his light. He was the sunshine to my grump. I miss the way he pushed me to loosen my buttons, to break out of my shell. I miss everything about him. Every day. But so much time has passed that I've grown used to being without the part of my soul that disappeared alongside him.

No regrets...

Would I regret not trying this thing with Parker?

Would I look back on this moment five years from now and think "what if?"

I stare blankly out the windows, letting my eyes get lost in the looming darkness outside.

I want to scream.

I want to go to Jax's and let loose a hundred punches against the bag.

I want to get rid of this feeling inside of me because it's tearing me apart.

It's tearing me apart because I know what I want and I'm scared of it.

I'm scared because I've twisted the lid and the feelings for Parker that I've kept bottled up are starting to leak out. I can't keep living in this state of confusion where I'm kissing him one moment and avoiding his touch the next. I need to reseal the lid or take it off completely.

Parker stirs under me, and his head lolls forward before it snaps back up and his eyes open. Startled glaciers blink around the room. When he looks down at me, I see the unfiltered adoration crinkle the corners of his eyes as a sleepy smile spreads across his face.

"Hey."

There's a gravely deepness to his voice that I've never heard before, and the way it sends a zing to my core is the final straw.

"Hey," I whisper back, the knowledge of my decision making my voice small.

He leans forward and places a soft kiss to my forehead. "I didn't want to risk waking you earlier, but let's get you into bed." His arms readjust under me, and he jostles me in the air before standing up with me in a princess carry.

It's a little ridiculous at this point. I feel lifetimes better than I did hours ago, let alone yesterday. The worst of the flu has passed, and there's nothing but a slight sore throat remaining.

He softly lays me back in bed, removing my blanket cocoon and tucking me under the sheets. It's pretty cute, and I once again just want to cry.

Maybe I'm getting my period early because my emotions are haywire.

He places a quick kiss on the tip of my nose before his thumb brushes over my cheek. When he goes to move away, I tear my arm free from the sheets and throw it out to grab onto any part of him.

"Wait." My fingers curl around his T-shirt. "Don't go."

Even in the darkness I see his eyes widen, the whiteness growing around his baby blues. There's a beat before he lets out a soft laugh.

"I won't go anywhere if that's what you want, love.

I'm just going to shut the balcony door."

I let go and suck my arm back under the covers so I can clutch it to my chest. Embarrassment threatens to send a flush over my body, but I push it away and just give him a nod.

He smiles and leaves the room. I count the seconds, listening for the telltale click of the door shutting and his returning footsteps. Part of me is worried he will leave because what good have I done?

He told me he liked me, and since then all I've done is make out with him on the beach and use his body as my own personal humping device before kicking him out of the room when Aleks showed up.

God.

Parker appears in the frame of my door, and my heart stutters as he comes to crouch at the side of my bed.

"What do you need, Sydney?"

It's a simple question on the surface, but it has more layers than an onion. It swims in his eyes, and I know that, no matter what I say, he'll give me a smile because that's Parker. He's been so patient with me.

I have my answer, but my throat closes and the nerves choke me.

No regrets.

The words ring out and give me that split second of confidence I need.

"You."

Chapter EIGHTEEN

PARKER

"You."

Her eyes shine with such brutal honesty that I forget how to breathe.

"You have me, Syd. I'm not going anywhere." It's the truth.

"No." She shakes her head and pushes up to lean on her elbow, turning on her side to face me. "No. Parker, that's not, I—" Her words get trapped as a sheen of wetness coats the bottom of her eyes. "I want to try this for real. Us."

"For real?"

"God." She groans in frustration and falls back against the sheets, raking her hands down her face.

It's been a whirlwind twenty-four hours, and frankly, I'm knackered. Other than the two hours on the couch just now, I haven't slept since Tuesday night. My blood, breath, and soul are Sydney currently. She's been my every thought since the second I walked into this apartment and found her burning up a storm in her bed.

She was a tangle of limbs, breathing heavily, her brows pulled in pain as she tossed in the sheets. The sheer panic I felt when I tried to wake her up and barely got a response is something that took ten years off my life. I was about to burn the whole world down just to get a spark from her.

She asked me to stay, but I was never going to leave.

After everything that's happened, I'm half tempted to drag her up to our apartment and make her live there until I know she is one hundred percent again. The thought of letting her out of my sight is unfathomable.

She wants me and I want her.

The way she kisses me already told me that. So, I'm a little lost as to what has her so frustrated.

Syd sits back up pushes herself to her knees. The silky nightdress rises up her thick thighs and rests just inches from her pussy. My pulse races as I remember her naked body in the shower.

It was near impossible to put her in the shower without looking. I tried for a few minutes, but I ended up brushing against her tits more times when I closed my eyes than when I had them open. Further proof that I like to torture myself when it comes to Sydney.

Her hands reach down to grip the collar of my T-shirt as she pulls me closer.

"Parker." Her breath is hot on my lips, and my name is a silent plea.

I clench my jaw and swallow, my hands coming up to

grip the edge of her bed. I keep telling myself to look at her eyes and not her plush mouth. The very same mouth I spent way too much time staring at when she fell asleep in my arms. If I hadn't been afraid of waking her up, I would've kissed her then.

I fucking miss her taste.

We're hidden in the silent darkness of her bedroom. There is just the dim haze of moonlight seeping through the open door from her living room. Paired with the white glow from her alarm clock, it's enough to clearly define the outline of her soft body. It makes everything feel just a little more confined. As though this very moment isn't real because we can hide behind the shadows.

It's that feeling of anonymity that has me reaching up to cup her face.

I shouldn't be doing this.

She should be resting.

But I can't stay away.

"Yeah, Syd?"

She pulls me closer. So fucking close that our lips are grazing against one another with the lightest touch. I inhale and get drunk on her cherry scent.

"Ask me again. Ask me what I want."

Her lips move against mine as she says the words, and I can barely focus on what she's saying. I just want to devour her.

"What do you want?" The words are strangled as they leave my throat.

"I want to be with you." Her lips press slightly against mine as she says it.

"You mean—"

"I mean I kind of like you," she huffs, and her breath becomes one with mine. The entire world blacks out, and the only light is her. "Like you, like you. I don't want any more gray areas. No more blurred lines. I want us together."

Hope sparks.

I want to believe her. God, I want to believe her so fucking badly.

But I honestly don't know if it's her talking. She's been through the ringer the last twenty-four hours, so I'm not sure if she even knows what she's saying. The last thing I want is to get my hopes up only for her to crush them in the light of day. I might put on a brave face, but I don't think even I could handle that blatant a rejection.

"Are you sure you're thinking clearly?" The words are painful as they leave my lips.

It would be so easy to just take her words as they are, but I respect us, what we could be, too much for that.

Raw rejection pierces her eyes, and her breath hitches. I feel her hands slip briefly from their hold on my top before they tighten again.

"I thought that—" Her voice cracks. "I thought that you wanted me."

Fuck.

Fuck, I'm fucking this all up.

I push myself up and onto the edge of her bed.

"I do." I tip forward so my forehead rests against hers, and my hands come up to rest on her bare thighs. "Sydney, I want you so fucking much that I would sell my soul just for a minute of your time. You're my Eve, and I want to keep you in my garden until the end of time. But I also know that you were half-delirious not even eight hours ago, so I just…I just want to make sure you know what you're saying."

She sighs, and my chest hollows out as fear attempts to seep in.

"I'm sure, Parker. It might scare me half to death, and this could go horribly wrong, but I'm sure." Her hands come to lie on top of mine, and she links our fingers together. "I promise that when we wake up, my decision won't have changed."

There are so many questions.

But I ignore them all for the carnal desire burning inside me.

I take Sydney's lips with mine.

The kiss is soft and slow, like pouring honey, and just as sweet.

My hands tangle in her hair as I cup her neck and draw her closer to me. Her chest presses against mine, her breasts flush against me as our breathing increases.

She mewls into me, and the sound has my cock hardening.

God, I'm down bad for this girl.

She could ask me for anything, and I would get on my knees as her loyal knight to do her bidding.

I trail my hands down to the globes of her ass and haul her onto my lap. Her ankles cross behind my back, and I groan at the feeling of her sweet cunt pressed against me.

Our slow and soft kisses descend into a fevered madness as we claw at each other with growing want. My hips rock up, my need for her clear.

She pulls back, panting. "I'm still not ready for that."

"Don't worry about that, love. You're still recovering, and I need you in top shape when I finally fuck you. Wouldn't want to rip you to shreds on our first go."

"Big talk."

"Big dick."

She rolls her eyes but doesn't deny it. I laugh, taking her into another heady kiss, memorizing the taste of her.

I place another quick kiss on her lips before rolling us flat on the bed. It takes a second for us to get the sheets fixed, but eventually she is snuggled in my arms.

I'm absolutely buzzing right now.

She molds perfectly to me, and there is not a doubt in my mind.

This girl was made for me.

Chapter
NINETEEN

SYDNEY

I wake up in the morning to an empty bed, and I panic.

Was everything just some fever-fueled hallucination?

I'd finally come to terms with my feelings only to imagine blurting them out to Parker?

Granted, it could have gone a lot more smoothly than it did, but…Parker and I are anything but smooth. Our relationship is a roller coaster, and there is no telling the highs or lows. But it is a relationship, that is undeniable.

I fling off my duvet and jump to my feet. The world sways, and little black dots fill my vision. I sink back and sit on my bed for a few seconds to collect myself.

A clink sounds, and I look up through my open bedroom door to see my apartment door opening.

The air whooshes out of my chest as I see my blond Adonis walk in. Parker hasn't changed, still wearing that causal outfit combination. Still effortlessly attractive.

He looks up and smiles when he sees me.

"How are you feeling, love?"

My heart flips over the term of endearment. One that he has always used for me but feels just that little bit more special now.

"A lot better."

He drops the white paper bag he is carrying on the kitchen counter and comes over to envelop me in a large hug. I instinctively nuzzle into his chest.

He pulls back and drops a kiss on my nose. It's something I've noticed he does a bunch.

I tilt my head in the direction of the paper bag. "What's that?"

Parker grins, and it fills me with a ray of light. A girl could get addicted to a smile like that. One that is basically a power-up against any bad mood.

"I got you a treat." He grips my wrist and pulls me into the kitchen.

The bag crinkles, and Parker lifts out a heavenly chocolate muffin. But it's not just any muffin, it's my favorite muffin in the whole world. A vegan double-choc chunk muffin from Terrestrial Coffee.

He hands it to me, and I let out a happy gasp when I feel that it is still warm.

I hop up onto my barstool and take a bite, groaning as the chocolatey taste melts on my tongue. The little chocolate chunks are all gooey, and I kick my feet with pleasure.

Parker opens my fridge and pulls out a glass jar filled with green liquid. He unscrews the cap and slides it across the marble.

"Don't forget your celery juice."

"You're the best," I mumble between bites.

Parker cups a hand around his ear and cocks his head. "I'm sorry, could you repeat that, please?"

I roll my eyes and take a loud sip of the juice. It's not as bitter as I expected; there are notes of lemon and ginger to break up the natural tang.

Parker slides onto the bar stool next to me and places a hand on my leg while he uses the other to dig a croissant out of the bag. Almond, by the look of it.

We sit in comfortable silence for a few minutes before a horrible realization creeps into my brain.

Parker must feel the tension that washes over me because he gives my thigh a squeeze.

"What's wrong?"

"Work!" I hop off the stool and run into my bedroom to find my phone.

Oh God. It's been, like, two days.

How much have I missed?

Did the guys stay on schedule? Did they do anything stupid?

Is everything still set for Parker's next tournament?

Crap, we have to leave for that tomorrow.

My thoughts continue to spiral as I frantically search. Not only is my phone missing, but so are my tablet and laptop.

Strong hands grip my shoulders, and Parker pulls me to his chest, running his hands down my arms in a soothing motion.

"Hey, stop."

I whip my head up to look at him. "Stop? But—"

"But nothing." He guides me over to the couch and forces me to sit down. He brings the last of my juice over and places it in my hands. "I talked with the guys. You're fine, Syd."

I clutch the glass, focusing my nervous energy on it.

"What do you mean?"

Parker sits on the couch next to me and tugs my legs across his lap. He begins massaging my feet, and all my thoughts get jumbled because, damn, that feels good.

"You need rest, Syd."

"I rested yesterday."

"No, yesterday you were recovering from a flu you ignored."

"Same thing."

"No, it's not."

I'm trying to get mad at him, but it's kind of impossible with the magic fingers he uses to ease all the tension out of my feet. God. I don't even remember the last time I had any sort of massage.

"I looked into it. You haven't used any of your PTO this year except for that weekend in April you always take. Even Mathias has used more PTO than you."

I snort because the PTO I did use wasn't even a relaxing one. I take the same weekend off every year because it's the anniversary. It was an emotionally draining weekend.

"So?"

Parker squeezes my foot hard and lets go. My eyes close, and a moan slips past my lips at the feeling.

"So, I'm forcing you to take time off. We all are."

I crack my eyes and stare at him.

"Parker, now isn't the time for me to take time off."

"There's never a perfect time, Syd."

I open my mouth to argue, except he has a point. I never take a break because it never seems like it's the right time. I keep waiting until there is enough of a lull or something comes up where it makes sense.

I let out a huff and pull my feet from his grasp, tucking them under my butt.

The pretty boy is trying to distract me.

"What do you want me to do, Parker?" I drain the last of my juice.

Parker takes the glass from my hands and places it on the coffee table before dragging me from my corner of the couch. He places me on top of his body and cocoons me in his arms, his legs cradling mine.

His warmth seeps into me and lulls me. My traitorous body relaxes into his hold, feeling safe with him.

"I want you to spend the day with me doing absolutely nothing. And then tomorrow, you are going with Stevie, Lee, and Deer for a spa day at a hot spring up in Napa."

"I can't just go to Napa."

"Sure, you can. I booked the helicopter and everything already."

I blink at the mention of a helicopter and force myself to ignore it.

"Helicopter aside, we have to leave for Miami tomorrow."

"Syd, I promise you, I am perfectly capable of going to the tournament by myself. You can't look after me if you aren't looking after yourself. The girls all agreed, so you can't back out. They'll hunt you down if you skip it."

Traitors.

There are a lot of things I can get around, but trying to avoid all three women? Basically impossible. Especially since Lee has been begging for us to do a girls' trip for eons.

What a sneaky man.

I hate him and love him.

"Fine. But I can't just laze around here all day, Parker. I need some compromise. I'll go stir crazy if I do nothing."

"I'm sure I can think of something to entertain you."

Parker runs his hand down my thigh, and I react instantly, my quads stiffening as my pussy clenches.

"Parker." It's supposed to be a warning, but it comes out all wrong, all pleading.

"Shh, just relax. Let me look after you."

His hand continues its slow perusal, trailing up and down my inner thigh. It skates over my skin with the barest touch, like a whisper. Each pass he travels lower and lower, closer and closer to the edge.

He uses his other hand to sweep my hair off my shoulder and begins peppering small kisses down the side of my neck. The dual sensation twists me inside. Anticipation builds in my blood.

A need like no other starts to burn within me. It's a tiny ember at first, flickering deep inside. Little sparks dart with every touch.

His finger grazes the side of my panties and trails up the side of my groin. Slowly, that finger explores more. It trails over the silk covering my pussy, dipping low. The pressure increases as he slides that finger up my slit, and I don't stop myself from clenching when the pad flicks against my clit.

"How does that feel?" Parker's rough voice melts around my ear.

"Good. Really good." I force the words out.

"Yeah?" He moves his finger in hard, lazy circles. "You like when I touch you like this?"

"I do." My leg lifts without my permission and hooks itself over the top of my couch.

"I can see. Greedy girl." His finger starts moving faster. "Does my greedy girl want more? Does she want this finger buried within her cunt?"

My breathing hitches.

Parker's always had a mouth on him. But this? This is something else. Something I didn't know I wanted.

"I can feel how hot you are. If I slip a finger under these panties, will I find you wet for me?"

As if he commanded it, that telltale wetness begins to pool.

I squirm in his hold. My ass brushes against something hard, and I realize it's his cock. This is turning him on just as much as me, and the knowledge of that sparks confidence in me.

I rub against his cock again, and Parker lets out a laugh.

"Do you feel how much I want you, Sydney.?" His lips nip at my ear. "Do you feel how hard you get me?"

His fingers continue their rhythmic motion. But I want more.

"Please, Parker." My hips buck slightly.

"Please, what?"

"Please…" My words stall as I fight the embarrassment. I can think the thoughts in my head, but voicing them is hard.

"Please put your fingers in my pussy, Parker. Please use that tongue to make me see stars," Parker growls the words in my ear. "Are those the words you're looking for?"

I nod senselessly, his words spurring me on. "Yes. Please make me come, Parker."

"Your words are my command."

His fingers dip under the silk, and the contact of his fingers against my mound sends chills up my skin. Two fingers slide up and down my slit, gathering the slick stickiness.

Those two fingers slip inside me with no resistance, and I almost cry out with relief. The feeling of his fingers inside me fills a void.

The palm of his hand continues to rub against my clit as his fingers swirl inside me.

He takes me in a deep, sighing kiss as his hands continue to work their magic. My hips grind against his palm, begging him to finger me deeper and deeper. His fingers curl in quick motions, hitting a sensitive spot within me.

It feels so damn good, and I want him to know that. I want to get off on this.

I squeeze against his fingers, chasing that feeling, that building pressure. But it feels like a wave, and every time it is about to crash on the sand, it just peters out.

Unintentionally, I groan in frustration.

Why does this always happen? Why do I always get so freaking close?

"What's wrong, love?"

"I'm so close," I whine. "I'm so close, but it just won't—" I cut off with a frustrated gasp.

This is why none of my relationships worked out. Okay, no, the main reason is because I am a workaholic and can never spare the time. But I also struggled to find satisfaction either. I get stuck in my own head. I overthink it. I worry. The noise just never quietens.

The other night with Parker was a fluke.

Something in me is broken.

"Relax, Sydney." His tongue trails the shell of my ear. "Relax. You're too tense."

"Relax?"

"Yeah, take a deep breath in and out."

"Seriously?"

"Sydney." It's a sexy reprimand, and the command is attractive as hell.

I do as he says. I take a deep breath in and out, telling my body to relax.

"That's it. Just clear your mind. Don't think about it. Just feel it. Feel my fingers, the pleasure. Keep breathing and stay in the moment."

I continue breathing deep breaths and empty my thoughts.

The second my pussy relaxes, the second it stops clenching so tight, I feel it. A new wave of arousal, a heightened sense of pleasure.

Shocks rocks through my body.

The heck is this?

By letting go of the pressure, it returns threefold. I have no clue what is going on down there, all I know is that it's amazing. It's nothing I've felt before.

I keep breathing, keep relaxing, and everything continues to build.

Parker murmurs words in between kisses, and it just keeps the wave growing.

"That's it. That's my girl. Take all you want. Fuck, your tight cunt feels like heaven."

The pressure builds in a final burst, and the longest orgasm I've ever experienced pulses out of me. My pussy ripples around Parker's fingers as I come. I gasp out a sharp moan, my head pressing back against Parker's shoulder as I lose myself to the sensation.

"There we go. Fucking milk my fingers, love."

God. Dirty Talk Parker is something else.

Parker is something else.

I come down from the high, my pussy still pulsing in the aftermath, greedy for more.

Parker removes his fingers, and I lament the loss. He brings his fingers to his mouth and sucks them clean.

"Mmm, cherries. Just like I expected."

I snort despite the haze. "That's a lie."

"Oh?" He cocks his head and smiles. That damn smile. "You doubt me?"

"My vagina does not taste like cherries, Parker."

He slips his fingers back into my panties and runs them across my sensitive folds. My clit throbs, and I gasp against the sudden touch.

He pulls them out, two fingers glistening in the midday sun.

"Care to test that theory?" He looks down at me with hooded eyes, and my mouth goes dry.

Every thought exits my brain as I stare at him blankly. I short-circuit.

And yet I keep my eyes on him as my mouth opens a

little wider. He gives me a wicked grin and curls those two fingers into my mouth. I taste myself on him, the slightly salty evidence of just how much this man turns me on.

"Fuck, that's hot."

His fingers hook against the back of my teeth, and he uses the force to pull me closer to him. My body twists, completely at his mercy. I get lost in the dark depths of his ocean eyes. The carnal desire and want reflected in the waters undo me.

I've never felt sexier than in this very moment.

Parker removes his fingers and grips my jaw before crushing me with a kiss. I lose all sense of reality, tasting myself on both of our tongues as I drown in the sensation.

"I didn't taste like cherries, by the way," I murmur.

He just laughs, and the sound explodes like sparkles inside me.

"Guess we'll have to try again. Maybe with my tongue this time?"

And try he does. He flips us over and grins up at me through the V of my legs. Parker feasts on me with his tongue until I'm a sobbing mess completely at his mercy.

We only stop because he worries about my dehydration.

He cradles me on his chest and flips on a new British reality show as we snuggle on the couch. I let myself relax into the evening, smiling at the comfort he brings.

My ray of sunshine.

Chapter
TWENTY

PARKER

"They're on our right," I shout into my mic. "Right. Right. Stop heading straight, fuckface. Are you even listening to me? What the fuck, seriously?"

I am going to murder someone.

Hopefully the enemy, but at this rate it is looking like I might kill my teammate instead.

We are down by four kills, and there are only three minutes left of the round.

The odds aren't looking great, but I refuse to give up. I just need this fucking noob to get his shit together.

I grind my teeth, remembering that this is all being live streamed. I'm not opposed to trash-talk, but I don't want to say anything that could get me canceled.

"Stop sucking your own dick and follow me," I growl

into my mic at the guy.

A notification pops up in the corner confirming a double kill from one of my other teammates, and the tension lessens a fraction. At least not everyone sucked.

"Okay, they're just around the corner; stay behind me."

My words are pointless because said noob fucking runs right around the corner and dies. I curse and throw a grenade into the room, cloaking the surroundings in smoke. I run in and get one headshot just as the timer hits zero.

It's still not enough.

"RED TEAM WINS" splays across the screen, and I slam my mouse on the table.

I shove my headset down, leaving it to hang around my neck as I twist my head to glare at the guy two seats down from me. Some random gamer who ended up on our team and couldn't play for shit. Dude kept bringing the team down and was the reason Red Team won because he basically died forty fucking times. Didn't matter how much I tried to carry him; it meant nothing. This is why randomized team battles suck.

Every inch of my body is thrumming with frustrated energy. It bubbles, threatening to break loose.

That match should've been a breeze; we should've won. I should've won.

"Yo, English, good game." A large hand claps my shoulder, and I turn to see CeleryGod grinning down at me.

I'm ninety percent sure his name is Andy, but we always go by our gamertags during streams, so it's easier to just stick to that.

"You only say that cause your team won." I shrug out

of his touch and snatch my mask from the table, slipping it on to hide the anger.

"Well, it is tough to beat a god."

I snort, some of the tension easing out of my body as I make my way offstage. "You wish, Celery. We would've wiped the field with you if it weren't for that noob."

Celery jogs next to me. "Yeah, that was shit luck. Guy was great target practice."

The farther I get from the stage, the more I begin to calm down. The more I'm less likely to punch that damn rookie.

This isn't me.

And this shouldn't be bothering me as much as it is.

But I'm a superstitious person.

The last two tournaments, I won my team battles clean through, and then I went on to win my speedrun matches. Losing the team battle sets me off kilter. It's not a good start.

Plus, I ran into CreepyPillows earlier, someone who shouldn't even be in the country right now.

Creep is another one of the top speedrunners and an all-around pain in my ass. Last year he won Best Speed-runner at the Streamzies even though it should have been me. And now he's here. I knew I'd be going up against him at the Divizion Championship Series, but that is still a month away. I thought I had more time.

Creep and I are both speedrunners at *Dreadlander*, but I've always beaten his time there. However, today's speed-run is for *Final Destiny*, which is his specialty. It's the one I've been clocking most of my hours in, practicing in an-ticipation for DCS. *Final Destiny* is my weak point, and I was hoping to test myself at this Miami tournament since I knew I'd be going against Creep later.

Not now. Not today.

Nerves eat their way through my body.

Fuck. I wish Sydney were here.

"You good, English?" Celery nudges my shoulder with his.

"Yeah, mate. I'm all right. Just distracted."

We flash our badges at a security guard who lets us into a roped-off area.

"Might want to un-distract yourself before the run."

"What a brilliant idea. Hadn't considered that." I deadpan him, but he can't exactly see my expression with the mask on. "Plus, you're one to talk. I merked you eight times that last round."

Celery rolls his eyes. "I still won. These matches are just for show, anyway."

I pat him on the back. "Whatever helps you sleep at night."

"All right, hotshot. Team battle next week, your guys versus mine."

"You're on. We'll bring in Lee and Wylder as our fourth and fifth." *FrozeLine* is a 5V5 game, and as much as Deer is becoming one of our crew, this game is not her strong suit. Wylder, on the other hand, is a pro gamer and good friend of ours. "Prepare for failure."

"You really think you're going to beat the Streamer of the Year?" He grabs an energy drink from the fridge and tosses it at me. I catch it and frown.

"You've been insufferable ever since you won that award." I toss the yellow can back to him, and he barely manages to grab it before it hits him in the face. "I like the blue flavor."

"Of course, you do." He throws a new one at me with more force this time.

I catch it gracefully and crack it open with the same hand, grinning at him as I go to take a drink.

The can knocks against my mask. He laughs, and I sigh at my rookie mistake.

I pull the mask down and take a sip. The blueberry flavor doesn't really taste like blueberry. It's more just...blue. But it's still better than the medicine flavor the red one has.

Celery has a point. I'm distracted.

I need to be back on stage for my run in ten minutes, and I have to be at my best if I'm going to put Creep in his place. I can't lose to him today, or he'll make my life hell at the championship.

My phone buzzes and I pull it from my pocket.

SYD

Don't worry about the match. Things happen. Just stay focused. You'll crush the run. I know you will :)

But also, don't crush it too hard. Remember, we're still keeping our cards close.

My fingers hover over the keyboard. I don't think she knows Creep is here. But I also don't want to be the one to inform her. She'll just worry, and she's supposed to be enjoying her time in Napa.

Hell, she shouldn't even be texting me right now. The

girls promised me that they'd give her a taste of her own medicine and put her in tech isolation. Hence, the reason why I think she has no clue Creep is here. He showed up this morning and was added to the roster, knocking some rookie speedrunner from the run.

ME

thanks love 😘

now put ur phone away

SYD

good luck 🍀

I sigh and chug the rest of my drink, feeling bad that I'm keeping her in the dark. I crush the can and shoot it into the nearest rubbish bin. It bounces off the rim, and I grimace. The fizzy drink settles uncomfortably in my stomach.

"Mr. English." I turn to see a security guard hovering on the other side of the roped-off area. "I'm here to escort you backstage."

"All right, sounds good." I pick up the can and dump it in the bin before sliding my mask back up my face.

My world once again turns blue, and I breathe a little easier. I roll my shoulders and remind myself that I'm EnglishCoffee. That I've got this.

I follow the black-suited man through the crowds and down the back hallways until we get to the second main stage. I immediately clock the other five gamers. None of them pose much of a threat other than Creep and Van.

OnlyVan is another speedrunner whom I always end

up pitted against for awards. I knew he'd be here, though, along with his sister, so I'm prepared. Plus, the only time Van's gotten close to my times is when he found a new skip, which I respect him for.

The announcer begins calling us on stage, and as each gamer walks up the stairs, it leaves less and less people as a buffer between Creep and myself.

"Glad to see you finally came out to play with the grown-ups," Creep says in his stupid Australian accent.

"You won't be glad when I leave you in the dust."

"Nah, mate. This is my stage." He grins and runs a hand through his sandy hair.

"Oh yeah? What did you do, lick it and claim it?"

"Actually, I made sweet, sweet love to it."

I laugh and then curse myself for letting my guard down. This is what he does. Stupid fucking Aussie charmer. I would like the guy if we weren't always pitted against each other. Until I win that damn championship, I've got to keep him squarely where he belongs.

"All the way from Down Under, let's hear it for CreepyPillows." The announcer's voice ends our conversation, and Creep rolls his eyes as one of the event staff ushers him to head up the staircase.

I jump up and down a few times, shaking myself out as I wait.

"And last, but certainly not least, he's the mysterious man in blue. The one, the only, EnglishCoffee."

I jog up the stairs and onto the stage. The bright lights are muted by my mask, and I make a show of waving to the crowd, blowing them kisses and being as extra as I can. People expect me to be larger than life, and I'm not here to give them any less, even if there's a pit of fear inside me.

I settle at my desk, which has been set up with all my gear. Van is on my left and his sister is on my right. Creep, thankfully, isn't anywhere in my direct eyesight.

I slide off my mask and pull my headphones back up. The noise canceling goes into effect immediately and drowns out sounds around me. I give my wrists a quick roll before getting my hands in position. The sensitivity levels seem to be right, but I give my mouse a few shakes, just to make sure.

My heart beats steadily in my chest as I wait.

The announcer counts down, and the second he says "one," I click on the Start button.

The game starts, and muscle memory kicks in. I know this game. I've practiced. I've got this.

Those first few minutes are always the most adrenaline inducing. If you don't start off perfectly, you might as well quit and not waste your time. My heartrate begins to level out as I keep playing, and I successfully get through the first mission without any hiccups.

The first hour passes in a blur, and so far, everything is on track. I haven't messed up any of the skips. I did heed Syd's advice, and I purposely ignored one of the new glitches I'd mastered, which would've shaved off a solid three minutes, instead opting to save it for the championship.

I just had to hope that everything else I'd improved on would be enough to beat Creep.

I pull out my revolvers and kill the store clerk in front of me, stealing his keys so I can bypass the mission objective. My morality meter takes a dip, but it's not an issue in the long run. I'll only need to worry about it if something goes wrong.

I would regret that thought.

I'm almost through the second hour when I catch movement from the corner of my eye. That split second distraction costs me. My character was in the middle of world traveling. I had to make sure to double bounce when I landed at my new destination in order to use the momentum to blast myself across the town to the next mission point.

Instead, I miss it.

"Shit," I mutter.

A fucking noob mistake.

I scramble to shove an NPC off their neo-bike and begin speeding it through the streets. Except I run over a few more NPCs in the process, and my morality meter begins dipping lower. When it turns deep red, a bounty logo pops up in the corner of my screen.

"Fuck."

I finally make it to the quest point and skip through the dialogue, but my heart rate isn't slowing down. I have no idea how much time I just cost myself. That was one of the worst things I could've missed.

Everything starts going downhill from there, and I just get more and more mad at myself. In my hyped-up state, I miss a shot and end up nerve-gassing myself. It happens three more times until I succeed in taking down a watchtower.

Each time I screw up, I fall deeper into the cracks of my brain. Spiraling further and further.

It's when I hear cheering so loud that it breaks through

my headphones that I know I've lost.

It's probably another twenty minutes until I finish the game.

The end credits roll, but I feel nothing.

I just want to slam my fist through the monitor. But that won't get me anything except a fucked-up hand, an upset publicist, and a trip to the med bay.

So, I do as I've been taught. I take a deep breath and weave a smile on my face as I turn to look at the cameras. I hold my hands up and shrug, effectively telling everyone, "Oh well."

I tug off my headphones, and the uninhibited sounds of the crowd shock me for a second. The noise is suffocating, choking me from the inside out. I wrestle with myself to push it all away.

I turn everything off before I grab my mask and slip it on. My shoulders relax a fraction behind the safety of the blue light. I stand up and give the crowd a dramatic bow before grabbing my shit and booking it offstage.

I don't bother looking up at the screens as I leave. I don't want to see what my time was. I don't want to know how much Creep defeated me by. I don't want to know who else did better than me.

I don't want to know what a failure I am.

I stop by the private lockers to grab my backpack and shove my stuff into it before bypassing the press area. I'm going to get an earful from Syd and Mathias, but I can't bring myself to care. I would do more damage in an interview right now, anyway.

And a part of me tells me Syd will understand.

Nausea churns in my gut as my gray-eyed angel flashes

in my mind.

Fuck, she'd been so confident in me.

But I'd screwed myself over.

Gotten so wrapped up in my own head that I'd gotten distracted.

Even if she won't be disappointed in me, I am.

There were only two tournaments left now, and if I didn't win at least one of them, I could kiss the championship goodbye.

I shove out the front door of the building and curse myself.

Idiot.

There are reporters everywhere, their cameras flashing in my face.

I was supposed to go through the exit where I was dropped off this morning, not here. For some unknown reason, I decide to power forward. Maybe to punish myself.

I push my way through the crowd, ignoring their questions and demands. Trying to block out their words that are jabbing into me. None of them are worse than the ones swimming in my own brain.

I don't have a plan, but I just need to get away from them.

"Parker."

Something about the voice breaks through barrage of people around me.

I look up and see a familiar head of blonde hair. A beacon. My head clears a little, and my feet begin pounding on the concrete as I run toward her. She opens the passenger door to a chrome Maserati. I dive in and slam the door as she rounds to the driver's seat and immediately takes off.

The engine revs as she weaves her way farther from the arena. The rumble of the low car soothes me, bringing me back to earth.

"Well, that could've gone worse."

I pull off my mask and look into the blue eyes that are a mirror of my own.

"Gee, thanks, Pheebs."

"Just saying." My sister shrugs as she pulls on the indicator and switches lanes.

"I didn't know you'd be here."

"I didn't want to add any pressure. Thought I'd just watch from the box and offer my silent support. I wasn't going to bring some big poster, like Paige would."

I let out a low laugh because that is exactly what our sister would do.

My stoic eldest sister softens at the noise, and it just makes me feel worse. Phoebe isn't one to offer pity often.

"I'm sorry, Parker."

"It's fine."

"Really?" she drolls, cocking a perfectly sculpted brow.

"No." I cross my arms over my chest and sink into the leather. "It's not fucking fine. I just lost to a complete as-swipe. It was my one chance before the championship, and I fucking blew it. Everyone's going to think I suck and make fun of me online, and Sydney is going to see all of it. She's going to think I'm a loser because even I think I'm a fucking loser right now."

Phoebe pats my knee like a child. "Feel better?"

I glare up at her. "No."

"You're not a loser, P. You're a lot of things, trust me,

but you're not a loser."

"I lost, Phoebe. That's the definition of a loser."

"Technically, that bloke, what was his name…Danger…something, whatever, technically he came in last, so he is the loser. You just weren't the winner."

I sigh, some of the fight leaving my body. Being mad is exhausting, and that's all I can feel in my bones. Exhaustion.

My phone begins vibrating in my pocket, and I pull it out to see an incoming call from Sydney.

Panic lances through me. I stare down at her photo, one I took of her just a few days ago when we were cuddled up on the couch. Half of me wants to answer the phone, the other half doesn't.

Honestly, I just don't want to deal with it right now. I don't want to deal with the shame and embarrassment. I don't want to deal with her sympathy. I don't want to feel worse.

I acted like hot shit only to end up as dog shit.

The Maserati comes to a stop out front of the Covington Miami. A handful of reporters and fans are milling about outside, but security begins ushering them out of the way once they notice my sister's car. Six men in suits flank the car as we exit and guide us inside the building. I keep my expression neutral until I'm safely inside my sister's penthouse suite.

"I was wondering who had booked the penthouse," I mumble as I dump my stuff on the couch and curl up. "I ended up settling for the King's Suite because of you."

Phoebe rolls her eyes as she pulls a bottle of LOUIS XIII cognac from the bar counter and pours three fingers worth of liquid into two tumblers. She sits on the couch next to me and hands me one of the glasses.

"I prefer my cognac on the rocks," I say as I eye the crystal.

"Well, I like mine neat. So, either suck it up, or I'll drink it."

I grumble, taking the tumbler and sipping the amber liquid. It coats my tongue with its spicy taste before gliding slowly down my throat.

"Why are you beating yourself up over this so much? It's unlike you."

"You know why."

"Parker, it was one tournament. Grandpa isn't going to leave you to the wolves just because you lost once. You have two more games to qualify for the championship, and even then, it's not like you're going to be poor if things don't go right." She takes a sip of cognac, crossing her legs.

"That doesn't make me feel any better."

"Well, it's the truth. You're acting like when you were ten and lost your first polo tournament. You sulked in your room for the entire weekend, refusing to eat or shower or anything."

"Paige would've been a lot nicer about this." I down the rest of the cognac, welcoming the burn. It stokes the fire within me, fueling the anger.

"Yes, well, unfortunately, you got stuck with me this time." She takes the empty crystal from me and goes to refill it. "Plus, if you remember, you went on to win silver in the under twelves that year even though you lost."

"Silver isn't gold. And this isn't some hobby for me,

like polo. This is my work, my life, Phoebe. I can't lose it."

"You won't lose it. No one's trying to take it away from you."

She holds out the tumbler to me, and I gulp all the amber liquid in one swoop. I use the back of my hand to wipe my mouth and then place the empty glass back in her hand.

"Sure doesn't feel that way. What good am I if I can't win a simple tournament? Maybe I should just give up, settle into a proper role like everyone wants."

She raises both of her brows slightly before letting out a soft breath.

"Parker, that's not what we want."

The sympathy in her voice cracks me.

I'm not mad at anyone except myself right now.

Sure, maybe I'm overreacting a little bit. But it's so much more than just a tournament I lost.

It's everything.

It's all the expectations clawing at my throat. All the pressure crushing my shoulders. The need to prove that I am worth something pulls on my ankles like chains. That I can stand on my own. That I am smart and capable and more than just a guy coasting through life. That I'm someone people can respect and look up to.

Phoebe looks down at me with her blue eyes, and the ocean within them feels like it's drowning me.

I shove off the couch and snatch up my backpack, storming past her.

"Parker!" she shouts. "Oi, get back here!"

But I don't look back.

I don't breathe until I shut the door to my own suite.

The room is dark, and the shadows close in on me,

swirling around my body. Every negative thought clouds around me in a suffocating haze.

My phone picks up it's buzzing in my pocket, and I growl as I throw it across the room. It narrowly lands on the corner of my bed before bouncing to the ground.

I don't miss the name on the screen, and it just makes me feel worse.

I'm supposed to be better than this. I'm supposed to be the guy everyone loves. The guy who doesn't take things too seriously.

I don't want her to see me like this.

In pieces.

I don't even want to see myself.

Chapter TWENTY-ONE

SYDNEY

'm worried.

I squint through the flashing purple and blue lights, trying to make sense of the clamoring bodies. Someone bumps into me, and I look down at a girl with glazed eyes. She just gives me a dizzy smile as she continues to sway to the music.

This is the last place I want to be.

My feet carry me through the crowd of sweaty people. Heat sticks to my skin, plastering my clothes to my body.

I'm so not dressed to be here either. My '90s bell-sleeve dress sticks out like a sore thumb in this upscale night club full of beautiful, scantily clad women.

The bouncer had given me quite the side-eye until he'd noticed how short the dress was, something that I am becoming more self-conscious of as I push through the crowd. In my rush to leave, I had just thrown it on over my bandeau bikini.

I was lucky that Deer was able to get me on a private jet over to Miami at a moment's notice. Suspicious of exactly where said jet came from but grateful, nonetheless.

Five and a half hours were spent gnawing on my thumb as I tried to get to the boy who was ignoring my every call.

I'd gone through every emotion under the sun during that flight, most of them the anger variety. I was livid that he wouldn't speak to me. Upset that he'd shut me out. Frustrated that I couldn't reach him.

But more than anything, I was worried.

And that worry, that deep-seated fear, won out over the anger. It flushed it away because all I care about is that he is okay.

There is a part of me that is mad at myself, too. Mad that I hadn't been here. Mad that I was states away soaking in a hot spring and getting massages while he suffered.

Parker likes to put on a brave face, but I know all that he hides underneath that. He isn't used to losing, to not getting what he wants, and I didn't know how he would handle it.

This is everything I'd feared when the tournaments started up.

I break through the crowd and spot an elevated area below the raised DJ booth. The security guy manning the roped-off area is a clear signal to the exclusivity. If Parker is anywhere, he'll be there.

I only make it a few steps before there is a loud hiss and smoke billows out from the raised DJ stage. I suck in my shock as the cold haze surrounds me. My head tilts up to see two men flanking the DJ with spray guns, shooting out a flurry of bubbles.

My gaze locks on one man in particular.

That glowing blue mask looks down at me, and it sends a chill through my skin. We stare at each other for a few seconds. I hold my breath, waiting a beat before taking a step toward him.

He bolts.

"God dammit," I mutter.

One second, he's standing above me in a cloud of smoke, the next, he's gone.

My eyes track through the crowds and spot him making a beeline through the roped-off area. He stumbles in his escape, leaning into some random guys before righting himself. His spray gun is thrown haphazardly onto a table.

That mask flashes again when he turns back briefly to see where I am before continuing on his way.

Hurt stabs into my chest like a poisoned dagger.

I push the feeling aside as I move to catch up to him. I don't know this club like he does, but I've chased after these boys my fair share of times, so I can track him like he's a rabbit on the loose.

I keep my eyes on the back of Parker's head as he races to get farther from me. I make it into a back hallway, and a security guard tries to stop me. I huff out a silent apology as I duck under his arm and kick him in the back of the legs.

A loud bang has me altering my course, and I round a corner in time to see one of the emergency exit doors swinging closed.

I follow suit, pushing out into the balmy night air.

"Parker!" I yell at the figure running down the alleyway. He pauses briefly at my words. "You can't run forever."

Part of me hopes that I've broken through.

That part of me is very naïve.

Parker keeps up his escape, but he's a mess. He isn't even running in a straight line; he keeps veering slightly off course. He manages to successfully exit the alley and runs onto the main street. Even at three in the morning, downtown Miami is still a busy city.

I am going to kill him for putting me through this.

The crowds of people slow him down and, finally, he stumbles and fails to correct his balance in time. Parker falls to his knees, and it gives me the window I need to catch up to him.

My hand closes around the crook of his elbow. I hold tight, knowing that I cannot afford to let him go.

People keep moving around us, but I see nothing except the scared man in front of me. He doesn't say a word. Doesn't move. I keep hold as I crouch before him, sinking back on my heels. My free hand comes up to caress the side of his mask, and I stare into those blue Xs that I know hide pain.

"I've got you," I whisper.

His head falls forward to rest against my own, and we stay like that for a few moments.

"I botched it, Syd." The words are slightly slurred, and they are muffled by the mask. But even still, I hear the ache, the disappointment.

"It was one run. You'll get it next time. And even then, if you don't, we will try again. It doesn't define you."

279

He shakes his head, the top of the mask rubbing against my bangs. "But it does."

"It doesn't."

"You don't get it." He rears back from me so quickly I almost fall on my ass. "It means everything."

My brows knit in confusion. I know he is torn up over the loss. It was his first one. But this is so much more. I don't get why it's affecting him so strongly, why he's letting it eat away at him. There are more chances to qualify.

I open my mouth to push but close it when I finally take note of all the people passing by us giving us odd looks.

Dammit.

"People are beginning to stare. Let's get you back to the hotel." I give his arm a light squeeze before pulling him to stand with me.

He tries to tug out of my grasp, but I level him with a hard glare before signaling for a nearby taxi. It takes extra effort than usual to get him inside. He's more than a little tipsy right now, which isn't a common occurrence for him.

We ride in silence through the traffic until we reach the Covington. I keep my expression neutral as I get him out of the car. There are still a handful of reporters camped outside, and this isn't going to be a good look.

One of the security guards from the hotel comes to assist me, but Parker shrugs him off with a grunt and stalks into the hotel on his own. Magically, he manages to walk in a straight line and mask his slightly inebriated state.

I bite my tongue as I rush to follow him, but I make sure to mentally catalog which reporters have their cameras trained on us, to follow up with later. I stay close on Parker's heels until we get to his hotel suite. He reaches

Forbidden GAME

into his pockets, searching for his key card, but comes up empty.

I sigh, pulling a copy from my handbag and scanning us inside. I'd gotten the key card from his sister when I'd come looking for him initially, just to find his hotel room empty and phone dead on the ground.

I'd only been able to locate him because Phoebe had made sure one of their security detail was following him.

We move in silence.

I go to the small fridge and pull out a bottle of water. He opens the balcony door and steps out into the night.

Parker leans against the railing, and my heart cracks in two.

I walk behind him, placing the bottle on the small outdoor table before tugging on his elbows.

He turns to face me. I reach up, the tips of my fingers grazing the sides of his mask. I push up on the balls of my feet to slide his mask off and drop it to the side.

My breath catches as I look up at the heartbreakingly beautiful man before me. Without the mask, there's nothing to hide the raw ache falling across his face. I search his eyes, looking for an answer in the hurt.

"What happened?"

He lets out a bitter laugh and turns away from me. He grips the railing with both hands, leaning his body back. His long arms keep him from falling over as he tips his head completely back, eyes closed. His hair turns the color of moonlight as it flops in the air.

A troubled prince with a crooked crown.

"Parker, don't shut me out. You can talk to me." I hug my arms around myself to ward off the growing chill.

281

"I can't."

"You can."

"No, Syd. I can't. I fucked up. It feels like the sky's falling, and there's nothing I can do to stop it." He opens his eyes, and I'm stopped by the dead look of defeat in them.

"I don't get it. It was just a match." My voice is small and confused.

I hug myself tighter.

Every part of me is screaming to do something to make this better. I'm freaked out because I've never seen him like this. I've never seen Parker so desolate, so without hope.

Sure, he messed up the run. I watched it twice through on my flight over and saw the exact moment his attention strayed. I also saw the tension he tried to hide the second he took the stage, the precursor to his mental state. They were things we could work on. I also knew Mathias would have his back, that he would have his own guys go through the tape and gameplay to help Parker improve before the championship. This wasn't the end of the world. It was just a small road bump.

"I couldn't beat Creep. How am I supposed to be the best if I can't beat him? How am I supposed to be the best when I mess up on stage? I get distracted by a flicker of light when my concentration is supposed to be steel."

"Parker—"

"I'm embarrassed, Sydney." His voice cracks, and my heart splinters with it. His eyes swirl with the force of a stormy ocean as he pushes himself to stand straight. "I told everyone I had this championship in the bag, but I don't know if that's the truth anymore. I'm scared. I'm scared everyone is going to think I'm a joke."

"You're not a joke." I tentatively reach out and hold the tips of his fingers. "And this wasn't the championship, Parker. It was one run."

"One run that I lost. What if I can't beat him? What if I lose the championship?"

"What if? You're not anything less if you don't win the championship. You are still one of the best. You are one of the top ten most-watched video gamers in the world, Parker. Creep and those others don't even come close to you. Why are you putting so much pressure on this?" I squeeze his hands, begging for him to let me in.

"Because I told my grandfather I would win." He pulls out of my grasp and walks back into the room, grabbing the water bottle and cracking it open as he goes. He sits on the foot and downs half the bottle before tossing it aside.

I know his family means the world to him; they are thick as thieves.

I shut the balcony door behind me and crawl onto the bed. He leans forward on his elbows, and his hand comes up to spin the hoops in his cartilage nervously. I kneel next to him and wait.

"I'm going to lose my inheritance."

The words are spoken so softly I almost miss them.

"Not the whole thing but—" He flops back on the bed and presses the heel of his palm to his eyes. "God, Syd, I'd been so desperate to prove myself, and it seemed like such a smart idea. Now I just feel dumb."

"What are you talking about?"

I wish I could read his mind, understand what is going

on right now. I'm trying to read between the lines, but I don't want to jump to conclusions. Not when he is in such a fragile state. I'm scared that I could break him when all I want to do is help him stay together.

He throws his arms out next to him and sighs.

"Remember that rumor a few weeks back? Before the Wyreless shoot."

Parker tilts his head to the side to look at me. I nod, thinking back to the conversation we had.

"Turns out there was some truth in that tea."

"Martin is trying to run you out of the company?"

Crap.

I should have looked into it more. What a rookie mistake on my part.

"Sort of." He pushes up on his elbows and gives me a sad smile. It's the worst expression he could have given me. "The entire board is trying to get rid of me."

"What? Why? Because they want more control?"

"Well, it turns out you can't be the heir to a company if you never plan to inherit it. The board doesn't want me to keep my stake in the company if I'm not going to do anything with it."

Oh. I mean. That does make sense, logically. But it doesn't really make sense for them to take away his shares as a result.

"Why can't they just remove you as the heir and be done with it?"

"There's a bunch of politics," he sighs. "I own twenty percent of the company as it currently stands. My grandfather is fighting with the board over it and doesn't want to rock the boat just yet."

"Wait, your grandfather supports this whole thing?"

"Yeah. He told me he doesn't see any value in my career as a gamer."

Oh God. That is awful. I know how close he is to his family. I can't even begin to imagine how blindsided he must have felt. I know his parents are supportive, so I'd just assumed that everyone in his life was. I thought he had it easy compared to the others.

I didn't know how wrong I'd been.

"I'm so sorry, Parker." I reach out and hold his hand in mine.

"He gave me a choice. Step into my role as the heir and work at the company or forfeit my shares and, essentially, my Covington inheritance."

I suck in a breath.

Dread pools in my stomach. Family is everything to Parker; there's no way he could accept being thrown out of it.

I start to get mad.

Why would he keep this from me? From all of us?

This would affect everything.

Why didn't he trust us, trust me?

"What did you pick?"

"Neither, for now."

"What?"

"I made him a deal. He's trying to force my hand because he thinks gaming isn't serious. So, I told him I would prove otherwise. I would prove that I am the best at what I do and that it matters. I told him I would win this championship. He said if I could do that, he would stop the board from taking my shares, that I could still be part of the Covington conglomerate even if I didn't work for them. I was going to have the best of both worlds. Turns out I can't have my cake and eat it too." He curls onto his side and tugs my hand close to his chest. "I lost to Creep. If I lose to him again, I lose everything."

Now it all makes sense.

I lie down on the bed and curl into a fetal position to match him, lining our bodies up as mirrors. Our hands are clasped between us, a connection of strength to ground ourselves.

"You're not going to lose, Parker."

"You can't promise that," he whispers.

"Okay, sure. I can't guarantee that you'll win. But I sure as hell can make sure that you compete to the best of your ability. I can make sure that you train so hard that when you step onto that stage, the likelihood of you losing is so low, it doesn't even register on the radar."

"And if I still lose?"

"If you still lose…then I'll respect whatever your decision is." The words taste like acid in my mouth.

"Wait, what do you mean?"

"I mean if you decide to work for your family, I'll support you."

He frowns, and his hands tighten on mine. "I wouldn't do that. I could never leave The System behind. I'd be miserable if I didn't game. It would be like living without my soul. I'd be a wandering husk of myself."

"Oh."

"And I wouldn't be able to see you every day if I left. I'm not sure I would survive without you in my life."

I smile, relief and something warm spreading through

my veins. "I'm not sure I would survive without your sunshine either."

He brings my hand to his lips and places a soft kiss on my knuckles.

"Why didn't you tell me you were dealing with all of this?" I ask him.

"It was my burden to carry." He shrugs. "I didn't want to drag anyone else down with the weight."

"Sometimes you have to share that weight, Parker, otherwise it will crush you."

"But it's my responsibility, and I didn't want you to think less of me."

"Parker. What if the tables were reversed? What if I were dealing with something like this? Wouldn't you want to know so you could help?"

"Of course. I would never let you suffer alone."

"That's how I feel." I squeeze his hand. "Don't shut me out again, please."

"All right."

"And don't run off without your phone again, or I'll beat you with it before getting a tracker sewn into your arm."

"Violence, love? Really?"

"Really. You scared me half to death with your disappearing act."

"I mean...I don't hate the idea of you branding me." He winks. "Although, I don't plan on being apart from you again if I can help it."

I grin, thankful that he is back to joking. "I'm not sure being attached at the hip is a sign of a healthy relationship. Seems a little codependent."

"Relationship?"

"I—isn't that what we're in? Isn't that what we discussed the other night?" Panic flares.

"It is." He grins. "It's just the first time you've actually said the word."

I shove our joined hands against his chest.

"Don't tease me like that."

"But you're so fun to tease." He leans forward and kisses the tip of my nose. "I like teasing my girlfriend."

I blink at him. "Girlfriend?"

"That's generally the term used for someone you're in an exclusive relationship with."

"I guess you're right."

It hadn't really occurred to me. Sure, it has only been three days since we had the conversation, but everything between us is so different than any other relationship I'd been in.

"And that would make me your…" He trails off with a smirk.

I press my lips together, biting them as the word sits on the tip of my tongue.

"Boyfriend." I grin so hard I'm worried my face will split.

"Aren't you a lucky one? *The* Parker Covington is your boyfriend."

He wiggles his eyebrows, and I roll my eyes.

Parker tugs me into his arms and tangles our legs together. My head snuggles into his chest, and I close my eyes, inhaling his scent as I drift off to sleep.

Sandalwood, crisp ocean, champagne…and home.

Parker smells like home.

But it's not just that. Everything about Parker feels like home, from the beat of his heart to his fingers on my skin. Parker has been part of my life for so long that I didn't realize how deeply ingrained he is until this weekend.

I had an amazing time with the girls at the spa resort, pampering ourselves to the max. I never knew how calming a mud bath could be until I had one.

Parker had been right; I was running myself into the ground, and I didn't need to.

He knew how to take care of me better than I could myself.

And, God, I missed him while I was gone. It was this little niggling feeling in my chest as I went about my day. Everything would be going great, and then I'd have these moments where I'd be thinking, "Oh, Parker would love this," or "He would laugh at this."

Small things.

But those small things are the most important, and I know that whatever is going on between us is a lot bigger than I'd thought.

It scares me. Especially after everything that happened today.

He is becoming more and more important to me and I just hope I don't end up burned.

Chapter
TWENTY-TWO

PARKER

The punch coming for me barely misses my chin.

I square my eyes at my opponent.

Bending my knees, I drop my lead arm into a ninety-degree angle before driving my fist up. I land the uppercut perfectly, and he goes staggering backward, his knee crashing onto the canvas to steady himself from falling completely.

I grin against my mouthguard, breathing heavily.

"All right, men. Let's call it." Jax taps on the ropes to get our attention.

"I can keep going." I shrug.

"I know you can, but David here needs a breather. Why don't you go help Sydney finish up her practice instead?"

I perk up at the thought and twist to see where she is.

Sydney lands a strong side kick to the punching bag in

the far-right corner of the gym. I hop out of the ring and tug off my gloves as I head over to her. She looks sinful in her tight workout gear. The light purple leggings hug her ass in a way that has me drooling.

I come up behind her and drop a puff of cold air against her bare neck.

She squeals and wheels around, striking me in the side with a kick. My forearm comes up to block her, but she's strong enough that I still let out a light grunt at the contact. Her doe eyes narrow when she looks up at me.

Sydney punches me lightly in the chest with her glove. "Don't sneak up on someone in the gym."

"You were just too tempting." I grin, gripping her left hip and tugging her a little closer to me.

She rolls her eyes but smiles back at me. Unable to help myself, I drop a kiss on her button nose. She's too fucking adorable. It's a chore to not be touching her all the time.

"All right, let's finish up so we can head home." I tap her hip and push her back toward the bag.

"Bossy." Her eyes light up as they scan up and down my body. "I like it."

Heat rushes to my dick, but I will it away as I help her finish her practice.

We run through a few combinations, focusing mainly on a double jab, right hook, left kick, left kick combo. She doesn't have the timing down yet, and the lag between the two kicks means she's not dealing enough damage as she should. It's a popular combo to learn, but a lot of people struggle with the finishing kicks. Even so, Syd is frustrated.

"Hey, you're getting close." I squeeze her shoulder.

"Not close enough," she huffs and blows her bangs off her forehead before removing her gloves.

I laugh and pick up my own gloves before throwing my arm around her shoulders and guiding her out of the gym and toward my car.

She wrinkles her nose and tries to push away from me. "Ugh, you're so sweaty."

"Me?" I look down at her. "You're the one glistening right now, love. I'm not even sure I should let you in my car. Don't want you ruining the leather."

"Ha ha, very funny."

I open the door for her, and she slides into the Lambo—which I did get cleaned after our ocean date. I get in the driver's side and throw our gloves on the ground of the passenger seat.

The drive back to the apartment complex is smooth. She only yells at me once when I hit one hundred on a particularly empty strip of highway and gives me a mild glare when I swerve a little to fast into my parking spot.

"My place or yours?" I ask her when we enter the private elevator, pulling her to my side.

"Well, I need to shower, as you so kindly pointed out earlier." Sarcasm drips from her tone as she stares up at me.

"You could always shower with me. I have many jets in my shower and *many* ways to use them." I wink, and she flushes.

"Yeah, sure, and how do you propose we explain why I'm using your shower instead of my own that's just fifty floors away?"

"No one's home." I shrug, hitting the button for the

penthouse. "Aleks and Stevie have a brunch date, and Jackson's at his sister's violin recital."

She purses her lips and pulls out her phone to open the tracking app. Sure enough, the little map shows Stevie and Aleks at a nearby café while Jackson is an hour away at his sister's school.

It is a rare occasion to have the apartment to myself.

I lean down and rest my chin on her shoulder. "See? Now why don't you come up and play with me?"

She shivers and peeks up at me through her lashes with a girlish smile. "Okay, hotshot."

I grin, pressing a kiss to her cheek. She turns into me, and our lips come together in a soft marriage. My hand snakes around the soft dip of her hip and pulls her closer.

In no time, I have her pressed up against the wall of the elevator, panting as our kisses become feverish. She moans into my mouth, and my cock stiffens at the noise.

The elevator doors open, and we stumble out into the apartment, kicking off our trainers as we keep kissing.

I waste no time throwing our gloves into the entryway and dipping down to pick her up. She lets out a twinkling laugh as I princess carry her into my bedroom. I use my knee to open the door to my ensuite and deposit her on the marble next to the sink. I drag my lips away from her as I step into the shower and crank up all the handles, releasing sprays from every direction.

The bathroom begins to fog up, and I turn back to the beauty behind me. Sydney swings her legs as she stares at me through hooded eyes. I run my hands down her thighs as I lean in to kiss her. My hands continue to trail up her waist, onto her bare skin, until the tips of my fingers toy with the bottom of her sports bra.

My heart beats heavily as I curl my fingers under the band.

"May I?"

"Please," she breathes.

I tug the lilac fabric from her body and toss it on the floor behind us. Her small breasts pop free, and those pale pink nipples harden. She's a sight to behold.

I dip my head to swirl one of them in my mouth. I taste her salty skin as my tongue circles her hard peak, and her chest arches farther into me. I lick a path up her chest and neck, sucking on a particularly sensitive spot that has her gasping and clenching beneath me.

Sydney's hands reach out to claw at the edges of my T-shirt. I let her tugs it off me. She pulls back and admires me. I like having her eyes on me, tracking every inch of my skin like she is trying to memorize it.

She reaches out and runs a single finger down my sternum.

"God, you're pretty," she says, cocking her head to the side.

"Pretty?"

"Mmm," she hums, letting that finger trail lower and lower. "It's like someone cut you out of a magazine."

My laugh turns to a strangled groan when that finger reaches the band of my shorts. My hand closes around hers, and I use both our hands to tug them off. My cock springs to attention, free from its constraints.

A spark of clarity breaks through Sydney's haze as she stares down at me.

"It's bigger than I remember." She looks almost horrified as she eyes my dick.

"All the better to fuck you with." I grin.

She hits my chest and hops off the marble, shimmying out of her leggings.

I stare, slack-jawed, as she stands before me. My eyes trace over every inch of her, cataloging every curve and dip on her short frame.

She gives me a shy smile before opening the door to the shower and stepping inside.

She stands under the spray, and the water sluices off her skin. She looks like a naiad, an ethereal beauty at home in the water. I'm at risk of drowning myself just so I can please her. I would kneel at her feet and offer her whatever she asked for.

I step behind her as she turns her face up to the rainfall shower head. Her blonde hair turns darker as it becomes drenched, and I reach around, placing my hands on the sides of her ribs. Her skin shines as the light hits it, and I become lost in her beauty.

I'm jealous of the water that touches every inch of her skin, wishing I could somehow do the same.

I twist Sydney around and pull her into a soft kiss. The water cascades around us, hitting from every direction. She wraps her arms around my neck, and I reach down, hooking my hands under her thighs and lifting her. I walk forward until her back rests against the cool tiles.

"You're so bloody gorgeous," I mutter.

Sydney's legs tighten around me, and my eyes roll back at the feeling of her cunt pressed against my stomach. I groan as the tip of my dick keeps bumping against her ass as she shifts.

Fuck, I want to be inside her.

I tug on her bottom lip and draw it into my mouth as I grip her harder. Her hands come up to thread through my wet hair, and I sigh into the feeling. Her kisses taste like the sweetest poison, killing me with pure pleasure.

"Parker, I want you. All of you."

And fuck me if I don't almost blow my load just hearing her utter those words.

I adjust my grip and carefully carry her out of the shower.

"I —What are you doing?"

"Putting you somewhere more comfortable."

"But I'm all wet!"

"That's what she said."

"Oh my God."

I crawl onto my bed with her still hooked around me and lay her on her back. She stares up at me, her golden strands splayed across my sheets and darkening them with water.

I drag my tongue down her body, tasting the water on her skin as I make my way to her sweet pussy. I lick a clean path up her slit and stare up at her.

"Cherries." I wink.

She attempts to kick me, but I take hold of her leg and press it open so she's butterflied before me.

Such a pretty sight.

My tongue dives into her heat, and she lets out a gasp. Her knees attempt to close, but I keep a firm grip on them. She squirms under my ministrations until she is a panting mess.

Forbidden fruit always tastes the sweetest, and my Eve

has completely surrendered herself to the garden of plea-sure.

I suck on her clit, and she moans my name. "Parker. Please."

"What's that, love?"

I slip two fingers into her hot cunt.

"Please. I said please."

"Please what?" I curl my fingers and stroke her faster.

"F—fuck me. Please. Oh God, please."

"You're so perfect when you beg."

I grin, reaching into my bedside drawer and pulling out a condom. Using my teeth, I rip open the foil and roll it onto my heavy cock.

Leaning forward, I brace my arms around her head. I clear her bangs from her forehead and look straight in her slate-gray eyes as I position the head of my cock at her entrance.

I don't break contact as I slowly push inside.

"Damn, you take me well," I whisper.

Her pouty lips form a small O and her lashes flutter, but she never lets them close completely. We stare into each other's eyes as we become one, and fuck me if it isn't the hottest, most intimate moment of my entire life.

"Holy crap." Her ankles hook behind the backs of my knees. "This feels amazing. You feel amazing."

"And I'm only halfway."

"What?" Her eyes blow wide. "Halfway?"

Her pussy tenses around my cock, and I let out a groan at the added pressure.

"Relax," I soothe, bringing my hand between us to roll her clit.

"You're going to split me apart," she splutters.

"I promise you, I'm not. Although, I'm flattered you think so." I press forward and kiss her.

She melts against my lips and her cunt releases its hold, letting me slip in another few inches. When I'm fully seated within her, I let out a deep breath, stilling so I can just bask in the feeling.

I move slowly at first, pulling out to the tip before pushing myself back to the hilt. It's torture but feels so fucking good. I'm drawing out the pleasure, losing myself in the feeling of her tight pussy clamping around my dick over and over and over.

"More," she gasps.

"More? More, what?" I ask.

"More, please."

"That's my girl."

I pick up the pace, pounding into her with more force. The bed starts to creak as we move faster and faster.

"You like that, baby?"

"Yes," she moans. "Don't stop."

My body heats with each stroke. I lift one of her knees higher, deepening my angle. The little noises she makes get louder and louder, and I don't stop the low grunt from pouring out of my mouth in response. When Sydney comes undone, it's the single most euphoric sight.

I feel my balls tightening as I go faster and faster, pistoning into her sweet heat.

"Parker?" Her voice is low and breathy.

"Yeah?"

"Can we flip?"

"Sounds hot." I smirk.

I wrap my arms around her ribs and roll us over. She doesn't even pause. Within seconds she's taking control, swirling her hips a few times.

Stars burst in my vision when she lifts her hips to the tip of my dick and slams herself back down.

"Holy fuck," I swear, arching my hips to meet hers.

I take my time roaming her body with my eyes, watching every part of her body bounce with the motion. The view from down here is heavenly.

Sydney loses herself in her movements, and it's a treasure to watch her take what she wants. There's nothing more powerful than the woman on top of me. She feeds the hunger inside her, never letting up.

I bring my hands up to grip the plush globes of her ass, holding them as she grinds harder and harder. It alters the angle slightly, and my dick manages to slip even deeper. I groan, gripping her tighter. The tip of my finger dips close to her hole, and she sucks in a breath, her eyes widening. But when she looks down at me, there's nothing but carnal desire flowing through her.

Interesting.

I'll keep that little piece of knowledge in my back pocket.

"It feels so good," she moans, throwing her head back as she continues to ride me into oblivion.

I lift my hips to push into her, following her movements and increasing the pace. Her hand snakes down to rub her clit, and I just about come.

"Fuck, you're sexy when you touch yourself."

She just gives me a sex-drunk grin in return, and I think I lose the last piece of my heart to her in that very moment.

Her moans become short gasps, and her pacing begins to falter. I reach my hand out to replace her own, two fingers swirling her swollen bud as she chases the high. I mentally plead with my cock to stay in control. There's no fucking way I'm not getting her off first this time. No matter how hard she makes it for me.

And I'm fucking hard.

"Oh my God."

It's the only warning I have before she completely comes apart. Sydney's eyes glaze over, and her lips part with a silent prayer. Her hands reach out mindlessly, grasping on to whatever they can as she crashes. Her fingers rake down my chest, and the pain unlocks the last thread of restraint I have.

Her name leaves my lips in a guttural groan. Pleasure pours out of me, and my hips buck up into her clenching cunt. This time it's my hands reaching out, grasping her thighs as I push farther and farther into her.

By the time my orgasm ends, we're both panting messes, holding on to each other for stability.

Sydney pushes off my body and flops next to me with a sigh. I immediately mourn the loss of her pussy pulsing around me. We lie in a comfortable silence as the endorphins course their way throughout our bodies.

"I knew I'd render you speechless with my dick." I tug her to my chest and peck her nose.

"You know what, I'll give it to you this time, Parker."

I look down and raise my brow.

She smiles and lifts her hand to trace the scar on my temple. "Best sex ever."

"We make a great team."

I pick her up and carry her back to the shower so we can actually wash off this time. We take a bit longer than necessary when I pull her back to me for another make out session until she weasels her way out of my grasp. She laughs as she washes my hair and styles it in a mohawk. I earn a stern glare when I lather her body with soap and spend a little too much time cleaning her tits.

We wrap ourselves in the soft blue towels hanging on the heated rack, and she hums to herself while dotting moisturizer over her face.

Everything in this moment seems unreal, like I'm living in a video game. I would hit save on life right now just so I could come back to this scene over and over.

I feel like the luckiest man alive.

"I need an energy drink. Race you to the kitchen?" I tug on a wet strand of her hair.

"Parker, I am not racing you to the kitchen."

"Ah. I wore you out, so you don't have the energy. Fair enough."

"All right, hotshot."

Sydney darts out of the bathroom without a second glance, and I curse, running after her. She pushes out of my bedroom and rounds the corner, but I reach out and throw my hands around her waist, gripping her towel. She squeals with laughter.

Then, she squeals in horror.

And someone else squeals in horror.

I look up and get a perfect view of Aleks' bare ass. Stevie is bent over the kitchen island before him, her golden skin on display.

"Oh, come on, mate. We eat there," I whine.

Sydney freaks out and tries to retreat into the safety of my room. Only issue is, I'm still holding her towel, and it gets caught in the sudden movement, ripping from her body and landing on the floorboards. She screeches again and crouches down into a ball to cover herself.

In an effort to save her from her sheer nudity, I throw my own towel over her.

Which…in hindsight…does not improve the situation that much.

In fact, I think Aleks might be more mad as he turns around to glare at me while blocking Stevie from view.

"Stop looking at my naked girlfriend!" he shouts, cupping his junk to hide it.

"Stop looking at *my* naked girlfriend!" I throw back, not bothering to hide anything.

"Seriously. You're both naked!" Stevie huffs over Aleks' shoulder.

I avert my gaze from her anyway and instead watch as Sydney subtly crawls back to my bedroom in the midst of the chaos.

"Clearly, I'm late to the party." Jackson's deep voice reverberates around us. "Not really sure I wanted to be invited though. Orgies aren't really my thing."

He stands in the hallway, leaning against the wall. A pair of rumpled black jeans dangle from his hands. He throws them in Aleks' direction, who grabs them midair with one hand.

"Thanks." He nods. "Mind tossing Stevie's stuff as well?"

Jackson laughs but bends to pick up more of the discarded clothes littering our floor.

"None of you were supposed to be home," I mutter, watching them all.

Assholes ruined everything. Here I was, about to have a fantastic afternoon with my cute girlfriend cuddled against me, and instead, I'm standing in my kitchen naked with my roommates.

"Was that Sydney?" Jackson walks past me and opens the fridge, grabbing the water filter pitcher and pouring himself a glass.

"Nope."

"Really? Looked suspiciously like her," Stevie coos, a black pleated mini skirt and oversized sweater covering her previously exposed skin.

"I know." I tilt my head and lower my voice dramatically, "It's just the uncanniest thing, isn't it?"

"Seriously, dude," Aleks deadpans as he throws up a hand to cover Stevie's eyes. "Can you not be naked?"

"No need to be jealous." I shrug, and stroll back to my room, happy to take the easy out. There is no way for me to avoid this conversation if I stay out here. They're all too nosy. Especially Stephanie. I saw that little glint in her eye.

Girl is too observant for her own good.

I slip into my room to find Sydney burning a hole in the ground as she paces the length of the room. She's thrown on one of my shirts; the fabric brushes her knees. *Hot.* She nibbles on her thumb, deep in thought.

She stops when she sees me and rushes over.

"I can't go back out there, Parker." Her eyes widen so much that the tips of her eyelashes brush her eyebrows.

"I'm not one hundred percent sure what your alternative is, though, love. Unless you want to dip onto the balcony and rappel fifty floors to your place. I've done it a bunch of times in *Devil's City*, and I'm sure Jackson has some ropes and a harness hidden in that compartment under his bed he thinks no one knows about."

I throw my thumb in the direction of the sliding doors that blend seamlessly into my floor-to-ceiling windows. In addition to my room being the largest in the apartment, it also leads directly onto the balcony. Owner privilege really does have its perks.

Sydney raises her hands, and they curl like she wants to strangle me. Which she probably does.

"Parker, this is serious." That telltale anxiety begins to pulse off her.

I reach forward and cup her hands between my own, forcing them to relax as I place a kiss on them. Tilting my head down to soothe her panicked expression, I give her a sincere smile.

"It's all going to be fine, Syd."

"They saw me!"

"They *think* they saw you," I correct.

It's the wrong thing to say. I knew it was, but the words still left my mouth.

Her eye twitches the way it does when she gets mad at me.

I pull her into a tight hug, attempting to diffuse her emotions. She tries to push out, but after a moment she goes slack and her arms reach around to curl around my waist.

"This was not the plan," she mutters into my chest.

"I know." I stroke her damp hair in a repetitive motion. "I know, but it's not the end of the world."

"What am I supposed to say to them?"

"Whatever you want. I'll take your lead."

She peers up at me and gnaws on her bottom lip. "It seems sort of pointless to try to lie."

"Then we don't."

"And you're okay with that?"

"Sydney. I couldn't be more bloody proud to be dating if you if I tried. I'd introduce you to the royal family if you'd let me."

"You're joking."

"I don't joke about royalty, babe."

She opens her mouth to say something before letting out a laugh and resting her cheek against my chest. I feel her shoulders relax, and it calms a piece of me as well. She's always so high-strung. Always thinking and worrying and planning. I just want to be able to provide a space where she can feel safe enough to turn off her brain and just be. I want to be her person.

"Unless you don't want to tell them we're dating?" I ask her the question because I saw her hesitation earlier. I ask her the question because I know how secretive she's been.

"I want to tell them, but…." She trails off. Her arms tighten around me, and she snuggles in closer. "But I'm worried about it getting out. It's the biggest PR taboo, and even though you think you have Mathias handled, it's still against my contract, Parker."

"I trust them. They won't say anything." I know that with every fiber of my being. The lads would never breathe a word, and the girls would never do anything to hurt Syd. "I'll deal with Mathias if it comes to that. I promise. You won't face him alone."

I'll have to find some way to get ahold of her contract so Paige can look it over. There would be a loophole somewhere where she wouldn't lose her job.

"Okay. I trust you."

My heart stops, those three words freezing time around me.

I have no clue whether she knows the true weight of what she just said, but it grounds everything. Earning Sydney's trust is like platinuming in a game. You spend hours doing everything possible to complete every single side quest, collect every token and relic, and finally, when it's all done, you get that little silver trophy next to your name and everything becomes worth it. Loving Sydney for five years, never giving up, was worth it just to hear those three words.

"Also, you need to put some clothes on before we go back out there." Sydney pulls back from my hold and gives me a pointed look.

I laugh, but my chest aches with the flurry of emotions pooling within me. "Why? I'm not ashamed."

"I know." She rolls her eyes and walks to my dresser, pulling out a pair of bright blue sweatpants and tossing them to me. "But the last thing I need is a literal dick measuring competition."

I grin, stepping into the fabric. "You know we—"

"No. No, I don't know. And I don't want to know."

"Are you sure?" I waggle my brows.

She sighs, pushing past me to the door. Her hand rests on the handle for a beat before she takes in an audible breath and wrenches it open.

Sydney walks into the apartment with practiced confidence. You would think she was walking into a boardroom to give a presentation to executives, not a living room full of gamers while wearing just an oversized shirt. Her shoulders are pulled back and her strides measured as she makes her way to the L-shaped couch and perches on the edge cushion nearest Stevie.

The three of them look up briefly from the couch before turning back to the racing game they're playing. But I catch the small smile tugging at the corner of Stevie's lips.

"Would you look at that. He does know how to wear clothes," Jackson mocks.

"Ha ha." I take a seat next to Aleks, stealing his controller. "Why does everyone have an aversion to seeing me naked? It's a privilege. You should feel special that I allow you the honor of seeing my goods."

"Dude, grab your own." Aleks wrenches the controller back, his character crashing in the process. He sends me a glare as he waits to respawn on the track.

"Parker, I'm surprised more people haven't seen you naked," Stevie sighs, maneuvering her vehicle smoothly into first place and overtaking Jackson.

"Please don't say that," Syd laments. "I don't want to bail him out of jail after hearing he went streaking just to prove your point."

I give her a wolfish grin. "What a great idea."

Jackson's character crosses the finish line, and he hisses out a "yes," balling his hand in a fist.

Stevie tsks, her car slotting in at third place across the finish line. "Cheater."

"Parker's the fucking cheater," Aleks growls from

eleventh place. "I could've won if he didn't steal the damn controller."

"Oh, babe." Stevie pats his leg. "You were already losing."

"Hate this fucking game."

Stevie lets out a shimmery laugh, her eyes full of such love as she stares at the broody gamer. She notices me staring and gives me a once over. Then, her sweet smile turns serpentine. "Nice shirt, Syd."

"Thanks." Syd keeps her face straight as she brushes imaginary lint from the sleeve.

The nonchalance sets off a glint in Aleks' eyes as they bounce from Stevie to Syd. "What's it made of?" He leans over and rubs the bottom of the shirt. "Feels like boyfriend material."

Jackson snorts something sounding like the word "loser," and I whack Aleks on the back of the head.

"Hands off my girlfriend, dude."

"I KNEW IT!" Stevie squeals as she jumps to her feet. "I told you he said girlfriend earlier." She points a finger at Aleks.

Sydney flushes but manages to keep her composure.

"Yeah, yeah, yeah." He wraps his arms around her waist and pulls her on top of his lap. "You're always right."

"Damn straight."

"I'm surprised it took the rest of you this long to notice." Jackson lifts his legs onto the coffee table and crosses them at the ankle with a smug look.

"What are you talking about?" Syd frowns across the couch at him.

"I've known for weeks."

"Bullshit," I accuse, getting up and moving seats to where Stevie previously was, hooking my arm around Syd's shoulders.

"What tipped you off?" she asks.

"Seattle, among other things."

Her lips curls, "Ugh," and she glares up at me. "I told you it was suspicious."

"Oh, come on. Aleks didn't realize, and he was right outside the door!"

"At this point, I think you could've opened the door, and he still wouldn't have put two and two together."

"Hey, hey," Aleks butts in. "Not cool. We gang up on Parker. We don't gang up on me. That's not how this works."

"Just wait until the girls find out. They're going to freak!" Stevie grins.

"Lee's going to kill me," Sydney whines.

"Well, she's going to figure it out during Halloween unless you find a way to keep Mr. Handsy here in line." Stevie inclines her head toward me.

I realize my hand has been tracing an absent path up and down Sydney's arm.

"Who wants to bet?" I smirk. "If Lee or Deer will figure it out first?"

"Parker." Sydney draws out my name in warning.

"I'm in," Aleks smirks back.

"Of course you are," Stevie sighs.

"If Deer figures it out first, I get to take the Lambo out." Aleks holds out a hand to me, the chipped black nail polish glinting.

"Fine. If it's Lee, then you to have to get my name tattooed on your ass." I grip his hand hard.

I am so going to win.

"Boys and their games," Stevie sings.

"This boy would like to get back to the actual game." Jackson points his controller at the TV, which has just been replaying the last race as we've been talking.

"Do you think I could play?" Syd's voice is quiet.

I look down at her, unveiled shock on my face.

"Oh my God, yes!" Stevie bounces up to grab one of the spare controllers. "I'll teach you everything. And then, we can kick their asses together."

"Hey." I snatch the black controller from her. "If anyone's teaching her, it's me."

Stevie mouths a word that looks a lot like "whipped" before plopping herself next to Aleks and picking up her gold controller. I stick my tongue out at her but smile.

"So long as it's not Aleks, I don't care. I want to learn how to win," Sydney comments.

"Burn," Jackson and I crow.

"All right, you fuckers keep this up, and we'll see who's laughing when I fuck you all up." He waves his controller at all of us.

"We're taking the piss," I say, batting his hand away.

Light dances in my chest as I hand the black controller to Sydney. This is the first time she's ever asked to play with us. Every time I've offered in the past, she would shrug it off. So much so that none of us really asked her anymore.

Sydney curves her hands around the controller, testing out the feel. I take the time to explain the basics and how there are power-ups on the course she can use.

She nods along, and her interest feels like winning a game when you've been down three points the entire time, just to score a Fury Kill in the last second.

I don't even care about playing myself; all my attention is on her, is on the way every single day she becomes more and more a part of my family, and I never want to let her go.

Chapter
TWENTY-THREE

SYDNEY

"I don't want to be here," Parker says for the fiftieth time, crossing his arms over his bare chest.

My eyes roam appreciatively over his sexy bloody angel costume.

He is wearing a pair of white wings with an open white shirt. The band of his Calvin Kleins peeks out the top of his white jeans, and Deer spent a solid thirty minutes painting bloody tears under his eyes.

God, he is attractive.

"Are you going to bitch the whole time?" Aleks asks.

"Oh, let him be, babe. You know he's a scaredy cat." Stevie threads her fingers through Aleks' and grins.

The two of them are dressed as Han Solo and Leia, although Stevie went for metal-bikini Leia. She looks drop-dead gorgeous, and more than a few people have stopped to stare at her. Aleks has given out his fair share of death glares tonight as a result.

Personally, I can't stop staring at the large hickey on her neck she's neglected to cover up.

"I am not a scaredy cat," Parker rejects.

"And I'm not about to punch you." Jackson hits Parker on the back, and the two begin arguing.

According to Parker, it had been a chore to get Jackson to put any costume on, let alone the one he has on now. Honestly, I didn't even realize it was a costume. He's wearing stone-gray sweatpants and an extremely tight navy T-shirt and is carrying a weird-looking sword. Parker explained that it's an anime character from a popular show. Togi? Toji? I don't know, I just nodded along.

Lee's outfit I recognized, at least. She's dressed as Sailor Mars and looks both cute and badass.

Deer, I thought, is just dressed as a sexy nurse. However, she got extremely offended when I said as much and made sure to correct me that she wasn't just any nurse but Nurse Joy from Pokémon.

Sometimes working with gamers gives me a headache.

There are too many things to remember. How anyone can keep track of every video game character or anime character seems impossible to me. I just make sure I keep up to date on what the boys play and leave everything else to the rest of Mathias' team.

I'd try to go simple with my Halloween outfit until Deer bombarded me with an Alice in Wonderland outfit she'd bought for me. Apparently, after she found out my original idea was to dress up as a cat, she decided to take matters into her own hands. I was heavily outvoted as I sat in Lee's bathroom getting ready earlier.

"We can hear you bickering all the way from the festival entrance."

We all stop to look at the newcomers. Deanna, Stevie's best friend, enters the fray with her girlfriend, Maya. They're dressed as Daphne and Velma.

I haven't hung out with Deanna much, but I know her girlfriend pretty well. Maya works for OMEN, one of the top *Gods League* esports teams. She's at a lot of the same events that I bring The System to, and her hours are even worse than mine.

"Dee!" Stevie abandons her boyfriend and flings herself at her best friend.

Everyone begins chatting as we move up the line for the haunted mansion.

The Huntington Halloween Festival opened last year and is all anyone can talk about. It is located a few hours from our apartment, just outside Palm Springs on this massive, abandoned lot that had been completely renovated. In addition to the haunted mansion, there is a man-made corn maze, a house of mirrors, a bunch of those carnival games where you toss rings or shoot fake guns, and a Ferris wheel.

The food is amazing, too. We'd already spent an hour going through all the stores and gorging ourselves until we almost burst. They have some of the best spiced caramel apples I've ever tried, and everyone else raved about this spiked pumpkin spice drink that came in a mini pumpkin.

It is hard to believe we are even in California; it looks like we have been transported to some remote town in the Midwest.

There is hay strewn over the dirt ground, cobwebs line barren trees, and fog machines throughout the grounds add to the ambiance. There are even employees who are dressed up as skeletons and scaring people as they walk about.

Everything is creepily perfect.

The line to get in here was nuts, but I worked my PR magic and got us passes that bypassed it.

Parker has been on edge the entire time. I'm pretty sure the only reason he came is because he didn't want to be left out. We flew back yesterday from Chicago from Parker's third win. He has officially secured his place in the Divizion Championship Series, and I couldn't be happier for him. I had certainly shown him how happy I was on the flight back.

Never had I been so thankful for a bedroom on a private jet before.

An ear-piercing scream rings out from inside the haunted mansion, and Parker blanches, turning as white as his outfit. Deer's eyes, however, brighten, and she clasps her hands together.

"This is going to be so much fun!" She hops from one foot to the other, her pink hair swinging from its elaborate style. Sometimes it is easy to forget how much she loves this kind of stuff, given her kawaii aesthetic.

"Totally! I heard they hired some special effects dude from Hollywood to help this year," Lee chimes in.

"Yeah, he's one of the guys who works on *Devil Nun*. Should be sick." Jackson grins, a gleam in his eye. If there's one way to get Jackson pumped up, it's horror movies.

"Not fucking *Devil Nun*," Aleks groans.

"There is something wrong with all of you." Parker glares at them.

"I think it's going to be cool." I smile. "Nothing like a good jump scare."

Parker gapes at me. "Et tu, Brute?"

I roll my eyes and nudge him with my shoulder. I am excited for the haunted mansion even though I feel bad for Parker. I'm not as into this stuff as Jackson, Deer, and Lee, but it still speaks to the crime buff in me. There is something about the adrenaline that comes with being scared.

Plus, it is fall. Which is my favorite season.

"Have I told you how much I love this outfit?" Parker's voice is low. "Blue always looks good on you."

"You should see what's underneath," I tease.

"Oh?" Molten curiosity spreads as his gaze rakes up my body.

He slings an arm over me and tugs me to his chest. Heat sparks in my belly at the feeling of his bare chest against my arm. My hands twitch to run all over him, but I refrain, not wanting to be too obvious.

I doubt there will be anyone here who would outright recognize the guys, since it is Halloween, but they are also gaining more popularity every week, and this festival is one of the hottest places to be.

Sigh.

Even when I'm not working, I'm working.

Plus, Aleks and Parker still have their bet going, and I promised him I wouldn't do anything to sabotage it. Not that I really know what that means. Parker doesn't seem to be doing anything different to dissuade the few curious looks I've been getting from Lee.

We finally make it to the front of the line, and the employee taking our tokens gives our group a once over.

"You're welcome to go in together, but it's more fun in pairs or smaller groups. The hallways are quite narrow at times," she says while dropping the tokens into a glass pumpkin.

"Then we're going first!" Lee links her arm with Deer, and the pair start running inside.

"Hell," Jackson mutters under his breath before he jogs up the stairs behind them.

"Guess that leaves you and me, babe." Aleks grins down at Stevie, wrapping his arms around her waist.

Stevie's fox eyes gleam. "Perfect," she purrs before tilting her head up into a kiss.

"Gross." Deanna shoves past them. "We'll see you on the other side." She and Maya hold hands as they disappear into the haunted mansion.

Stevie and Aleks follow a few minutes later, and then it's our turn to wait for entry.

Parker's quiet. I can feel the nerves vibrating off his body. He even starts toying with the twin hoops in his ear as his eyes dart all over the creepy monstrosity before us. It's like he is trying to see through the decrepit wood to the inside so he can map out an escape, and we haven't even gone in.

"Don't worry." I pat his chest, my fingers tingling at the contact with his skin. "I'll protect you."

He scoffs, standing straight and gripping the collar of his shirt to puff it out.

"I'm not worried."

"Sure," I drawl.

"Next," the employee calls out.

"Come on, Alice. Let's enter the rabbit hole." He tugs my hand and starts to lead us inside. "Maybe I'll even show you my caterpillar later."

"Oh, Parker." I frown. "No, that's," laughter bubbles out of me, "that's awful."

He gives me a boyish smirk, but it quickly fades away as we walk into the entryway of the mansion. It's somehow bigger and smaller than I expected. There's the hum of music swirling around us, a solemn piano tune mixing with quiet laughter. The creepy kind, not the joyous kind. It's also colder here, and goosebumps rise on my arms.

Parker stills, every part of him on high alert.

"Come on, let's go this way." I nod to the room on our right, one that looks like a dining room from the crack through the door.

Excitement burns through me. It feels like I'm part of my beloved haunted house podcast, investigating a creepy ghost story.

We're making our way through the living room when the chandelier starts to flicker. The room is plunged in and out of darkness over and over.

It looks like there are spiders crawling on the ceiling, and a dripping noise begins playing through the speakers.

"Oh, fuck no," Parker swears, grabbing my hand and pulling us through the next door.

We just about make it through when a nearby cabinet pops open and a bloody head rolls out. It looks pretty realistic. Parker flinches and immediately starts running us down the dark hallway.

I snicker quietly under my breath.

"This was a shit idea," he mutters, finally slowing down.

"I think it's fun." I trail my hand up his arm absently, looking around and trying to make out shapes in the distance. There looks to be another set of doors just up ahead.

Parker's hand closes around mine. "I think my idea of fun is better."

The husk in his voice pulls my attention, and I look up at him. The blue of his eyes is so much brighter against the deep red paint dripping down his face. My breath hitches as my hand comes up to trail his sharp jaw.

Creaks and groans sound around us. There's even a whistling of wind. It all adds to the moment, increasing the urgency.

Parker backs me against the wall in the narrow hallway, his hands clasped around my wrists as he lifts my arms above my head. My chest heaves.

Parker leans down, not once breaking eye contact. The tip of his nose dances lightly against my own, and that contact of skin makes me break out in shivers. His lips remain a breath away, but I can feel the ghost of them.

I squeeze my thighs together, something thick and warm mixing low in my abdomen. Desire surges through me as Parker closes the distance and brushes his lips against mine. I try to deepen the kiss, pushing forward, but he doesn't let me. He just continues to tease me with the soft brushing of his lips.

My hands twitch, begging to touch him, somewhere, anywhere. But they're trapped. I groan in frustration.

Parker smirks. I'm about to complain, but then his tongue coaxes the seams of my lips. I open myself to him, humming in pleasure as he deepens the kiss. I lift one of my legs to wrap my ankle around his calf, pulling us closer. Everything fades away, and I start to forget exactly where we are.

The freedom he instills within me is euphoric and dangerous.

That is until Parker screams into my mouth and reels back.

Shock ripples through my body, and it mixes with my growing arousal, creating a cacophony of confusion in my brain.

What looks to be some sort of zombie clown looms over Parker. Even my own heart starts to beat faster in its presence. They weren't kidding about the special effects being out of this world. The guy looks as if someone had taken *IT* and thrown acid at him.

As soon as Parker makes eye contact with the clown, he screams again and starts running down the hallway.

Without me.

It takes a second before my brain catches up through the love-drunk fog and I start after him into the darkness.

"Parker," I yell at the disappearing angel. "Parker!"

It's useless.

My core is still tight with the memories of a few moments ago, unreleased want leaving me wired, but fear begins to crawl through my system as I attempt to follow him through the haunted mansion.

Room after room of jump scares. It's one thing to be going through this with someone, but navigating it on my own is way worse. Don't get me wrong, it's fun but in a seriously terrifying way. The mansion gets darker the farther

I go, and it feels like it gets colder, too.

I round a corner and shriek when some creepy doll girl pops out of nowhere with an axe, true fear bleeding into me for the first time.

Shivers wrack through my body, but I push on, picking up the pace and looking over my shoulder to make sure the doll isn't following me.

What I thought was a cool idea has turned very, *very* uncool.

I am going to kill Parker.

A screech rings out from nearby that sounds oddly like my boyfriend.

I pivot and head in the opposite direction. I didn't think you could get lost in the haunted mansion; it isn't supposed to be a maze. But the more I run, the less confident I become.

I'm halfway up a set of rickety stairs, doubting every decision I've ever made, when a burst of white starts barreling down the stairs.

For a second, I just pause.

The bloody angel running toward me is beautiful.

"Run!" Parker's hand closes around my wrist, and he pulls me with him.

I let him lead us through the mansion. He alters direction whenever we come across an employee, his throat going hoarse with each screech. I think lose my sense of self along the way because I start laughing.

"This isn't funny, Sydney," he hisses.

More laughter spills from me.

"Fucking clowns, and dolls, and skeletons, and ghouls," he mutters.

Parker continues to complain and curse until we come across a door with an exit sign. He practically body slams it to get out.

We spill into the cool night, the amber lights of the festival grounds a welcome brightness around us compared to the imposing darkness of the haunted mansion.

Parker releases me as he falls to his knees, bracing his hands on the ground.

"That wasn't too bad, was it?" I laugh, crouching next to him.

His head whips up, and he rocks back onto his ankles, glaring at me.

"That was awful."

"All of it?" I smile.

His shoulders drop, and a lazy grin spreads across his moonlit features. "Not all of it."

He reaches forward and pushes my hair over my shoulder, the tips of his fingers grazing my neck. That warmth from earlier returns, stirring within me.

"Y'all dating?"

We freeze.

As one, Parker and I crane our necks to look up at Deanna. Her cool chocolate eyes have a calculating glint.

"Don't be silly." Deer sidles up next to her. "That's just them."

"Yeah," Lee backs her up.

My eyes slip to Jackson hanging behind them. An unfiltered grin splits across his face. He's more than enjoying the show.

Deer's eyes bounce between us, and her pale brows furrow.

"Wait," Parker cuts in. "Wwhere are Stevie and Aleks? They went in before us."

We all pause, scanning the surrounding area.

As if we summoned them, the duo comes running out of the mansion exit. The creepy zombie clown from earlier is hot on their heels. We stare, confused, as the zombie clown stops in the frame of the exit door.

"Keep your horny hands out of our mansion!" he shouts before disappearing back inside.

My eyes narrow on the couple, zeroing in on Stevie's smudged nude lipstick and Alek's untucked cream top.

"Please tell me you did not have sex in the haunted mansion."

"We didn't have sex in the haunted mansion." Stevie raises her hands in front of herself in defense.

"Not for a lack of trying." Aleks grins.

She elbows him in the ribs, giving me a placid smile. I cock my head, assessing them further. It's the faint remnants of glistening tears clinging to her bottom lashes that gives them away. They act like teenagers sometimes.

"That clown is a real cockblock." Aleks snakes his arm around Stevie's ribs, his fingers toying with the bottom of her bra top.

"Tell me about it," Parker huffs, rising to his feet before holding a hand out to me. I sigh, taking it.

Standing, I brush myself off, unruffling the poofy blue dress.

"Oh my Gods, they were right." Deer points an acrylic nail at me. "You're fucking!"

My jaw goes slack. "What?"

"Yes," Aleks hisses, fist bumping the air. "I win."

"No way, the bet was whoever figured out we were dating first. Dating," Parker counters.

"You're dating?" Lee gapes at me.

"See, now I win."

"Dude, that's not how it works." Aleks steps closer to Parker, and they come chest to chest. "I get to drive the Lambo, fair and square."

"Not my fault you weren't less specific about the terms."

"Shut up, both of you." Lee pushes them apart and holds a hand in front of each of their chests. She gives me an exaggerated pout. "Sydney?" She says it all whiney and hurt.

I give her a weak smile. "Surprise?"

"Girl." She gives my shoulder a push before crushing me in a hug. "I hate you, but I'm so happy for you." She whispers it so only I hear her.

"Thank you."

She pulls back, smiling at me. "You have to tell me everything."

"Everything?"

"Ew, no." Her nose scrunches, and she loops her arm in mine.

"Well, I want to hear everything." Stevie grins.

"Yeah, like is it as big as Stevie said?" Deer bounces in front us and starts walking backward with a smirk.

"You guys," I groan, flushing.

Deer lets out a sparkly laugh, crinkling her eyes. Her expression falters for a split second, and her eyes flare slightly as she looks over my shoulder. I follow her gaze but see nothing out of the ordinary. When I look at her again, she's nothing but smiles, pushing herself between Stevie and me before looping her arm around my free elbow.

"Come on, Syd. You can share. What is it, eight inches?"

"I'm more than happy to prove that," Parker calls from behind us.

"No public nudity," I shout back.

"But, babe."

We all fall into a fit of laughter as we weave our way back into the throng of the festival crowds. The girls keep chittering around me, peppering me with questions. My heart lightens as I fill them in with details. I didn't realize how much I had wanted to talk with them about this. I was so used to keeping a thin barrier between me and everyone else. But Parker had shattered that and shown me freedom.

I turn and look at the naughty angel behind me. He winks, mouthing the word "later." The promise burns into my skin, sending a fire to my thighs. I look forward, pressing my lips together to hide the smile.

This boy is trouble in the best ways.

Chapter
TWENTY-FOUR

PARKER

"Now, if you look at that leaderboard, you'll see—"

"Shut up, English," Jackson cuts in.

"You'll see that I am at the top. Four games in a row now."

"Fuck off," Aleks growls.

"How's the weather down there, boys?"

I grin like a child, the taste of victory fresh. I was crushing everyone in *Kill Strike* tonight. It didn't matter what the lads tried, I just kept coming out on top. I was one-shot, one-killing like a madman.

This was probably my best stream in weeks.

We play another round, and I manage to get off a triple kill in no time.

"Do you see that, my little coffeemakers? Your boy is

326

sending it today." I flick my eyes to the comments and grin.

Jackson and Aleks groan and grumble, trash talking in their growing frustration.

The round ends with me sitting MVP again.

"That's it, I'm done. Have fun stroking your dick." Jackson exits the lobby.

We've been streaming for five hours, so we are due to end anyway.

"All right, let's end it," Aleks agrees.

We say our goodbyes, and I spend a few extra minutes on my own stream, chatting with the commenters before clicking off.

I push my headset around my neck and reach across my desk to flip my phone over.

A text from my grandfather shines back at me, and instead of feeling like I'm on cloud nine, it's like I'm falling through the sky. I'm plummeting to the ground at breakneck speed, and I have no idea if the parachute on my back is going to save me or not.

I shove the phone in my pocket.

I hang up my headset and give my neck a crack as I grab the screen recording of the stream and drop it into my shared folder. Our editors would work on doing their magic with it and posting it to the appropriate social channels. I power off my monitors and then push back from my desk with a sigh.

I lean my head back against the chair and just bask in the blue LED-lit room.

My streaming room is one of my favorite places in the world. There's just something about it that calms me, that brings me back to center. Sure, the games can be stressful, and I spend hours shouting with the lads, but that's just part of the appeal. This is my home base. It's my core.

I use my feet to twirl the chair around and around, spinning in the blue darkness.

Tomorrow we fly out to Vegas for the championship.

Everyone's going, and I can't tell if that makes me more or less nervous.

Since Halloween, I've spent every waking second grinding. The team and I even decided to skip the last practice tournament in Dallas so that I could get more hours in with *Final Destiny*.

Mathias had the team review Creep's gameplay from the Miami game, and they'd come up with an intensive training schedule for me that I'd been following to a T the last three weeks. Honestly, once the championship is over, I never want to play *Final Destiny* again.

All I need to do is defeat Creep once. That is it.

Mathias keeps reminding me that I don't necessarily need to beat Creep's time in *Final Destiny* so long as my times for *Dreadlander* and *Styx* are up to par. But I don't care. Because I know I am better than him in *Dreadlander* and *Styx*. He isn't the competition I am trying to beat there.

OnlyVan would give me a run for my money in *Styx*, and JustAGame would come at me in *Dreadlander*, but Creep is undisputed in his times for *Final Destiny*. Even if I crush Creep in *Dreadlander* and *Styx*, it would mean nothing if I have a repeat of Miami.

Twenty minutes would end me.

Statistically speaking, less than five minutes would separate the top three speedrunners at the end of the night. So, if I don't stick close to Creep, nothing else matters.

The door to my room cracks open, and bright light cuts through the blue haze.

Aleks leans against the door frame, his tattooed arms crossed over his chest. "You good?"

"Yeah." I push up from the chair and follow him out into the kitchen.

Jackson is pulling a tray of chicken parm from the oven, but even the smell of food doesn't quell the mild nausea in my gut.

Aleks continues to side-eye me as we take our seats at the island, but I ignore him, opting to pull out my phone and scroll instead. My grandfather's text notification burns back at me.

In typical Jackson fashion, he plates everything for us, even going so far as to pour us each a glass of water before joining us on his own stool to the right of Aleks.

Some might think it was dickish of me not to offer help. But I'm not really allowed in the kitchen. You could even say I'd been banned.

Alicia, our personal chef, is a goddess and makes us meals during the week that we can reheat since our streaming schedules left us out of whack. But even the simplicity of reheating a meal didn't always go right when I was involved. I can tell you that, if I'd been in charge of reheating that chicken parm, it would have burnt to an indecipherable crisp.

I cut the chicken into bite-size pieces, hoping that the effort would spark some desire to eat in me.

It does not. It just makes me look like a child playing with their food.

Distracted, a heavy sigh leaves my body.

Aleks lets his fork clatter against the marble, and he turns to stare.

"Either talk or stop being a broody bitch."

"Dude, just let him be. He's nervous," Jackson mumbles between bites.

"I'm not nervous," I retort.

Jackson leans forward so I can see him, and he gives a strong look. "Liar."

"Whatever." I push back from the island and hop off the stool, stalking to my bedroom.

I don't even bother taking off my clothes. I just lift up the bed sheets before throwing myself under them, encasing myself in darkness.

"You're just gonna feel worse if you stew in it." Aleks' voice is muffled by my cocoon, but I can still make out his words.

"I told you, I'm fine."

"You didn't, and you're not." The bed dips with his weight as he invades my space.

"Go away, I just want to sleep." I'm getting pissed now.

"I'll leave but only after I say my piece."

I groan, but I refrain from kicking out my leg and shoving him off the bed. He'd probably just sit on the floor and continue to preach, anyway. I hate when he puts his leader mask on.

"You've been working your ass off for this championship, grinding hours. Stop getting all in your head about it. You'll come out on top because you always do, Parker. We're The System, and we're the fucking best there is. You'll head out on stage and show everyone that. We'll be in the stands, cheering your ugly ass on, and after we'll go out and celebrate by getting absolutely blacked. You've got this, brother."

He doesn't wait for me to say anything. The weight disappears, and my bed springs up. The soft click of the door is the only sign I have that he has left the room.

I peek my head out from the sheets and breathe in cool air.

My head continues to spin.

Even though Aleks doesn't have the full grasp of how much weight is on this championship, he is right. Whatever is going to happen, would happen. I've been working my ass off, and that is the best I could do. Nothing would change the outcome now.

It is like writing code. You have to let the system run through it and test the parameters before you make any changes. There is no point tweaking it within an inch of its life before knowing the results.

I roll over, facing the wall, and will myself to fall asleep.

But that's the thing; when you want to fall asleep, your body won't let you. My brain just keeps playing through what the next forty-eight hours will entail.

The only way I'd been able to distract myself today was by streaming with the lads. Now that I don't have a game in front of me, my brain won't shut up. It keeps running through every scenario.

Eventually, I hear the snick of my door opening again.

I should have locked the damn thing.

"Aleksander, I'm trying to sleep," I growl. "Come near me, and I'll kick you in the balls. We'll see how much Stevie likes you with a purple dick."

"He's just looking out for you. Which is why he texted me."

I still at Sydney's voice. A cool breeze grazes my back as she lifts the sheets and climbs in behind me. It takes her a second to scoot all the way across the large bed, but, finally, I feel her next to me. Her cherry scent washes over me, and I take a deep inhale, letting it flood my system.

She lines her chest up with my back and conforms her body around mine. I lift my arm so she can wrap hers around me, and then I clutch her hand in mine.

The contact of her skin against mine quiets the buzzing in my brain.

She doesn't say anything. She just lies there. And somehow, it's exactly what I need. It's the reassurance that she's there for me.

I focus on the feeling of her chest rising and falling against my back. The soft rhythm paints a pattern that I follow.

"My family is going to be there," I tell her.

The text from my grandfather earlier had been a confirmation that he was heading over from Kensington with my parents and Paige.

"And so will thousands of other people."

"Yes, but those thousands of people don't know that if I lose, the board will eat my shares like the Last Supper."

She's quiet for a beat, and I can't help but fill the silence this time with something. Everything feels too real.

"I'm going to be poor if I lose."

"You're never going to be poor, Parker," she snorts.

"If I lose my inheritance, I won't be a multibillionaire. I'm not even sure I'll still be a billionaire."

"You won't be poor even if you're a millionaire, Parker; that's not how the world works. And I'd like you regardless, unfortunately."

"For the record, I would never be a millionaire, love. I'd at least be a multimillionaire." I wrinkle my nose in offense. My streaming income and the revenue I make off this apartment complex guaranteed that.

"So dramatic." I can feel her rolling her eyes at me, and some of the tension releases.

"It's not about the money," I whisper, my voice threatening to crack.

"I know."

"You know?"

"Yeah, Parker, I know. I haven't spent the last five years with you to not understand you." She lets out a sigh, and her chin nuzzles against my shoulder. "It's your pride."

Her accuracy is on point, her shot sniping me right in the heart. I struggle to speak for a second, panic rising at how naked I feel. It feels like all my cards are on the table, and she's just flipped them all over, revealing every part of me.

"I don't want to disappoint them." *I don't want to disappoint myself.* "I want to prove that I can still be a Covington even if I forge my own path."

"And you'll prove that," she whispers. "I've seen how much you've improved in just the last twelve weeks. Imagine where you'll be in a year." There's such reverence in her voice. Such belief. "You could take over the world, Parker, if you wanted to. Your family will see that."

I squeeze her hand. "If I could take over the world, I'd hand it over to you. Because you rule every breath I take, every thought I think."

"Are you getting sappy on me, Parker Covington?"

"Only when it comes to you, love."

She chuckles, and with it, my worries bleed away. My body sinks into the plush mattress, and my heart beats in time with hers. The stress that's been coursing through me dissipates, and exhaustion is left in its place. My lids turn heavy as I finally let myself shut down.

"Thank you, Sydney."

"Always, Parker."

Chapter
TWENTY-FIVE

PARKER

"Stop pushing me." I elbow Aleks as we descend the stairs of my private jet.

"You stop pushing me." He elbows back.

"Seriously, you're holding everyone up." Jackson shoves between the two of us.

My hand flies out to grip the railing so I don't totally eat shit. Aleks stumbles down a step, but Sydney's hand shoots out to grab him.

"Children, please," she sighs.

I watch her ass she walks in front of us, her tight pencil skirt hugging her curves. I start to follow her, but Deer bounds down the steps, jumping off the last one and miraculously landing on her sky-high heels.

"Come on, move your booty." Lee uses her knee to nudge mine.

I pound down the remaining steps onto the runway. I not-so-accidentally clip Jackson with my backpack as I stroll to Sydney. He gives me a glare and I grin, throwing my arm around her shoulders.

She looks up at me with a smile. "Hi."

"Hi."

I drop a kiss on her cheekbone, and her smile grows before she looks back down at her tablet. She continues to type away, checking in on everything for the championship.

It takes a few minutes for all our luggage to get unloaded—especially Deer's forty-ton custom pink Louis Vuitton suitcase. The girl is just as bad as me, not that I'd tell anyone.

Four black SUVs roll to a stop. Security files out and opens the doors to the middle two vehicles for us to pile into.

Lee and Deer jump into the first one. Jackson jumps into the passenger seat of the one behind it, and Aleks and I follow suit, getting in the back. I hold my hand out for Sydney.

"Syd, come hang with us!" Lee calls, waving her hand out the door of her car.

Sydney's stormy eyes bounce between the vehicles.

"It's fine," I reassure her, kissing her hand before letting it go. "You can make it up to me tonight."

"Okay," she snorts.

I smile as she jogs to her best friend, but my view is cut off by the chest of a leggy brunette pushing into my face, a dove necklace swaying off her neck.

"'Scuse me."

Stevie shoves her way into the car, her manicured hand digging into my shoulder as she forces herself between Aleks and me. When her bum is firmly on the seat between us, she hooks one of her legs over Aleks. "Thanks." She grins at me.

I rub my shoulder. "Yeah, no problem."

We leave the airport flanked by our two security cars.

I stare out the window at the red mountains in the distance as we make our way to The Covington on the Strip. The traffic is bumper-to-bumper, roads closed off for the championship.

I swallow down my nerves, trying to stop myself from thinking about how I'll be playing in less than twenty-four hours. I focus on counting every desert palm tree we drive past and ignoring the cooing noises from the couple next to me.

My eyes snag on a Bugatti La Voiture Noire, and I just about piss myself. There's only one in existence, and no one knows who owns it. I reach my hand out to tap Aleks and show him. He leans across Stevie, and we foam at the mouth. This is one of the many reasons I love Vegas; you can see some of the sickest cars here.

I distantly pick up on the sound of a revving engine over our conversation.

My eyes flick around, trying to locate the car, the deep rumble getting louder.

Everything stops as I watch a black Escalade blow right through the red light, right toward us.

I yell out a warning, but it's futile.

Because the car swerves and hits the one in front of us.

The one with the girls in it.

The one with Sydney in it.
And I lose it.

"Sir, I will need to sedate you if you do not calm down."

I shove against the security barring me from the room and glare at the doctor before me.

"She's my girlfriend," I growl. "Get them to take their hands off me."

"I'm sorry, only family—"

"She is my family," I bark.

"That's not how it works." The spindly man frowns.

They would regret this. They don't know who I am. I will fucking find out their names and get them all fired. This doctor wouldn't work at another hospital in his life.

The security guard's hold lessens a little, and I use the chance to rip away from him. All decorum flees my body as I bodycheck the doctor and push my way into the room.

My heart shatters on the floor at the vision of the bruised woman before me.

Sydney's body lies on a bed in the middle of the private hospital suite. An IV snakes into her hand, while a breathing tube feeds into her nose.

My knees give out.

I just about crash onto the vinyl when a strong hand grips me.

I look up into a set of dark blue eyes.

"Dad." My voice breaks.

"It's okay, son. I'm here."

He steadies me and wraps his arms around me in a heavy hug. Sobs wrack my chest as I fold like a child against him, all my strength crumbling in his presence.

"Oh, Parker, darling." My mother rushes into the room and cups my face in her delicate hands. "We came as soon as we heard there'd been an accident."

I pull from my father into my mother's embrace. Her hand rubs my back as she lets out soft, cooing reassurances.

It's impossible for me to even form words. My brain is spinning nonstop, the crash playing on repeat in my mind, over and over and over.

The guys had had to hold me back at the accident site, stopping me from charging into the debris.

It was painful waiting for emergency services to arrive, and when they pulled her limp body from the wreckage, I just about threw up. I'd managed to bully my way into the ambulance, holding her hand and watching the monitor as her heart continued to beat. But the doctors had shut me out the second they took her into the ER.

I'd done the only thing I could do, and that was use all the money and power at my disposal to get her and the other girls their own private hospital suites.

I'd told the doctors to spare no expense, I'd cover any cost, they just needed to run every test, no matter how minor. I didn't want them to miss anything. I needed her to be okay. I'd also made sure Sydney's father was contacted and booked him on the first Imperial flight out of Missouri.

But that was all I could do, and I fucking hate it.

I can't make her wake up.

The doctors said it should happen, but until her eyes

open and I know she is okay, I wouldn't rest. I couldn't rest.

The driver died on impact and the police are still investigating, but all I can think about is that someone almost caused me to lose the single most important person in my life.

Sydney is my lifeblood; she gives me strength and power. She is the person who makes life that little bit better just by being by my side, the cherry on top of my sundae.

I can't lose her.

I can't imagine the world without her in it.

I'd just gotten her, finally. They can't take her away.

The tears flowing from my body turn to quick, sucking breaths.

"Darling, you need to calm down. It's going to be okay. The doctors said she would be okay." Mum pulls away from me, running her thumbs across my cheeks to clear some of the wetness. Her seafoam eyes shine with empathy.

"Oh, baby." She places a kiss on my forehead. "I'm so sorry you're going through this. It breaks my heart."

I stumble from her grip and hazily make my way to Sydney's bedside. My knees crack on the linoleum as I crouch next to her. I shakily take her small hand in mine, trying to warm her up with my touch, hoping that it will wake her up.

"Please, Sydney," I beg. "Please."

Chapter
TWENTY-SIX

SYDNEY

"**C**arson, turn the music down. You're going to blow out my speakers."

"Oh, come on, Sydney. Lighten up." My brother grins at me from the passenger seat, the moonlight shining on his sandy hair. "This is my favorite part." He starts singing along to the refrain, bopping his head and hands in time with the guitar.

I roll my eyes. For someone eight years older than me, he has his moments when he acts like the younger sibling. You'd think he is eighteen, not me.

"Also, this car is so old, I doubt my music is going to ruin what's already broken."

"Don't make fun of my car." I glare at him and then give the console a quick pat. It had taken me forever to save up for it. "You're not old, girl, he's just mean."

"Oh, Sydney." He looks at me with pity. "You're talking to the car, still? This is why you need to get out of this town and head to college ASAP so you can make real friends. Live life more."

"I have real friends."

"Dad and I don't count."

I gape at him. "Rude."

But I smile as I continue driving along the dark road. I have a few good friends in high school, mainly the other students in Yearbook, but I'm not close to anyone like I am with Carson and Dad. Not even my boyfriend, whom I am planning to break up before we leave for college.

Carson is probably my best friend. I don't care that that is the truth. My family is the best, even if they think I am a little high-strung.

I am just glad that Carson came home for Easter this year. He loves his work and rarely leaves California to come back to Missouri. I am determined to join him out there once I graduate college. Maybe I could even get a job at the same company.

"You know, Vince is taking me to prom, and we're going to this fancy lake house for prom weekend. So, I am living, thank you very much."

"Ooooo." He waggles his eyebrows. "Just make sure he wraps it. I can even get you some if you need."

"Seriously, C?" My face heats, and I keep all my focus on the road in front of me.

"I won't tell Dad." He pokes my arm, but then his tone sobers. "I'm serious, S. Have fun. I told you, I've got you and Dad. You don't need to spend all your time working and studying. It's your senior year. You have to live for

yourself, Syd. No one else is going to do it for you. We can't be perfect. You can't be perfect. Something is always going to go wrong, so just embrace what you can. No regrets."

"And you should be living your life, not sending half your money to us." I level him with the same serious tone.

"Trust me, I live my life plenty."

He chuckles and rolls down the window. Out of my peripheral, I see him throw an arm out the window. The chill night breeze fills the car.

When I roll to a stop at the next light, I poke him back. "Love you."

He looks at me with a silly smile and reaches out to ruffle my short blonde hair. "Love you, too. No regrets, okay?"

"No regrets." I grin.

A beep behind me signals the light change. I turn back to the road and start rolling through the intersection.

"Sydney!"

Carson's panicked yell is the only warning I have before the car starts spinning.

Everything moves fast and slow.

I don't understand what's going on. The world seems to endlessly swirl around me before coming to an abrupt stop. My body jerks with the force, and my vision blurs. Everything hurts. My head is pounding, and I slowly realize we were just hit. I can't see, everything is fading around me. I force my eyes to stay open, and make my head turn to look at my brother.

A guttural scream leaves my throat, and then the pain takes me under.

My eyes fly open.

There's a loud, quick beeping around me. Panic wracks my body as I take in the pristine white walls. My eyes flick to the IV in my hand and the hospital bed I'm resting on.

No.

No. No. No.

The sound of a door opening has my head swiveling.

My dad drops the coffee in his hand, and it splashes all over the white tiles as races toward me. Tears fill his eyes as he grips my hand lightly.

"Bug?"

"Carson?" I croak.

His eyes soften with sadness and then bleed with worry.

"Sydney," he says tentatively. "How old are you?"

I frown, confused by the question. But it's enough to rip me out of the painful memory. I haven't had a nightmare about the accident in years, and never one as real as that had been. Everything comes flooding back, but recent memories are still hazy. I fight through them.

"Twenty—" My voice stutters, and I see his eyes widen. "Twenty-six. Sorry," I rush out.

"Don't be. That's good. That's really good."

Relief floods his wrinkled face, and he lets out a sigh, patting my hand before pulling a chair to the side of the hospital bed.

My body itches at the familiarity of the scene. I hate hospitals. Hate being in them. Hate what they remind me of.

"Thank God, Sydney. You had me worried there." A watery tear drips down his face.

"What happened?"

"There was an accident; a car hit yours."

A new wave of panic rolls over me as flashes come back to me.

"The girls." The words leave me with such raw pain.

"They're fine. Just a bit bruised up, like you, but fine. The vehicle hit your side first, but the car you were in was quite the tank; it took most of the damage. The other driver died on impact though."

My chest hollows at the mention of death, but the relief I feel that the girls are all right wins out.

I let out a sigh only to wince at the pain it creates. My ribs feel like they're on fire.

My hand comes up to cup my side, but it sets off a jolt of pain in my shoulder. Stars burst in my vision.

"Are you sure nothing's broken?" I wheeze.

"Trust me, that boyfriend of yours made sure you had every test possible." He gives me a pointed look that says I have some explaining to do. "Your shoulder was dislo-cated, so they had to reset it. Your ribs have bruising, but there's nothing they can do other than monitor it. The oth-ers have some whiplash."

Suddenly, I break down in tears, everything becoming way too much. My dad starts crying as well, and it just spurs me on further. It hurts, but the emotions wrack my body with violent sobs.

I know better than to keep it in.

"Sydney."

I look up through blurred eyes, but I don't need to see to know who it is. That voice is written in my DNA.

"Parker," I sob.

The bed dips with his weight as his hands come around my face. The whites of his eyes are lined with red, making them look even more icy blue than usual.

"How are you feeling?"

"A little sore."

"Sorry." He immediately removes his touch.

"No." I fight through the fire in my shoulder to grab his hands. Our connection is what I need right now. Seeing him is what I need. "Don't be sorry."

He grips my hands more tightly and brings them up to his forehead briefly before placing a kiss on them. He looks up at me from our joined hands. Worry lines are thick between his brows.

"But I am. I am so fucking sorry, love."

"Why? It's not your fault."

"I should've made you stay in the car with us."

I shake my head, ignoring the way it thuds with the motion.

"If it wasn't me, it would've been Stevie." My heart tears at that thought, but I push the "what if" out of my mind. "You couldn't have stopped the car, Parker."

It is something that has taken me years to learn, and I wouldn't let the same emotions eat Parker alive like they had me.

Nothing that night would have stopped that drunk driver from smashing into Carson and me. Even though there were parts of me that had said it wouldn't have happened if I'd driven a few miles slower, or taken a different route home, or even if we'd stopped to get Carson the drive-through fries he'd wanted. There were always a million alternatives, but I couldn't live with regrets. Carson would hate me if I did. So, I would be that person for Parker.

"Besides, I'm fine."

Clearly, the watery smile I give him isn't very convincing because his gaze hardens.

"You scared me half to death. You weren't waking up, Syd. You weren't waking up. The doctor's said you would be fine but... Lee and Deer came to last night, and you just—" His voice cracks and a stray tear rolls down his cheek. "Fuck, love."

"I'm here, Parker."

"You can't go anywhere."

"I'm not. You're stuck with me."

"I thought you said it wasn't healthy to be codependent."

His teasing makes me smile, and he leans down and places a soft kiss to my nose. Warmth spreads throughout my body, healing me from the inside out.

"I didn't know, Syd."

I cock my head at the words, not understanding. "What?"

"Your brother."

My chest aches momentarily, and I glare at my dad with a sigh. "Really?"

"I was emotional. My anger might have been a little misplaced." He avoids my stare, looking very interested at a patch of light on the ceiling. "I was worried I'd lost another one."

I can't get mad at him for that. Plus, I knew I was going

to have to talk about it with Parker eventually.

"I'm sorry, Dad."

"It's fine, Bug. *You're fine.*"

The doctor comes in then and gives me a check-up, adjusting my IV and making sure I don't have a concussion or anything worse now that I'm awake. As he starts to leave, he is almost knocked over by the tattooed man barreling into the room.

"Is she awake?" Aleks asks.

Stevie and Jackson are hot on his heels, wheeling Lee and Deer in with them. My chest rips and repairs looking at the small smattering of bruises on my girls.

Aleks' green eyes light up when he sees me, and he all but shoves Parker aside to wrap me in a hug.

"Ow," I wince.

"Dude, careful." Jackson wrenches him off me, and he goes tumbling onto the floor with an oomph.

"Really, babe?" Stevie holds a hand out to lift him up.

I laugh at the scene, grateful for the slice of normalcy.

"How are you?" Stevie rounds Jackson and sits on the side of my bed opposite Parker.

I had a feeling I was going to be answering some iteration of that same question a lot.

"I don't feel that bad, honest."

I mean, it certainly felt like I'd just been hit by a car, but I wasn't going to worry anyone more than necessary.

"I'm sorry." Her chocolate eyes melt with guilt.

"I shouldn't have made you get in the car with us." Tears drip off Lee's bottom lashes as she wheels herself closer to the bed.

Deer is nibbling her bottom lip within an inch of its

life.

I look at all the worried faces around me.

All right. That is enough.

"Don't you all start." I push myself up, gritting through the pain. "Look, I'm going to say this once and once only. What happened isn't anyone's fault. There are a million things that can happen in any day, and we can't prevent them all." I steel them all with a hard look. "You're all going to do more damage worrying about the what ifs. Life can't move on if you are stuck in the past. What happened, happened, and everyone's okay. So, no regrets."

My dad rubs my arm, and I turn to him to see that knowing look in his eyes.

"No regrets," he whispers back to me.

I place my hand over his and squeeze. I've dealt with my demons, and sure, it is still hard for me to get behind the wheel, but I've done it. I would make sure the people around me don't suffer from the same mistakes I'd made.

"You're the best fucking thing in our lives, love. We'd be lost without you." Parker fiddles with my blanket.

"Yeah, without you, who would keep these fuckers in line?" Aleks jerks a thumb at his teammates.

"Me? You're the problem child, asshole," Jackson retorts.

"Boys, what have I told you about cursing?"

A beautiful blonde woman stands in the doorway. She has a regal elegance about her that has nothing to do with the flowing olive-green silk dress she's wearing.

"Priscilla, you were supposed to knock first."

"I was worried." She purses her pink lips and side-eyes the man who places a hand on her shoulder. Looking between the two of them, I am reminded exactly where Parker gets his stunning looks from. The entire Covington clan is unnaturally beautiful. "I'm glad to see you awake, dear."

"Thank you." I smile back at her, accepting the soothing air she radiates.

"Oh, is she alive?" Phoebe strolls in, shattering the calm.

"Pheebs, really?" Paige winces, following closely behind. The Covington sisters are opposites as always, one sharp and one soft.

There are entirely too many people in my room right now.

It is a little overwhelming, but I accept the love for what it is.

Although, now that I'm paying attention, this room is oddly large for a hospital room. Something tells me that the golden family before me had something to do with that.

Seeing all the Covingtons together triggers something in my brain. Something that has nausea rolling through me all over again.

"What day is it?"

A quiet look is shared between everyone, including my boyfriend, who is pointedly not looking at me.

I shoot my gaze at the one person who I know will answer me.

"What is the date and time?"

Phoebe's assessing eyes flick over me before she peers at her watch. "Sunday. Eleven eighteen a.m."

"Parker," I blanch, gripping his arm. "The championship. What the hell are you doing here?"

"It's fine." He gives me a soft smile.

"It's not."

I close my eyes as my brain whizzes, running through the championship schedule. Sunday is the *Final Destiny* run. It doesn't start until one, so he still has time. Relief runs through me. I don't know what hospital I am at or how far it is from the arena, but it can't be that far.

"You need to leave now. You can't miss the run."

He shakes his head. "I'm disqualified, Syd."

"What?"

How is he disqualified? Parker would never cheat, so there should be no reason for his disqualification.

"I didn't go."

I blink a few times, trying to process his words. Slowly, tears fill my eyes as I realize what he is saying.

"What? No. What do you mean?" I shoot a watery glare at everyone in the room. "Why did none of you do something about this?"

"I barely managed to get the boy to leave and eat some food. I doubt anyone could've gotten him to leave the building," my dad scoffs.

"He's right, honey," Pricilla adds. "He's stubborn like his father."

"He just wanted to make sure you were all right." Stevie's voice is soft as she runs a hand over my forearm.

I shake her off and push Parker with all the strength left in my body. My shoulder explodes with pain, but I welcome it, letting it fuel my fury.

"What's wrong with you? Why would you do that?"

"Sydney—"

"No." Guilt strangles my throat, cutting off my air. "Oh God. I ruined everything."

"Hey, hey," he hushes, bringing my face to his. "You did nothing."

"I—"

"What did you just say, Sydney Lake? What happened, happened, and everyone's okay. No regrets. And I don't have any regrets skipping the runs. I can always compete next year. There's always another championship. But there's not another you. And not being by your side? That I would've regretted. I wouldn't have been able to live with myself if I left you and something happened."

"It was more than just the championship," I whisper to him.

"And you told me you'd like me even if I was poor," he whispers back.

"But your family—"

"You are my family, too."

I love this boy in front of me.

I love him, and I know I have the power to fix at least some of this.

"You need to go." My voice is solid and sure.

"What?"

"You might not be able to win the championship, but you can still compete in the run."

"Sydney—"

"Parker Covington, I'm not fucking around."

Silence fills the room.

Jackson lets out a low whistle. "She just swore, dude."

"Shut up." Parker glares at him briefly before looking back at me. "I'm not leaving you."

"Don't be dumb, Parker. I'm perfectly fine. But if you don't go to that run right this very second, I promise you that I won't be the only person in a hospital bed."

Phoebe lets out a snort, and Paige pinches her.

"Go show Creep that he's no match for you. Show the world that you can beat him." I push a soft kiss to his lips. "You need to do this."

Because he would regret it if he didn't.

Parker would come to terms with his family because, at the end of the day, he would always have their love. While a part of him had worried about disappointing them, I know that would never be the case. They have the same love between them as my father and I have. So long as Parker is happy, they would be. And Parker's happiness lies with his gaming career. He would feel more disappointed in himself if he is left in the balance with Creep, if he doesn't give this a shot. He knew going into this championship that winning those first two runs was in the bag. It is the unknown of *Final Destiny* that will hang over him until he faces it.

I am going to make him face it.

"Listen to the girl," a rich British voice rumbles into the room.

Parker's hands fall from my jaw as everyone turns to look at the newcomer.

Suddenly, the room feels too full.

The formidable man strolling into the room has a thick head of silver hair and clear blue eyes. The very same eyes as four other people in this room. Philip Covington stops at the end of my bed, and I do my best to keep eye contact with him. Something tells me that I'll lose if I look away.

"Dad, what're you doing here?" Patrick Covington asks.

"My meeting with the Keltons ended early, so I thought I would stop by." He cocks his head, assessing me. "It's a pleasure to you meet you, Sydney."

"You too, sir." I swallow the ball in my throat.

He's a lot more intimidating than I expected. No wonder Parker felt pressure from him.

"What shall you do, Parker?"

His icy stare shifts from me to his grandson. I watch the rise of Parker's chest as he remains silent for a few beats. And then I see it, that slight uptick of his mouth, the barest hint of a smirk.

"I'm going to need a boatload of energy drinks."

Chapter
TWENTY-SEVEN

PARKER

"**R**un faster," Aleks yells at me.

"I'm faster than you!"

"You're both slow," Jackson calls from ahead of us.

The three of us are sprinting through the convention center. The good thing is we'd all slipped on our masks, so people are parting like the Red Sea for us as we navigate our way to the B stage.

I'd barely had enough time to stop by the hotel to pick up my gear before coming here. The two energy drinks I'd downed are not sitting happily in my stomach. I'd attempted a third one, but Jackson literally slapped it out of my hand, saying I would crash.

I am running on no sleep.

The last forty-eight hours were some of the worst of

my entire life.

I hadn't even second-guessed myself when Saturday morning rolled around. Everyone around me asked countless times if I was sure I didn't want to go to the championship. My family especially.

Eventually, I had locked the door to Sydney's hospital suite so it was only her father and me because I didn't want to deal with them. I'd just wanted Sydney. I'd just wanted her to be all right. All my worries were nothing compared to the fear I'd felt.

I didn't care about winning the championship, and I certainly didn't care about pleasing the whims of the fucking board.

But Sydney had been right.

I do care about this run.

I care because I want to prove to myself that I am the best. I want to prove that I can do this. It doesn't matter what anyone else thinks so long as I have that belief in myself.

It killed me to leave her in that hospital bed, but I saw that gleam in her eye. I saw how much she wanted this for me, and that's why I love her. We are a team.

There is a part of me that mourns the impending loss. My severance from the Covington Hotel Group won't be easy. My safety net will officially be gone. I will have nothing to fall back on other than myself.

Except I'm not alone.

The two guys running beside me are proof of that.

The girl in the hospital bed will always be mine. If I have Sydney, I can get through anything.

"And next, please welcome to the stage JustAGame."

The announcer's voice booms across the crowd as we push through the double doors and into the B room. We begin running down the stairs, passing bleacher after bleacher.

There are already five gamers on stage. JustAGame would be the sixth.

I have minutes to get myself up there.

"Lastly, he's your top pick and the self-proclaimed *Final Destiny* king, CreepyPillows."

Creep bounds onto the stage, raising his arms to hype the crowd. They cheer for him, shaking the air around us.

"Get your ass up here, English."

The crowd hushes, and everyone looks around until their gazes land on us. I halt in my progress, looking up to see that Creep has snatched the microphone from the announcer on stage. He grins down at me with that punchable face.

This is it. My moment of no return.

Aleks and Jackson clap a hand on either shoulder.

"You've got this, brother." Jackson nods.

"Kick their asses." Aleks pushes me forward.

I pick up my pace, racing down the stairs and then swerving around the mosh pit. A security guard joins me, guiding me quickly backstage and then to a set of stairs to lead me onto the stage.

"Please give a welcome to EnglishCoffee."

Nerves rattle through me.

I step onto the stage to the thunderous crowd chanting my name. There is no doubt they know what I've been going through. Every media outlet has been covering the accident.

I take my place at the only free monitor.

The one right next to Creep.

Fuck.

I swallow, peeling off my mask and letting my eyes adjust to the lighting. I shove it in my backpack and pull out my headset.

"You look like shit."

I side-eye Creep with a sarcastic smile. "Thanks."

"You better give it your all, English."

As if I would give anything less.

"Just watch."

Creep gives me a grin as he slides on his neon orange headset. I follow suit, clicking my noise-cancelling into place.

I might be fighting this battle at half HP, but that won't stop me.

I brace my left hand on the keyboard, my right hand curving around the mouse. The cursor hovers over the start button, and I close my eyes. I picture the woman who pushed me here.

I feel her with me, her support and warmth. Syd's cherry scent still clings to my skin, and it sets me at equilibrium. My power surges, and I open my eyes, ready and full of fight.

That and the energy drinks start to kick in. Ungodly high amounts of caffeine are filtering through my bloodstream. They basically function like a stat potion, souping me up for the battle.

"Three. Two."

Jitters run through me.

I definitely drank way too much caffeine.

"One."

My pointer finger reacts on instinct, clicking on the Start button.

The second the opening sequence begins to play out, my nerves freeze and die. A practiced cool falls over me. I let my field of vision zero in on just the monitor before me.

I remember who I am. I remember what I've been training for.

This time around, I use everything in my arsenal. That skip I didn't implement last time? I execute it perfectly. A five-minute boost. The neo-grenade trick one of Mathias' guys saw Creep use in the replay? I use it as well. I use it better.

I don't leave any card unturned.

I'm halfway through the second hour when I get to the same part I faltered at in Miami. My jaw clenches as my hawk eyes zone in on my character world traveling. Butterflies flurry in my stomach as I keep my finger poised on the right click, waiting to double-tap it. My character drops to the ground, and I mash the mouse, my shotgun exploding into the dirt.

The glitch activates.

I watch as my dystopian cowboy goes flying across the barren town. When he lands at the mission point, I let out a small sigh of relief.

A small victory, but there's still more I need to do.

I curse when one of my frag bombs goes awry, but I smile when the nerve gas mission completes without a hitch.

I'm getting closer and closer to the end, and I have no clue if I've done enough.

But I still have one last trick up my sleeve.

There's a clip that I know will guarantee my win, but the added time to execute it will end me if it doesn't all go perfectly.

I weigh my options.

Take the risk or not?

Fuck it.

No regrets.

I successfully clip my character through a wall into a house that would otherwise be inaccessible. From here I can get to the guard, who is normally sleeping at this time of night, and murder him for his helicopter key.

"Sorry, mate."

I headshot him with my revolver and then access his inventory for the key. My morality meter takes a dip, but this time, it's still within the yellow. A few minutes later, I make it to the helicopter and pray that this is going to work.

I get in and begin flying it to the corner of the map. I keep going and going, aiming for a specific pixelated triangle in the mountain range. My finger doesn't let up from the D key.

Sweat breaks out across my forehead.

I'm also eighty percent sure I need to piss right now. Those energy drinks did wonders keeping me awake, but they went right through me. Noob mistake before a three-hour run.

I just need to get this right, and then I'll be done in no time.

My breath hitches as I watch the helicopter spin out of control, clipping through the mountain range into some unforeseen blackness on screen. It spits back out on the other side, into what looks like a control room. I quickly jump out of the helicopter before it crashes in the small space and goes up in flames. Adrenaline pumping through me, I run my character toward the NPC sitting at the large desk and merk him with my revolver.

There's a pause as the game attempts to catch up to my actions. Finally, the code realizes I've just killed the final boss and sets itself back on course.

The final cutscene plays, and I grin.

I fucking did it.

I rip off my headphones and stand, letting loose a howling cheer.

A quick glance to my right shows that everyone else is still finishing. I look up at the jumbo screen, and tears bead my eyes when I see my time. Three hours and two minutes. My body shakes.

A new fucking record.

And it's on the official books.

I did it.

The crowd chants around me, and I feel nothing but pure euphoria in this moment. Dopamine and pride flood my system. The only thing that would make this better is if Sydney were here. I have no doubt she is watching the livestream from the hospital.

God, I can't wait to see her.

Two bodies crash into me, almost knocking me to the ground as they envelop me in a hug.

"You crushed that." Jackson squeezes tighter, attempting to remove all the air from my body.

"Thanks," I wheeze out.

"Yeah, congrats, dude!" Aleks grins down at me. "How

are we going to celebrate?"

"Honestly, I just want to see Syd."

"Fair." Aleks shrugs. "But we're going to do something eventually."

"Oh, yeah. We'll get proper pissed later."

"That's my boy."

"All right, let's leave the winner to do his glory round." Jackson inclines his head to the reporters standing by. "We'll catch you later, 'kay?"

I give them a nod, and they file offstage.

I do my due diligence and thank the crowd before standing off to the side to chat with the announcers about the run.

A cheer has my head swiveling back up to the screen, and I see Creep's time finalized. My eyes drift down to sandy-haired Australian, who gives me a droll look before he stands up and lazily makes his way over to me.

"I kind of hate you right now."

"Why?" I tilt my head with a smirk. "Because you know if I'd competed in the whole championship, I would've left you in the dust?"

"Yeah."

I blink, his honesty catching me off guard.

"You better show up next year." He pokes me in the chest.

"Just tell me you're obsessed with me, Creep."

"In your fucking dreams, English." He begins to walk past me but throws his head back briefly. "Enjoy the victory while you can; I'll be reclaiming my crown soon enough."

I smile, triumph settling warmly in my chest as I move to take a few photos for the waiting paparazzi and answer their questions. I finish up by crouching down and shaking the hands of some fans in the front row, smiling for the numerous selfies.

I sling my backpack over my shoulder and exit backstage to find the nearest toilet because I'm about to piss straight energy drink at this point.

When I exit the loo, my eyes snag on my grandfather. He stands off to the side, arms crossed over his chest, watching me intently. I gulp, giving him a tense wave as he nods at me.

I take one step toward him, watching him straighten, before I quickly pivot.

With breakneck speed, I take off, weaving through the smattering of people huddled backstage.

Yeah. Nah.

Don't really want to deal with that right now.

My entire body jerks as someone yanks on my backpack. I let out a grunt as my shoulder is almost torn from its socket.

I whip my head around, ready to bite the person's head off, but the fire dies when I look at the wiry man peering down at me.

"Mister Covington, really?" Frank admonishes.

"Worth a shot." I grin at him, but inside I'm glaring daggers.

The man is a snake with a freakishly strong grip. He wouldn't be my grandfather's right hand if he didn't anticipate my moves, though.

"I'm not sure what your plan was. You do remember we drove here." Frank continues to keep ahold of my backpack as he leads me back through the crowds.

"There's this really great invention called a rideshare app. Ever heard of it?"

Frank sighs and says nothing more as he returns me to my grandfather. I feel like a five-year-old who just got caught with their hand in the cookie jar.

I open my mouth to speak, but my grandfather holds up a hand.

"Good job."

"Thank you," I stammer. I say nothing else, waiting for the other shoe to drop.

"I thought we could chat in the car back to the hospital. I figured that's where you would want to go." He angles his head to the side and starts walking off.

My body doesn't move for a few seconds, catching up to the unexpected turn of events. I jog to catch up to my grandfather, narrowing my eyes at him, trying to decipher what he was playing at.

We go through the back exit, and Frank opens the door to the rental limo for us. I slip onto the fresh, black leather, my hands tight around my backpack in silence. Traffic is thick on the Strip, and I stare out at the moving lights while I wait for grandfather to make the first move.

"That was impressive, Parker."

"Pardon?" I whip my head around.

"Your game, it was impressive to see it in person." Grandfather lifts his eyes from his cellphone and gives me a warm smile. "I still don't fully understand it, but it was entertaining to watch."

"Thank you." Hope bubbles in my chest.

"The crowd was excited by everything you did. They loved you. They *do* love you. It's quite the community you have, and it's clear how influential you are."

I grin now. "The community is what makes it the best. It's not just the fans, but the other gamers, too. In the speedrun community, we work together on new ways to outsmart the system."

Grandfather hums, crossing his ankles. "And you broke a record, correct?"

"I did. I now hold the world's fastest speedrun for *Final Destiny*."

I have no doubt that Creep would try to dethrone me as quickly as possible, but I don't care. I'd accomplished what I'd set out to achieve, and I'd take the win.

"You didn't give up, Parker. I'm proud of you."

Chills race over my skin at the praise. But because I'm a masochist, I say, "Even though I didn't win the championship?"

"This was never meant to be a punishment, Parker. I didn't enter into this agreement hoping you would fail."

I wince, knowing I had done just that.

His face softens as he purses his thin lips. "Come here." He pats the seat next to him.

I crouch and shuffle my way to the other side of the limo to sit beside him.

"I'm not going to stop the vote, Parker. You have to take responsibility for your choices. Part of becoming an adult is accepting your failures just as much as your wins; it's the only way you'll continue to grow."

I know he is right. It is how I made it this far in my gaming career. I could've lost the Miami tournament and thrown in the towel. I could have vowed to never play *Final Destiny* again or to never face Creep. Instead, I used the anger of my loss to train harder. I took that loss, and I turned it into one of the biggest wins of my career.

Hearing the crowd chant "English" over and over reminded me that I'm not just a Covington. That I really have made a name for myself, one that I am proud of.

"I was holding myself back," I whisper in realization.

Grandfather pats my leg. "Took you long enough."

"What do you mean?"

"I mean you can't reach for the stars if you keep one foot on the ground, son. If you are going to commit to your career, if you are going to be the best, you have to give it your all. And I'll never be disappointed in you so long as you are giving it one hundred percent. You showed that today. You showed me that, even against the odds, you'll fight, and you'll come out on top." He grins at me now, and the truth of his words sinks into my bones, rewriting the very way I look at life. "I told you, I'm proud of you, Parker. Just because you're no longer the heir doesn't mean you're not part of this family. You're still a Covington. You're still my grandson."

"Damn straight, I'm still a Covington." I grin back.

He is right. I am fucking proud of myself. I might not have won the championship, but proving myself against Creep had been way more important.

"There seems to be quite a bit of money in this industry of yours. Maybe we'll look at sponsoring one of those esports teams."

"Always looking to make more money, aren't you?" I roll my eyes.

"I told you, it's always about the money."

The car rolls to a stop, and Frank hops out to open the

door.

"How long do I have?" I ask my grandfather as we make our way through the hospital.

"The board votes in four weeks, just before the holidays."

"A lovely Christmas gift for them," I snort, hitting the lift for the floor of private suites Syd is located on.

There is one thing my grandfather missed.

I'm not just going to sit around and wait for the board to strip me of my power.

I accept the fact that I have to step down as heir. If I keep holding on to that shield, I would never move forward. I need to be free of that weight so I can soar to new heights on my own. I am EnglishCoffee, and I would become the best gamer there is.

But I would do it on my own terms; I wouldn't do it just because the board bullied me into it.

In fact, I would make them regret pushing me.

All this time, I thought I couldn't have my cake and eat it, too. Technically, I can't. But that doesn't mean I can't give my cake to someone else.

I stop short of Sydney's room and smile at the blonde frowning at her phone in the corridor.

"Paige, can I talk to you?"

Chapter
TWENTY-EIGHT

SYDNEY

66 don't get how you drink this stuff." Parker screws his nose up as he sips on the red juice. "It tastes like dirt."

"That's because the only things you ingest are champagne and energy drinks. I think your body rejects anything healthy." I make a loud sucking noise as I finish my own juice.

It's a carrot, beet, orange, and ginger blend, and it's my favorite. But no matter how many times I order it for the boys, Jackson and Parker won't stop acting like I'm making them drink battery acid.

Aleksander pretends he hates it, but he always finishes his before even I do. That's a win at least.

"I'm healthy," he challenges, kicking a stray pebble on the sandy sidewalk.

"Sure," I drawl, tossing my empty cup into the nearest recycling bin.

The action causes my jaw to clench slightly at the slight tug of pain.

My ribs are still a little bruised. I've been taking it easy, hoping it would speed up the recovery, and it's worked, mostly. I still can't lift anything heavy, but I can officially reach up and grab things off the top shelf without feeling like someone is punching me in the process.

I can also take full breaths again, which is why I wanted to walk along the ocean and enjoy the salty, fresh air.

It's taken three weeks to get to this point.

I'd spent most of that time resting up in Missouri after Vegas. Partially, it was because I was heading there for Thanksgiving anyway, and partially, it was because I didn't want my dad to be more worried than he already was. It gave him a sense of comfort to be able to watch over me.

Of course, Parker had flown out to join us between all his press events. He is in even higher demand since his record-breaking win at the Divizion Championship Series. I, personally, am proud of myself for not joining him at those events.

All right, I'd tried to, but my body physically hadn't let me.

On the plus side, being practically bedridden had shown me that I don't need to micromanage the boys as much as I have been. Surprisingly, they'd behaved at all their events. I'm not sure how long it will last, but I am grateful for it.

Parker throws the last third of his juice in a nearby

trash can, and I scowl at him as he slings an arm over my shoulders.

I huddle into his warmth, saving myself from the cool December air rolling off the dark blue ocean.

"What's going on in that mind of yours, love?"

"Just thinking how impressed I am none of you boys have done anything ridiculous for almost a month."

"That you know of."

My eyes flick up, and I pinch my brows together.

"Kidding, kidding," he laughs.

"You better be."

We finally make it back to the beach parking lot, and Parker unlocks the Porsche, opening the door for me.

I hesitate in front of the car for a second before sliding into the passenger seat, scolding myself in the process. I'd done a lot better this time around after the accident. There are still those moments of panic that have resurfaced after so many years, but another added bonus to going back to Missouri is that I'd been able to start therapy back up to make sure I wouldn't fall prey to my old fears.

I am doing pretty well, if I say so myself.

The nightmares are dwindling, I hadn't had any panic attacks, and I'm not avoiding cars.

Although, my desire to get back behind the wheel is becoming nonexistent.

"Mind if I take us somewhere?"

I pull my attention from the ocean breezing past and look at the blond prince beside me. Somehow, he gets more and more hot every single day.

"Sure."

We pull off the highway and start weaving around a

couple of side streets. My eyes dart around our surroundings, trying to figure out where we are going. Eventually, my eyes catch on a sign for an out-of-service highway, and the car rolls to a stop just at the entrance, as he shifts it into park.

I keep my mouth shut, not wanting to sound skeptical. I'm not going to lie. The way he'd framed it, I thought it was going to be somewhere a little more romantic than, well, this.

My juice might taste like dirt to him, but this road literally is dirt.

"How long has it been?"

"What?"

"Since you've driven. How long has it been?" he clarifies slowly.

"Uh, I stopped around the time you hired me."

"Were you driving a lot before that?"

Alarm bells begin ringing in my head.

"Not really." I shake my head. "Why?"

He nods his head a few times, thinking about something. Something that I instinctively know I'm not going to like.

"Do you want to drive again?"

It isn't the question I'd expected.

There is such clear honesty swirling in his eyes that it makes my chest tighten.

I let out a sigh and let my head fall back against the headrest.

"I don't know."

It is the truth. I don't really need to drive. There is the company rideshare account, plus Francis and the boys.

Even Stevie drives me sometimes, although she is an awful driver. Sure, it means I am reliant on people but…

An ugly spore sprouts deep within my chest the more I toil with the thoughts. It begins to stain me from the inside out, clawing at me to look at it. To acknowledge what I'd been ignoring.

That I'd fallen back into my old pattern.

It isn't that bad, honestly. It's not like I am avoiding being in cars all together. But just glancing at the wheel of the car and imagining my own hands on it has a knot forming at the base of my throat.

Crap.

"Does it scare you?"

Parker places his hands on top of mine, and it's then that I realize I've been fidgeting with my fingers.

"I don't know." My voice is softer this time.

It's also a lie.

Parker unbuckles his seatbelt and gets out of the car. I watch as he crosses to my door and pulls it open. He holds a hand out to me, and I watch it warily.

"Do you trust me?"

"Yes."

"Then *trust* me."

I know where this is going. I'm not oblivious. And yet there is a part of me that is thankful. Because I know I don't have the strength to force myself to do this alone. But Parker? Having him tell me that it is okay, that I can do this, somehow that makes it all better. I am relieved to give the power to someone else.

I undo my seatbelt and take his hand. I let him lead me to the driver's side, and my heart rate begins to spike.

My eyes dart all over the interior of the car as he lowers me into the seat and fiddles to get it into position for me. I don't move an inch, staying perfectly still as he leans in and clicks my belt in for me.

That click resounds in my ears, like a gun being cocked.

"Breathe, love."

I zone back in and notice Parker has taken a seat next to me.

"I'm not really sure a Porsche is the best car to get back into driving," I deflect.

"It's a straight shot. Six miles of nothing but road that comes to a stop. You can't mess it up."

"And if I do?"

"This is my cheapest car, it's fine."

He says it as though he has forgotten I know exactly how much effort—and money—he went through to get these custom blue sports cars. I am grateful this isn't his new Lamborghini, I guess.

"My license is expired," I tell him.

"There are no police here. It's an abandoned highway."

"I don't think I can do this."

My palms sweat.

"I know you can."

"Why does this matter so much to you?"

"Because you matter to me." I shiver at the sincerity, his words rippling over my skin in a cool wave. "I hate the thought that this fear might still rule you. I want to help you get control of that again. Just like you helped me."

"I didn't help you."

"Ah, that's where you're wrong, love. I wouldn't have gone to the run in Vegas if you didn't push me to leave that hospital room, and I would've regretted it."

Regret.

I would regret letting this fear fester.

I want to take that control back.

My hands curl around the steering wheel, and I let my-self just feel the smooth leather for a moment. My chest constricts, but I take several deep breaths, letting myself even out.

I move my foot to the gas pedal and pause.

Wait.

Which side was it on again?

"Right." Parker slides his hand behind my neck and begins massaging it.

Heat flushes my cheeks, but some of the tension starts to ease away at his contact.

"You have to use your thumb to push down on the cen-ter of the gear shift, and then you can move it into drive."

I nod, repeating the instructions silently in my mind as my hand rests on the knob.

Looking ahead, the road seems a lot longer than six miles.

I just focus on the feeling of Parker's hands.

Mechanically, I shift the car into drive. My foot presses down on the pedal, and the car purrs to life. The sound of the engine startles me, and I immediately slam my foot on the brake. The car jerks forward slightly. My body catches on the seatbelt.

I want the ground to swallow me up right now.

"Good start," Parker encourages.

I look at him doubtfully, but his smile doesn't wane.

"Try again."

A small puff of air passes my lips, and I slowly let the tension out of my foot, easing it off the brake. The car rolls forward.

My heart pounds in my ears.

"That's it. Now, the gas pedal."

I rest my foot over the pedal and apply the least amount of pressure possible. This time, I'm ready for the feel of the engine around me. The car gently continues its progression forward.

"Nice, just a little more."

I bite my lip.

"Come on, Syd." Parker keeps up his ministration, kneading my tight neck muscles. "You've got this."

"Okay."

The speedometer crawls higher as I press my foot down. I get used to the feeling of the car humming around my body and the way the driver's seat hugs me.

Soon, we're moving at a casual fifteen miles per hour up the derelict highway. It's not as awful looking as I'd first perceived it to be. The higher we get, the clearer the view becomes, and my curiosity heightens at what awaits me at the top.

"Perfect, at this speed we'll reach the top in twenty minutes," he softly teases.

I purse my lips. "I thought I could take my time."

"You can, or you can go a little faster; we're not in a school zone."

I risk a glance in the rearview mirror, then the side mirrors. There is no one else around.

Nerves wriggle their way through my body, and I flex the iron grip I have on the wheel. So far, it has been going well.

I push down a little more, watching as the number climbs.

Every time I think I might freak out, every time my shoulders tense and my thighs lock, Parker's there with soft words and deft fingers, chasing the fear away.

I focus on the feeling of his thumb rubbing strong circles up the length of my neck. The way his fingers occasionally drum out a calming beat across my skin.

After a few more minutes pass, he reaches forward and turns up the music volume, allowing a small trickling of sound to filter through the car. A smile tugs at my lips as I recognize one of my current favorite songs.

I'm cruising at a solid thirty miles per hour by the time the car crests the hill. I notice that the highway begins to fall away to the natural elements, the asphalt broken up by sprouting weeds and dirt.

"You can stop here."

I nod, bringing my foot to the brake and inching the car to a stop. Parker reaches down to shift the vehicle into park with his free hand, but he uses the one on my neck to angle my face toward him.

The golden smile on his face is contagious, and I feel the corners of my lips tugging as my own face splits into a grin.

"You did it. You fucking did it, Syd."

His free hand cups my jaw, and he pulls me into a dizzying kiss. All the nerves running through me pop and fizzle like champagne, turning into sheer joy. My heart warms, and my tongue slides against his for the briefest moment.

Then, I laugh.

I laugh with no regret, the sound bubbling out of me. My head tilts back, and I close my eyes as my chest continues to rumble with the giggles.

Parker's thumb glides across my cheek, and I distantly register the wetness. Tears pool in the corners of my eyes, spilling from me with no stop.

I just laugh harder until it turns into a sob.

Parker rushes from the car, running to my side and pulling open the door. He undoes my seatbelt and pulls me into his arms. I curl into his chest, letting him slowly lift me up as the tears continue to flow freely from my body.

They aren't sad tears, not completely. Yes, there's a part of them that still mourns my brother, that weeps for the fear and pain I went through in each accident.

But more than anything, they are tears of freedom.

They're the realization that I'm moving forward. That I'm letting go of the last tendrils of hurt that I was clutching onto. That I am finally allowing myself to heed my brother's words and *live*.

No regrets.

These tears are grateful. Grateful for the man holding me. The man who vowed to never leave my side and has proven just that. The man who has pushed me just as much as I've pushed him. The man I've held feelings for, for far too long.

The man I just might be in love with.

I blink through groggy eyes as I land on a soft mattress. My eyes adjust to the darkness, and I register Parker tucking me into his bed.

"What time is it?"

"Half past."

The last thing I remember is being curled up in his arms as we sat on a bench and watched the sunset fall behind the ocean, chatting ideally about life. I told him about my brother, our childhood and everything between. The nights when I would catch him sneaking in after curfew. The afternoons he would pick me up from school and take me for fro-yo. That he'd indulged me and played dolls as a preteen when anyone else would have laughed. The way he'd also played video games, and I would sit with him on the couch as he played and would doodle in my coloring books. How Carson had been my knight, but that I'd been the one in control of the car when his life ended. How his death broke me for years. That I'd moved to California in memory of him.

"Thank you," I whisper. "For everything."

"I'd move the moon for you, Sydney. You don't even need to ask."

He curls into bed behind me, and I drift off in the comfort of his arms and the knowledge that I never want to leave them.

I watch him sleeping next to me. I memorize every inch of his face. The strong blond brows, the small scar on his temple, the barest hint of stubble on his chin.

My hand itches to reach out to trace the gentle slope of his nose. My thumb begs to rub over his full bottom lip.

The more I look at him, the more I want him.

His lashes flutter seconds before his eyes open. Those baby blues are the kind of color women go mad for. They hold every emotion under the sun, clear as day. Right now, they speak a story of adoration, and I smile in response.

"Hey, beautiful." Parker juts his neck forward to place a kiss on the tip of my nose.

"Why do you always do that?" The question leaves my mouth instead of staying in my brain. I wince before giving him a sheepish grin. "Morning, handsome."

Parker huffs out a laugh, the corners of his eyes crinkling before he plops another kiss atop my nose.

"I do this because it's instinct. Every time I look at you, the air is stolen from my lungs, and all that remains is this need to be with you, to be touching you." I suck in a breath at his words. "That, and you have the cutest button nose that just begs to be kissed. It's not my fault you have such a kissable face. Just reap the benefits, love." He throws me a cheeky grin before he lifts out of the sheets. I lament the loss of his warmth as he pads into the ensuite.

I watch him through hooded eyes as he walks back into the bedroom. Parker quirks a brow, running a hand through his messy platinum hair.

"If you keep looking at me like that, I might just eat you for breakfast."

"Maybe that's what I want."

Heat blazes across his baby blues as that growing want swirls low in my belly.

"Be careful, Sydney." His voice is low and thick.

I let my gaze trail his naked figure. I don't know why I ever got mad at him for sleeping nude. He is sculpted like a statue.

Slowly, I lift the sheets from my body. When Parker had put me to bed last night, he'd taken off my clothes, so I am just in my lingerie.

I drag my ring finger languidly up my bare stomach and through the shallow valley of my breasts and across my shoulder. I butterfly my left leg and drop my other hand to trace a path up my inner thigh, pausing right at the seam of my panties.

Parker reaches down and strokes his thickening cock, watching my every move with the precision of a pro gamer.

My eyes are locked on his the entire time, and the tension between us grows hot and heavy.

I bite my lip and let my finger dip under the lace. I inhale deeply as I feel the gathering wetness between my thighs.

Parker pounces on the bed at a speed I can't even track, positioning himself between my legs.

"Come on, Sydney. Show me how much that pretty cunt glistens for me."

My stomach flips at his words.

He tears off my panties and runs two fingers up my slit, bringing my want to his mouth and sucking on it.

"My favorite meal." He grins before hauling me above him and switching our positions. "Now sit on my face and ride me. I want to drown in your taste."

His tongue dips into me, and I try not to crush him.

"Fucking suffocate me," he growls from below before

he grips my hips and forces me down.

I squirm almost instantly at the intense pressure his tongue creates dipping into me. For all his teasing words, this boy has a mouth that works wonders. I don't even have to remind myself to relax into the feeling. When I'm with Parker, he's the only thing on my mind.

There is no doubt that he has ruined me for anyone else.

My breath hitches as his finger starts to rub quick, hard circles on my clit. His tongue and finger work in tandem, like a synchronized swimming team, teasing me closer and closer to the edge. My hips move on their own, matching his pace.

It feels like I am racing up a spiral staircase; with each step, my orgasm crests higher and higher.

I lose myself in the feeling, tipping my head back and taking everything for my own. He said to suffocate him, and suffocate him I would. My hips grind against his mouth, plunging his tongue deeper and deeper.

The intensity sends me jumping off the top of the staircase, and I dive into the abyss.

My thighs tighten around Parker as my pelvis pushes off the mattress with the orgasm pulsing through me. Parker's fingers dip into the rolls on my hips as he keeps me from lifting off him completely, drinking me in.

Just as the high starts to wane, he flicks his tongue over my sensitive clit and my hips buck again. He pulls out from under me and grins. "Delicious."

He sits up and leans forward, capturing me in a blinding kiss. My hands curve into his shoulders, my nails biting into his skin as I pull him to me. He tugs on my lower lip, and the small flash of pain has my body heating again.

Parker trails his tongue up my neck before sucking on my earlobe. His voice is low and raspy as he whispers into my ear.

"I want to watch that ass jiggle as I pound into your sweet cunt from behind."

His dirty words steal the breath from my lungs and send a fresh wave of desire through me.

Need is the only thing on my mind, the need for him to be inside me.

I immediately flip over, pushing myself on all fours. My pussy still pulses as the remnants of my orgasm beat through me.

I look at him over my shoulder. Parker watches at me with the heat of a thousand suns, stroking his cock languidly.

My mouth waters at the sight of his strong hands on his enormous length. Pride ignites within me at the knowledge that I'm the one who makes him that hard.

"Come on, or were you all talk?" I tease, but it comes out all breathy.

He smirks, pulling a condom from his nightstand and rolling it on.

I keep my eyes on him the entire time, never leaving him once. His icy blues stay on me as one hand grips the globe of my ass. He guides his thick cock up my wet center, and I bite back a moan at the sensation.

I'm hungry for him. Hungry for all of him.

His tip pushes in, teasing.

Then he slams into me fully, and I cry out in relief, watching as he smirks. He pistons in and out, filling me to the brim.

My arms give out, and my chest pushes into the mattress as he picks up his rhythm. The new angle deepens his thrusts, and we both moan at the sensation.

I love the way he stretches me completely, becoming one with me. I lose myself in the feeling.

Parker's grip on my ass tightens, and his thumb inches dangerously close to a very different hole.

"Oh my God," I gasp as it sends a zing through my body.

Parker lets out a deep laugh. "Oh?"

His thumb rubs a bit closer, and my stomach does a flip.

"This okay?"

"Yes," I breathe.

His finger continues to rim the outside of my ass as he pounds into me, and my core tightens as my senses short-circuit.

"Oh God, oh God, oh God," I chant, my voice pitching higher with each repetition.

"Am I your god now?"

"You can be whatever you want if you keep that up."

"What if I told you it could be better?"

"I—" I gasp as he slams back into me, stars bursting in my eyes. "I'd say show me."

He pauses in his pounding and reaches across to pull his nightstand open. Through watery eyes I recognize the bottle of lube. I suck in a breath as the cold liquid hits me, the feeling strangely sensitive.

Parker resumes moving inside me, but it's slower this time as his finger continues to rim me in time with his rhythm. My core tightens in expectation.

My body begins to relax as my orgasm continues its steady build. The tip of Parker's finger pushes, and I gasp so loudly, it's like I steal all the air around us. The sensation is odd at first, but I quickly become acclimated.

"How does it feel?"

"Good," I hum, pressing farther into him, aching for release.

His speed picks up, and his finger pushes in more. My body completely overloads with pleasure at the dual sensations. I've never felt anything like this before, and I don't want it to stop. I want more. I want everything he can give me.

"God, I love this ass," he grunts. "You're so fucking sexy."

The guttural tone of his voice and the praise send me over the edge. My orgasm cascades over me like the final note in a sonata. My body chimes with satisfaction as I come.

"Oh, God, Parker."

I'm not sure how, but it seems like every orgasm with Parker is better than the last.

I won't tell him because I don't need to feed his self-love any more than necessary, but I am starting think he wields some sort of sex magic.

"Fuck, Syd, I'm coming."

His hands grip my ass cheeks so hard they burn as he pounds into me, pushing me farther into the mattress. He comes with a grunt, and I look over my shoulder to watch him fall off the edge.

He tips his head back, and I admire my prince as he

gives me a lazy grin.

"Best sex."

"Definitely one for the books." I smile.

He pulls out of me and places a kiss on my nose before he throws the condom in his trash can. He grabs a pair of discarded sweatpants from the floor and slips them on.

"Where are you going?" I ask.

"To get us some breakfast from the kitchen. I need some fuel before we go round two."

"Round two?" I squeak.

I'm not sure my vagina can handle that.

He sits on the corner of the bed and pushes my sweaty bangs from my forehead.

"I can't get enough of you, Sydney."

I smile at him. "You better bring back a feast and lots of coffee."

He boops my nose, and I watch as he leaves the room, keeping my eyes on his ass the entire time. I guess we really are a perfect match. An ass-obsessed couple.

I laugh to myself and roll over, staring up at the ceiling.

I have no regrets.

Chapter
TWENTY-NINE

SYDNEY

"You're fired."

I blink at the man on the screen in front of me.

"I'm sorry, what?"

"I said you're fired, Sydney. Effective immediately. You violated your contract; there's nothing I can do."

"Mathias, I—"

"Happy holidays."

The screen goes black, and I just stare at myself in the reflection.

What the hell?

I attempt to call him back, but he just declines it.

Who fires someone like that? That can't be legal. In fact, I am sure it isn't.

Not only that, but I'd worked for the man for five years.

Five. Years.

And that's how he fires me?

Seriously?

Happy holidays, my butt.

Anger bubbles in my blood as I pull up my email and begin typing an extremely passive-aggressive message.

"Everything okay, love?" Parker pads into the bedroom, buttoning up his navy blue shirt.

"Mathias just freaking fired me," I seethe. I try to keep myself from screeching the words. The last thing I need is for the entire Covington clan to hear this.

Parker, Phoebe, my father, and I had flown to London on the private jet a few days ago. We spent some time exploring the city.

I've never been to the UK before, and Parker hadn't minded indulging my every whim as I'd giddily dragged us to every tourist attraction.

Of course, in true Parker fashion, he had to take it to the next level, even booking us a private helicopter ride and exclusive museum tours. We'd stayed at the Covington townhouse in Kensington, spending the early mornings strolling the leafy walking paths of Holland Park. We made the drive up to Buckinghamshire, where their other residence is, yesterday for the holidays.

I'd had expectations of what the Covington mansion would look like.

I'd been totally wrong.

It is an entire estate, acres and acres of land sprawled out, with a central mansion that can house a hundred people, without fail.

It looks like something out of a historical romance

novel. Every room is beautifully detailed in the English Baroque style, giving it a regal palace feel. There is even a sprawling garden that I know would take me days to fully explore.

The images I'd concocted in my mind hadn't held a candle to what the place truly looks like. If this is how beautiful it looks in the winter, I can't wait to see it in the summer when all the trees and flowers are in bloom.

"He said I broke my contract, but I have no idea how he even found out we were dating." I continue typing my email.

I had known this would come to a head eventually, but I hadn't been prepared for it to happen now. I'm not ready. Sure, I have a little nest egg tucked away, but… I've been trying to find a loophole that would let me keep working with the guys. I had been planning to talk with Paige about it, see if maybe I could get around it by just being Aleks and Jackson's publicist.

"Oh, I told him we were dating."

My hands freeze on the keys, and I jerk my head up at Parker.

"What?"

"Well, Mathias had to fire you."

My brain short-circuits, thinking it has heard him wrong.

"It was the only way to get you a new contract."

"I'm sorry, what?" I blink as confusion wars with anger.

"Yeah, unfortunately, the one you signed with Mathias was pretty ironclad." Parker cocks his head in the full-length mirror, fixing a stray piece of hair. "Paige couldn't find a loophole even after pouring over it for hours. However, she still came up with a solution. A pretty good one, honestly."

"Which was getting me fired? Seriously."

"No. Well, technically, yes."

"Parker." I sigh at the lack of clear communication.

"Instead of having you work for us through Mathias' firm, we're hiring you directly. Congratulations, your unemployment lasted three minutes and eleven seconds." He turns and grins at me.

"So, you fired me...just to hire me." I say the words slowly, testing them on my tongue. "I lost my job, but I didn't lose my job."

"Correct. Paige said she'd get you a new contract by end of day." Parker pulls a designer tie from a drawer in his ridiculously large walk-in closet before winking at me. "You're looking at your new boss, baby."

I roll my eyes and watch as he loops it around his neck with deft fingers, using the time to wrap my head around his words. Technically, Parker had always been my boss, it was just that Mathias was also my boss on top of the boys. Ugh. It is too much to think about.

"Mathias still didn't have to be that rude about it." I attempt to hold onto some of my anger, but it fizzles out to ambivalent annoyance. "And you could have warned me."

"In fairness, I didn't think he'd call you today." He shrugs, checking himself in the mirror. "Not exactly in the Christmas spirit."

God. He looks amazing.

And he knows it.

"Come on, love. Dinner is about to be served." Parker

389

kneels before me and holds out my silver heels. I sigh, shutting my laptop and slipping my feet into the expensive shoes. Parker buckles them around my ankles before running his hand up my calf, sending shivers along my skin.

"Parker," I warn him.

"What?" he says innocently, but there's no hiding his devilish smirk.

He continues to trace the tips of his fingers across the back of my leg, and I stand up shakily, forcing myself not to melt into his touch. I fall prey to Parker's whims more and more every day. It is becoming a chore to keep myself from falling completely off the deep end. One of us has to remain somewhat sensible.

I grab my perfume and spritz my wrist before I touch up my makeup in the mirror. I fix my bangs before triple checking that the elaborate bun I'd spent an hour on this morning is still in place. One of the pins is poking me at an odd angle, but I'm not going to risk moving it.

Parker wraps his arms around my waist, resting his chin on my shoulder. The color of his shirt matches my dress, making us look like the perfect pair.

I won't admit it to him, but my wardrobe is slowly turning more and more blue.

"You are proper stunning. Like a freshly polished gem glinting in the sun."

I tilt my head against his. "Thank you."

"What? No compliment for me?"

I chuckle as he pulls back and holds his elbow out for me. I press my fingers daintily into the crook and smile. "I think you're well aware that you are one of the most attractive men in existence. I don't want to inflate your ego any more than it already is."

"One of?" He gives me a fake look of pain. "I am *the* most attractive man."

I shrug. "We'll see if you win hottest streamer of the year or not."

He gapes at me. "Cold, Sydney."

The mansion is abuzz with people moving about and getting ready as Parker and I weave our way through the many hallways. The Covingtons' Christmas Eve dinner is an intimate affair, but they host an extravagant annual party on Boxing Day, where they raise money for charity as part of the holiday. Hence the staff working around the clock.

We enter the formal dining room, which has a gilded, domed ceiling that features a stunning teardrop crystal chandelier hanging from the center. Grandiose deep green curtains frame the windows, and a decidedly expensive piece of art hangs above a fireplace.

I make a note to take a picture of the art and send it to Stevie; I have no doubt she would flip over it. I'd already sent her images of the ceiling in one of the reception rooms that has an angelic Renaissance scene painted on it. I'd stared up at it for so long, my neck hurt.

Heads swivel from the elegantly set table at our arrival.

"Oh, don't you look beautiful." Pricilla stands from her seat to give me a kiss on the cheek.

"Thank you. I love your dress."

Pricilla runs a hand down her maroon dress with a soft smile. She never has a hair out of place and always looks like she is ready for high tea.

Parker pulls out my seat for me to sit before taking his

next to me. My father grins at me from across the table before returning to his conversation with Parker's dad.

Philip Covington enters the room with a stern look, immediately setting me on edge.

Parker's grandfather had been quite jovial yesterday when we arrived even though the board vote had come in only hours earlier, removing Parker from his position as heir. The two seem to be getting along fine. It also helps that his nana dotes on him with clear favor.

Parker's maternal grandparents wouldn't be arriving until tomorrow; they split the holidays between Pricilla and her sister.

Philip pulls a seat out for his wife before taking his place at the head of the table. Parker's parents shoot each other a silent look, confirming that the displeasure radiating off his grandfather isn't something I am merely imagining.

The only person missing is Paige, who strolls in a few minutes later in a satin green dress, her long blonde hair flowing in perfect waves. She gives Parker a wink before slipping her purse around her chair and sliding in next to Phoebe, who eyes her younger siblings through slightly narrowed eyes.

Two staff members slip into the room, one pouring a glass of champagne for each person while the other places fresh bread and butter at intervals along the table.

Parker slips his hand over my flute before reminding the woman of my preferences. She apologizes before dipping out of the room and returning with a non-alcoholic alternative. I bite my lip, feeling a little bad.

The rest of the meal proceeds without a hitch, conversation flowing as we stuff ourselves with decadent food.

Although, every once in a while, I catch Parker's grandfather eyeing him with a puzzled look, like he can't quite figure something out. When it comes time for dessert, my eyes widen at the limitless number of puddings that are deposited onto the table. Phoebe hums as she digs into her Christmas pudding, and my dad doesn't hesitate before going back for seconds of the figgy pudding.

"Here, Sydney, you have to have one of the mince pies." Pricilla uses a set of tongs to lift a crumbly pastry onto my plate.

"Oh, no, I can't have meat." I hold my hands out to stop her, but she just bypasses them.

A series of chuckles sound across the table, and I frown at Parker in confusion.

"There's no meat in it," he explains.

"Oh."

I watch as Parker grabs one for himself and cuts it in half. A fruity filling trickles out. He cuts it again and holds it out on a fork to me.

"We also had them make the pastry vegan for you."

"I can feed myself." I flush, trying to take the fork from him.

"Don't be embarrassed, darling." Pricilla pats my forearm before taking another sip of champagne.

This family is too affectionate.

I give Parker a stern look before pointedly cutting into my own little pie and taking a bite. Flavors burst along my tongue. The tartness of the dried fruits mixes with the sweetness of the sugary filling, all brought together with the flaky pastry.

Damn, it is good.

I immediately cut another bite, enjoying myself in the moment.

"I think she likes it," Pricilla whispers to Parker.

"I agree," he whispers back.

I give him a side kick under the table with my heel, and he laughs.

The staff clears our plates when we finish, and Parker's grandfather stands up almost instantly, inclining his head to Parker.

"Can I have a word with you?"

A quite hush falls over the table.

"Oh, Philip, do you need to do this now?" his wife laments, patting him on the hand.

"It's important."

"We're all family; can't you chat with me here?" Parker leans farther back in his chair.

My senses go on alert, recognizing the telltale signs. Parker's up to something.

Philip's eyes narrow, assessing his grandson. I think he might put up a fight, but he sits back down.

"I had our lawyer begin the paperwork to transfer your shares yesterday," he starts.

"Working quickly, I see." Parker grabs his cup of tea and takes a sip.

Yeah, he's definitely up to something.

My eyes dart around the table, reading the family's concerned looks. Except Phoebe, whose suspicious blue gaze is sternly fixed on Parker, and Paige, who is trying to hide a small smile behind her wine glass.

"Yes, but they ran into an issue."

When Parker doesn't say anything, his grandfather's gaze narrows even further, the wrinkles around his face becoming more prominent.

"They couldn't find them."

"Well, that's unfortunate, now, isn't it?" Parker hums.

"Oh, Parker," Patrick Covington sighs at his son. "What did you do?"

"My shares were an heir's share, so I gave them to the heir." He shrugs.

There is a soft snick, and we all turn our attention to Paige, who opens her purse and pulls out an envelope. She holds the creamy white paper out to her older sister.

Shock ripples over Phoebe's normally calculating features.

"The fuck is this?" she breathes.

"Phoebe Anne," Pricilla chastises. "Language, please."

Phoebe snatches the envelope and rips it open. She shuffles through the pieces of paper, her eyes widening.

"You gave me your shares?" She blinks at her younger brother, disbelief in her tone.

"Merry Christmas, sis." Parker lifts his teacup in a salute.

"Parker James Covington, you did not have approval to do this," his grandfather's voice cuts through the room.

"I didn't need approval; everything was legal. Right, Paigey?"

"Right, Sparky." His coconspirator smiles. She pulls another envelope from her purse and holds it out to me this time. "Your new contract, by the way."

I blink, taking it from her.

All this time, I had thought Paige was the angel of the

Covington siblings, but she is just as cunning as the other two, behind that elegant exterior.

"Why?" his grandfather asks, steepling his hands beneath his chin.

"Well, why should my shares be redistributed to the board? Why should they get more power over our company? That's bullshit."

"Language," Pricilla sings again.

"I simply gave my shares to the person they belonged to, the next CEO of Covington Hotels." Warmth shines in Parker's eyes as he grins at Phoebe. "We all know it should be her, and this way the board can never dispute it."

"Thank you." A soft smile spills onto Phoebe's face.

Philip sighs, leaning back in his chair. "I do wish you'd asked me first."

"So you could have stopped me?"

"No, so I could have told you this was already my plan."

The whole table looks at him in puzzlement.

I take a sip of my tea, watching them all. My gaze lands on my dad, and he raises his brows at me. I stifle a smile. It's like the two of us are watching a family drama in real time. I swear the Covingtons have forgotten we're even here.

"What do you mean, Dad?" Patrick cuts in.

"It wasn't my immediate plan. I was going to put the shares in your name, son, for the next few months as we transitioned Phoebe into the CFO role. Then, I would have transferred her the shares when the time came. Now, I'm going to have to deal with the board sooner than I wanted."

"I'm not going to say sorry," Parker grumbles.

Paige lets out a laugh, and her sister follows closely behind. Soon the entire table is giggling and laughing at the entire situation.

"It's all right, babe. It's the thought that counts." I squeeze Parker's forearm.

"Sure." He moves to grip my hands in his, letting out a huff.

I join in with the laughter, and Parker caves, smiling.

There would never be a dull moment around him.

Chapter THIRTY

PARKER

"What are you doing out here, love?"

I open the doors to see my girlfriend leaning against one of the large exterior columns. She's cloaked in partial darkness, but when she turns to face me, the moonlight hits her cheekbone and lights her up. She glows like a moon goddess visiting Earth, her deep sea-blue dress shifting with her movement.

I don't think there will be a day when the vision of her wouldn't take my breath away.

"I was just admiring the view." She folds her arms across her chest.

"In the dark?" I shuck off my suit jacket and place it around her shoulders.

She smiles up at me. "It's gorgeous."

I look out at the view she seems so enraptured with,

noticing for the first time that it's begun to snow. The moonlight reflects off the light smattering of snow that is sticking to the grass.

Distantly, I can hear the running water of the central garden fountain. It is a sight I am used to; our family has had this estate since I was a young boy, but there is always something about coming home that makes me feel a little more whole.

"Maybe we should stay a little longer."

I wrap my arms around her, and she leans back into me. Our trip is for two weeks, and we only have a few days left before we head back to the States. I typically always leave after the Boxing Day party, but this trip feels different.

Probably because I have Sydney all to myself here.

"I'd agree if I didn't think Stevie would bite our heads off for skipping New Year's."

"She is planning a banger," I muse.

The breeze picks up, and Sydney shivers. I run my hands up her arms.

"Come on, let's head inside. I'll show you around to-morrow."

She nods. "I feel like this place is never-ending."

"Just wait until you see the tennis court."

I wrap my arm around her shoulders, and we head back into the warmth, her heels clicking quietly on the floor as we make our way through the now quiet house.

"I've never played tennis before."

"Perfect, I love stealing your firsts."

She snorts. "You haven't stolen any of my firsts, Park-er."

"You mean someone else stuck their finger in your ass

before me?"

She gapes at me, whipping her head around in case anyone overheard. But it is quarter to midnight, and everyone else has already retired to their rooms. Her cheeks flush a strawberry pink as her eyes narrow.

"Parker Covington, seriously?"

She punches me lightly in the chest and takes the staircase two at a time. I jog after her, sweeping her into my arms on the landing and twirling her around.

She lets out a light squeal, and when she looks down at me, it is as if my heart melts.

I tentatively kiss her lips, and she sighs into me.

Our hands don't leave one another as we stumble into my bedroom. Our clothing falls to the ground as we paw it off, shoes tumbling to the side and lingerie landing on the couch. Sydney's knees hit the bed, and she tips backward. I kneel on the bed, gripping her plush ass and pushing her farther back as I crawl on top of her.

My cock is heavy with want as I trap her between my knees. She meets me kiss for kiss, sucking and tugging on my lips. My hand slips between our bodies, trailing that slick line of wetness at her center. She groans into my mouth, her hips pitching up.

I slip two fingers into her, and my dick twitches at the feeling of her clenching around me. Her breathing picks up as my fingers move more quickly. She grinds herself against my palm, taking her pleasure. Just as her legs begin to quiver, I pull out.

Her eyes flash open, and I see the silent protest on the tip of her tongue. I reach over and grab a condom from my side drawer, rolling it on before I slam into her.

She sucks in a gasp, her mouth forming the perfect O.

I bring one of her legs to hook around my back as I move rhythmically, pumping in and out.

"You always look so pretty when I'm inside you," I praise her.

She smiles at me with a love-drunk expression, and it just spurs me further, inciting this need to keep claiming her as mine. Mine. Mine.

'Cause she is.

I will never give her up, not in a million years. I will fight for her until my HP is fully depleted and I am out of lives. And even then, I would find a resurrection bug so I can respawn and love her all over again.

Sydney's nails dig into my deltoid, and I recognize that glint in her eye. I move with her as she flips our positions. She takes control, and I watch as she bounces on my cock.

Fuck, it's a sexy sight.

Her hands curl around my shoulders as she uses me for stability, increasing her speed. I reach behind and grip her ass and move my hips up in time to meet hers. The sound of our bodies slapping together mixes with our moans. She grinds her cunt against me as she reaches her peak.

I let myself tumble off the edge with her, emptying myself with a low grunt.

She flops on top of me as our labored breathing evens out. I focus on the feeling of her as pleasure continues to haze my body. I think of how perfect these last few days have been. How grateful I am to have her here with me.

"Hey, Sydney."

"Yeah?"

I swallow, letting the words flow out, "I love you."

She stills in my arms, and I worry for a second until I look down and see her gray eyes shining up at me with unshed tears.

"I love you, too," she whispers, lifting her chest off mine to smile.

I cup her face, tracing her jaw and admiring the beauty before me.

"Yeah, but I really, really love you. I love you so much it makes me delirious. I wake up every day, and you're the first person I think of, the first person I want to see. You've become the breath in my lungs, the blood in my veins, and I don't think it would be possible to survive without you."

"Parker." She speaks my name with such emotion before tipping her head up to take me in a soft kiss. "You're my anchor in the storm, my ray of sun on a cloudy day. It's us, no matter what."

She nuzzles into my chest, and I pull her against me tightly.

I stay awake, listening as she drifts off to sleep.

From the moment I met her, she stole a piece of my heart, and every day since, I have given her more and more of me, and I will continue to give her everything I have until there is nothing left. And even then, I will find a glitch in the system to give her more.

There is no Parker without Sydney; she is my forever person—no regrets.

THE END

Exclusive
BONUS SCENE

PARKER

Five Years Ago...

My phone buzzes for the tenth time in the last five minutes, and I contemplate throwing it in the fish tank with all the lobsters in it. It wouldn't cost much to replace the damn thing, and at least I would get a few moments of peace. But because I'm a nice person, I give in and answer the incoming call from one of my soon-to-be roommates.

"I'm at the bloody restaurant, Jackson. It's not my fault the que is a hundred meters long," I growl into the speaker. "Tell Aleksander that if he texts me one more time, I'll piss in his wonton soup."

"First, we call it a line," Jackson muses. "Second, that's gross, dude."

"Semantics."

"I'm just saying, you're the one who moved to this country. You're going to have to learn the proper terminology."

I am beginning to regret leaving England already, and I've only been here for two months.

I've just turned nineteen, and my family isn't exactly thrilled that I had changed universities and moved to a completely different country to live with lads I'd never actually met before to pursue a career that could crash and burn. But still, they are open to supporting me so long as I complete my studies and don't end up murdered by my roommates or held for ransom.

"Whatever. I'll text you guys when I'm headed back to the warehouse."

"Fine, I'll try to keep Aleks distracted in the meantime, but I can't promise anything."

"Just play a round of Zombies or something. Bye." I hang up the phone with a sigh and shove it back into my pocket.

I love Aleks and Jackson, but I also want to murder them half the time. Makes me a little worried for when we move into our new place in a few weeks.

"Sounds stressful," a soft voice comments.

I look down and see the prettiest bird I've ever laid eyes on. Red-tinted lips, shiny blonde hair, cloud-gray eyes, and the cutest button nose.

"My new roommates. They aren't exactly a patient lot." I smile, turning on the charm.

"I just moved here myself. I'm Sydney." She holds out her hand.

"Parker." I take her delicate hand in my own and give it a shake. "How do you like California so far, Sydney?"

"I like it. I'm from a small town in Missouri, so it's been a bit of a change. But I can't complain about the weather though. Seventy degrees in March? Heaven."

"I'm going to pretend that I know where Missouri is and what seventy degrees means and just agree with you."

She laughs, those glossy red lips spreading into a smile that lights up her whole face, and I know I'm a goner. My parents say they fell in love at first sight, and I always thought it was a load of bullocks. Until now.

Call me ridiculous, but I look at this girl and I can see years into the future.

"How long have you lived in America?" she asks as she shuffles farther up the que.

"Just a few months; I moved after Christmas."

"Wow, big change. What are you doing here?"

"I'm attending UCLA."

It's my blanket response for anyone who asks, and it is the partial truth. It's not like I can tell everyone I'm a video game streamer when my identity is a secret. I've only been posting online as EnglishCoffee for two years. It just started out as a way to track my speedruns until it took on a life of its own. I've been streaming for the last year, and I'm addicted to it.

"What about you?"

"I just got a new job." She beams. "I've always wanted to move out to California, and it's the perfect job. I start tomorrow, which is why I thought I'd treat myself to take-out from Chá House. A splurge to celebrate. Although, I didn't realize how long the wait would be, especially for a Sunday."

Damn, she's cute.

"Yeah, this que is mad."

She stifles a laugh.

"What?" I tilt my head.

"Nothing, it's just…the way you talk, it reminds me of those dating shows." Her cheeks turn pink.

"Haha, very funny. Next thing I know, you're going to ask me if girls really say, 'fanny flutters.'"

"Do they?"

I mime zipping my lips, and she gives me a playful push. I lightly grab her wrist before she fully pulls it away and run my thumb over her hand. She looks up at me, her pupils dilating.

"Next." The brisk voice punctures our little bubble.

Sydney whips around, and I let go of her as she shuffles up to greet the host at the desk in front of us.

"Pickup for Sydney Lake, please."

"All right, one moment." The guy grabs a small white bag from a row and hands it to her. "It's not prepaid. Your total is thirty-eight eighty."

"Right. One second." She takes her handbag off her shoulder and begins digging through it. I take the opportunity to pull my wallet from my pocket and tap my black card to the payment device. Sydney's head jerks up at the little beep it makes when the payment processes.

"Consider it a congratulations on your new job." I wink.

"Oh." She tucks a stray tendril of hair behind her ear. "Thank you."

"Next."

"Parker Covington." I tilt my chin in a nod.

The guy goes back to the row of takeaway bags on the counter behind him and leafs through them before turning around with a frown. He picks up his tablet and scrolls through it.

"Don't have anything for a Parker Covington here."

I match the guy's frown before pulling out my phone

and shooting a text to the boys.

ME

what name is the order under???

JACK-ASS

idk, Aleks placed it

BLADE

oh right

it's under DE'EZMA NUTS

JACK-ASS

lmao

ME

wtf

I am going to murder them.

Then again, this is probably in retaliation for the fact that I'd signed Aleks up for an erectile dysfunction trial and they won't stop calling him.

I step closer to the desk and lean into the host with a tight smile. "It's under De'Ezma Nuts."

The guy blinks at me. "What."

"The name for the order. It's De'Ezma Nuts." I try to keep my voice low, but I hear Sydney laugh next to me.

"Right," the guy deadpans before turning back to the row of takeaway bags. He picks two of them up and hands them to me. "Here you go."

"Thanks, mate."

Dread sinks into my chest, and I close my eyes for a second.

When I open them and turn around, the shining blonde is still there.

"Your roommates sound like a wild time." She smiles.

Ten minutes with her, and I already know she is too good for this world.

"You have no idea." I angle my head to the door. "Did you drive here?"

Her lips thin imperceptibly, but she nods. "Yeah, I parked out front."

"Same. Mind if I walk you out?"

"Sure." She smiles at me again, and bloody hell, I never want her to stop.

"Don't like driving in California?" I venture as we exit into the cool night.

"Something like that." She shrugs. "I'm surprised you can drive here. Don't they drive on the other side of the road in England?"

I don't miss the subject change, but I let it be.

"We do, but I'm a bit of a petrolhead. There's nothing I can't drive."

"Nothing?" Her brows rise teasingly.

"Nothing."

"Normally, I'd doubt that, but I have a feeling you're the kind of guy who accepts any challenge, Parker."

The way my name sounds on her lips has my cock tightening in my pants.

She stops suddenly.

"This is me."

I'm unable to hide the shock as I look down at her car. Complete disbelief fills me as I look at the deathtrap. The silver Volvo has paint chipping off it, and there is a massive dent in the rear bumper. My guess is it had to be a 2005 or 2004. She'd be better off walking.

"Um, well, thank you."

"Wait." I reach out and grab her arm.

Her eyes blink up at me.

Shit.

"Could I get your number?"

She bites her bottom lip, and I pray that my misstep didn't ruin everything.

"Sure."

I let out a breath and smile, handing her my phone. She types in her number and holds it back out to me.

I look at the contact.

Sydney Lake.

Pretty name. Of course.

"It was a pleasure to meet you, Sydney Lake."

"And you, Parker."

She slips into her car, and I stand a few feet back, waiting for her to pull out.

Except, she doesn't.

The engine splutters a few times, attempting to come to life but failing with every single shot.

I knew this thing was a deathtrap.

After a few minutes, I walk up to the driver's side window and rap on it.

Sydney slowly rolls the window down with a thinly veiled grimace.

"It happens sometimes."

"Really?" I cock my brow.

"Yup, it's the cold. It'll be fine in no time. Really, you don't need to worry."

Bullshit.

"Pop the bonnet for me."

"The what?"

"The hood, pop the hood."

"Oh, oh no. No, it's fine. Seriously."

"Because you already know it's a mess under there, don't you?" It's a shot in the dark.

"The drive from Missouri didn't exactly do me any favors," she whispers.

I have no idea where Missouri is but that sounds far as hell.

I reach down and open the door, "Come on. Let me drive you home. I'll call a company to tow it to a nearby auto shop."

"Really, it's fine."

"Sydney, it's not up for debate."

"I don't get into cars with strangers."

"Seriously."

She crosses her arms, and I see the defiance written all over her face.

I sigh.

"Look, you can call a friend and talk to them the whole time or, I don't know, have 911 on standby. I don't care. But it'll be a hell of a lot safer than you waiting out here all night or attempting to get somewhere in this deathtrap."

"Fine." She steps out of the car and locks it. "But if you make even one wrong turn, you're done."

I place my hand over my chest. "I swear."

Thankfully, she follows behind me, and I lead her to my McLaren. She eyes the blue car suspiciously.

"This is yours?"

"Yup." I open the passenger door for her, and she frowns before crouching in.

I get in the driver's side, and she jolts when I start the engine.

"Here, type in your address." I tap the center console, pulling up the GPS.

She begins tapping away as I pull out of the lot.

When she finishes, I take a glance at the final address and internally curse.

She isn't far from the restaurant, but…she is in the opposite direction of the warehouse.

The guys are going to murder me.

We ride in silence for the first few minutes, and I don't push it. I know from my sisters that it isn't a chick's natural inclination to get into the car of a bloke she just met. No matter the sparks I felt when we first met.

"Thank you."

I look at her out of the corner of my eye. "It's no biggie."

"Most people wouldn't offer to drive a stranger home."

"I'm not most people."

She chuckles. "No. No, you're definitely something else, Parker."

There she goes again, gracing her pretty lips with my name.

"So, what do you do for fun?"

"Hmm, I like to listen to crime podcasts."

"Like those serial killer ones?"

"Exactly!"

"Your enthusiasm has me deeply concerned for my well-being."

She snorts, "I won't lie, I've learned many different ways to dispose of a body."

"Not helping."

We continue to trade stories, and every time I manage to make her laugh, something in my chest pulls.

Too soon, I make the final turn onto her street and roll to a stop in front of a shady apartment building.

"Home sweet home," she chimes.

Her apartment complex is just as shitty as her car. There is no way it is safe for her out here. Isn't there anyone looking out for her? Isn't there anyone who told her to maybe look at a safer neighborhood?

"Thanks for the ride." She smiles.

"Any time." I reach out and tuck a piece of hair behind her ear. "Seriously, if you ever need anything, just give me a call."

She stares at me for a beat, pressing her plush lips into a thin line.

God, I want to kiss her.

Her eyes flick from my eyes down to my lips, and before I can blink, she leans forward and plants a quick kiss on my cheek.

I'm stunned, but only for a second. Before she can pull away, I bring her to my lips.

Cherries.

She tastes like cherries.

The world turns silent and when I pull away, I see the stars in her eyes. She blinks up at me a few times, that deep flush building on her cheeks.

"Thanks again," she whispers before bolting from the car.

I sit in my car for a solid five minutes, staring out into the night.

My thoughts are only broken up when my speakers start blaring with an incoming phone call.

I hit accept, still in a haze.

"Where the fuck are you?" Aleks barks.

"I'm on my way, chill."

I shift the car into drive and peel onto the street.

But I don't stop myself from looking in my rearview mirror at the apartment building, imagining the sweet blonde inside.

Sydney Lake.

That girl seems like a keeper.

READY FOR MORE OF THE SYSTEM?

Order *Fake Game* now for Jackson & Deer's story.
And turn the page for a **sneak peek** ;)

***

Curious about how Parker proposes to Sydney?
Download the epilogue by visiting:
https://BookHip.com/PDTBFCM

Wondering about how Parker & Syd's had their first kiss?
Read about their original meet-cute in a **bonus chapter**
available in the <u>discreet paperback</u> **edition!**

Thank you for reading, *Forbidden Game*.
If you enjoyed this book, I would be grateful if you could
leave a review on the platform(s) of your choice. Reviews
are one of the best ways to support an author!

Kisses,
Madison Fox

Fake
GAME

THE
SYSTEM
BOOK 3

DEER

There's a man in a black hoodie and black facemask parked on one of the couches by the community pool table. Most people wouldn't give him a second glance, but I do. Because I recognize him just by his eyes.

My chunky platform heels click softly on the tiles as I make my way over. It's only when I stop right in front of him that he looks up from the mobile game on his phone. My skin heats from the intensity of his gaze, swirling pools of bottomless black framed by thick lashes.

That was the thing about Jackson Lau, he said so much without uttering a word.

"Why are you here?"

"You headed out?" he counters.

I blink down at him, "um, yeah. I'm going over to Lee's."

"'Kay, let's go." He stands up, his chest coming to rest mere inches from my nose.

I take a startled step back as he steps around me to head out of the complex. My brain glitches for a second as I stare at his retreating from.

"Uh…what?" I call out, jogging after him. The fresh outside air fills my lungs as I pass through the revolving door and into the late afternoon sun.

"I'll drive you."

"You came all the way here just to drive me to Crime

416

Night?" I quirk a brow.

Jackson hands a ticket to the valet outside my apartment before turning back to give me a bored look.

"I was in the area and Lee asked." After a beat he adds, "for safety."

"Right."

Safety.

I chew on my bottom lip, trying to decide whether he is telling the truth. It annoys me that he can read me like a book while I struggle to even read his blurb.

An army green Jeep comes to a stop before us, and Jackson opens the passenger door, "get in."

I let out a huff and ignore him, hauling my ass into the passenger seat. "I could have driven myself," I mutter as he gets into the driver's side.

Jackson says nothing, he just removes his facemask and hood before putting the car in drive. I pull my phone out of my handbag to fiddle with it, but really, I'm just using it as an excuse while I stare at him out the corner of my eye.

It was frustrating how attractive he was.

His long black hair wasn't tied in a bun for once, and the ends grazed the top of his shoulders. My fingers twitched to rake my nails through it. This wasn't the first time I'd had the urge, and if the last year had taught me anything, it was that this urge wasn't going anywhere soon.

My eyes trail down his arms to the strong hands gripping the steering wheel.

He was the kind of guy who could toss you over his shoulder without a second thought.

And I had thought about it.

I'd be lying if I didn't admit that there was a time when I harbored a tiny little crush on him. But *super* tiny. And the more I got to know him, the more convinced I became that he didn't really have that much interest in me unless other people were involved. We only played video games together when Lee or the guys were with us, and we never hung out alone—minus this car ride, which was at the expense of Lee anyway.

No. Jackson Lau, I was sure, saw me as a by-product of his other friendships. An acquaintance at best. He was the type of person you would refer to as your friend, only to have him scowl in response.

Whatever, I wasn't salty about it or anything.

"What?"

"Huh?" I startle out of my thoughts to notice Jackson looking at me.

"You're staring." There's a glint in his eye as he drawls the words.

"So?"

"Just making an observance," he muses, turning his attention back to the road. "You seemed preoccupied."

"I was just thinking about how they say men with big hands tends to have big penises."

The car jerks as Jackson's head whips to me, his eyes wide. I feel a slither of satisfaction as his mouth opens and closes.

"Although, I'm not really sure there is any scientific evidence backing that statement. Not that I've Googled it or anything, but it's food for thought," I continue to babble.

Jackson clenches his jaw. "You're spending too much time around Stevie."

"I'm always like this." I shrug, pretending to clean under my nails.

Jackson doesn't say anything else for the rest of the ride, and I can't tell whether or not he is just a tad miffed with me. Whatever. It's not like I made him drive me here.

The car rolls to a stop outside Lee's opulent apartment complex and I waste no time unbuckling my seatbelt and popping open the door.

"Well, thanks for the ride. I'll be sure to give you a four-star rating."

"What time will you be done?"

I halt, one foot on the asphalt, and turn back to him. "What do you mean?"

"Your little Crime Night, when does it finish?"

I frown, "I don't know. Depends on how much we drink. Why?"

Typically, if we had a particularly tipsy Crime Night, I ended up just crashing at Lee's instead of waiting to sober up and drive back. Occasionally, Syd would drop me home, but then I had to deal with getting my car the next day and that always ended up being a pain. If it was a pretty sober night, I would drive myself home, but there was never any telling how a Crime Night would go. That was the beauty of them.

"So I can drive you home."

"Why? One of the girls can."

His eyes give me a quick once over before turns away from me, "fine."

"Okay, bye."

I shut the door half expecting him to take off and leave me in a cloud of dust, but instead he just waits. When another second passes and he just stares at me through the window, I give up and turn around to walk into the building.

I really did not understand that man.

[to be continued]

www.authormadisonfox.com/books

ACKNOWLEDGEMENTS

GOOD JOB TO MYSELF.

Ya know, people always told me writing your sophomore novel is hard. While I believed them, I didn't realise how hard it would be. Parker and Syd were a journey. Their story really took on a life of its own and it kept changing as I was writing.

I look back at this baby and I see just how much I have grown as an author. With each book I write, I see myself growing.

Sophie Lark is someone who always told me that writing is something you have to train and practice at. The more you do it, the better you get. And she is 110% correct.

OF COURSE, THANK YOU, THE READER, FOR PICKING THIS BOOK UP. It is because you support me that I am able to do something I truly love.

A big hug to all my beta readers—Jen, Katie, and Dilan. Jen, your airplane knowledge was the tidbit I didn't know I needed. Katie, thanks for giving me all the vibes. Dilan, thank you for checking that I didn't do a disservice to any Brits with Parker.

Cat, my cover designer and my sparkle. Surprise, I dedicated this book to you. Can't wait for you to find out. Thank you for ALSO beta-reading and for your architecture and design knowledge—bougee hospitals are important.

Thanks to my lil bro for letting me chill on his bed and listen to him play games online with his friends so I could take notes.

Jade, I love you. Thanks for being my fellow baby author friend and letting me vent.

A big hug to Catherine Cowles for being my biggest supporter from day zero.

Kylie, thank you for letting me ramble about the whole billionaire inheritance issue I was having.

Thank you to my fellow amazing author friends— Carlie Jean, Kat Singleton, Tate James, Catharina Maura, Jenny B, and Cali Melle.

Zafina, my fellow gamer girl, thanks for having my back,

Alyssa, as always, you're a goddess for formatting this while both of our lives are more hectic than a rollercoaster that won't stop.

My editor, Katie, thank you for adoring Parker & Syd from Day One and always giving me your TED Talks.

Thank you to my girl Becca, for letting me be a hot mess as I keep growing in this career.

The gals at Eternal Embers, you are such a hype team.

Lastly, My Little Doves, my ARC team, thank you for being awesome! And thank you to every creator and reviewer who has ever posted about my books online. It means the world.

Also, Piper, taadaa, see I did get my acknowledgements done on the plane ;)

xoxo

ABOUT THE AUTHOR

Madison Fox was born and raised in Australia but has been living in the United States for the past decade. While she still watches Australian football every Sunday, she currently resides in Nevada as a cat mum to Zelda (yes, based on the video game).

Madison has always been obsessed with books. As a child, she would stash chapter novels in her pillowcases before bedtime so she could read after her parents went to bed.

When Madison isn't reading or writing a new book, she can be found drowning in one of her other obsessions, such as k-dramas, manga, anime, video games, and espresso martinis.

GOOD GAME is her debut romance novel.

**FOLLOW ME ON SOCIAL MEDIA
FOR ALL THE FUN!**

I post fun updates on my socials pertaining not only to my upcoming releases, but also my life in general and the books that I am reading. I would love to connect with you <3

authormadisonfox.com

Milton Keynes UK
Ingram Content Group UK Ltd.
UKHW020935110624
444053UK00015B/929